# Love and Russian Literature

# Love and Russian Literature

*From Benjamin to Woolf*

Ira Nadel

BLOOMSBURY ACADEMIC
LONDON • NEW YORK • OXFORD • NEW DELHI • SYDNEY

BLOOMSBURY ACADEMIC
Bloomsbury Publishing Plc, 50 Bedford Square, London, WC1B 3DP, UK
Bloomsbury Publishing Inc, 1385 Broadway, New York, NY 10018, USA
Bloomsbury Publishing Ireland, 29 Earlsfort Terrace, Dublin 2, D02 AY28, Ireland

BLOOMSBURY, BLOOMSBURY ACADEMIC and the Diana logo
are trademarks of Bloomsbury Publishing Plc

First published in Great Britain 2024
This paperback edition published 2025

Copyright © Ira Nadel, 2024

Ira Nadel has asserted his right under the Copyright, Designs and
Patents Act, 1988, to be identified as Author of this work.

For legal purposes the Acknowledgments on p. x constitute an
extension of this copyright page.

Cover design: Rebecca Heselton
Cover image by Amedeo Modigliani, found in the collection of A. Akhmatova Memorial
Museum, St Petersburg © Fine Art Images/Heritage Images/Getty Images

All rights reserved. No part of this publication may be: i) reproduced or transmitted
in any form, electronic or mechanical, including photocopying, recording or by means of
any information storage or retrieval system without prior permission in writing from the
publishers; or ii) used or reproduced in any way for the training, development or operation
of artificial intelligence (AI) technologies, including generative AI technologies. The rights
holders expressly reserve this publication from the text and data mining exception as per
Article 4(3) of the Digital Single Market Directive (EU) 2019/790.

Bloomsbury Publishing Plc does not have any control over, or responsibility for,
any third-party websites referred to or in this book. All internet addresses given
in this book were correct at the time of going to press. The author and publisher
regret any inconvenience caused if addresses have changed or sites have
ceased to exist, but can accept no responsibility for any such changes.

A catalogue record for this book is available from the British Library.

A catalog record for this book is available from the Library of Congress.

Names: Nadel, Ira Bruce, author.
Title: Love and Russian literature : from Benjamin to Woolf / Ira B. Nadel.
Description: New York : Bloomsbury Publishing Plc, 2023. |
Includes bibliographical references and index.
Identifiers: LCCN 2023030521 (print) | LCCN 2023030522 (ebook) |
ISBN 9781350115019 (hardback) | ISBN 9781350425583 (paperback) |
ISBN 9781350115026 (pdf) | ISBN 9781350115033 (ebook)
Subjects: LCSH: English literature–Great Britain–20th century–Russian
influences. | English literature–Great Britain–20th century–Themes,
motives. | Love in literature. | Authors, English–20th
century–Relations with women. | Love–Russia. | Love–Soviet Union.
Classification: LCC PR129.R8 N33 2023 (print) | LCC PR129.R8 (ebook) |
DDC 820.9/9410904–dc23/eng/20230808
LC record available at https://lccn.loc.gov/2023030521
LC ebook record available at https://lccn.loc.gov/2023030522

ISBN: HB: 978-1-3501-1501-9
PB: 978-1-3504-2558-3
ePDF: 978-1-3501-1502-6
eBook: 978-1-3501-1503-3

Typeset by Integra Software Services Pvt. Ltd.

For product safety related questions contact productsafety@bloomsbury.com.

To find out more about our authors and books visit www.bloomsbury.com
and sign up for our newsletters.

*For Anne*
*&*
*Gideon, Levi, and Coby*

*In Russia it is always the unexpected which happens.*
        Bruce Lockhart, *The Two Revolutions,*
          *Eye-witness Study of Russia, 1917*


*Every love, happy as well as unhappy, is a real disaster when you give yourself over to it entirely.*
         Turgenev, *A Month in the Country*

# Contents

| | |
|---|---:|
| Acknowledgments | x |
| | |
| Introduction: "Magnanimous Despair" (Marvell) | 1 |
| *Prelude*: Walter Benjamin in Love | 23 |
| 1  Somerset Maugham: Love and Russian Literature | 45 |
| 2  R.H. Bruce Lockhart: Love and Revolution | 71 |
| 3  Jane Ellen Harrison: In Love with Language | 93 |
| 4  William Gerhardie: Flattery Is Not Enough or War de Luxe | 113 |
| *Interlude*: Edmund Wilson: In Love with Lenin | 135 |
| 5  H.G. Wells: Triangles | 165 |
| 6  Virginia Woolf: The Sound of Russian Love | 185 |
| *Postscript*: Isaiah Berlin: From the Finland Station | 207 |
| | |
| Bibliography | 228 |
| Index | 240 |

# Acknowledgments

A text as diverse as *Love and Russian Literature* required a supporting cast of myriad scholars, friends, and family and the following were instrumental: Katia Bowers, Director of the University of British Columbia's Centre for European Studies, Dostoevsky expert and tolerant of my attending her seminar on St. Petersburg; Galya Diment, scholar of Russian/Jewish thought and literature at the University of Washington and author of a comprehensive biography of Samuel Koteliansky; Rebecca Beasley of Oxford and the source of repeated insights on the reception of Russian culture in Britain and beyond. Steven Zipperstein of Stanford has also been a remarkable resource on matters Russian, literary and biographical offering sensible responses to my often fanciful ideas. Olga Panova of the Gorky Institute of World Literature, Moscow, and Vassily M. Tolmatchoff of Lomonosov Moscow State University were stimulating and welcoming academic hosts. Michael Earley, former publisher, Principal of Rose Bruford College, and Dean of Performing Arts at the LASALLE College of the Arts, Singapore, has consistently encouraged my multiple and sometimes contradictory pursuits.

Additional support came from Jesse Tisch, Ruaridh MacKenzie (vigilant reader of *War and Peace*), Ryan Nadel, Isabelle Rash, Dara and Jon Pavlich and their energetic team of Gideon, Levi, and Coby. Anne MacKenzie has participated in this project from the start and showed patience and curiosity whether in St. Petersburg or Vancouver. Her frequent question—"Just what *is* Russian love?"—might finally find an answer here.

# Introduction: "Magnanimous Despair" (Marvell)

## i

*"Can one really die of love?"*
Polozov, in Chernyshevsky, What Is to Be Done?

Andrew Marvell's phrase "Magnanimous Despair" from his 1681 poem "The Definition of Love" encapsulates the paradoxical nature of the love stories recounted here by a set of Anglo-German-American authors in diaries, autobiographies, fiction, memoirs, and letters. For Walter Benjamin, love was a Latvian actress pursued in Moscow; for Somerset Maugham, it was intrigue with a mysterious woman he could not resist; for H. Bruce Lockhart, admiration for a possible double-agent; for the scholar Jane Harrison, an affair with the Russian language; for William Gerhardi, it became war; for Edmund Wilson, a love of Lenin; for H.G. Wells, a double or triple agent, also Maxim Gorky's secretary; for Virginia Woolf, Russian literature and film; and for Isaiah Berlin, the elegant, tragic Anna Akhmatova. What these diplomats, journalists, writers, and visitors shared was an intoxication with Russian love, underscored by Russia's dramatic history, violent politics, and cultural history.

But did the reading of Russian literature influence these Russian lovers? It's impossible to know exactly but these nine figures were certainly well-read. To a large degree, they shared a grasp of Turgenev, Gogol, Dostoevsky, Tolstoy, Chekhov, and later Akhmatova and Pasternak, some more deeply than others. The literature played a part in their conception and practice of Russian love. Indeed, an understanding of Russian writing may have been a prerequisite for Russian love.

The uniqueness of Russian love has much to do with the double nature of Russian women, metaphorically representing Russia as an unattainable bride often pursued by westernized figures at the same time they embody independent, forceful voices.[1] While the plot of the individual narratives outlined in this text duplicates the pattern of various nineteenth-century Russian novels—a Russian heroine in opposition to a westernized protagonist often in competition with another male—the individual stories here are unique, involving mystery, pursuit, and curious satisfaction even in defeat. It is Walter Benjamin contending for the love of Asja Lācis while she is attached to Bernhard Reich, or H.G. Wells competing for the love of Moura Budberg while involved with Maxim Gorky. Amorous failures are a given but do not deter the lovers. Politics and revolution may have been the initial appeal of Russia for the protagonists but romance repeatedly interfered with their diplomatic, literary, or personal goals.

Elizabeth Hardwick's essay on *Hedda Gabler* may clarify the situation. Commenting on how "creatures of the will move step-by-step toward victory and loss almost at the same time," she exposes the duality that marks the nature of Russian love. Because the "contingencies of existence" constantly interfere with love, characters are "never boring. There is never a relaxation of tension."[2] This is the nature of Russian love as shown in the fiction and experience of the nine figures here. They, and their literary counterparts, experience

> restlessness, mood, obsession. Everything comes at us in fragments, disturbing bits and pieces. You feel life cannot sustain their degree of willfulness, and part of the suspense of their character is the anxious waiting to learn in just what way they will fall.
>
> (Hardwick 53)

The situation of the lovers is one of simultaneous attraction and rejection: a pull toward, and a push away, occurring at the same time. It is the moment in *Anna Karenina* when the ill Anna "with one hot hand ... held his [Alexei's] hand, and with the other she pushed him away." Her lover Vronsky watches from the shadows.[3] It is a battle between circumstance and will resulting in a characteristic hesitation and denial despite compelling emotions and passions. The paradox tests the characters and excites the readers while they face what Dostoevsky called the "coquetry of happiness" experienced directly by Benjamin, Lockhart, Wells, and others.[4]

Hardwick further elaborates the condition of Russian love when she writes that "negative forces are more devastating to Hedda's integrity than positive wishes unfulfilled"—even when the topic is love (55). Unlike Hedda, who is in love with no one, Russian characters tend to be in love with everyone. Romantic posturing is inescapable. In Hedda, character and action unite; in Russian love stories, they do not. Actions do not connect with feelings. In response to the romantic projections of Olga in Goncharov's *Oblomov*, for example, the hero spends hours on his couch "endlessly interpreting and reinterpreting in his head that morning's conversation with[her]." Can it be she loves me? Could her passionate singing be for me? But doubt replaces certainty and he fails to act. He responds by not responding, paralyzed by the thought of possible love, while she soon feels both embarrassment and resentment.[5]

## ii

*"I could not simplify myself."*

Turgenev, *Virgin Soil*

Women of energy and agency made an enticing if not heady mix for susceptible foreigners. The independence yet struggle of Russian women, balancing freedom with discipline, speech with silence, initiated a "double-voiced discourse," one of autonomy circumscribed by obedience.[6] They were equally outspoken and silent as seen in Dostoevsky's positioning of women in *The Idiot* where the proud, candid but exploited Nastasya (*femme fatale* or fallen woman?), once the ward and then mistress of Totsky, is caught between love for Prince Myshkin and Rogozhin. Aglaya is the idealistic romantic similarly in love with Prince Myshkin but rejected and who, in the end, runs off with a supposed Polish count. Between them stands Alexandra, twenty-five, regal, unmarried, and seemingly unmoved by passion. The three archetypes embody the female condition as presented in the literature and encountered by the set of lovers represented here who experience Russian love not as romance or redemption but as an affliction, the product of the clash between desire and disillusionment.

Western lovers of Russian women remain naïve romantics blind to dissemblers in any form. But as Masha explains in Tolstoy's *Family Happiness*, deception may be a form of survival: "without wishing to deceive him [Sergei], I did deceive him, and I became better myself while deceiving him." Her self-improvement coupled with a will to power expressed in the final clause creates the complexity of not only Masha but other women, confirming Tolstoy's ironic belief that "men make of love something enormous, but women are always *terre-à-terre*."[7]

In such a world, even a kiss can be misinterpreted resulting in emotional disaster elaborated by Chekhov in "The Kiss" (1887). There, the narrator reports on the distress of a shy, colorless, socially inexperienced Second Captain Ryabovich who thought an accidental kiss by an unknown woman in the dark was an unexpected but destined sign of love.[8] Suddenly elated, energetic, and with a new, positive outlook on life, love strikes a chord. He then tries to imagine the young woman and creates a composite image, an image "he desired, but which was nowhere to be seen at the table" (Kiss 122). On his return to his encampment, he fantasizes on the identity of the woman while "an intense, groundless joy took possession of him" (Kiss 123). The next day, the brigade departs, marching past the manor house where Ryabovich had his encounter. His imaginings continue with greater intensity until several weeks later a general interrupts his reverie telling Ryabovich that many have shared such feelings; Ryabovich then realizes that instant love passes (Kiss 126, 127).

That evening, he decides to share his adventure with his fellow officers, unexpectedly summarizing his entire adventure in a minute, no more. He thought it would take hours to tell but it did not, even if it is a tale of a *first* kiss. His friends react skeptically and describe their own misadventures and unexpected encounters. But no matter: Ryabovich still felt and acted "like a man in love" (Kiss 128). A month or so later, he and the company returned to the Von Rabbek estate where the incident occurred, convinced he would meet the mysterious woman again, directed by an inner voice "which so often deceives lovers" (Kiss 129). But the host does not send for him, nor his comrades. Anxiety takes over and at night he restlessly walks to the town church and then to the garden near the manor house. But no inviting light appears.

Ryabovich returns depressed and realizes again how foolish he has been. He now understands that he manufactured his love, his disappointment reflected in a universe now an "incomprehensible, aimless jest." To be caressed by an unnamed woman happened by chance but left a lasting impression, although without those dreams, his life "now seemed singularly meager, wretched and drab" (Kiss 130). Ryabovich disappoints himself by the very story he tells, his self-knowledge implying dissatisfaction even in the story Chekhov has given him to narrate.[9] Ryabovich's adventure takes only a minute to tell but a lifetime to understand.

Disappointment has overtaken love and Chekhov has fulfilled what he believed to be the writer's task: to "stand up for the guilty if they have already been condemned and punished."[10] This is the principal condition of Russian lovers, hopeful but ever discontent, rejection invalidating one's feelings but always with a story to tell. The trope replays itself not only in a series of Russian texts focusing on courtship, romance, and even love but in the experiences of the nine figures outlined here. Love *is* Russian literature, even when imagined.[11]

"Decent Russians like ourselves have a passion for problems that have never been solved," writes Chekhov—and Russian love is the ultimate problem.[12] Details remain unsolved as Wood observed: Chekhov's "stories are like tales of crime in which nobody is a criminal" partly because his characters forget to act as *"purposeful fictional characters.* They mislay their scripts," while their inner life bumps against the outer where experience, framed by fiction, contradicts expectations (Wood 81, 90).

Love becomes, then, the ultimate subject precisely because it is unsolvable. It generates passion that has no outlet as seen in "The Kiss." It creates fantasies that remain unresolved. It becomes a vessel of disappointment, in both major and minor ways. All Chekhov could advise about love was that "if you wish women to love you, be original" (in Wood 81). Love seeks agency in a tumultuous world defined by suffering: tension is relentless resulting in a powerful but exuberant Russian sense of self-exhaustion. This is precisely the condition of the young military officer in "The Kiss" and of countless other Russian men and women experiencing unfulfilled love, pithily summarized by Belinsky in Tom Stoppard's "Voyage" from *The Coast of Utopia*: "for me, suffering and thinking are the same thing."[13]

Distress over love has been a persistent theme in Russian literary studies because of its emotional power and candid portrayal of failure. Its cultural narrative is one of dismay expressed romantically in the cliché "crimes of the heart."[14] The clarity with which writers from Pushkin to Tolstoy recount the challenges of love distinguishes their texts summarized in such early twentieth-century accounts of Russian writing as Prince Mirsky's *A History of Russian Literature* (1927). The repeated theme of romantic engagement and disengagement is inescapable which led the poet Marina Tsvetaeva to defiantly exclaim in 1919, "What an unloving country."[15]

But in the context of critical studies past and present, this account differs because it concentrates on nine individual Russian love affairs. Earlier work such as Joanna Hubbs's *Mother Russia: The Feminine Myth in Russian Culture* (1988) or Laura Engelstein's *The Keys to Happiness: Sex and the Search for Modernity in Fin-de-Siècle Russia* (1992) comprehensively analyzes the treatment of women and love but from a historical or sociological perspective. More recently, *Mapping the Feminine: Russian Women and Cultural Difference* (2008), edited by Irina Reyfman, plus Matthew Taunton's *Red Britain: The Russian Revolution in*

*Mid-century Culture* (2019) and Rebecca Beasley's *Russomania, Russian Culture and the Creation of British Modernism, 1881–1922* (2020) tangentially address the topic summarized in Anna McDonough's article "Love and Heartache in 19th Century Russian Literature" (2020).[16] But few if any of these works consider the actual love affairs of the figures presented in this study. Their focus is largely on the literary or cultural, not the actual encounters between lovers.

### iii

*"What necessity carries this man to Russia?"*
Walter Benjamin, "Dostoevsky's The Idiot" (1917)

The writers in this account are pragmatists in love who, being outsiders, bring a Western sense of experiential action to the dialectic of Russian love, minimally investing in the idea of Russian self-scrutiny. They are parallel to the character Natalia Haldin describes in *Under Western Eyes*: "He seems to be a man who has suffered more from his thoughts than from evil fortune," adding that "that is natural enough in a Russian .... so many of them are unfit for action, and yet unable to rest."[17] "In our country there are no practical people," the narrator of *The Idiot* reminds us.[18] But this became *the* conundrum for the major figures here who were fit for action but also trapped by love. Maugham, Lockhart, Gerhardi, or Wells were placed in, or created, situations where acting practically was essential but impeded by love. Yet, if they did not act, they would be arrested, deported, or tried.

The preponderance of non-fictional forms in the responses of these writers to Russian love may reflect a Chekhovian rather than Tolstoyian swerve. Few of them sought the sweep or panorama of history found in Tolstoy, or the spiritual challenges that characterized Dostoevsky. In the words of William Gerhardi, a Russian-born, Oxford-educated British military attaché stationed in St. Petersburg who wrote an early study of Chekhov, these figures focus on "creating convincing illusions of the life that is ... in the material sense of reality, ... *plus* all the sneaking, private, half-conscious perceptions, suspicions, sensations that go side by side with the 'official' barren life of fact." Gerhardi then elaborates, exposing the incompatibility between the reality of life and

> our romantic, smoother private visions of what life ought to be, and that, together, makes our life seem what it is, with its makeshifts, self-deception, contradiction, and emotional misunderstanding of individual and mutual sensibilities, which has seized him [Chekhov] and because he saw beauty in it ....[19]

The writers at the center of this study do not, indeed cannot, turn away from the life, the women, or the events that surround and immerse them in pre- and post-revolutionary Russia.

This situation, of course, is not new as the literature confirms. The idea of lovesickness or unfulfilled love has remained a crucial theme in Russian writing for almost three centuries. Passionate love is repeatedly met by passive heroes, the paradigm of unrequited love even taking on physiological expression. This preoccupied the Anglo-American and European writers in this account whose experience with Russian romance was direct, their reaction measured in a series of varied literary genres from diaries and autobiographies to fiction and drama. In their work, romance mixes with politics, ideology, and experience. Polozov's question in Chernyshevsky's *What Is to Be Done?*, "Can one *really* die of love?" or Rudin's admission in chapter IX of Turgenev's early novel that he was unable to say truthfully if he actually loved Natalya, are two recognized responses. But, Rudin asks, would he really suffer when he left her? And why did he wait for her with "secret anxiety?" The narrator answers, offering the basic paradox of Russian love: "no one is as easily carried away by his emotions as a dispassionate man."[20]

Such behavior is more than posturing. It is a deeply felt emotional response to early signs of love which Vladimir in Turgenev's novella *First Love* experienced. There, the capricious, sometimes mocking Zinaida inaugurates a powerful, youthful love which she dismisses and yet values which the narrator constantly re-evaluates: "I didn't want to know whether I was loved, and I didn't want to admit to myself that I was not."[21] He has shockingly learned that the young woman he loves is actually his father's mistress. But it is more than a romance. Such feelings and attachments signify a greater importance which the narrator of Conrad's *Under Western Eyes* understands when he describes the revolutionary Victor Haldin's sister: "I saw the gigantic shadow of Russian life deepening around her like the darkness of an advancing night" (UWE 168).

Unrequited love may be scorned or satirized but it is always keenly felt among Russian characters as Kitty rhetorically declares to her sister Dolly in *Anna Karenina*: "What, what is it you want to make me feel, what? .... 'that I was in love with a man who cared nothing for me, and that I'm dying of love for him?'"[22] But the emotional impact of unfulfilled love is beyond physical remedy: "Her heart was broken. And what did they want to do, treat her with pills and powders" (Karenina 119)? In the course of the novel, she declines a marriage proposal from Levin believing the more exciting Vronsky, infatuated with Anna Karenina, will ask her.[23] Such behavior in response to the condition of love fulfills a statement made in Turgenev's "A Correspondence" which also deals with failed romance: "We Russians have set ourselves no other task but the cultivation of our personalities" where, ironically, "habits of self-consciousness distort the very striving for truth."[24] Love is complex and brings jealousies and guilt, or as Vladimir's father writes in an unfinished letter to his son at the end of *First Love*, "beware of the love of women; beware of that Ecstasy—that slow poison" (First Love 103). Ecstasy and poison unite.

Epitomizing the intersection of revolution and romance is Ralph Fox's novel *Storming Heaven* (1928). A well-known British Communist and Oxford graduate, Fox visited the Soviet Union many times and met his wife there, marrying in Moscow in 1926 but returning to England in time for the General Strike. Four years later, he became a librarian at the Marx-Engels's Institute in Moscow (1930–1932) and then a columnist for the *Daily Worker* in London. His biography of Lenin appeared in 1933. He died fighting in the Spanish Civil War at age thirty-six.

*Storming Heaven* reframes the idea of Russian love by attaching it clearly to politics and ideology. The novel is an account of an American torn between two lovers: Nadya, an uncomplicated, innocent girl from the countryside, and Neura, an actor and *femme fatale*. These two women represent female tropes repeated often in Russian literature but now affiliated politically with the idea of free love: "Liberty in love, only liberty worth having," a character exclaims in an effort to "smash the bourgeois sex tyranny."[25] Johnson, the male hero, is caught in the middle, and cannot decide between the two: Nadya, with her factory job and nights spent attending classes or meetings or the appealing Neura who performs, on and off the stage, enticing John until a new lover, an Englishman with money, turns up.

Two events accentuate the themes: the death of Lenin with vivid descriptions of the lying-in-state and funeral, and a visit to a prison. The former provides a colorful account of Moscow's response: it "seemed the whole nation was in the streets" with their banners, marchers, shouts, and grief. The social details accompanying the demonstrations offer a detailed glimpse of repression and unhealthy urban conditions. But politics activates love. Nadya explains this via the classic love dilemma: the first night I saw you I loved you but I did not know you. Now that I know you and still love you, "part of you is the fact that you'll leave me" (SH 231).

Disappointment is anticipated and tension prevails, accelerated by the temptations of Neura whose beauty and passion are "emphatic" (SH 249). In the background is Marxism, neatly stated by Fox in *The Novel and The People* when he writes that Marx "believed that the material mode of life in the end determined the intellectual," although he did not believe the connection was direct. Fox also believed that the novel is "the most typical creation of bourgeois literature" and "its greatest creation."[26]

After John rejects Nadya (I can never settle down, he tells her), the hero turns to Neura only to discover that she has been jesting with his love and has turned to the Englishman. Feeling angry and betrayed, he returns one evening to discover Neura with her guest; in a fit of jealous rage, he murders her, echoing the scene at the end of *The Idiot* where Rogozhin murders Nastasya. Only by killing her can Rogozhin possess Natasya and only by murder can John control Neura. To no one's surprise, John ends up in a Moscow prison, the very prison he had earlier visited.

The novel is less a record of Moscow life in the 1920s than a representation of Russian love, divided between the ideal and the corporal. The hero struggles between the two and destroys the one offering physical passion because it is denied to him. But the outcome is not a transcendent, ideal bliss but a Russian jail. The story is a variation of Tolstoy's "Kreutzer Sonata" where jealous violence shapes the action but with a different outcome. Importantly, both stories register the intensity of Russian love translated into action. "Russian natures have a singular power of resistance against the unfair strains of life," Conrad wrote, suggesting that the Russian response is uncontrollable action motivated by emotion (UWE 147). At the end of Fox's novel, John recalls what a priest had said in Pavlovak: "Life was storming heaven" (SH 310). John's assault on heaven did not succeed, his quest for love on earth a failure. Fox presents two contested views of love with Bolshevik love a seeming success, wanton love no more than a dangerous liaison. What his novel and the experiences of Benjamin, Maugham, and Berlin confirm is (slightly rewriting Marx) that the material mode of life in the end determines love. Surrounding and effecting the heart are social, cultural, and political barriers.

iv

*What does love mean; is love the same for Russians and for [the] English?*
        Virginia Woolf, "Tchekhov on Pope" (Unpublished), 1925

In Russian love individuals repeatedly love an imagined, not an actual, self. Gurov in Chekhov's "The Lady with the Little Dog" realizes this when Anna Sergeevna visits him in Moscow and acknowledges the power of their secret love, hiding from people "like thieves." But, he asks, "was their life not broken"?[27] Late in the story, Gurov, seeing himself in the mirror, realizes that he's aged and wonders what women see in him. He then understands it was "a man their imagination had created, whom they had greedily sought all their lives" (Lady 427). But now, he was truly in love despite his wife and his mistress's husband. The couple wants to end their secret and deceptive life but as the story concludes, the final sentence creates suspense: "the most complicated and difficult part was just beginning" (Lady 427). This enigmatic end confirms Gurov's view that every intimacy and affair becomes "a major task, extremely complicated" and finally "burdensome" (Lady 415). But offsetting his anxiety is Chekhov's final phrase suggesting hope: "the end was still, far, far off" (Lady 427).The act of attenuated love repeats itself in the actual experiences of those foreign writers with Russian lovers where there is always a longing that is unfulfilled. This is quintessentially Russian—not just between the disappointed love between Walter Benjamin and the actor Lācis but between H.G. Wells and Moura Budbeg or Isaiah Berlin and Anna Akhmatova. An anecdote involving Boris Pasternak and Akhmatova summarizes the complicated and contradictory experience of love partly expressed by the term *malentendu*. In the 1920s, Pasternak repeatedly visited Akhmatova and expressed his feelings for her, declaring that he could not live without her. Akhmatova remained indifferent. Pasternak would then tire of his declarations and call his wife to come and bring him home.[28]

But the idea of a love triangle seemed one solution, embedded in the theory of Russian love. In the figures at the center of this study, it appears repeatedly, initiated perhaps by Turgenev who as a young man fell in love Pauline Viardot, an opera singer, and pursued her across Europe. She at one point invited him to join her and her husband in Paris and he did, later sending his son to live with her. As noted earlier, Asja Lācis similarly invited Walter Benjamin to join her while in a relationship with Bernhardt Reich. Moura Budberg suggested a similar arrangement while in a relationship with Gorky; even Isaiah Berlin found himself in a parallel situation with Aline Halban who would eventually leave her husband and marry Berlin, but not without her husband first inviting him to join a *ménage à trois*, something of a Russian habit—but rarely a success.[29]

The origin of this behavior, at least for the women, was likely the financial and legal independence of Russian women of the *haute bourgeoise* and aristocracy established in the eighteenth century. The specific change providing financial security for women was the Law of Single Inheritance instituted in 1714 by Peter the Great. Women could legally inherit patrimonial estates, both finances and, by 1731, land. Women from the nobility and merchant class benefited and were able to manage their own wealth offering them new independence. Not only did Russian law permit them to maintain any financial or landed inheritance but it allowed them to conduct business, exchange properties, and sign contracts.

Such freedom led to social and romantic independence, a life separate from their often authoritarian or jealous husbands. At their own apartments or even villas, the women entertained, took lovers, and led a liberated life while maintaining their marriages. Of course, not all had the financial means to live so well but the trickle-down ideal of freedom in love meant women revolutionaries, artists, and bohemians had precedent for their own freewheeling lives.

The Irish Wilmot sisters who visited Russia at the beginning of the nineteenth century were among the first to observe and react to this behavior. In their *Russian Journals*, they expressed surprise, if not shock, at this somewhat common practice known as "marriage à la russe" or "in the Russian way." It was not uncommon to have a General or gentleman's mistress attend a ball or be at home with his mistress and his wife as the Wilmot's recorded. To their chagrin, a woman of means could live "separated from her Husband *in the Russian way*, that is keeping different establishments but on very good terms & writing Letters to each other by every Post."[30] The collapse of social boundaries between a mistress and the family upset the moralistic Wilmots but hardly altered the practice. The celebrated equality of women later promoted by the Bolsheviks may be the annexation of this nineteenth-century habit of women's social and sexual independence translated into the "set of three" that characterizes a variety of relations narrated in this account of Russian love.[31]

Tolstoy, however, took this situation of three lovers into the realm of jealousy and violence in "The Kreutzer Sonata" (1889) where Russian love and Russian emotions conflict. When the unhappily married wife of Pozdnyshev begins a flirtation with the violinist and music teacher Troukhatchevsky, her husband at first does not object, but then the triangle cracks. Such flirting harmed the family's honor. The husband, soon believing there *was* an affair, becomes jealous and attacks both when he discovers them alone at the piano; his rage turns violent, beating and stabbing his wife as his jealously overpowers him. As she dies, the husband expects her to repent; she does not. "Hate," not "forgive me," is her final word transforming unrequited love into remorseless love, the triangle oddly surviving in death, not life. Ironically, the husband is acquitted of murder because of the wife's perceived adultery. "Love or not, but do not disturb the household. Every husband can govern his wife. He has the necessary power. It is only the imbecile who does not succeed in doing so," says the husband who narrates the story in the opening scene in a train car.[32]

The subsequent conversation of three figures in a train car confronts the complex and seemingly temporal nature of Russian love as the following illustrates. Attempting to define love, a woman claims it is

> "a preference for one man or one woman to the exclusion of all others …."
>
> "A preference for how long? … For a month, two days, or half an hour?" said the nervous gentleman, with special irritation.
>
> "No, permit me, you evidently are not talking of the same thing."
>
> "Yes, I am talking absolutely of the same thing. Of the preference for one man or one woman to the exclusion of all others. But I ask: a preference for how long?"
>
> "For how long? For a long time, for a life-time sometimes."
>
> "But that happens only in novels. In life, never. In life this preference for one to the exclusion of all others lasts in rare cases several years, oftener several months, or even weeks, days, hours …".
>
> ("Kreutzer," Ch.2)

Love is temporal and does not exist argues a lawyer: "To talk of loving a man or woman for life is like saying that a candle can burn forever." But the true issue, as a second gentleman declares, is that to affirm "that love, real love, does not consecrate marriage, as we are in the habit of believing, but that, on the contrary, it ruins it" ("Kreutzer," Ch. 2).[33] Yeats sensed this situation in another but applicable context when he wrote that "We had fed the heart on fantasies / The heart's grown brutal from the fare; / More substance in our enmities / Than in our love."[34]

But the story indicts sex which can only lead to violence, the narrator implicitly condemning sexual passion even between married couples. The suggestion of an affair undermining marriage, however, led to the novella being banned in Russia and the United States. Abstinence became the new goal but Tolstoy's wife, Sofiya, and others read the story as an attack on her integrity. She resisted and successfully petitioned the Tsar to lift the publication ban in an effort to persuade the world it was not about her. The Tsar granted her request and in her diary she congratulated herself on her accomplishment as a woman. Sofiya herself then wrote a novella, "Whose Fault?" a rebuttal to her husband's position, although it also narrates the death of the female protagonist, albeit more from alienation rather than sex.[35]

Beyond Russian love are Russian emotions identified by Isaiah Berlin when writing to the widow of the American critic Edmund Wilson whom he first met and admired in 1946: "I felt Russian emotions in his presence: love, acute interest in every word, a sense of pride about knowing him at all;" he also respected Wilson's grasp of Russian and Hebrew.[36] Virginia Woolf, in her comments on Russian literature, explicitly identified and praised the representation of Russian emotions: in a passage omitted from a later version of "Mr. Bennett and Mrs. Brown," Woolf says that "after reading *Crime and Punishment* and *The Idiot*, how could any young novelist believe in 'characters' as the Victorians had painted them?" For figures like Raskolnikov, Myshkin, or Stavrogin, we "go down into them as we descend into some enormous cavern …. it is all dark, terrible and uncharted" but also thrilling.[37]

Woolf read *Anna Karenina* three times and in 1933 read through eleven volumes of Turgenev's fiction, as well as a biography, memoir, and set of letters for her essay "The Novels of Turgenev." She had read *Crime and Punishment* in French on her honeymoon. In a 1918 review in the *TLS*, she wrote that "the Russians might well overcome us, for they seemed to possess an entirely new conception of the novel and one that was … much more profound than ours."[38] She also understood that the power of the Russian writers originated in "their deep sense of human suffering and their unwavering sympathy with it." "Don't they see through everything—the Russians? All the little disguises we've put up?" Woolf asked in her comments on *Uncle Vanya* (1937).[39]

Woolf repeatedly speculated on the differences between English and Russian cultural identities. Her 1918 essay on George Meredith recorded her thoughts clearly. The Russians, she wrote, "accumulate: they accept ugliness; they seek to understand: they penetrate further and further into the human soul with their terrible power of sustained insight and their undeviating reverence for truth."[40] In this, Russian emotion and literary energy find their source.

But there was also a social side to "Russomania" beyond soul-searching. Somerset Maugham captured this in his volume *Ashenden*. There, he writes that when his protagonist met Anastasia Alexandrovna, an exile in England,

> It was at the time when Europe discovered Russia. Everyone was reading the Russian novelists, the Russian dancers captivated the civilised world, and the Russian composers set shivering the sensibility of persons who were beginning to want a change from Wagner. Russian art seized upon Europe with the virulence of an epidemic of influenza. New phases became the fashion, new colours, new emotions ….

To seem Russian, at least in behavior, was an aspiration. The impact of the culture was so great that Ashenden comically "changed the cushions of his sitting-room, hung an eikon on the wall, read Chekov and went to the ballet," while "women of letters tremulously put their lips to a glass of vodka."[41] The tone is satiric but the meaning apt.

## V

Geometry may be one way of conceptualizing Russian love which employs geometric relationships, although its categories can never quite sustain geometric rigor. Strict patterns break apart and the geometry of love, recurrently a triangle, constantly re-defines itself. The geometry of Russian love is always irregular, struggling under constant pressure to have angles and lines intersect. But oblique lines can only meet in angles; parallel lines "though infinite, can never meet" as Marvell writes in "The Definition of Love," eight four-line stanzas, where he outlines the struggle in its opening stanza:

> My Love is of a birth as rare
> As 'tis for object strange and high:
> It was begotten by Despair
> Upon Impossibility.

The language of astronomical measurement frames the idea of unrequited love outlined in the seventh stanza:

> As lines so Loves *oblique* may well
> Themselves in every angle greet:
> But ours so truly *parallel*
> Though infinite can never meet.

In Russian love, parallel lines never meet. Geometry becomes a metaphor of love but its principles ensure a love that can never be fulfilled. Conjunction and opposition rule:

> Therefore the Love which us doth bind,
> But fate so enviously debars,
> Is the Conjunction of the mind,
> And Opposition of the stars.

The impossibility of love is what makes it powerful, rare, and inescapable, simultaneously hopeless and desirable resulting in "Magnanimous Despair" (1.5).[42]

Epitomizing the condition of disappointed love is Turgenev's "Diary of a Superfluous Man" (1850) where the narrator, Stocking, a government bureaucrat, rises to romantic heights falling in love with the daughter of a landowner with four hundred peasants in a rural town, only to be supplanted by a dashing Prince from St. Petersburg who dazzles the youthful Liza. Seeking revenge at the undoing of his idealized idea of love, Stocking insults the Prince at a ball; a dual follows where Stocking only grazes the Prince who then graciously calls off the fight and forgives the original insult. The magnanimity of the Prince further undermines Stocking, overshadowing any sense of reprisal on Stocking's part.

Humiliated, Stocking is only emboldened to try again at love when the Prince peremptorily leaves and makes no expected marriage offer. Stocking now believes he has a second chance to display his own magnanimity in taking back the lovelorn Liza. But she dismisses him and, in the end, decides to marry the common place Bizmyonkov. The story dissects love, the narrator asking at one point "is love really a natural feeling?" and answers that "love is a disease and disease knows no laws."[43] A few pages earlier, however, he exclaims that "my whole life was radiated with love, every part of it down to the smallest details, as if it had been a dark box-room into which a candle had been brought" (Diary 38).

But in the story, disappointment rules framed by irony. Despite the uplift of love, the narrator knows that Liza was "not in the least in love with me" (Diary 40). And when he learns of the Prince's betrayal, he exhibits the Russian reaction to the loss of love: satisfaction in disappointment. "I finally realized how much pleasure a man can take in being aware of his own misfortune;" "even in the midst of my sadness I was glad in some way" (Diary 62, 64). "They say that in some cases, when someone really loves you, it is even useful to torment the beloved," he adds (Diary 47). Even Liza shares this paradoxical state, telling Bizmyonkov, a petty town official, that "I wouldn't exchange my unhappiness for their happiness .... he [the Prince] didn't love me for long, but he loved me" (Diary 69)! Compounding the irony is the impending death Stocking senses at the end of his diary: "My heart, so ready and willing to love, will soon stop beating" (Diary 71). He ironically dies loveless on April Fool's day, remaining the superfluous man he always claimed to be (Diary 71, 72). For him, love arrived and then evaporated. The contest between magnanimity and loss, united through love, is the actual subject of the story.

The philosopher Vladimir Solovev's work *The Meaning of Love* (1892–4) summarizes a great deal of the Russian absorption with love. Written in response to Tolstoy's "*The Kreutzer Sonata*," it celebrates erotic love. Both authors were puzzled by the conflict between the philosophical meaning of love and the physical expression of sexual desire. Solovev could not accept asceticism or the celibate ideal. His effort to channel the sex drive toward the abolition of death is a Russian alternative to Freud's concept of the death instinct.[44] But what is important is less Solovev's theories and his effort to outline an "erotic utopia," than the constant focus on love as the center between a life of fulfillment and a life of unhappiness.

The impact of Russian love has a biographical and cultural importance equal to the literary which T.S. Eliot recognizes at the opening of his 1917 essay, "Reflections on Vers Libre" Eliot quotes an acquaintance who exclaims that "since the Russians came in I can read nothing else. I have finished Dostoevski, and I do not know what to do."[45] Virginia Woolf felt a similar *frisson* but she knew what to do: read and translate Tolstoy, write about Chekhov and Turgenev. She summarized her reaction in part in her 1925 essay "The Russian Point of View" reprinted in *The Common Reader* celebrating the cultural power of the Russians.

Reaction to the Russian imaginary of love was as varied as it was complex. While the public applauded the Russian national anthem during the First World War at the proms, Conrad exposed the contradictory impulses of the country's authoritarianism and revolt. Having one's illusions destroyed by the Russian aristocracy—"I live in hope of seeing all the Ministries destroyed" one character in *Under Western Eyes* announces—emphasizes defeat through cynicism and "moral negation" (UWE 130, 136). Men and women who suffer more from their thoughts than from evil action are "natural enough for a Russian" (UWE 140) but *not* for Maugham, Wells, or Woolf. They confronted Russia with love and skepticism despite its character as a politically unstable enigma soon to be ruled by autocrats. For them, Russia was a fascinating riddle imaginatively expressed through the darkness of Dostoevsky, the sweep of Tolstoy, the precision of Turgenev, and the domestic tensions of Chekhov. As Lezhnev says in *Rudin*, "Russia can get on without any of us, but not one of us can get on without Russia" (Rudin 158).

How Russian love, often expressed through the prism of lovesickness, effected the lives and writing of this set of authors is the concern of this study, understood clearly by John le Carré. On his first visit to Russia, a KGB border guard asked him, "Why do you look older than the photo in your passport?" "Because I've been disappointed in love," he answered.[46] The key word is "disappointed."

## Notes

1. On this particular trope, see Ellen Rutten, *Unattainable Bride Russia, Gendering Nation, State and Intelligentsia in Russian Intellectual Culture* (Evanston, IL: Northwestern University Press, 2010), 36–41. Rutten develops the idea of a gendered love triangle between the bride of Russia, the masculine state, and the intelligentsia (Rutten 42). I am arguing that this contested situation plays out in the actual relations documented by the nine figures in this study, although a marriage between a feminized Russia and the West (represented by the males in this study), despite their individual feelings, is impossible. Rutten also outlines the mythopoetic, folkloric elements attached to the trope but also stresses that sexuality and revolutionary crises do not mix. In some instances, the noble and long-suffering Russian woman cannot coalesce with the largely ineffectual western "visitor/hero."
2. Elizabeth Hardwick, "Hedda Gabler," *Seduction and Betrayal: Women and Literature* (New York: Vintage, 1975), 52–3. Hereafter Hardwick.
3. This is the moment when Anna nearly dies after childbirth and asks for forgiveness which she knows is impossible. Her husband Alexei and Vronsky are in her bedroom at the same time. Tolstoy, *Anna Karenina*, tr. Richard Pevear and Larissa Volokhonsky (New York: Penguin, 2002), 413. in Part IV, Ch. 17.
4. Dostoevsky, "White Nights," *White Nights and Other Stories*, tr. Constance Garnett (New York: Grove Press, 1960), 37.
5. Ivan Goncharov, *Oblomov*, tr. Stephen Pearl (Richmond, Surrey: Alma Classics, 2015), 245. Also see 304–8.
6. The phrase "double-voiced discourse" appears in Susan Lanser and Evelyn Torton Beck, "[Why] Are There No Great Women Critics?" *The Prism of Sex: Essays in the Sociology of Knowledge*, ed. Beck and Julia A. Sherman (Madison, WI: University of Wisconsin Press, 1979), 86.

    Also useful is Barbara Heldt, *Terrible Perfection: Women and Russian Literature* (Bloomington: Indiana University Press, 1987). For a valuable survey, see Arja Rosenhom and Irina Savkina, "'How Women Should Write;' Russian Women's Writing in the Nineteenth Century," *Women in Nineteenth-Century Russia, Lives and Culture*, ed. Wendy Rosslyn and Alessandra Tosi (Cambridge: Open Edition Books, 2012), 161–207. https://books.openedition.org/obp/1253?lang=en.
7. Tolstoy, *Family Happiness* (1859), tr. Louise and Aylmer Maude. Part I Ch. 2. http://www.magister.msk.ru/library/tolstoy/english/tolsl19e.htm. Tolstoy, *Anna Karenina*, tr. Pevear and Volokhonsky, 312.
8. Anton Chekhov, "The Kiss," tr. Ann Dunnigan, *Anton Chekhov's Selected Stories*, ed. Cathy Popkin (New York: Norton, 2014), 120–1. Hereafter, Kiss.
9. As James Wood writes, Ryabovich has wriggled out of Chekhov's story "into the bottomless freedom of disappointment," trying to make his own story independent

of Chekhov: "the soldier forgets that he is in Chekhov's story because he has become so involved in his own." James Wood, "What Chekhov Meant by Life," *The Broken Estate, Essays on Literature and Belief* (New York: Picador, 2010), 90. Hereafter Wood.

For further commentary, see Cathy Popkin, "Kiss and Tell," *Sexuality and the Body in Russian Culture*, ed. Jane T. Costlow, et al. (Stanford: Stanford University Press, 1993), 139–55.

10   Chekhov in Wood 89. Chekhov explained this in an 1898 letter to his friend Alexi Suvorin.

11   Two more examples are *The Idiot* (1869) and Chekhov's "A Little Game" (1886). The former presents complex relationships of love crossed, undone, and unfulfilled, especially for Prince Myshkin, who, like the women, hesitates.

In "A Little Game," "words of love" may or may not have been uttered by the male protagonist or the wind to a young woman while sledding. She is uncertain. Did she hear them or not and who said them? But the words become "a habit for Nadenka, like wine or morphine. She cannot live without them," actually prompting her to undertake dangerous downhill sledding in an attempt to have them repeated. But this, too, passes and remains unknown. Nonetheless, the desire for love persists (Chekhov, "A Little Game," tr. Katherine Tiernan O'Connor, *Selected Stories*, 59–60).

12   Chekhov, "Concerning Love," *The Kiss and Other Stories*, tr. Ronald Wilks (London: Penguin, 1982), 146. The full story is 145–53. This 1898 short story continues the dilemma of Russian love with Chekhov at one point ironically and tersely writing that

> with love, if you start theorizing about it, you must have a nobler, more meaningful starting-point than mere happiness or unhappiness, sin or virtue, as they are commonly understood. Otherwise its best not to theorize at all. (153)

Love is again disappointment and sadness as Ratikin's cynical statement from Turgenev's *A Month in the Country* confirms: "Every love, happy as well as unhappy, is a real disaster when you give yourself over to it entirely."

13   Tom Stoppard, "Voyage," *The Coast of Utopia* (New York: Grove Press, 2007), 110.

14   The phrase appears in Svetlana Boym, "Loving in Bad Taste," *Sexuality and the Body in Russian Culture*, ed. Jane T. Costlow et al. (Stanford: Stanford University Press, 1993), 156.

15   Marina Tsvetaeva, "Diary" of 1919 in Boym, "Loving in Bad Taste," *Sexuality and the Body*, 156.

16 Anna McDonough, "Love and Heartache in 19th Century Russian Literature," *Emory Journal of Asian Studies* II. Special Edition (April 2020). https://ejasonline.org/wp-content/uploads/2020/04/REALC_2020_McDonogh.pdf.

Also useful are *A Plot of Her Own: The Female Protagonist in Russian Literature*, ed. Sona Stephan Hoisington (Evanston, IL: Northwestern University Press, 1995) and Gregory Carleton's *Sexual Revolution in Bolshevik Russia* (Pittsburgh, PA: University of Pittsburgh Press, 2004).

17 Joseph Conrad, *Under Western Eyes*, ed. Stephen Donovan, Intrd. Allan H. Simmons (London: Penguin, 2007), 140. Hereafter UWE.

18 Dostoevsky, *The Idiot*, tr. Richard Pevear and Larissa Volokhonsky (New York: Vintage, 2003), 325.

19 William Gerhardi, *Anton Chekov: A Critical Study* (London: Cobden-Sanderson, 1923), 16.

20 Turgenev, *Rudin*, tr. Richard Freeborn (London: Penguin 1975), 124. Hereafter Rudin.

21 Turgenev, *First Love*, tr. Isaiah Berlin (London: Penguin, 1978), 92. Turgenev, "A Correspondence," V.S. Pritchett, "Introduction," *First Love* 13; *First Love* 103.

Berlin translated *First Love* five years after he had his monumental encounter with Anna Akhmatova. In the novella, the narrator witnesses his father strike Zinaida with his whip. Shocked, he then watches her silently raise her arm and kiss the scar "which glowed crimson upon it" (First Love 101). Love is grateful pain always accompanied by "tense excitement" (Turgenev, First Love 89) "She did exactly what she liked with me," the narrator confesses (First Love 91). Berlin would also translate Turgenev's *A Month in the Country*.

The impact of Turgenev on Berlin's liberal views of social and political change was profound according to his biographer Michael Ignatieff. See Ignatieff, *A Life of Isaiah Berlin* (Toronto: Viking, 1998), 71. Berlin and Akhmatova disagreed on the significance of Turgenev, however: he celebrated the author's irony and delicacy; she was impatient with the writer's outlook. Dostoevsky was her preference. See Ignatieff 159.

22 Leo Tolstoy, *Anna Karenina*, tr. Richard Pevear and Larissa Volokhonsky (London: Penguin, 2001), 124.

23 For a discussion of the physiological and psychological impact of love in nineteenth-century Russian writing, see Valeria Sobol, *Febris Erotica, Lovesickness in the Russian Literary Imagination* (Seattle: University of Washington Press, 2009), especially Chapters 6 and 7. Sobol's emphasis is medical whereas mine is literary.

24 Turgenev, "A Correspondence, Letter VI," *The Diary of a Superfluous Man and Other Stories*, tr. Constance Garnett. Project Gutenberg. https://www.gutenberg.org/cache/epub/9615/pg9615.html.

25 Ralph Fox, *Storming Heaven* (London: Constable, 1928), 25, 26. Hereafter SH. For a useful biographical summary of Fox's career, see Graham Stevenson, "Fox,

Ralph," *Encyclopedia of Communist Biographies*, September 19, 2008. https://grahamstevenson.me.uk/2008/09/19/ralph-fox/.

26  Ralph Fox, *The Novel and the People*, Preface Jeremy Hawthorn (London: Lawrence and Wishart, 1937), 29, 42.
27  Anton Chekhov, "The Lady with the Little Dog," *Anton Chekhov's Selected Stories*, ed. Cathy Popkin, tr. Richard Pevear and Olga Volokhonsky (New York: Norton, 2014), 426. Hereafter Lady.
28  Ignatieff, *A Life of Isaiah Berlin*, 160.
29  Ignatieff, *A Life of Isaiah Berlin*, 215–16. Sociologically, Chernyshevsky's ideas about replacing conjugal couples with a *ménage à trois* in *What Is to Be Done?* (1863) is a nineteenth-century source.

   An earlier prototype may have been the eighteenth-century *ménage à trois* between the Regent Anna, her lady-in-waiting Julie Mengden and their joint lover, Count Lynar outlined by Simon Montefiore in *The Romanovs: 1613–1918* (New York: Alfred A. Knopf, 2016).

   During the Russian Revolution, high-ranking women in the Communist Party advocated free love as a government policy in an effort to destroy bourgeois institutions such as monogamy and marriage. Alexandra Kollontai, the first Commissar of Social Welfare, co-founder of the Women's Department in the Communist Party, Soviet ambassador to Sweden and the author of the novel *Red Love* (1923), was a leading spokesperson for this idea summarized as "comradely love." See Teresa L. Ebert, "Alexandra Kollontai and Red Love," *Against the Current* 81 (July 1, 1999). https://againstthecurrent.org/atc081/p1724/ and Paula Erizanu, "The Revolutionary Sex," *Aeon* (2018). https://aeon.co/essays/the-shining-moment-when-russian-revolutionary-women-reinvented-sex and Prince D.S. Mirsky describes another *ménage* in his *History of Russian Literature* relating to the publisher/ poet/radical Nikolay Nekrásov born in 1821. His love affair with Mme Panayeva lasted nearly ten years and for a time Nekrásov lived with Panayevas, "a form of George Sandian liberalism" popular in the nineteenth century, Mirsky adding that they "got much more suffering than joy from their liaison." Mirsky, *A History of Russian Literature* (New York: Knopf, 1927), 297. The dedicatee of the history is Jane Ellen Harrison. One further example is the poet Mayakovsky who lived with his muse, Lilya Brik, and her husband, the Marxist critic Osip Brik.
30  Martha Wilmont in *The Russian Journals of Martha and Catherine Wilmot, 1803–1808*, ed. Marchioness of Londonderry and H.M. Hyde (London: Macmillan, 1934), 286–7. Hereafter RussJournals.

   Also see Judith Vowles's "Marriage à la russe," *Sexuality and the Body in Russian Culture*, ed. Jane T. Costlow, Stephanie Sandler, and Judith Vowles (Stanford: Stanford University Press, 1993), 53–72. Vowles discusses the independence of upper middle-class Russian women in the late eighteenth and early nineteenth centuries noting in particular that a woman of means could carry on a series of affairs and not jeopardize her marriage.

According to Martha Wilmot, the control of women over their own fortunes created a "'remarkable degree of liberty & a degree of independence'" to such an extent that they acted as men and became the active party in love matters (RussJournals 271). But such independence in the eyes of some made women ungovernable and unlovable but dependent women were prone to male tyranny, infidelity, and abandonment (Vowles 65). A clear sign of fallen Russian morals for the Wilmots is Prince Zenovia who, needing funds, has "Let a wing of his House as a Brothel" and "lives *with his family* in the remainder of his Palace" (RussJournals 294)!

31   The Russian Revolution of 1917 reinforced the legal equality of women and men and encouraged them to enter the work force, freeing them from economic dependency on men. The right to vote and hold public office was granted to Russian women over twenty in July 1917 just before the October Revolution, while the Family Code of 1918 instituted further rights for women. In 1920 Russia became the first country in the world to legalize abortion, although it was eliminated in 1936 under Stalin but legalized again in 1955 after Stalin's death. See Megan Stewart, "Curbing Reliance on Abortion in Russia," *Human Rights Brief* 11.2 (2004): 51–4.

Useful sources: Barbara Alpern-Engel, *Mothers and Daughters: Women of the Intelligentsia in Nineteenth Century Russia* (Evanston, IL: Northwestern University Press, 2000) and her *Women in Russia, 1700–2000* (Cambridge: Cambridge University Press, 2004) plus Rochelle Ruthchild's *Equality & Revolution: Women's Rights in the Russian Empire, 1905–1917* (Pittsburgh, PA: University of Pittsburgh Press, 2010) and *The Palgrave Handbook of Women and Gender in Twentieth-Century Russia and the Soviet Union*, ed. Melanie Illic (London: Palgrave Macmillan, 2018).

32   Tolstoy, Ch. 1, *The Kreutzer Sonata and Other Stories*, tr. Benjamin R. Tucker (Boston: Tucker Publisher, 1890). Project Gutenberg. https://www.gutenberg.org/files/689/689-h/689-h.htm#pref01. Hereafter Chapters indicated.

33   For an update on the love triangle, see Nabokov's short story "Spring in Fialta" (1936) with an accidental death at the end. The male protagonist lacks the conviction of true love and lets his early lover Nina drift away, although his feelings persist.

For a fascinating follow-up to the story in Tolstoy's own family, see *The Kreutzer Sonata Variations*, tr. and ed. Michael Katz (New Haven: Yale University Press, 2014). It includes Tolstoy's original story plus two counter-stories including Sofiya Tolstoy's "Whose fault?".

34   W.B. Yeats, "Meditations in Time of Civil War," *Selected Poems* (London: Penguin, 2000), 140. D.M. Thomas used this passage as the epigraph to his novel *The White Hotel*.

35  See Sophia Pinkham, "Sofiya's Tolstoy's Defense," *New Yorker*, October 21, 2014. https://www.newyorker.com/books/page-turner/sofiya-tolstoys-defense.
36  Isaiah Berlin in Jeffrey Meyers, *Edmund Wilson: A Biography* (Boston: Houghton Mifflin, 1995), 347.
37  Woolf, *The Essays of Virginia Woolf*, vol. 3, ed. Andrew McNeillie (New York: Harcourt Brace Jovanovich, 1988), 386. For additional details on Woolf and Russia, see I.B. Nadel, "The Russian Woolf," *Modernist Cultures* 13 (2018): 546–67.
38  Woolf, *TLS*, July 25, 1918; Essays 2: 273.
39  Woolf, "'The Russian View,' 1918," *Essays* 2: 341–2; Virginia Woolf, "Uncle Vanya," *The Complete Shorter Fiction*, 2nd ed., ed. Susan Dick (San Diego: Harcourt Brace Jovanovich, 1989), 247.
40  Virginia Woolf, "On Rereading Meredith" (1918), *Granite and Rainbow: Essays* (London: Hogarth Press, 1958), 50.
41  Somerset Maugham, *Ashenden* (London: Vintage, 2000), 293, 294. For a comparison of Maugham and Woolf's view of Russia, see I.B. Nadel, "Maugham and Woolf in Russia: *Ashenden* and *Orlando*," *Journal of English Language and Literature* 66.1 (2020): 23–43. Also helpful is Natalya Reinhold, "Virginia Woolf's Russian Voyage Out," *Woolf Studies Annual* 9 (2003): 1–27.
42  Andrew Marvell, "The Definition of Love," *Norton Anthology of English Literature*, vol. 1, 7th ed., ed. M.H. Abrams (New York: Norton, 2000), 1693.

    In 1965, the American writer John Cheever published "The Geometry of Love," an account of an engineer who tries to understand his rocky relationship with his wife in terms of geometric forms. At one moment, looking out a window, he sees a small truck advertising "Euclid's Dry Cleaning and Dyeing" and immediately thinks of "the principles of geometric analysis and the doctrine of proportion .... if he could make a geometric analysis of his problems, mightn't he solve them, or at least create an atmosphere of solution?" John Cheever, *Collected Stories and Other Writings* (New York: Library of America, 2009), 716–17.
43  Turgenev, "Diary of a Superfluous Man," *First Love and Other Stories*, tr. Richard Freeborn (Oxford: Oxford World's Classics, 2008), 44. Hereafter Diary.
44  Olga Matich, *Erotic Utopia, The Decadent Imagination in Russia's Fin de Siècle* (Madison: University of Wisconsin Press, 2005), 60. In Solovev there is a desire to transcend the empirical world. *Doctor Zhivago* marks the popularity of Tolstoy's *Kreutzer Sonata* and Solovev's *The Meaning of Love*: in the work, the young heroes read both authors in tandem.
45  T.S. Eliot, "Reflections on Vers Libre," *To Criticize the Critic and Other Writings* (New York: Farrar, Straus & Giroux, 1965), 183. The essay originally appeared in *The New Statesman* March 3, 1917.
46  Adam Sisman, *John Le Carré, The Biography* (Toronto: Knopf, 2015), 453.

# *Prelude*: Walter Benjamin in Love

> "*All forward-thinking people in their right mind are going to Moscow these days!*"
>
> Asja Lācis, *A Revolutionary by Profession* (1971)

Walter Benjamin was married when he traveled to Moscow in the winter of 1926 in pursuit of the Latvian actress and Marxist children's theater director Asja Lācis.[1] His *Moscow Diary* records his passionate pursuit of this remarkable woman, herself in a relationship at the time with Bernhard Reich, a German director and theater critic.[2] The likelihood of a love triangle was in the making. Benjamin may have originally thought he wanted the experience of Moscow—"I want to write a description of Moscow at the present moment in which 'all factuality is already theory,'" Benjamin wrote to Martin Buber in 1927—but that was not the cause of his journey. It was a Slavic/Russian romance, one that required a mix of diplomacy and passion that brought him to Moscow, having already surprised Lācis in Riga in 1925 after their initial meeting in Capri in 1924.

Nevertheless, on a broader level, Benjamin's travels through the streets of Moscow reveal the complex interplay between territory and national identity. His diary documents a sense of an increasing alienation of Russians from self and society, particularly evident in his personally registering Moscow's atmosphere and weather. The effects of coldness on his body and skin are a constant litany of discomfort, echoing his struggle to adapt to a complex sociopolitical moment. In mapping and charting these relations, he learns to extract various codes and reveal how cities are signifying machines. He first outlined this in *One-Way Street* and then his essay "Naples" (1925) co-authored with Asja. In his 1927 essay "Moscow," Benjamin emphasizes that one understands Europe better for having spent time in Russia, although the country forces one to "choose his standpoint …. In Russia above all, you can only see if you have already decided."³ Benjamin's Moscow romance, however, tested his claim. His mind seemed to be made up concerning Asja but his actions and her response undermined his intentions.

Benjamin and love is an absorbing topic. In 1913, while attending the University of Berlin, he wrote a Platonic dialogue on love entitled "Conversation on Love" which did not appear until after his death. Agathon (virtuous one), Sophia (wisdom), and Vincent discuss the value and virtues of love in a loose imitation of Plato's dialogue on love in *The Symposium* where Agathon hosts a philosophical drinking party on the forms of love. But for Benjamin, love is always disappointment: for example, Asja surprises him one day in his Moscow hotel room and as she enters, he wants to kiss her but, "as usual, it proved unsuccessful." He then hands her a card and in doing so tries to kiss her again: another failure. But after a moment, she surprisingly kisses him.⁴ Love is erratic, impetuous, and unstable.

For Benjamin, the issue in his dialogue is whether or not there is only *one* love, *one* term that covers its manifest forms. Vincent believes that "love cannot augment itself" and that friendship is not love, nor marriage. Love transcends such forms, stripping itself of personal relations.⁵ In its purest form, love "is always a longing," Vincent claims (Love 140). But are there rights in love, Agathon asks. The modern Vincent declares, no, there are no rights: "marriage confers rights; love does not," which has as its sole right "expression" (Love 140). It must become visible, always seeking to reveal itself to the beloved otherwise it is invalid.

Benjamin then addresses unrequited love with Vincent stating there is "unrequited infatuation ... but is there unrequited love" (Love 141)? Sophia explains that if love is not expressed, jealousy emerges: "the silence that is not animated—the constrained, impressed silence—engenders distrust" (as Pushkin and Turgenev show; Love 141). Sophia then explains that love will go astray in a weak person when "it sees its sole right unfulfilled! Where wanton self-will has taken this right from it, trust begins to waver, and jealousy first becomes possible" (Love 141). Here, Benjamin seems to anticipate himself and his later relation with Asja and echo N.N.'s behavior with Ásya in Turgenev's story. Suddenly, the right to woo another fades, but, Vincent states, wooing has "in view not love but the declaration of love" (Love 141). And then, Agathon's crucial question: "Can one love many" (Love 141)? Vincent replies yes, partly because "love is something imminent; you love this one time—and always—" (Love 142). This becomes a Benjamin doctrine.

Love was not possession but actualization Benjamin believed, developed further in his 1914 essay, "Erotic Education." For Benjamin, the intellectual and sexual overlap expanded more fully in a 1920 fragment, "On Love and Related Matters."[6] A further passage on love can be found in *One-Way Street*. Under "Old-map," he explains that in a love affair "most seek an eternal homeland. Others, but very few, eternal voyaging" but these latter are "melancholics" who "seek the person who will keep far from them the homeland's sadness." And to that person "they remain faithful."[7] This describes Benjamin exactly, a constant voyager seeking a love that is equally distant and near.

According to Benjamin, the erotic finds defeat by the mundane, subjugating eroticism to privacy but in marriage, "value does not lie in the sterile 'harmony' of the partners: it is as the eccentric offshoot of their struggles and rivalries enacted elsewhere that … the spiritual force of marriages is manifest" (One-Way 101). Marriage exists under a Strindbergian cloud that alternates between obscurity and acuity: "All close relations are lit up by an almost intolerable, piercing clarity in which they are scarcely able to survive," he concludes (One-Way 55).

## ii

*Do not feign innocence when you have gambled everything away.*
Benjamin, *One-Way Street*

Benjamin first met Asja in Capri in March 1924 and offered three different accounts of their encounter written in Latvian, Russian, and German. The German text is the fullest, possibly because Asja and Benjamin communicated in German.[8] The Russian version records their laughter when Benjamin drops her packages which he has gallantly offered to carry for her having met in the equivalent of a patisserie. Born in Latvia as Anna Liepina, her nickname originated in Turgenev's 1857 novella, "Ásya."[9] The name, a shortened form of Anna in the story, is that of radical young woman traveling with her half-brother, Gágin. Asja Lācis's actual name was Anna. At turns buoyant and effervescent, and then demure and private, she was physically a vibrant woman of presence with a wide smile and large eyes. A photograph from 1924 shows her in a mannish hat and overcoat but with an inviting, confident, dominant smile. Across from her photo in the same volume is the image of a scholarly Benjamin sitting upright in a chair wearing a suit; his eyes are hesitant, avoiding the camera. He appears as a man with secrets or at least hidden emotions. Below his photo is one of his wife Dora and son Stefan in 1921, also a woman of stature.[10]

The actions of Turgenev's character find expression in the actual Asja, the object of Benjamin's passion. For Turgenev, Ásya is playing a role: she is of mixed identity and illegitimate; her father was an aristocrat, her mother a maid to his first wife named Tatyána, on his estate. Asja also plays multiple roles between Benjamin and her constant lover/companion, Bernhard Reich. And like Turgenev's character, Asja doesn't experience emotions partway. As Gágin says of Ásya, "none of her emotions go by halves" (Ásya 280). She also believes, like that of the narrator, N.N., that "there is no tomorrow for happiness" (Ásya 315). But she is also forthright: "I have been accustomed to blurt out everything which comes into my head," she announces to the narrator (Ásya 287).

But like Benjamin's Asja, Turgenev's independent and stubborn Ásya always wants to astonish (Ásya 257). Her step or half-brother tells the narrator N.N. that she must "have a hero, a remarkable man—or a picturesque shepherd in a mountain gorge" (Ásya 282). And the narrator realizes her hold over him: "everything in her being aspired toward truth," something Benjamin would also sense about Asja (Ásya 283). What attracts the narrator in Turgenev's story is that Ásya's "half-savage charm diffused over all her slender body: her soul pleased me" (Ásya 283). But then she unexpectedly tells the narrator she would like to be Tatyana in *Eugene Onegin*. In reaction, the narrator asks, "can it be that she loves me?" (Ásya 287, 296). And then Gágin reports her literal "love sickness": fever, chills, restlessness, as she tells Gágin that she loves N.N. but as a consequence must disappear (Ásya 299). She cannot handle love but also cannot dissemble, much like Tatyana in *Onegin*. But like Benjamin in response to Asja, "her love both delighted and upset me," the narrator says (Ásya 302).

A last-minute meeting with Ásya leads to a confrontation about commitment but not before the paradoxes of Russian love appear: although she frightens him, N.N. loves her, yet cannot marry her—but she must not know that I love her the narrator thinks (Ásya 304). Chapter XVI is a crisis moment when he visits her. Tremulously kissing her hand, she moves toward him and rests her head on his breast. But he quickly rejects her, despite being gripped by love. They must part as one accuses the other of distrust, the narrator boasting that "I had had the heart—to repulse her, even to upbraid her …. [but] now her image haunted me" (Ásya 310). This is the condition of the Russian romantic hero: in love but berating himself for being in love. But could he in fact live without her? His indecision does not allow an answer.

Turgenev's early story is the germ of Russian love: denial of its acceptance while acknowledging its power. This is love's fundamental paradox at the heart of Russian love: emotion unleashed but denied. Struggle meets with self-reproach. She came to me with her heart and I deprived myself of her joy, the narrator admits (Ásya 313). The thought nearly drives him mad plus the thought that he in fact did ask for Ásya's hand, contrary to what he promised Gágain (wisely, she demurred). He promises to reveal all his feelings tomorrow but, as he notes, "there is no tomorrow for happiness"; it is ephemeral and exists only in the moment (Ásya 315). Brother and step-sister disappear the next morning while the narrator reads a note from Ásya which declares that if he had only acted, had said the word "love," she would have remained. "You did not say it," she writes with devastating exactness (Ásya 318). It was on his lips but he could not pronounce the words: "It had flamed up with irresistible force only some moments later, when affrighted by the possibility of unhappiness" (Ásya 318). Inaction ruled.

In the novella, N.N. refers to Ásya, at one point as the most Russian creature he knows because of her temperament, hidden feelings, appearance, disguised love, and principles (Ásya 265). But she also makes excessive demands on her proposed lover, as Asja would do on Benjamin, essentially telling him that a *ménage à trois* (herself, Reich, and Benjamin) would easily work. Accept it. Benjamin could not. Ironically, when N.N. gestures toward the love he has for Ásya, it creates a counter-reaction: departure not union.

If only Ásya had said it was impossible, he could accept his fate thinks N.N. But she did not say so, and their future remains incomplete. At the end, the brother and half-sister leave for Cologne and then London but then disappear after the narrator perfunctorily pursues them. But the hero admits he did not grieve too long, believing that he probably would not have been happy with her. The future is more promising with another love in a "still more beautiful form" (Ásya 320). But his original feeling for Ásya cannot be reproduced in another. He ends the story as a bachelor but one who still treasures her notes and a spray of geranium she once tossed to him. So, too, Benjamin who will also end life alone.

### iii

Asja encouraged Benjamin to act on his feelings despite the presence of Reich and likely envisioned a three-way relationship. Turgenev's Ásya's anticipates such behavior, her seeming to say that "you consider my behaviour improper" at the same time it says "I know that you are admiring me" (Ásya 258–9). This was the dilemma encountered by Benjamin, again summarized by Turgenev. In Ásya, the narrator explains that "vain to the last degree, she attracted me even when I was angry with her" (Ásya 269). Love, as Benjamin well understood, is a paradox.

Ásya's reference to Tatyana from Pushkin's *Eugene Onegin* foretells Asja's behavior with Benjamin. In Pushkin, Tatyana (the older sister of Olga, in love with Lensky) loved Onegin who did not love her back but rejected him late in the work once he did. As Tatyana explains, "happiness, before it glided / Away forever, was so near! … But now my fate is quite decided."[11] Onegin, in a move typical of young Russian heroes, initially rejects Tatyana, claiming he was not made for happiness which was foreign to his soul.[12] She, in turn, consults mystics and dreams of walking in the snow then being kidnapped by a bear and taken to a house with Onegin at the head of a table.

*Onegin* romanticizes and dramatizes disappointment in love, anticipating the unfulfilled love in "Ásya" and experienced by Benjamin, but jealousy often leads to bloodshed as in "The Kreutzer Sonata." The irony, of course, is that Pushkin was himself killed in a duel on the outskirts of St. Petersburg at age thirty-seven by his brother-in-law, George-Charles D'Anthès (a French officer in the Russian Guard). Pushkin believed D'Anthès had an affair with his wife, considered one of the most beautiful women in the country who also supposedly flirted with Tsar Nicholas.[13] No evidence emerged that Natalya Pushkina had ever been unfaithful. But impetuous Pushkin, akin to Lensky, forced D'Anthès to accept the challenge of a duel.

The literature, or at least romances, has a key role in both Pushkin and Turgenev. Tatyana's reading such books causes an identification with heroines, transposing Onegin into a character, not an individual. In browsing through his library, she hopes to understand him. Lensky, too (a disciple of Schiller), writes odes to Olga with idealistic sentiments Onegin rejects. But Ásya also has idealistic dreams of romance from books. But idealism has no place in Onegin's world (although it does in Benjamin's who, in his attachment to Asja, is more akin to Lensky than Onegin). Benjamin's innocence stands in contrast to that of Bernhard Reich or even Asja herself. He cannot, nor does not, know how to, respond to Asja's loving rejection of him other than to continue in his pursuit of her.[14]

When Onegin finally admits his love for Tatyana, she has the maturity and experience to reject him. His pleading in Chapter 8, a letter to balance her earlier letter to him with cries like "How justly now I am afflicted …. If you but knew how agonizing / It is to parch with hot desire … the blood that burns with frantic fire," brings no resolution as Benjamin's pursuit of Asja; even divorcing his wife Dora brings him no closer to her (Onegin 291–2). Tatyana even chastises Onegin for still wanting her, as Asja often reprimands Benjamin for his passion.

For Pushkin, as for Turgenev, the only true love is unrequited love, Russian love. At the end, with Tatyana still in love with Onegin and he with her, their love must remain unfulfilled to maintain their passion: the fullness of longing is preferable to a period empty of happiness, duplicated for N.N. at the end of "Ásya." For Pushkin—and Russian love—what is important is not to possess the object of love but to continuously long for and desire it, acknowledging its impossible realization. But its impossibility is what gives it value. Tatyana and Onegin know their love exists but also that it will remain unattainable.[15]

Ironically, Benjamin may not have realized that his condition of unfulfilled love paralleled one of the greatest themes in Russian writing. His lack of success with Asja matched that of a series of Russian protagonists, from Eugene Onegin to N.N. to Ratikin in *A Month in the Country* which also portrays a love triangle between two old friends (Islayev and Rakitin) and Islayev's wife, Natalya.[16] Benjamin, himself, becomes a character in a Russian love story, although he failed to realize it.

## iv

*The only way of knowing a person is to love them without hope.*
Benjamin, "Arc Lamp," *One-Way Street*

Asja at first found Benjamin curious: meeting her in a shop in Capri when he helped her buy almonds, he courteously pursues her and learns of her background and revolutionary, Communist ideals. At the time, she was with Reich but he had returned to his duties at the Munich *Kammerspiele*. Benjamin's intellectuality, not physicality, in turn, captivated her. He was trying to write his early book on German drama but while intellectually knowledgeable, he was socially naïve. At the time, he had been married to Dora Kellner for seven years and had a six-year-old son but quickly discovered emotions with Asja he could not control. But while Asja found him physically unattractive, she could not resist his ideas.

They began to plot a union, at least intellectually, preparing a series of city essays, the first, "Naples," appearing in 1925 in the *Frankfurter Zeitung*. In November that year, Benjamin then turned up unannounced in Riga where Lācis was directing illegal agitprop theater. Several notes in *One-Way Street* suggest the nature of his evolving love and Asja: in "Stereoscope," he writes of paper rods in a Riga market that they are "like being scolded by the most beloved voice—such are these rods" (One-Way 86). In "Ordinance," also from *One-Way Street*, he conveys his ignitable passion in a city completely unfamiliar and walking in solitude but

> From every gate a flame darted, each cornerstone sprayed sparks and every streetcar came toward me like a fire engine. For she might have stepped out of the gateway, around a corner .... for had she touched me with the match of her eyes, I might have gone up like a magazine.
>
> (One-Way 68–9)

Obsession and denial initiate the rhythm of his Russian love expanded in December 1926 in the period recorded in his *Moscow Diary*.[17]

Benjamin found Moscow a rich culture to explore with at least eight essays or broadcasts the result, despite his not knowing Russian. His publications began with the article "Moscow," and then his "Young Russian Writers" broadcast; "Recent Literature in Russia," a 1927 essay, plus "Russian Toys," originally to be illustrated (a truncated version appeared in *Sudwestdestschen Rundfunkzeitung* in 1930) followed. Supplementing these quickly written works were "The Political Groupings of Russian Writers," "On the Present Situation of Russian Film," and his review of Gladkov's 1927 novel *Cement*, which he calls "the first novel of the period of reconstruction" (Sel. Writings 47). Collectively, they attest to the importance of Benjamin's Russian experience, although its personal impact did not emerge until the appearance of his *Moscow Diary* in 1980.[18]

Benjamin wrote many of these pieces while living with his wife and then eight-year-old son in Berlin in an apartment in his parent's Grunewald villa but he soon left for France to keep up with developments in French literature. But what was to be a two- or three-month visit lasted eight.[19] At one point, he thought of settling permanently in Paris and invited Dora and his son for a visit which included the Riviera where in June he won enough at the casinos of Monte Carlo—he had a fondness for roulette—to finance a week's vacation in Corsica.[20] He argued that this was part of his interest in experimentation, which included hashish and intoxication. He liked to take chances, his affair with Asja another example.

His publications also marked shifting ideas about art and social responsibility, partly the result of time with Asja and her Soviet views (Eiland/Jennings 277). He also witnessed the insecurity and uncertainty of Moscow life seen in the beggars and their markets which he frequented. This marginal form of life may reflect his own feelings concerning his status with Asja as an outsider. In Moscow he also detects a constant remaking of space, domestically in the almost weekly rearrangement of furniture in barely furnished apartments and in the frequent relocation of government offices, museums, and institutes. Street vendors also seem to "turnup in different places every day" (MD 36). This fluidity and instability visually and objectively project Benjamin's feelings about his relationship with Asja with its constant tension between argument and affection.

Even the cold of Moscow becomes a metaphor of his relationship with Asja writing that he has little idea whether or not he could "bear living with her, given her astonishing hardness and, despite all her sweetness, her lovelessness" (MD 35).[21] But she still has a power over him: "I cannot remember a woman granting gazes or kisses this long" (MD 35). He responds by telling her they should have a child. But there are daily challenges if not contradictions: "Just yesterday, as I was in the process of leaving her room to avoid an argument, she grabbed hold of me violently and ran her hands through my hair" adding that it was his fault they were not living together on a desert island (MD 35). He admits that this was his fault and that on two or three occasions he "directly or indirectly avoided sharing a future with her" (MD 35). But the cause of his hesitation is not financial or even social but fear "of those hostile elements in her which only now do I feel I can confront." Yet, everything happening to him in Moscow has combined "to make the idea of living apart from her more intolerable to me than it ever was before" (MD 35). The paradox strangely paralyzes him: he rationalizes not leaving her, although he finds reasons to do so.

Late in his diary, Benjamin idealizes a life with Asja centered in his native Berlin:

> We kissed again and spoke of living together in Berlin, of getting married, of taking at least one trip together. Asja said that there had never been another city as difficult for her to leave as Berlin, did this have something to do with me?
> (MD 110)

City space becomes defined in terms of love, holding a future that is alternately impossible and yet imaginable.

Fearing future complications because of her relation with Reich, Benjamin, nonetheless, believes that the bond of a child will solve any difficulties. A comment about physical life in Moscow duplicates his internal struggle: "People live on the street as if in a frosty hall of mirrors, and every decision, every stop becomes incredibly difficult: it takes half a day of deliberation to go drop a letter in a mailbox" (MD 35). Benjamin writes this revealing entry on his relationship with Asja while seated next to Reich.

Moscow has become an impenetrable citadel, psychologically and physically, as this long sentence summarizes:

> Moscow is now a fortress; the harsh climate which is wearing me down, no matter how healthy it might be for me, my ignorance of the language, Reich's presence, Asja's utterly circumscribed mode of existence all constitute so many bastions, and it is only the total impossibility of advancing any further, only the fact that Asja's illness, or at least her weakness, pushes our personal affairs into the background, that keeps me from becoming completely depressed by all this.
>
> (MD 34–5)

In the Russian version of her autobiography, Asja reports that Benjamin badly wanted to move to Moscow despite its chaotic living conditions. The only thing he wanted to bring with him was his library. He saw Moscow as the "first capital in the world with a socialist government."[22] He also believed that Russia alone offered nourishment for the impoverished Western intelligentsia "in comparison to the countless constellations that offer themselves to an individual here in the space of a month" (MD 72). Meetings, committees, debates, resolutions, and ballotings may take over one's life but that is the goal, to force one to take a position and become a participant, not a spectator (MD 72). Such a world, he believed, would offer a framework in which he could write.

But one cannot neglect Benjamin's melancholy something that plagued him throughout his life. It prevented yet encouraged his will, largely through the narcotic of work. As Susan Sontag noted, melancholiacs "make the best addicts, for the true addictive experience is always … solitary." As she later writes, aiding in our understanding of Benjamin's contrary behavior in love, "the need to be solitary—along with bitterness over one's loneliness—is characteristic of the melancholic."[23] His heroes—Kierkegaard, Baudelaire, Proust, and Kafka—never married, and he came to regard his own marriage as a fatal mistake (married in 1917, estranged from his wife after 1921, divorced in 1930). Unable to overcome the feeling of isolation may cause the melancholic lover, Russian or otherwise, to deny love even while recognizing its power over him.

Benjamin, the cultural historian, continued to observe and note selective artistic developments in Moscow, despite his personal upheavals. One of them was children's theater. His "Program for a Proletarian Children's Theater," written in late 1928 or early 1929 under the guidance of Asja's influence who directed such programs, was the result. In the essay, he argues that "proletarian education must be based on the party program—or, more precisely, on class consciousness." He then goes on to outline the method and value of children's theater: to create the collective imagination which he believes is "the power of observation" (SW, Vol. 2: 201–2).

He then brings the topic of the collective imagination back to love, claiming that "this alone is the heart of unsentimental love." It is guided by improvisation and is of the moment, ideas not far from Benjamin's broader conception of love—plus the idea that in performance the children teach the audience. Through play and performance, childhood and love fulfill each other (SW, Vol.2: 203–5).[24]

V

*I read Proust in my room while eating marzipan.*
　　　　　　　　　　　Benjamin, *Moscow Diary* December 10, 1926.

But what of the diary directly? What does Benjamin note, question, celebrate, or criticize? What did he learn from Moscow and what do we learn from his comments on love? Gershom Scholem in his Preface to the 1986 edition claims it is "mercilessly frank" and the most personal document we have of Benjamin at a crucial moment of his life (MD 5). But is it as free of "self-censorship" as Scholem suggests? Importantly, other than two letters, one to Scholem and the other to Jula Radt-Cohn, Benjamin provides no further documents of his time in Moscow.

There were three causes for his trip—passion for Asja, a wish to get a closer look at Russia and the Communist experiment, and an obligation to write something of the city for a publisher which resulted in his essay "Moscow" published in *Die Kreatur* II (1927, 71–101), a journal edited by Martin Buber. The essay refines notes and details he made in the diary. Benjamin partially financed his trip through advances for pieces yet to be written. One of his goals was to consolidate relations with representatives of the literary and artistic communities of Russia, perhaps becoming a correspondent on German writing and culture for Russian publications. He was also re-examining whether or not he should become a member of the German Communist party. Optimistic at the outset of his visit, he gradually, like Lucien Chardon in Balzac's novel, lost his illusions. Impatient and ambitious, Benjamin had to temper his enthusiasm. Combining his disappointment in love and failure to secure a literary commission, Benjamin becomes an antihero in his own narrative, at one point claiming he feels like a disillusioned character out of a novel by the Danish writer Jens Peter Jacobsen, likely *Niels Lyhne* praised by Rilke (MD 13).

Benjamin's literary goals for his diary and essay shifted as he explained to Buber in a letter of February 23, 1927, in which he declares that he wants to let the city speak for itself: "I want to write a description of Moscow ... in which 'all factuality is already theory'" echoing Goethe's remark that "everything actual is already theory."[25] Scholem also anticipates what the diary will reveal: Benjamin's tense relationship with Bernhard Reich, companion to Asja and whom she would marry in her later years. But Reich, who met Benjamin at the station when he arrived, played a crucial role in assembling and facilitating Benjamin's Moscow contacts. Asja did not have the same access, although Benjamin broke with Reich by January 1927 precipitating his departure. On that first day, December 6, 1926, however, Asja also appeared as they drove down Tverskaia. At one moment, Reich got out of a sleigh and Asja jumped in.

Rather than focus on the political or cultural impact of Moscow, it is Asja who claims Benjamin's attention. Scholem, in the interim, attempts to curb Benjamin's Russian love for a woman Benjamin describes in letters from Capri in May 1924, as only a "Bolshevik Latvian from Riga" (MD 7). But this remarkable woman decisively influenced Benjamin's life from 1924 until at least 1930 according to Scholem—not unlike the importance of Moura Budberg for H.G. Wells some years later (MD 7).

After having met in Capri in 1924, Benjamin and Asja were together again in Berlin in 1924 and in Riga in 1925 and perhaps in Berlin again before he went to Moscow in late 1926. Their association was established and flourishing in its way before his Russian journey confirmed by his dedication of *One-Way Street* to her. Composed of sixty short prose pieces, Benjamin showed her the manuscript with its dedication on his second day in Moscow. It reads "This street is named Asja Lacis Street, after the engineer who laid it through the author" (MD 12 ftnt. 17). In retrospect, the title may mean there is only one direction in his love for Asja which is straight to her heart.

Ironically, during his visit Asja was confined either to a sanatorium recovering from a neural condition, or recuperating in her room.[26] She visited Benjamin in his hotel room only on a few occasions. She remained romantically elusive and at times his adversary in a series of political and intellectual disagreements. Yet he constantly pursued her and she constantly rejected him displaying an "erotic cynicism" (MD 8). Together, they quarreled. This continued through 1930 when she came to Berlin and Frankfurt to see Benjamin while he was starting his divorce. Why, then, did he continue to favor her?

The diary does an inadequate job in answering, although it reveals his psychological dependency on Asja needed to reaffirm his own masculinity, sense of the physical nature of love and determination to succeed when thwarted by love. His account is the epitome of unrequited love, his meetings with Asja at the sanatorium and occasionally on the street truncated and undeveloped. Yet his accounts of his city activities are detailed, from the cost of a seat at the Institute of Culture (1.50 rubles) to the route to the Organization of Proletarian Writers. Anecdotes and tales of Moscow follow, from crimes to Stanislavsky's encounter with Stalin (MD 10–11).

Curiously, when Asja does make the effort to see Benjamin, he is never alone. Reich or someone else is always present (MD 11). Discussion over whether or not Reich should join the party often ensues with Benjamin offering digressive but insightful critiques on the method of writing in Russia which he summarizes as "the broad exposition of an argument and, if possible, nothing further" (MD 12). The cultural level of the public is so low, he believes, that any further formulations would be "incomprehensible" (MD 12). The opposite is true in Germany he pridefully states.

On her intermittent visits, Benjamin gives Asja gifts, while she encourages him, telling him he's definitely not undergoing a crisis. He responds by reading her a passage from *One-Way Street* which argues that love must involve attraction to the defaults, not beauties, of a woman: "it is just here, in what is defective and censurable, that the fleeting darts of adoration nestle." Love is not mental or psychological but "in the place where we see it, then we are, in looking at our beloved, too, outside ourselves. But in a torment of tension and ravishment .... feelings escape into the shaded wrinkles, the awkward movements and inconspicuous blemishes of the body we love."[27] Love is a physical and emotional paradox.

A curious Benjamin rhythm begins: brief calls on Asja, walks and discussions with Reich, visits to theaters and cultural offices, and time alone in his room reading or writing. Occasionally, he's permitted a night out at a Moscow theater with Asja, arranged by Reich, to see, for example, a production of Rimsky-Korsakov's *The Czar's Bride*. The theater administrator then invites him back to see Tchaikovsky's *Eugene Onegin*.

Interspersed with accounts of his time (but not emotions) with Asja are descriptive details of Moscow, from walking on the icy streets to the architecture which gives one the appearance "of a summer vacation colony, [although] looking at them one feels doubly cold" (MD 17). But the sidewalks are narrow, staples are in short supply, and people wait in long lines (MD 17). But in the middle of a large pastry shop, while having a coffee and Asja a cup of whipped cream, he suddenly realizes how much his projects depend on contact with her (MD 18). They interact further: he asks her to buy him a pipe, while the next day he returns for toys for his son and Asja's daughter. Constant meetings with Reich, who, at one point sleeps in his room, disrupt his limited time with Asja. But the adventures never stop: "My hair is very electric here," he summarizes (MD 18).

Complicating the matter is Asja's personal attention to Benjamin, unpacking his suitcases, tidying up his room, picking out his ties. Equally erratic is Benjamin's writing in the diary with sudden shifts from one topic to another. At one point, he moves from all three characters in a café to an argument where Reich made it clear he was planning to cut all ties with Germany and concentrate on Russian matters. An evening alone with Reich in his room follows where Benjamin studies a guidebook and Reich works on a review of the dress rehearsal of Meyerhold's *The Inspector General*. In the diary, this is suddenly followed by the remark that there are no trucks or delivery vans in Moscow: every purchase, big or small, must go "by a tiny sled or *izvozchik*." (MD 19). But unexpected, wonderful details pop-up such as the man who sells letters from an alphabet board on the street which were to be affixed to galoshes to prevent mix-ups (MD 19). "Everywhere, even advertisements, the people characteristically demand that some tangible action be represented," Asya tells him; abstractions have no place (MD 20).

But increasingly, Benjamin reports on his frustration in seeing Asja and inability to see her alone. Either the sanatorium refuses to allow her out or Reich limits their encounters. Yet, he confesses that he hardly pays attention to any of her remarks because "I am examining her so intently" (MD 21). But his "dwindling prospects," personally and professionally, begin to undermine his trip (MD 22). Nonetheless, as he walks about the city, Benjamin's eye lyrically captures remarkable details, from antiques to furs, from handicrafts to display windows. The crosses above the domes of St. Basil's Cathedral, he notes, "resemble gigantic earrings attached to the sky" (MD 22). But in contrast to the luxury noticed in a fashion boutique or chocolate store are the beggars forming "a corporation of the dying:" street corners have bundles of rags, beds for the homeless "in the great open-air sickbay called Moscow" (MD 22). This double vision of Benjamin's makes his diary a cultural and personal account of discovery. Even the churches are cold and poorly maintained. But in the collage that is his diary, there are suddenly tips on writing (MD 23).

But Benjamin's frustrations grow, especially in his inability to be alone with Asja as one anecdote from a trip to a theater reveals. He sits next to Asja for the first tableau. Reich then appears to sit by him, thinking the strain of translating from Russian to German for Benjamin too great a burden for Asja (MD 25). She then had to move, Reich replacing her. Benjamin's comment on St. Basil's applies: "this building is always holding something back, and could only be ambushed by the eye from the height of an airplane" (MD 25). The inside of the church "has not only been emptied, but eviscerated" and turned into a museum. This metaphorically represents Asja whose passion for him appears to have evaporated (MD 25).

Interiors speak to Benjamin and visiting a home on Strasnoi Square he is struck by the large rooms with little furniture: "completeness is an essential feature of the décor of the petit-bourgeois interior," he remarks, walls covered with pictures, sofas with cushions—but there is little of that in the Moscow he sees (MD 26). He tellingly writes that "if people manage to bear rooms which look like infirmaries after inspection it is because their way of life has so alienated them from domestic existence. The place in which they live is the office, the club, the street" (MD 26).

But Benjamin also uses the diary for big ideas. One example is the thought that the history of the educated ought to be materialistically presented as a function of "a history of 'uneducation.'" Revolutionary energy is released "from its religious cocoon by the uneducated classes" with the intelligentsia revealed not as an army of deserters from the bourgeoisie but an advance guard of "uneducation" (MD 29). The very next sentence, however, surprisingly reads "the sleigh ride refreshed me considerably" (MD 29). Benjamin characteristically cuts off one thought with another. At this moment, he was traveling to dine with the journalist Joseph Roth who would admit to Benjamin that he "had come to Russia as a (nearly) confirmed Bolshevik and was leaving it a royalist" (MD 29).

Benjamin's frustration with Russia grows, explaining that nothing happens as planned or as expected, leading to a certain negative, Russian fatalism. "Within the collectivity, its initial effects will only further complicate individual existence," he concludes (MD 30). Better to have a house with candles than with lights if there are constant power failures he writes. When on a streetcar, the frosted-over windows mean you can never make out where you are but "if you did find out, then the way to the exit is blocked by a mass of bulkily clad people" suggesting a metaphoric reading of what prevents the proper movements of independent minds (MD 31). Furthermore, the narrow sidewalks mean people walk in a zig zag pattern giving Moscow "the character of an improvised metropolis that has fallen into place overnight" (MD 31). On another day, he watches children playing soccer between the ranks of Red Army soldiers on drills, a contest between play and order (MD32).

Only momentarily during his romance does Benjamin draw a parallel to this wife, Dora. When Reich suffers a heart attack, he finds Asja agitated and scolding Reich for getting ill, making him feel guilty for having gotten sick. This was similar to the way Benjamin treated Dora when she became ill (MD 32): it was clearly her fault. But no development follows; rather, there is an account of the shortened production of Meyerhold's *The Inspector General*, a production supposedly presenting the adaptation of a classical play for the revolutionary theater. The Party had opposed the work, however.

Later in his *Diary*, Benjamin voices criticism of Communism in a debate with himself about joining the Party or not. He understands that to be a Communist "in a state where the proletariat rules means completely giving up your private independence" (MD 73). The Party organizes your life. Is this a positive or negative? Should you be an outsider or insider? Will you be thought to go over to the bourgeoisie if you don't join? Should he avoid "certain extremes of 'materialism'" or work out his disagreements with them within the Party (MD 73)? He debates his choices.

Symbolizing the nature of his relationship with Asja, and by extension Reich, is the final scene of the Diary. Crying, he departs the hotel "with Asja following me with Reich's coat under her arm" (MD 121). Like the end of a Gogol or Turgenev story, three elements (Benjamin's emotions, Asja's presence, and the ghost of Reich) unite in a single object, Reich's coat. Asja then joins Benjamin in the sleigh until the corner of Tverskaia. She leaves but not before he romantically draws her hand to his lips in the middle of the street. He then departs, and she stands in the street waving. He rides to the station in tears (MD 121).

There are actually, several scenes of departure in the diary, as if Benjamin is replaying the event. Earlier, it's a goodbye at the theater. At the end of the performance, she wanted to hop on a streetcar but did not: "animosity and love were shifting within me like winds; finally we said good-bye, she from the platform of the streetcar, I remaining behind, debating whether or not to follow her, leap after her" (MD 116–17). In another translation, the dilemma of love, the conflict in Russian love between hesitation and emotion, is more dramatic:

> Displeasure with her and love for her leapt around in me at tremendous speed, in the end we said goodbye, she from the platform of her tram—with me remaining behind, wondering whether I should not run after her and jump up to join her.[28]

This was actually not the end of his contact with Asja. Benjamin returned to Berlin and continued his fraught relationship with his wife, but also continued to correspond with Asja who, with Reich in November 1928, went to Berlin where

Brecht was finishing the *Three-Penny Opera*. Asja worked at the Soviet Embassy as a trade representative for Soviet films. During this period, from roughly 1928–1930, she lived with Benjamin for two months and in May 1929 arranged a long-sought meeting between Benjamin and Brecht; the two developed an extensive friendship.

But despite his divorce in 1930, Benjamin lost sight of Asja, although he wrote to her in 1935 and sent a reprint of an essay from *Zeitschrift für Sozialforschung*. She had returned to Moscow in 1930, and the following year became involved with Erwin Piscator's filming of *Aufstan der Fischer von S. Barbara* with John Heartfield and Lotte Lenya. In 1935, she published a book on German avant-garde theater but in 1936 Stalin had her arrested and deported to Kazakhstan for more than a decade. Reich also suffered either banishment or imprisonment: in 1937, he was released and then rearrested. After the Stalin era, Asja and Reich appeared together in both Berlin and Moscow partly as Brecht's Moscow advisors to the Berliner Ensemble. Allowed to work as a director only after 1956, Asja produced Brecht on the Latvian stage. Reich wrote a monograph in Russian on Brecht.

The love triangle intimated by Asja actually recalled 1921 when Benjamin was caught between his wife Dora and his seeming love for Jula Radt-Cohn. Dora was actually interested at the time in Ernst Schoen and conjugal relations between the husband and wife ended. During his difficult period with Asja in Moscow, he wrote to Jula again after a disagreement with Reich in January 1927 over Asja, suggesting that he renew his love for her. He ends with "Two kisses. After you have wiped them off, please tear up this letter right away" (Eiland/Jennings 269). But that relationship did not restart. In 1928, Benjamin learned that Asja would be coming to Berlin to work at the Soviet Embassy. She arrived with Reich who stayed only for a short while and for two months, Asja and Benjamin lived together (December 1928–January 1929) in an apartment less than two miles from his parents' villa where Dora and his son lived (Eiland/Jennings 314). But by February, he had returned to the villa, asked to leave by Asja, although she continued to exert an influence on his intellectual life. The love triangle was malleable enough to allow Benjamin to attend a birthday party for Dora while living with Asja.

But relations with Dora deteriorated and by the spring of 1929 he asked her for a divorce to marry Asja, although it is unclear if *she* wanted to marry *him*. It had been seven years since his early affair with Jula Radt-Cohen and Dora's with Ernst Schoen. Nevertheless, divorce proceedings began at the end of June. It was a bitter fight lasting until March 27, 1930, when the divorce became final with Benjamin losing heavily: he had accused his wife of infidelity despite multiple examples of his own faithlessness and reckless behavior regularly drawing on his wife's income for himself. He also refused all requests to support his son, Stefan. The court ordered him to pay Dora 40,000 marks which meant signing over his entire inheritance plus a valuable collection of children's books and his share of the family villa (Eiland/Jennings 315). Reluctantly, he acquiesced.

In a June 27, 1929, letter to Gershom Scholem, Dora complained of Benjamin's dissembling state of mind: "all he is at this point is brains and sex; everything else has ceased to function." By then, Asja's residency permit expired, and he wanted to marry her quickly to provide German citizenship, she explains. He then audaciously asked Dora for funds; unexpectedly, she agreed to give him half of her inheritance. Her personal letter then criticized his "smutty affairs," money he owes her and their separate lives. Behind him stands Asja "who, as he himself has said to me, ... doesn't love him but merely makes use of him" (Eiland/Jennings 315). She also notes that Benjamin is paying the rent for Asja's apartment where he stayed until he was kicked out. He returned to Dora and boldly suggested that she should have Asja come live with her and their son to ease his financial burden. Dora makes him out, however, as the victim of his own sexual drives and Asja's desires, downplaying his irresponsibility and unscrupulous behavior. Within a year of the divorce, she forgot about him but still respected his intellectual accomplishments (Eiland/Jennings 317). Dora kept the house and lived off the proceeds from its sale after she left Germany in 1934.

The year 1929, however, was also notable not only for the start of the divorce but for his remarkable productivity with a more pronounced Marxist outlook. The presence of Asja in Berlin had a part in the change: not only did she shepherd him to meet revolutionary proletarian writers but to performances by proletarian theater groups. At her request, he also drafted his "Program for a Proletarian Children's Theater," unpublished in his lifetime (Eiland/Jennings 320). And before her return to Moscow in 1930, Asja tried to arrange for Benjamin's immigration to the Soviet Union, also advising him against moving to Jerusalem. But by the end of the twenties, they did not see each other again, although they continued to correspond until 1936 when she was arrested and began a ten-year internment in Kazakhstan.

Love triangles seemed to fascinate Benjamin partly because one marriage could continue without the drama of a breakup, while a new relationship could emerge. But his pursuit of other women seemed relentless, part of his program of "radical knowing" (Eiland/Jennings 317). In Ibiza in May/June 1932, for example, he spent time with the Russian-German Olga Parem, attractive and vivacious. They had originally met in 1928. She later told Scholem that Benjamin's intellect and charm appealed, something also noted by Asja: "He had an enchanting laugh; when he laughed, a whole world opened up," wrote Parem to Scholem (Eiland/Jennings 375). But her refusal to accept his marriage proposal may have contributed to his thoughts of suicide later in 1932 which partly led to his writing to Jula Radt-Cohn again. From a Nice hotel room, he told her that "my life has no great gifts in its possession than those conferred on it by moments of suffering over you" (Eiland/Jennings 378). Suffering is love for Benjamin and women, whether prostitutes, divorcees, or married, a form of narcissistic celebration and protest.

Benjamin also had a beautiful woman in Barcelona, the divorced wife of a Berlin physician. During this period, May or June 1932, he apparently asked Olga to marry. She also refused (Eiland/Jennings 376). The next month he turned forty and wrote a melancholic letter to Scholem expressing his sense of failure (Eiland/Jennings 377). A faithless husband, lover, and partner, he nevertheless sought new relations that confirmed his own sense of sexual attraction and experience. His frequent absences from his earlier marriage had allowed for his permissive behavior, euphemistically called "erotic entanglements" by his biographers (Eiland/Jennings 314).

Benjamin's Russian romance reoriented his political, intellectual, and emotional life while offering a framework for Russian love as experienced by a series of foreign writers, spies, and visitors. Their experiences set a pattern of intense feelings frequently met by unfulfilled desires which ironically deepened a love shaped by frustration expressed by Dostoevsky's narrator in the final sentence of "White Nights": "My God, a whole moment of happiness! Is that too little for the whole of a man's life?"[29]

## Notes

1 He arrived on December 6, 1926, and departed on February 1, 1927. Asja, it should be noted, had studied in Moscow in the studio of Komissarzhevsky and later, in Orel, used an obscure Meyerhold play in her successful children's theater.

2 Asja's first husband was Julijs Lācis but they had divorced when she took up with Reich, father of her daughter Daga. She later wrote two autobiographies: *Revolutionär im Beruf. A Revolutionary by Profession* in English and then *The Red Carnation* in Russian. Each provides a different perspective on her life.

3   Walter Benjamin, "Moscow," *Reflections, Essays, Aphorisms, Autobiographical Writings*, tr. Edmund Jephcott, ed. Peter Demetz (New York: Schocken Books, 2007), 97. The essay first appeared in *die Kreatur II* (1927), 71–101.
4   Benjamin, *Moscow Diary*, ed. Gary Smith, tr. Richard Sieburth (Cambridge: Harvard University Press, 1986), 27. Hereafter MD. Smith points out that the *Diary* is Benjamin's longest extant autobiographical document (MD 137). It was first published in 1980. Two reasons prevented its earlier appearance: the publishing house would not print it while Asja Lācis was alive and, secondly, it was to appear as the sixth volume of Benjamin's selected works. The actual fifty-six page ms. of the diary is at the Adorno archive in Frankfurt. The last entries, January 29, 1927, were made in Berlin.
5   Benjamin, "Conversations on Love," *Early Writings 1910–1917*, tr. Howard Eiland et al. (Cambridge: Harvard University Press, 2011), 139–40. Hereafter Love. For further clarity on the Asja-Benjamin relationship, see Justine McGill, "The Porous Coupling of Walter Benjamin and Asja Lacis," *Angelaki: Journal of the Theoretical Humanities* 13.2 (2008): 59–72.
6   In this short essay, Benjamin attempts to fuse the erotic with prostitution arguing that there is a spirituality that has been overlooked. See Benjamin, "Erotic Education," *Early Writings, 1910–1917*, tr. Howard Eiland et al. (Cambridge: Harvard University Press, 2011), 166–7. For "On Love and Related Matters (A European Problem)," see Benjamin, *Selected Writings*, Vol. 1 1913–1926, ed. Marcus Bullock and Michael W. Jennings (Cambridge: Harvard University Press, 1996), 229–30.

   In the second piece, Benjamin argues that the old forms of love and relations are changing in response to an unusual unity of "the erotic and the sexual in women" which he believes is a supernatural, not natural, power causing men to flee. The result is the dissolution of man's primitive instincts. Impotence and desire are in conflict, dissolving potent love. Through abstractions, Benjamin suggests a new, spiritual love. But importantly, the two-page fragment shows Benjamin's engagement and attempt to define love.
7   Benjamin, *One-Way Street and Other Writings*, intro. Susan Sontag, tr. Edmund Jephcott and Kingsley Shorter (London: NLB, 1979), 75. Hereafter, One-Way.
8   For the original German and a translation, see Jānis Taurens, "Asja Lācis and Walter Benjamin: Translating Different Cities," *Canadian Review of Comparative Literature* 45.1 (March 2018): 18 and 27, ftnt 9.
9   Turgenev, "Asya," *Phantoms and Other Stories*, tr. Isabel F. Hapgood (New York: Scribner's Sons, 1904), 239–321.
10  See Wolfram Eilenberger, *Time of the Magicians, Wittgenstein, Benjamin, Cassirer, Heidegger and the Decade that Reinvented Philosophy*, tr. Shaun Whiteside (New York: Penguin, 2020) photo Insert 178–9.

11  Pushkin, "Eugene Onegin," tr. Babette Deutsch, *Poems, Prose and Plays of Alexander Pushkin*, ed. Avrahm Yarmolinsky (New York: Modern Library, 1964), 300. Hereafter Onegin.

12  "Onegin," Ch. 4, Verse 14: 186. He may also believe that "A woman's love for us increases / The less we love her." Ch. 4, Verse I: 183.

　　　Later at a dance, Onegin flirts with Olga getting back at Lensky who may have started a rumor about a union between Onegin and Tatyana. Suddenly, Olga returns his favors, agreeing to dance with him implying a possible liaison if not love triangle. In response, Tatyana rushes out of the room, Lensky chastises Olga and abuses Onegin. The two supposed lovers claim innocence but the suspicious Lensky challenges Onegin to a duel which Onegin is honor-bound to fight. The two reject a late attempt at reconciliation and at the duel Lensky aims first but is killed by Onegin before Lensky he can pull his trigger. Pushkin shows that idealistic Lensky was foolish to challenge Onegin to a duel.

　　　Onegin escapes to the south, while Olga searches for a new husband; Tatyana resists pressure to find a new man (she's still in love with Onegin) and visits his estate and reads the books in his library, studying his annotations. She then leaves for Moscow and possibly a new husband. The final scene is in St. Petersburg honoring a wounded general. Onegin appears only to discover that the general's wife is Tatyana. Onegin then realizes at last he is in love with Tatyana but cannot win her back. A final encounter reveals her constant feelings for Onegin but that she cannot leave the general, Prince Gremin. She rushes out and Onegin is left alone.

13  Pushkin was wounded with a bullet in his abdomen. Two days after the duel, held on January 27, 1837, Pushkin died of peritonitis. At his wife's request, he was put in the coffin in evening dress. On Natalya and Tsar Nicholas, see "Pushkin's death and its aftermath," British Library. https://www.bl.uk/onlinegallery/features/blackeuro/pushkindeath.html.

14  Two letters discovered after the duel written by D'Anthès describe his infatuation with Natalya and that she felt the same toward him and that her husband was "furiously jealous." But she felt duty bound, however, to her husband, similar to Tatyana and her husband at the end of *Onegin*. In July 1841, Mikhail Lermontov also died in a duel with his fellow officer Nikolai Martynov.

15  Among many discussions of unrequited love in Russian literature, treated almost exclusively in individual authors and rarely thematically, see Viv Groskop, "Surviving Unrequited Love with Ivan Turgenev," *Paris Review*, October 19, 2018. https://www.theparisreview.org/blog/2018/10/19/surviving-unrequited-love-with-ivan-turgenev/ and "Longing for Love: Does Romantic Love Exist?" https://thefifthe.wordpress.com/2013/01/16/longing-love-does-romantic-love-exist/.

16 The situation broadly paralleled Turgenev's personal life: from the 1840s to the end of his life in 1883, Turgenev adored the married opera singer Pauline Viardot. The exact nature of their relationship is unknown but Turgenev's love was one-sided, represented by the resigned Rakitin in the play.

17 Benjamin was not alone: among other German visitors at this time were the Bavarian dramatist Ernst Toller, welcomed with pomp but then denounced; Egon Kisch, (1925–6) who published his account in Berlin in 1927; Joseph Roth, who traveled through Russia in 1926 and dined with Benjamin; his report appeared in the *Frankfurter Zeitung* in eighteen segments.

18 Benjamin, "Review of Gladkov's *Cement*," *Selected Writings* Vol. 2 1927–34, tr. Rodney Livingstone et al., ed. Michael W. Jennings, Howard Eiland and Gary Smith (Cambridge: Harvard University Press, 1999), 47. Hereafter SW, Vol. 2.

19 Howard Eiland and Michael W. Jennings, *Walter Benjamin: A Critical Life* (Cambridge: Harvard University Press, 2014), 279. Hereafter Eiland/Jennings.

20 An early draft of the *Arcades Project* included a passage on gambling according to his biographers (Eiland/Jennings 280).

21 Compare the adjusted translation by Jānis Taurens, "Asja Lācis and Walter Benjamin: Translating Different Cities," *Canadian Review of Comparative Literature* (March 2018): 27 ftnt. 15.

22 See Benjamin in Susan Ingram, "The Writing of Asja Lacis," *New German Critique* 86 (2002): 174.

23 Susan Sontag, "Introduction," Benjamin, *One Way Street and Other Writings*, tr. Edmund Jephcott and Kinsley Shorter (London: NLB, 1979), 23.

24 See also Andris Brinkmanis, "Introduction," Lācis and Benjamin, "Signals from Another World; Proletarian Theater as a Site for Education," https://www.documenta14.de/en/south/25225_signals_from_another_world_proletarian_theater_as_a_site_for_education_texts_by_asja_la_cis_and_walter_benjamin_with_an_introduction_by_andris_brinkmanis.

25 Benjamin, *Moscow Diary*, 6; Goethe quoted in Eiland/Jennings 272.

26 See Ingram, "Writing of Lacis," 172.

27 Benjamin, *One-Way Street*, 52.

28 Benjamin, *Moscow Diary*, tr. Wolfram Eilenberger in Eilenberger, *Time of the Magicians, Wittgenstein, Benjamin, Cassirer, Heidegger and the Decade that Reinvented Philosophy*, tr. Shaun Whiteside (Penguin Books, 2021), 288–9.

29 Dostoevsky, "White Nights," *White Nights and Other Stories*, tr. Constance Garnett (New York: Grove Press, 1960), 56.

# 1

# Somerset Maugham: Love and Russian Literature

"Passion thrives not on satisfaction but impediment."

Maugham, *The Razor's Edge*

i

When Winston Churchill complained that the ms. of *Ashenden* broke the Official Secrets Act, Somerset Maugham burned fourteen unpublished stories and held off publication of the rest until 1928. His volume of linked stories, one third dealing with Russia and the Revolution, nevertheless charts Maugham's time there as a spy, or as Rebecca Beasley phrases it, "the Allies' chief secret agent in Russia in 1917."[1] But why was Maugham in Russia and how do his stories embody elements of Russian love? The answer as to "why" is the Foreign Office; and for "love," the daughter of an exiled Russian revolutionary, Peter Kropotkin. It may be no surprise, then, that *Ashenden* became required reading for MI6 agents during the Second World War and students of Russian romance.

Why did Maugham go to Russia? At the beginning of the First World War, he had volunteered for service in an ambulance unit and was posted to France, spending several months there where he met his soon-to-be American lover Gerald Haxton. But on leave in England, he accompanied his then mistress, Syrie Wellcome, to Rome where she had their daughter Liza in September 1915.[2] Four weeks later, they were back in England where his new play *Caroline* would premiere in February 1916, the same month Syrie's divorce case went to court. In the previous summer, through one of Syrie's girlfriends who was the mistress of Major John Wallinger, an officer in the foreign section of the Secret Service Bureau, Maugham had met Wallinger who supervised a network of agents in

Germany and Switzerland. Impressed by Maugham and his fluency in French and German, plus his popularity as a playwright (an excellent cover), he offered him a position in Geneva.

At the same time, divorce proceedings against Syrie were becoming public with Maugham named as co-respondent. Such notoriety would almost certainly create pressure to marry her, an unappealing prospect given his bisexuality but a seemingly inescapable social obligation, although he had made no final commitment. She knew of his homosexuality and the names of some of his lovers which she just might use to blackmail him if he did *not* marry her. The chance to escape to Geneva in November 1915, acting for the Foreign Office, was irresistible, while also postponing any further obligations to Syrie. He took the post and she joined him there briefly but their time together was unremittingly unhappy, surpassed only by his need to be in London for the divorce case in February 1916, their adultery now public. The opening of his new play *Caroline* a week before the trial ensured sustained publicity. The tension between the opening night and the courtroom was stressful and at first chance he returned to Geneva to continue his work as a spy.

Maugham found neutral Switzerland a congenial location since it attracted unusual figures on the fringes, or in the shadows, of war. Wallinger, however, had few successes as Maugham took up the post, replacing an agent who had had a nervous breakdown. Maugham's task was to facilitate information gathering rather than produce it, relaying messages to and from other agents working within Germany and France. His natural diffidence made him eminently suitable for the job. His code name was "Somerville" and his headquarters the elegant *Grand Hôtel d'Angleterre*. He arrived in the late autumn of 1915 and remained nearly eight months mixing hazard with tedium, the latter caused by hours of coding cables.[3] He found the danger exciting and for protection he often carried a small revolver which his hero Ashenden would duplicate (Hastings 205). And despite Wallinger's stumbles, Maugham respected him; he appears as Colonel R. in the *Ashenden* stories.

After Switzerland, Maugham went to America in October 1916 to escape Syrie again and to oversee a new production of *Caroline* plus a new work, *Our Betters*. This was six months before America joined the war and the country seemed indifferent about the conflict. Maugham, whose health was questionable—there were signs of tuberculosis—then thought a warm climate might help, preferably the South Seas. He contacted Gerald Haxton in Chicago and suggested that he accompany him. Syrie then made a surprise visit to New York days before he was to leave. After a ferocious scene where he insisted that they would marry on his return, he and Haxton trained to San Francisco and then by boat to Hawaii, Samoa, Fiji, Tonga, New Zealand, and eventually Tahiti. The night before the ship left Hawaii, a Miss Sadie Thompson rushed on board, a prostitute who had fled from the police but left a lasting impression on Maugham. She would become the center of his 1921 eponymous short story, later retitled as the popular "Rain."[4] Maugham absorbed every detail of his extended journey, discovering new inspiration for his tales during what turned out to be a six-month voyage.

He returned to New York in 1917 where he was unhappily married on May 26, 1917, in New Jersey. From the start, he knew it was a mistake with deception everywhere. The bride gave her age as thirty-two when in fact she was thirty-seven (Hastings 221). Their daughter, Liza, was two. But during a summer vacation in East Hampton, he unexpectedly received a call from Captain William Wiseman, working for the American branch of the SIS, asking if he was interested in further war work. Could he ensure the success of the Mensheviks over the Bolsheviks since the former were committed to continue the fight against Germany? Lenin and the Bolsheviks were not. The Allies wanted to support the so-called and seemingly moderate Provisional Government of Kerensky.

American and British intelligence had approved a secret mission to back Kerensky with the added creditability of $150,000, $75,000 from each government. Kerensky appeared insecure in the face of attacks by the vociferous Bolsheviks. Wiseman needed an emissary to Petrograd to support and convince the Russian leader to stay in the war, while also disseminating propaganda and report back on the volatile political situation. Maugham was Wiseman's choice (Hastings 222).

A surprised Maugham accepted the assignment: it would allow him to return to the war, visit Russia and free himself from what was marital disaster. He was also suffering further signs of tuberculosis and was generally unwell. But the possibility of a new adventure and travel was too strong to turn down. He also understood its artistic value: "the writer cannot afford to wait for experience to come to him: he must go out in search of it" (in Hastings 215). He accepted the offer and began his preparations, briefed in New York by various experts, including Rabbi Stephen Wise, an important Reform rabbi in close touch with Jewish communities in Petrograd. Other assistance came from Polish and Czech leaders and agents. Maugham continued with his code name, "Somerville," and his official cover of a journalist writing for the British press. He also received a salary and expenses, items he had turned down in Switzerland.

Maugham left New York for San Francisco carrying bills of exchange worth $21,000 to be distributed as he saw fit in Russia. He traveled with three Americans sent to join the US Embassy in Petrograd. Several Czech nationalists also joined him but he was to feign no knowledge of them. He was also traveling as a private agent, a journalist/playwright interested in Russia's transformation; both governments would disavow any knowledge of his activities if he was caught. The ship went from San Francisco to Yokohama, Maugham's first visit to the Far East. In Japan, he transferred to a Russian ship headed to Vladivostok, then on to the trans-Siberian train for Petrograd which took eleven days. On his arrival at the end of August 1917, he went directly to the Hotel Europa on Nevsky Prospekt to prepare for a meeting with the British Ambassador the next day. He found him taciturn and withdrawn.

Maugham also found Petrograd a disappointment, complaining that Nevsky Prospekt cannot match Bond Street, London, Fifth Avenue in New York or the rue de la Paix in Paris. Yet, because of its people and buildings, Nevsky Prospekt has more character. There is something "haphazard about the street" which has an "unfinished air," while stock in the shop windows "look[s] like bankrupt stock from the suburbs of Vienna or Berlin."[5] Yet the street is always crowded with a great variety of individuals, from students and soldiers to workmen, peasants, and the bourgeoisie. Most fascinating for Maugham is the diversity of appearance: "it is as though the passions of the soul were written more plainly on their faces, and the faces were not a mask but an index." What you see is a gallery of the characters from Russian fiction, "strangely primitive in the completeness with which they surrender themselves to emotion" (NtBk. 152). In a further comment, related to the Russians and love, he remarks that "with the Russians it looks as though each emotion took complete possession of the individual and swayed him wholly" (NtBk. 153). This entire section contains some of Maugham's most astute remarks on the Russian character.

Six months before Maugham arrived, the revolution forced the abdication of the Tsar, but anarchy and riot followed with gunfire common and soldiers, who had deserted the army in the face of German advances, roaming the streets. Battles between the Cossacks, loyal to the Provisional Government, and the Bolsheviks, loyal to Lenin, regularly occurred. Crime was everywhere but provisions were not. Kerensky, former Minister of Justice and then Minister of War in the provisional government of Prince Lvov, soon found himself the new Prime Minister after Lenin's attempt to overthrow Lvov failed but forced his resignation. The Germans had allowed Lenin to cross by train into Russia in the hope that he would remove the country from war. Kerensky vacillated and did not outlaw the Bolsheviks who would take control by November. Maugham arrived in the midst of the mayhem but culture, strangely, continued with movies, ballets, concerts, and restaurants open.

The British Embassy was not fully informed about the purpose of Maugham's secret mission and reluctantly assisted as he sent back coded reports to the British Consul General in New York, cover for the British spy operations. The British Ambassador to Russia, Sir George Buchanan, greeted him coldly because he had no exact idea as to Maugham's goal and no knowledge of the contents of the coded cables. Maugham's aim, according to Wiseman, was to "expose the German political intrigues in Russia" and disseminate propaganda encouraging Russia to continue the war against Germany (Jeffreys-Jones 92). But Maugham did not have policy-making power or free reign as Ashenden suggests he has.

As Jeffreys-Jones comments, Maugham likely realized he could achieve only limited ends; as a consequence, he took literary license with Ashenden's intensions, adding a grandiose manner for dramatic effect. He also believed that Wiseman's instructions gave him a greater challenge than was officially intended (Jeffreys-Jones 92). But Maugham also over-stressed his failure after the mission. His goals were to identify the new leadership, determine its value for the Allies, and work as an intermediary. In this sense he succeeded, although through oversight, he made no attempt to deal with the Bolsheviks who were clearly gaining power. He preferred to prop up the Mensheviks and then the Cossacks and Slav nationalist groups, largely through the Czech Emanuel Voska, actually a US intelligence officer, whose group often posed as waiters in German restaurants to spy on customers (Jeffreys-Jones 93–4). Voska would become in charge of counterespionage among the Poles, Czechs, and Cossacks in Russia; Maugham worked with him and Thomas Masaryk, later to become the first President of Czechoslovakia.

This was a challenging time: the Russian army was mutinous, famine was beginning, and the Kerensky government was ineffectual. The future was bleak: winter was approaching and there was no fuel. Lenin was hiding somewhere in Petrograd, while Kerensky was filled with doubt, more worried about doing the wrong thing than not doing the right. Voska provides a vivid picture of the situation in his memoir:

> In Petrograd I had been seeing the Russian republic crumble and fade away. All news was bad news. Day by day the Bolsheviki ... came more and more to the fore. It was to end with shooting; but it began with talk. On every street corner, in every public square and every hall, orators—some of them speaking Russian with a German accent—bawled out the same theme: This was a people's

revolution …. The Bolsheviki were talking themselves into power and no one was talking back.⁶

Shooting was soon everywhere: "Petrograd seemed to live always in sound of rifle fire," with the Bolsheviks randomly shooting at second story windows and then at groups of bourgeoise in the streets (Voska 231). "You would see figures dotted along the pavement in that unmistakable huddle which marks the dead," Voska writes (Voska 231). But people continued to live: "People went through their accustomed motions like soldiers, [and] considered the prospect of instant death as part of the business of living" (Voska 231). A few blocks from the telegraph building, under siege by Imperial Cadets, stood a cinema showing American films. While posters of Charlie Chaplin, Douglas Fairbanks, and Mary Pickford "smirked at the fighting," a long line of patrons patiently waited for the doors to open while bullets flew around them (Voska 232). Roving bands of deserters soon shot at officers and priests. Stopping any well-dressed man, they "inspected the palms of his hands. If these proved to be soft, a shot ended the interview" (Voska 234). "Human life seemed the cheapest commodity in Russia," he later wrote (Voska 237).⁷

Maugham's view of the Russians combines cliché with insight. In his *Writer's Notebook*, he comments on the Russian preference for "self-abasement" because humiliation offers a "singular sensual gratification" (NtBk. 142). The literature offers a "poverty of types:" one always meets the same types under a variety of names. The characters Alyosha (*The Brothers Karamazov*) and Stavrogin (*The Possessed*) represent the two most dominant categories, the two sides of the Russian character, "the two persons whom every Russian feels more or less in himself" (NtBk. 142). But these irreconcilable selves make the Russians "unbalanced" and "contradictory" (NtBk. 142). One result is the overpowering of art by moral purpose as in Tolstoy's *Resurrection* (NtBk. 147). Fiction, which he admires and dislikes in equal measure, is clearly the main source of Maugham's view of Russian character. However, its irony is coarse, while repartee, sarcasm, or even epigrams are absent. This negative attitude finds expression when he writes that "when a Russian laughs, he laughs at people and not with them; Dostoevsky's humor is that of a bar-loafer," yet he can admire his "tortured passion" (NtBk.142, 150).

*A Writer's Notebook* records a series of Maugham's Russian activities, admitting that what originally stimulated his interest in Russia was specifically Dostoevsky and particularly Alyosha Karamazov: "he affects one like a June morning in England" (NtBk. 159). A selfless, eager love is "the passion that fills his soul" but his morals are mixed: "pure but also dissolute" (NtBk. 159–60). In his notebook for 1917, Maugham writes in a bewildering way that the Russians are "strangely primitive in the completeness with which they surrender themselves to emotion." Unlike the British where emotion modifies character, with the Russians "it looks as though each emotion took complete possession of the individual and swayed him wholly" (NtBk. 152–3).

Remarks on the Democratic Convention at the Alexandrovsky Theater with Kerensky follow, the audience composed of representatives of the working classes from across the country. Nearly two thousand attended, Maugham feeling uncomfortable with their backward demeanor; they listened to the speeches with apathy. The "monotonous fervour" of each speech did not even offer "the relief of a plain fact," only "generalizations and exhortation" (Ntbk. 161). An address by Tsesetellim, Minister of Foreign Affairs, confirmed the mediocrity of the leaders and the gathering. Only Kerensky roused the crowd.

Seeking a vote of confidence, the khaki-dressed leader anxiously walked quickly down the central aisle of the theater to his political fate. He spoke emotionally for an hour but his sincerity won over the crowd (Ntbk. 162–3). Maugham then adds that Kerensky was essentially a man of words, of "morbid verbosity," not action, and who disliked disagreement (Ntbk. 165). For Maugham, it was Kerensky's "emotionalism" that aided his rise to power, always a strength in Russia "where the facile expression of feeling has an overwhelming effect." This, however, is disconcerting for "English modesty" (NtBk 167). Noble sentiments, expressed with candor, is the difference between the Russians and English.

Maugham began to keep notes as his position became more tenuous, and it became clear that Kerensky's government could not keep control. The Bolsheviks increasingly gained power. A coded message by Maugham in late September 1917 suggested the urgency of the situation, noting that Kerensky was losing his grip on the country and that chaos reigned in the army, that a secret agreement for Sweden and Finland to join Germany on the capture of Petrograd may exist and that there will be no separate peace with Germany, only "chaos and passive resistance on the Russian front."[8]

During his time in Petrograd, Maugham made various new contacts, from John Reed and his wife Louise Bryant, recent converts to Communism—Reed would soon write *Ten Days That Shook the World* on the October Revolution—to the English suffragette Emmeline Pankhurst, who held a daily tea in her room at the Europa, and the gay novelist Hugh Walpole, who originally went to Russia for the Red Cross but was now running an intelligence gathering service called the Anglo-Russian Propaganda Bureau. Walpole and Maugham knew each other from London and he later offered this remark about Maugham's Russian observations: "he watched Russia as we would watch a play, finding the theme, and then intent on observing how the master artist would develop it" (in Morgan 231).

Maugham does respect, however, the power of Russian love, declaring that the "message that Russia has given to the world seems to be the simple one that in love lies the secret of the universe" (NtBk. 142). But the will is often set in opposition to it as Russian novelists continue to reveal. Love only brings catastrophe. With religious overtones, Maugham complains that love fascinates characters in Russian literature but are fearful of its "satanic power." They look upon it with a strange compassion but believe it is divided against itself and rejoice when it "abdicates its power" and refuses to direct their lives (NtBk 143). Unrequited love is best.

But love in Russia troubles Maugham which this passage from the 1917 section of his *Writer's Notebook* elaborates when contrasting will and love. Love essentially means

> Placing one romantic figment of the imagination in face of another. They are both appearances .... they begin and end in feeling. Love, so far as it is active, partakes of the nature of the will, and so cannot reasonably be set up against it as a rival answer to the riddle of existence; but it is its passive side, its self-abnegation, its humility which have attracted the Russian temperament; it is there they find the answer they seek to the mystery which torments them .... it is a surrender of thought to emotion; when they say that in love is the secret of the universe they confess that they have given up the search for it .... intellectually they all suffer from the malady of Oblomovism [but] the supremacy of love has had a good press.
>
> (NtBk. 143)

He goes on to suggest that the intellectual life of Europe had stagnated: the world was disappointed with science; France was weary; the naturalistic school had become mechanical; Schopenhauer and Nietzsche had lost their novelty. Mysticism was in the air and when Europeans (and Russians) were told love offered a solution to their doubts, they accepted the concept which suggested that the term would make clear "everything that had puzzled them" giving them "an emotion which they were quite ready to take for an explanation." What never occurred to them was "that they were trying to explain a leg of mutton in terms of a top hat." Love was a troubling idea, "a grateful theme for rhetoric" but no more (Ntbk. 144).

The literature, however, provides clues, with Chekhov favored: he "will tell you more about the Russians than Dostoevsky," he admits (NtBk. 134–5). But the fashion for Russian writers has exaggerated their merit "merely because they write in Russian" (NtBk. 132). Kuprin, Korolenko, and Sologub are all criticized. Artzibachev, however, is better because *Sanine* has some sunshine: "the characters do not pass their lives in the freezing drizzle" (NtBk. 132). But in general, he finds an overall poverty in Russian writing but because they have so "small a literature," Russians know it thoroughly, a clear, backhanded compliment (133). Gogol, however, is good because he introduces no one of intelligence. His rogues and fools justify his stories. English and French fiction, by contrast, became fiction fit for a "middle-class civilization, well-fed, well-clothed, well housed" (NtBk. 126). Only Dostoevsky wrote with honesty about the disenfranchised, the marginalized, and the confused. Ironically, despite his critique of the Russian writers, they influenced Maugham's style, notably Chekhov who is able to offer the completeness of character with minimal details.

One other feature they possessed was an acute sense of sin. Russians repeatedly experience remorse; others have regrets but many, notably the English, do not carry the burden of sin beyond the church Maugham writes. But the introspective Russians have an urgent sense of sin (NtBk. 137). Dimitri Karamazov is representative: boisterous and quick tempered without self-control, he is also besieged by sin and feels remorse. But, Maugham notes, he does not bear malice. He drinks but then all Russians "take their liquor sadly. They weep when they are drunk. They are very often drunk" (NtBk. 138). But Maugham has no patience with portraying suffering which he has witnessed as a medical student and during the First World War. Suffering never improves the character and does not ennoble a man or woman. One suffers "poverty and the anguish of unrequited love, disappointment, disillusion" but this only creates envy and selfishness he believes (NtBk. 139). Suffering lessens a man.

The strength of the Russians is their resistance to convention. They do not do what's expected of them. Personal freedom is upheld, despite political coercion, freeing them from rules (NtBk.140). Yet, there is a constant streak of masochism. Citing Leopold von Sacher-Masoch, he points out that his short stories have women who are audacious, strong, and energetic and use men as seen in Russian fiction. Dostoevsky's heroines are similarly over bearing; tenderness and charm do not appeal to the men who love them. The heroes find "a horrible delight in the outrage to which they are exposed. They want to abase themselves" (NtBk. 141). A stream of masochism exists with men constantly ill-treated by the women they love, yet they find a "horrible delight in the outrages to which they are exposed. They want to base themselves" (Ntbk. 128). Women constantly treat men aggressively, obtaining an almost "sensual pleasure in humiliating them before others" but also become "femininely passive" (Ntbk. 128–9).

For Maugham, this is the condition of Russian love displayed, as we see, in Turgenev's *First Love*, Walter Benjamin's pursuit of his Latvian actor and Isaiah Berlin's unrepentant feelings for Anna Akhmatova. It is Dostoevsky's gravestone, the sculpted face "devastated by passion" (Ntbk 136). Women treat men in Russian fiction and life aggressively, often contentiously, becoming if not brutal in their conversations and actions which the men endure, then strict and domineering (NtBk.141). Maugham's ideas open a seam of understanding in the nature of Russian love.

Maugham's unsympathetic view of Russian love has several sources, beginning, perhaps, with his own unhappy marriage and then his realization that true love (for Maugham, gay love) is something he would not likely experience, despite his recollection of his powerful, always remembered love for Gerald Haxton, the dedicatee of *A Writer's Notebook*. Thoughts of an earlier love in England with Princess Sasha Kropotkin may have also colored his jaundiced view, as well as his unhappy time with Syrie who gave birth to their daughter in Rome, Italy selected to keep their relationship secret (she was not yet divorced; Hastings 199). Nevertheless, in his remarks Maugham has identified the overwhelming element of what both attracts and repels him from Russia and its literature: love. Writing *Ashenden* became the means of working out his own relationship with love, its absence, and his Russian intrigues.

But secret agents working in hidden ways, as he had to hide his homosexuality, naturally appealed, from their strength of character to their ruthless purposes. They were terrifying but creative in their dark methods. With equanimity, the agent would face danger, discomfort, and boredom. But he was a disciplined patriot, Maugham declaring that the patriotism of the Russians is "a singular thing," even if there is a great deal of conceit in it (NtBk.127–8). Yet it reinforces their mysteriousness and complexity as they even become proud of their faults (NtBk.128). But perhaps Russia is too vast for intimate sentiments, he thinks, like patriotism: "its character [is] too indefinite … for the imagination to embrace the country, its history and culture, in a single emotion" (NtBk. 129). He then offers a slanted view of Russian pride and diminished sense of nationality adding that the Russians would accept life under "Central Powers" with only a shrug (NtBk. 129). By contrast, the Czechs seem better disciplined and purposeful: "they are organized like a department store" (NtBk 129).

Comments on Russian literature again follow, noting that *Anna Karenina* seems "hard and dry," *Fathers and Sons* too related to French fiction, Turgenev too idealistic and sentimental. Only Dostoevsky had meaning, then Chekhov and Gorky whose singularity came from his origins: he wrote of the proletariat as a proletarian. Chekhov was a writer you could understand intimately, not "a wild force like Dostoevsky" (NtBk. 131). From Chekhov one could learn "the secret of Russia" because his knowledge of life was direct (as was Maugham's: both trained as doctors and witnessed pain [NtBk. 131]). With Chekhov, he writes, "you do not seem to be reading stories at all" (NtBk. 131). All of these attitudes create the context for Maugham's actions and reactions to his Russian experiences, largely oriented around love.

But *Ashenden* is not entirely about Russia. Several episodes deal with the hero's escapades in Europe, while three are based on the experiences of Gerald Kelly, a friend and agent in Spain. "The Hairless Mexican," "The Dark Woman," and "The Greek" deal with Kelly's adventures, two with a Mexican general recruited by "R." to kill a German agent but who kills the wrong man. Six deal with Petrograd with personal relations his focus, plus the dangers of revolutionary change.

In Petrograd and needing to meet Kerensky, Maugham contacted his former lover and now political activist, Alexandra (Sasha) Kropotkin, rekindling an earlier romance, a Russian romance. Maugham had, in fact, experienced Russian love in London. The daughter of Prince Peter Kropotkin, an anarchist then living in exile and who in 1905 published *The Ideals and Realities in Russian Literature* (London: Duckworth, 1905), Sasha Kropotkin was a voluptuous woman both clever and intense. She was part of a circle of Russian artists and revolutionaries. At her London parties, Maugham met Diaghilev and Pavlova. Together, the two went to Paris for a few days, staying on the Left Bank. They visited the Louvre and *Comédie Française*, went dancing in a Russian nightclub, and enjoyed enormous meals which surprised him. Maugham would draw on this experience (especially the food) in "Love and Russian Literature," the penultimate story in *Ashenden*. Their affair lasted only a few weeks but for Maugham it was a vibrant introduction to Russian love which would, itself, soon travel from London to Petrograd, his adventures transposed to fiction.

In more detail, Sasha Kropotkin, having returned with her husband (Boris Lebedev, m. 1910) and father to Russia in 1917, spent time there befriending a series of political leaders. In Petrograd, she was known as Madame Lebedev and began to involve herself with the revolution and the Mensheviks. She knew Kerensky well and offered to introduce Maugham, although Kerensky was himself ill and indecisive, even at the young age of thirty-six. Nevertheless, Maugham met Kerensky with Sasha once a week at the Mjedved, one of the finest restaurants in Petrograd; she was hostess and interpreter. Maugham regularly offered his guests caviar and vodka "at the expense of the two governments who had sent me to Petrograd, and they devoured it with relish" (in Hastings 226). Conversation would continue in Sasha's apartment. Maugham summarizes her importance in the final story in *Ashenden* where she understood that through him (and his government funds), she might acquire "an influence in the affairs of Russia .... She had a passion for intrigue and a desire for power" (Ashenden 307).

The Allies had been pressuring Kerensky to continue to fight against Germany, while the people, facing famine and winter, demanded peace. With an absent American ambassador, a former grain merchant from St. Louis, and an obdurate British Ambassador outfitted with a monocle and mustache, there was little further assistance. A disorganized government and confused army did not help. Maugham became the only viable go-between between the Allies and Kerensky (Hastings 227, 225).

In September 1917, Maugham and Sasha attended a large, formal gathering of nearly 2,000 including foreign dignitaries where Kerensky spoke. He was unimpressive and ran from the stage when a heckler shouted from the audience of the Alexandrovsky Theater. Nonetheless, Maugham continued his weekly meetings with the politician in the hopes of propping up the weakened leader. Maugham summarizes many of the political conflicts and vacillations in sections of "Mr. Harrington's Washing" in *Ashenden*, especially 314–6.

"Love and Russian Literature," the fifteenth story in the *Ashenden* collection, focuses on Russian love but with a comic touch. Maugham again turns to actual events: the story begins with Ashenden visited by three Czech nationalists who traveled with him from California. Emanuel Voska was the principal figure, the Czech refugee working for US intelligence and eager to free his country from the Austro-Hungarian Empire. The three men followed Voska, one of whom becomes Dr. Orth in the story. He provided essential information on the political situation for Ashenden, who proposes him as a translator for Harrington. He then thinks of Anastasia Alexandrovna Leonidov, daughter of a revolutionary who escaped to England, Alexander Denisiev (Ash 291, 293). In actuality, this is Sasha Kropotkin and her father, Peter.

Three pages on, Ashenden outlines his relation with Anastasia, summarizing Maugham's actual relation with Sasha in London and Paris, acknowledging "the pangs of unrequited love" (Ash 292). She mesmerized him: "In her dark melancholy eyes," he saw all of Russia.⁹ Maugham here satirizes the impact of Russia on the British consciousness through the supposed intensity of Ashenden's love for Anastasia (Ash 295). Meeting her after her marriage to a Vladimir Leonidov in the story, he notes that they originally met

> at the time when Europe discovered Russia. Everyone was reading the Russian novelists, the Russian dancers captivated the civilised world .... Russian art seized upon Europe with the virulence of an epidemic.
>
> (Ash 293)

Anastasia was also part of the intelligentsia, "a difficult word to spell but an easy one to say" (Ash 293). But as the daughter of a revolutionary, would she ever remarry? To Ashenden's shock, she says yes.

But would her husband allow her to divorce and marry Ashenden? No, he would never get over his unhappiness, she declares: "That is the Russian spirit" (Ash 296)! Leaving him would mean he has lost everything but he wouldn't want to stand in the way of her happiness. Optimistically, she explains that "he's far too great for that. He'll see that when it's a question of my own self-development I haven't the right to hesitate" (Ash 296). And then she calmly explains that when she tells Vladimir that she has decided to marry Ashenden, "he will commit suicide" (Ash 296). The scene, he thinks, is straight out of Dostoevsky "and he saw the moving and terrible pages" where everyone made long speeches: "It was all very dreadful and wonderful and shattering" (Ash 297). Satire has overtaken the seriousness of Russian love now framed by suffering.

She continues: Vladimir would never expose her to the "vulgar notoriety of the divorce court" but, instead, prefer suicide. When asked how Vladimir would kill himself, she says he will blow his brains out. Ashenden immediately thinks of Ibsen's *Rosmersholm*: with his death on their conscience, they would always suffer. "Life is like that," Anastasia replies in a tempered, fatalistic Russian style, adding that "there is his happiness to be considered too. He will prefer to commit suicide" (Ash 297).

We must be sure we are doing the right thing she then announces. She would never forgive herself if she allowed Vladimir to commit suicide "and then found I'd make a mistake." To find out if they really love each other, she suggests a week in Paris which she will keep secret from Vladimir because it "would only distress him" (Ash 299, 298). This blends Russian emotion with French romance and English comedy underscored when she asks "surely you have no bourgeois prejudices" (Ash 299, 298)? They meet at Victoria Station, pleased with their first-class tickets: "father and Vladimir travel third on account of their principles" (Ash 299).

In Paris, they settle in a small hotel and talk about Gorky and Marx plus "human destiny, love and the brotherhood of man; and drank innumerable cups of Russian tea" (Ash 300). Breakfast in a dingy dining room meant scrambled eggs for Anastasia, a hearty eater. Sightseeing followed, including a Russian cabaret. The next morning, however, it was scrambled eggs again. So, too, the third day, Ashenden frustrated by her unwillingness to try something different. On the fourth, he partially surrenders and switches to fried eggs. But isn't that inconsiderate, she asks:

> Do you think it's fair to give the cook unnecessary work? You English, you're all the same, you look upon servants as machines …. how can you be surprised that the proletariat are seething with discontent when the bourgeoisie like you are so monstrously selfish?
>
> (Ash 302)

Accused of having no feelings because he is insensitive to the extra work involved—"you wouldn't talk like that if you had been through the events of 1905 in Petersburg" with "crowds in front of the Winter Palace kneeling in the snow while the Cossacks charged them"—she challenges him as politics and eggs intertwine (Ash 302). Ashenden succumbs, the bourgeois gentlemen capitulating: scrambled eggs every morning.

A week later, they return to London where at their parting she announces that, yes, she would marry him but the prospect of scrambled eggs each morning comically obscures his romantic feelings. After she departs, he immediately goes to a Cunard office to book passage on the first ship to America (Ash 303). Love and Russian life, as determined by Sasha and experienced by Ashenden, are incompatible in what is a satiric twist on a Chekhovian situation of two secret lovers where their future is unknown but presumably entwined (see "The Lady with a Little Dog"). The gap between how the literature presents love as inconsolable, intense, and deeply emotional finds comic relief at Maugham's breakfast table and the inevitable scrambled eggs. Ironically, the actual Sasha Kropotkin published a Russian cook book with a section on eggs, but not scrambled.[10] But in his exposé, Maugham discloses the major contradictions of Russian love and its limitations.

The final Ashenden story further involves Anastasia but in a political manner. It deals with Mr. Harrington and his determination to retrieve his laundry as the Kerensky government is overturned and fighting breaks out.

Harrington's decision will have fatal consequences as actually happened to the American banker Maugham met on his train trip to Petrograd. In the story, Sasha becomes Harrington's guide and interpreter. In Voska's memoir, a Russian lady "in reduced circumstance" served as the banker's interpreter; Maugham duplicates her account of running into a street skirmish after they retrieve his laundry before separating. Voska, in fact, actually ran to the street and found the banker dead in the gutter but holding his washing (Voska 232–3). Maugham uses the story as his plot.

Maugham structures the drama of the story so that just after Harrington gets the signatures he needed to guarantee a loan to the Provisional Government, Kerensky's administration falls. The documents are now worthless because of the overthrow and Anastasia may possibly be on a list to be arrested and killed (Ash 317). In disbelief at this change, Harrington suddenly asks Anastasia to go with him to America. She refuses, declaring that "I'm a Russian. My place is here. I will not leave my country when most my country needs me" (Ash 318). Russian love becomes love of Russia, even when danger is self-evident. But Harrington challenges her jingoism, and she admits that what she said is not entirely true. She wants to stay in Russia so as not to miss the action.

Harrington leaves to pack, and Ashenden and Anastasia discuss the general situation. Depressed, Ashenden knows his schemes have failed, but she was elated by the rapid change in political fortunes. She tried to be serious but Ashenden knew that she looked upon the events "very much as a thrilling play" (Ash 319). Harrington returns but declares that he won't go without his laundry which included four shirts, "two union suits, a pair of pyjamas and four collars" (Ash 320). Harrington then asks what did Ashenden think of Russia now in the midst of its revolution? His response is a diatribe against the Russian writers and the so-called intelligentsia ending with "I'm sick of fine phrases, and oratory and attitudinising" (Ash 321).

Rifle fire interrupts his discourse, but Harrington expresses new determination to get his laundry; Anastasia agrees to accompany him, while Ashenden remains to send encoded cables. Shortly after, a distraught Anastasia bursts-in looking for Harrington who had found his washing unwashed. On their return, she wanted to pause at a demonstration but in the midst of the gathering, soldiers turned a corner and fired. Harrington disappeared in the melee; Anastasia and Ashenden begin a search on streets strewn with broken windows and lost items. They discover Harrington dead and this tragic/comic sentence ends the story: "Mr. Harrington had not let his washing go" (Ash 326). The incident is identical to the story told to Maugham by Emanuel Voska.[11]

## ii

Love in various forms permeates *Ashenden*, essentially an English novelist's understanding of Russian love. One of the most curious examples is "His Excellency," the twelfth story, which narrates the love affair of the British ambassador to Russia who confesses his early passion for a French courtesan who is an acrobat. This unexpected narrative of desire undermines the proper and dignified image of the ambassador, who reluctantly rejects a bohemian life after traveling three months with the woman and her company. Instead, he chooses a well-placed marriage which furthers his career. But he knows, and tells Ashenden, that his life has been unfulfilled. "How long does love last?" is his persistent question, because his obsession with the "whiskey voiced" Alix never left him (Ash 249–51). The ambassador's proper marriage has brought only an empty life with a woman he dislikes.

Anticipating this tale is the narrative of the agent Byring who was the *amant de coeur* of a "famous harlot" which he admitted but would not end (Ash 233). Ashenden himself meets this mistress who turns out to be well-read and sophisticated. This story, shared with the ambassador, is a prelude to the ambassador's own confession. At the end of the narrative, the ambassador admits that it might be wiser for a man "to do what he wants very much to do and let the consequences take care of themselves," the attitude of Byring whose career will end because of his affair. But it will be worthwhile: "he will have been satisfied. He will have fulfilled himself" (Ash 236, 261).

This is a reckless statement for an ambassador but he self-consciously recognizes the contradictions of his own disappointed love: "he was disgusted by the sordidness of his intrigue" but cannot give up the acrobat, Alix. Maugham emphasizes that desire, not status, should guide one's emotional life (Ash 252). But the behavior of the ambassador repeats the conditions of Russian love where hesitation and doubt overpower feeling. In the end, the ambassador sacrificed his love for Alix to marry his well-placed fiancée, suppressing his emotional life. Russians want to act for love and are fully committed to love; even if disappointment means a life apart, one still remains devoted to the lover as in *Onegin* or, later, Turgenev's "Asya."

Other forms of love are also present in *Ashenden*. "Giulia Lazzari" displays false love, centering on a Spanish dancer *cum* prostitute and her passion for an exiled Indian nationalist, and also a spy, Chandra Lai. Love is here a lever, Giulia writing a letter, under Ashenden's direction, drawing Lai back across the border into France. Both know he'll be arrested immediately. Learning of this betrayal,

Giulia commits suicide. Here, love is a trap, shown as a magnet to bring people together but falsely, relying on duplicity.

In "The Dark Woman," love, danger, betrayal, and death mix. Overcome by love, a former Mexican general, Manual Carmona, now a spy allied with Ashenden, tells of his obsessive love for a singular woman, a love so strong that it takes away your appetite for food. Love then becomes a frenzy: "a man like me is capable of every folly and every crime when he is in love" (Ash 79). His folly is his sharing with his lover plans to overthrow the government but he suddenly senses that she is a spy and if she left, he and others would die. With an almost religious fervor and a love that brings "exquisite pain," he knows he has no choice: she must die and slits her throat (Ash 84). This passionate, extravagant, criminal love knows no limit and contrasts with unfulfilled, often secret or at best incomplete Russian love. Maugham parades these alternate forms of love in his collection to display the range of love witnessed and experienced by a spy alternately indifferent to but also entrapped by love.

Maugham loves intrigue, and these stories are replete with deceptions, false clues, and tricks. In "Miss King," we learn that twice a week in the market place, Ashenden receives instructions from an old peasant woman, corpulent and red-faced. Yet tucked between her ample breasts were coded notes for Ashenden (Ash 24–5). Ashenden was also cavalier, sometimes blasé about his situation, thinking that he might, indeed, be arrested before he could finish his current play and he very much "disliked the notion of leaving it half done for an indefinite period" (Ash 21–2). Stylish detail fills Ashenden's narrative with a certain *savoir faire*: putting on slippers and a dressing gown, he drops a small revolver into his pocket "as an after-thought" but believes "much more in his acuteness than in a firearm, which is apt to go off at the wrong time ..." (Ash 39).

Surprisingly, during his time as an agent, Maugham was still able to write. Not only did he gather material for *Ashenden*, but he wrote three plays: *Our Betters* (in Rome, 1915), *The Unattainable* (in Geneva, 1915), and *Love in a Cottage* (in Petrograd, 1917). And it was in Petrograd where he wrote the substantial Russian sections of his *Writer's Notebook*.

After Maugham's hasty departure from Russia following the early November overthrow of Kerensky's government—he had to relay in person a secret message from Kerensky to the British Prime Minister, Lloyd George—he gave up any further direct contact with Sasha Kropotkin, although she remained a presence in his work as the woman in whose "dark melancholy eyes Ashenden saw the boundless steppes of Russia" (Ash 294; also see 315). Earlier, she had appeared as the Archduchess Anastasia, a reference in his play *Jack Straw*.

In *Penelope*, she becomes a figure invented by the principal character to gain the interest of others and later, Sasha would become the Grand Duchess Anna Alexandrova in Maugham's unpublished play, *The Road Uphill*. His encounter with Russian Love, which began in London, lasted through Petrograd and beyond.

### iii

In Petrograd in the fall of 1917, Maugham was busy: when not trying to support Kerensky and his aides, he was sending nightly coded reports to New York which were then sent on to Washington and London. They were accurate and politically sensitive. Maugham also had several subagents working for him, using them at one point to try to infiltrate a secret Bolshevik meeting. It failed but he continued to maintain a set of important contacts in Petrograd, including Boris Savinkov, the Minister of War who in 1918 would organize a secret resistance movement against the Bolsheviks (Hastings 227–8). Savinkov would appear briefly in Maugham's *The Razor's Edge,* when the narrator drinks Russian tea in a Petrograd apartment.

By September 1917, Maugham realized that Kerensky and his government were hopeless. Lenin and the Bolsheviks were gaining public support, while a mood of fear ran through the Provisional Government. In a later comment, Maugham wrote that there was endless talk, not action, and soon the

> vacillations, the apathy when apathy could only result in destruction, the high-flown protestations, the insincerity and half-heartedness that I found everywhere sicken me with Russia and the Russians.[12]

Maugham often spent his mornings taking Russian lessons, which he had started years ago in Capri, but the political situation was becoming dire and on October 16 he wired Wiseman urging fuller support of the Mensheviks with a program of pro-Menshevik espionage and propaganda activities which would likely cost $50,000. But he also made time to visit Dostoevsky's grave (as does Mr. Harrington in *Ashenden*) and went to the theater to discover that his own play, *Jack Straw*, had been translated into Russian. On October 18, Kerensky summoned Maugham and passed on a secret message for Lloyd George, so sensitive it could not be written down. Maugham had to go to London immediately to ask for more weapons and ammunition, and to replace the current British Ambassador.[13]

On October 22, 1917, Maugham left Petrograd from the Finland Station; two days later, the Bolshevik Revolution began but he was on his way to Norway and then on to Scotland before reaching London on November 17. On the 18th, he went to Downing Street. Having written down Kerensky's requests, he thrust the paper into the hand of the Prime Minister, who glanced at the sheet and simply said, "I can't do that" (Morgan 232–3). Before Maugham could return, events moved forward: Kerensky had been overthrown on November 7, the Bolsheviks then took power, and Russia sought peace with Germany. Maugham was depressed and disheartened: "his careful schemes had come to nothing" as Ashenden admits (Ash 319). Maugham believed that if he had started six months earlier, the outcome might have been different. On November 20, he had a second high-level Russian meeting held in the office of the editor of *The Times* and chaired by the Lord Chief Justice. Also present was the director of British military intelligence and William Wiseman, recently returned from America. He passed on his report. He had their respect and was shortly after offered a new assignment in Bucharest. He was tempted but his health did not permit acceptance.

In his political history of American espionage, Jeffreys-Jones is complementary about Maugham. Unlike other intelligent sources at the time, Maugham gave proper warning of Kerensky's infirmity, of Bolshevik strength, and of the possibilities of a Czech and Polish uprising. The Root commission (a US group sent to Russia after the ousting of Nicholas II to determine if Russia would continue to fight the Germans) mistakenly misread the power of the Bolsheviks and failed to warn President Wilson of the shift in power. The US ambassador, David F. Francis, a political appointment, was inept as a diplomat and enamored of Kerensky; the British Consul General in Moscow, Bruce Lockhart, similarly supported Kerensky. Other committees and reports passed on or initiated by Washington were either second-hand or incomplete.

By contrast, Maugham's summaries were accurate, well-written, and clear. But Wilson could not consider the Russian and Slav problem on the basis of intelligence reports alone, Jeffreys-Jones writes. He had to consider American politics but the "Allies' chief agent in Russia" must be given credit for precise accounts of a fluid situation; he also offered sensible steps on political and financial methods to follow in order to become proactive in East Central Europe (Jeffreys-Jones 100). His suggestion of clandestine funds to subsidize certain national movements of self-determination became a controversial but enacted program (Jeffreys-Jones 101).

Maugham did not return to Russia after the Bolsheviks took control but began to transpose his experiences into the linked short stories centered on Ashenden's espionage activities in France, Switzerland, Italy, and Russia. He began to write them while in a sanatorium in northern Scotland, where he would stay for over a year recuperating from his tuberculosis, worsened by his two-and-a-half months in Russia. Most importantly, *Asheden* represents two forms of Russian love: the first is Maugham's attachment to Sasha Kropotkin begun in London and rekindled in Petrograd (Ash 306). Her appearance in several Ashenden stories attests to her centrality in Maugham's conception of Russian love, life, and culture.

His second love was intrigue. He enjoyed the deceptions, dangers, and difficulties of running agents, transmitting secrets and carrying out sensitive political plans. For a dramatist, this was both natural and theatrical. As he wrote in "The Traitor" (the tenth and longest story in the collection), assuming a disguise offered a new sense of self:

> He was travelling with a brand-new passport in his pocket, under a borrowed name, and this gave him an agreeable sense of owning a new personality ... it diverted him for a while to be merely a creature of R.'s facile invention.
>
> (Ash 171)

What other job would see Maugham move so easily from the titular Prime Minister of Russia, Kerensky, to the Prime Minister of England, Lloyd George?

*Ashenden* did not appear, however, until 1928, the same year as Woolf's *Orlando*. Government concern over revealing too much about espionage delayed its publication. In the interval, however, he revised his views on Russia and Russian writing resulting in the occasional caricatures and satiric view of Russian intelligentsia. But the presence of Sasha Kropotkin, mixed with the world of intrigue, remained. Both were Russian loves that could not be forgotten. But what of Sasha Kropotkin's life continued to fascinate?

Detained during the Revolution, Sasha managed to leave Russia in 1921 for Paris, ending up in New York where, by 1927, she remarried and began a successful career as a journalist retaining her royal title ("Princess Alexandra Kropotkin") as a byline for her woman's column, "To the Ladies," for *Liberty* magazine. She also wrote for *New Outlook* and undertook various translations including *Crime and Punishment* and *The Brothers Karamazov*; she also translated several of Shaw's plays into Russian. Her arrival in New York occasioned a story in the *New York Times* headlined "RUSSIAN PRINCESS COMES TO STUDY US; Daughter of Prince Kropotkin Says She May Base Lectures on Her Observations. APPROVES SOVIET SYSTEM/ She Opposes Communist Rulers, Predicting Their Downfall as Peasants Rise" (April 6, 1927).

The opening sentence of the article identifies her as the "daughter of Prince Peter Kropotkin, Russian scientist and revolutionist and descendant of Rurik, first ruler of Russia." In the piece, she emphasizes her objection to the return of a Czarist government but opposition to the Communists now in control: "The Soviet system is good but the Communist dictatorship is the evil." The peasants have acquired land and "property rights are the death knell of communism."[14] Two years later, she was a guest speaker on Russia at the Town Hall Club, also reported in the *New York Times*.

Sasha also published a popular cookbook, *How to Cook and Eat in Russian* (1947), whose significance was as much political as it was culinary. This remarkable book—the author is listed as Alexandra Kropotkin, not her married name, nor as a Princess—offers political commentary, while revealing social practices. With Russian food the focus, it also provides details on Russian life from the Revolution through the 1940s with clarity and occasionally humor. It opens with "On Russian Eating and Russian People" before Chapter 1 deals with "Russian Eating Materials." Later chapters turn directly to food: "Pirogs and Piroshki Kasha" (Ch. 4), "Russian Pancakes" (Ch.5), "Sauces" (Ch.11), and "Preserves and Pickles" (Ch.14). "Around the Samovar" is the final chapter.

But politics is never far from the stove: the preface begins by directly addressing public reaction to Russia:

> Nowadays any mention of Russia brings on a red-hot argument, but to me there is nothing new in all this. All my life I have listened to Russian controversies and have taken part in them. The tsar and his government provided the issue when I was a girl .... now the tsar has become a faded memory, yet the debate continues to be furious between those who admire the Russian government and those who disapprove of it or fail to understand it.

But "in the noise and anger of the ideological clash, the Russian people usually are forgotten."

Extending her political and social thinking, she writes in the next paragraph that the Russians are

> pretty nice people. Though their admixture of Oriental blood may lend an aspect of deviousness, at times, to their behavior, fundamentally they are friendly and patient folk, alive with curiosities, tirelessly energetic, sometimes incredibly lazy. Strange and moody, no doubt. Interesting nevertheless.

(How v)

But in highly charged language, she claims that the political representatives of the people were another story. Long before the Revolution, "the debonair manners of Russian officialdom covered a puffed-up provincial insolence" typical of other countries as well. To truly know a country and its people, study their home life, family habits, and cooking. "The table and kitchen customs of the Russian home" will be her subject through which she hopes to "win American friends" (How v–vi). Her choices are "the most characteristic Russian specialities" discarding only those that seem impractical to make for American homemakers. In her thanks, she acknowledges not only Colonel Serge Obolensky, but the staff of the New York Consulate of the USSR: "their enthusiasm for Russian dishes proves once again that politics don't count—when eating is concerned" (How vi).

The text begins with an emphasis on the communal spirit of Russians who love to eat in company: "The Russian spirit is a community spirit" (How 1). And it is a Russian convention that there must always be leftovers: "enough isn't enough in Russia." Unless there is surplus, the host might be thought stingy, as much a crime as robbery. You can call a Russian a liar or a thief—he will soon be forgiven—but to call him a *skriaga,* cheap, and he will hold it against you (How 1). "Hospitality is an ingrained Russian trait," she adds (2). And Russians love lengthy banquets with the traditional dinner time between three and five o'clock; those who ate later were imitating foreign customs and habits.

And food crosses political boundaries: the most popular national dishes have not changed from the Tsarists to the Communists: "if they are really Russians, they all like the same things to eat, however violently they may disagree in politics." All agree on the virtues of Russian black bread, cabbage soup, baked buckwheat or pastilla candies which taste like fruit (How 2–3). Russians are also hearty eaters: "no Russian would dream of dieting if he wasn't flat on his back sick in bed. Russians would rather be robustly fat than fashionably lean," which may actually be a reaction to the frequent Russian famines (How 3).

Her colloquial style and idioms increased the popularity of the book. But politics still emerges. In her discussion of caviar (48–50), for example, she records that Kerensky and the Provisional Government, under siege at the Winter Palace, had no food but the distinguished St. Petersburg grocer Elisseeff, on hearing of the situation, arrived with Caviar, their only staple for seven days![15]

Chapter 15, "Around the Samovar," outlines the social importance of the nightly gatherings around the urn which usually began at 10 p.m. when the entire family gathered to talk. Friends dropped in between ten and midnight to gossip, talk politics, religion, science, art, war and peace. "Perhaps because Russians have never at any time enjoyed the freedom of airing their opinions openly in public," she adds, "the evening tea hour plays the part actually of a national forum" (How 252). Arguments can be heated but around the samovar there is a "frame of fairly reasonable compromise …. That, I suppose, is the reason why Russians all over the world, in whatever country they may be, like best to be entertained with an evening around the samovar," the final sentence of her book (How 253).

Russia's imprint on Maugham was long lasting, personally and professionally. Although he ended his espionage activities, he did return to travel, often to Southeast Asia and writing. But he never forgot Petrograd, nor the impact of Russian love.

## Notes

1 On Churchill's reaction to Maugham's volume, see John Le Carré, *The Pigeon Tunnel, Stories from My Life* (New York: Viking, 2016), 17. Le Carré cites Christopher Andrew, *Secret Service* (London: Guild Publishing, 1985). Ted Morgan reports the same on p. 206 of *Maugham* (New York: Simon and Shuster, 1980), as does Selina Hastings in *The Secret Lives of Somerset Maugham* (London: John Murray, 2009), 237.

    For the Beasley quote see *Russomania* 37. In his account of American espionage, Rhodri Jeffreys-Jones refers to Maugham's "uncelebrated but vital mission as secret agent in revolutionary Russia." See Rhodri Jeffreys-Jones, *American Espionage, From Secret Service to CIA* (New York: The Free Press, 1977), 85. Hereafter Jeffreys-Jones.

    The title of Jeffreys-Jones seventh chapter is "Maugham in Russia" and largely celebrates Maugham's efforts to keep Russia in the war, even if the overall mission was a failure. He also examines the use of a British agent for American information gathering; Sir William Wiseman, Maugham's superior, regularly shared intelligence between the Foreign Office and the State Department, especially transmitting Russian intelligence to the Americans. As a decoy to foreign intelligence agencies, Maugham's coded messages were sent to the British Consul in New York.

2 In the 1960s, Maugham tried to deny his paternity in an effort to transfer his estate to his then male secretary. A notorious 21-month court case followed. His daughter won and was awarded nearly £1.4 million in damages.

3 For Maugham's activities in Geneva see Selina Hastings, *The Secret Lives of Somerset Maugham* (London: John Murray, 2009), 204–8. Hereafter Hastings.

4 On the success of the short story, filmed, rewritten as a play and even made into a musical, see Hastings 220.

5   W. Somerset Maugham, *A Writer's Notebook* (London: Vintage, 2001), 151. Hereafter NtBk. It originally appeared in 1949.
6   Emanuel Voska and Will Irwin, *Spy and Counter Spy* (New York: Doubleday, Doran, 1940), 226, 228. Hereafter Voska.
7   In another passage, he describes his first night in Petrograd: "crowds, parading aimlessly, jammed the sidewalks and pavements. Talk popped like the rattle of machine guns. It was as though Russia were letting off in one blast the thought bottled up through a thousand years of rule by czars, nobles and police spies …. at every street corner, in every square, orators were haranguing crowds which talked back at 'them'" (Voska 219).
8   Maugham in Ted Morgan, *Maugham* (New York: Simon and Schuster, 1980), 230. Hereafter Morgan.
9   Ashenden 294. There are parallels with Virginia Woolf's *Orlando* (1928) where the character Orlando also calls his Russian princess Sasha and who is also a gateway to the Russian imaginary (Woolf, *Orlando*, ed. Rachel Bowlby [Oxford: Oxford World's Classics, 2008], 43). Woolf spends nearly ten pages on Sasha, including her ability to bark like a wolf heard on the steppes (52).
10  In her cookbook, eggs appear with mushroom piroshki, chopped herring with egg and egg slices with Kilki on. Earlier on p. 28, she notes, "Vast quantities of eggs are featured on the national menu. At breakfast we like them soft-boiled. At lunch or supper we like them fried, and any Russian will relish an omelet at any hour of the day or night. No one in Russia would ever think of eating fewer than 3 fried eggs at a time, nor would anyone make an omelet with less than 4 eggs." But mention of scrambled eggs is absent. See Alexandra Kropotkin, *How to Cook and Eat in Russian* (New York: G. P. Putnam's Sons, 1947), 28–9. Hereafter How.
11  Morgan 232; Voska in Hastings 239; Voska 232–3.
12  Maugham, *The Summing Up*, Section 54 (London: Heineman, 1938), 75. https://gutenberg.ca/ebooks/maughamws-summingup/maughamws-summingup-00-h.html.
13  Morgan offers a slightly different scenario: learning that Maugham would likely be recalled by the Foreign Office, Kerensky summoned him to the Winter Palace telling him in a message to be memorized that Britain should offer peace to Germany but a peace without annexations or compensation. This way Kerensky thought he could keep his army in the field, especially if Britain would provide additional armament and supplies. He also demanded the replacement of the British Ambassador. Immediately after the meeting, Maugham sent a coded message to London; the reply indicated that a destroyer would be sent to Christiania (now Oslo) to bring him back for consultations (Morgan 232).
14  See NYT: https://www.nytimes.com/1927/04/06/archives/russian-princess-comes-to-study-us-daughter-of-prince-kropotkin.html. The article originally appeared on

p. 26 of the Amusements section. The article also notes that her ship, the Cunard's *Aurania*, arrived from Liverpool and Belfast with 1,161 passengers.

15 Soup, synonymous with dinner for Russians, also becomes political, suggesting that meat served to Russian army recruits during the First World War was responsible for fall of Tsardom. If peasant rookies could have meat in their soup every day, instead of two or three times a year, then why couldn't the Tsar and his government provide peasant families with meat soup at least once a week with more equal distribution of wealth (How 66–7)? Failure to do so partially led to revolution.

# 2

# R.H. Bruce Lockhart: Love and Revolution

Best known for his autobiography *Memoirs of a British Agent*, a 1932 bestseller dealing principally with diplomatic adventures and the Russian Revolution, and turned into a popular film starring Leslie Howard and Kay Francis, R.H. Bruce Lockhart was one of the youngest British diplomats in Russia, becoming Acting Consul General in Moscow at age twenty-eight.

Lockhart's life was as dramatic as it was adventurous. He began his career as a British diplomat/spy in 1912 when he was appointed Britain's Vice-Consul in Moscow, becoming Acting Consul General from 1914 to 1917 (the Ambassador and Consul General were withdrawn because of the impending Russian Revolution). After returning to Britain, he was sent again to Russia in 1918 at the expressed wish of Lloyd George as an unofficial British representative to the Bolshevik Government to assess the power of Lenin and Trotsky; he was also tasked with keeping Russia in the Great War.[1] At thirty-one, he was called the "Boy Ambassador."

Russia after the revolution, specifically in the summer of 1918, was largely his focus in *Memoirs of a British Agent*, the Bolsheviks his major concern. He repeatedly argued with the Foreign Office that the Bolsheviks had the power and that they would not fall; London disagreed, preferring to support the White Russians. He also opposed an Allied intervention in the internal affairs of the country but could not stop the aborted invasion by British and American troops arriving in Vladivostok in 1918/19 (Memoirs 196–7).

As tensions increased between Russia and England, with fighting in Archangel and then an attempt on Lenin, Lockhart was arrested accused of spying. Imprisonment in Lubyanka and then the Kremlin followed, while the papers suddenly promoted the so-called "Lockhart plot," a supposed plan by Lockhart and the Odessa-born British spy Sidney Reilly (actually born Sigmund Rosenblum) to murder Lenin, immediately labeled as Soviet propaganda by the British.[2] The danger and uncertainty of Lockhart's fate meant a negotiated release: after a month in a Kremlin cell, he was exchanged for Maxim Litvinoff, Soviet representative to Britain, arrested in London as reprisal for holding Lockhart. This was the precursor of prisoner exchanges between the USSR and Britain.[3]

After returning to Britain, Moscow tried and sentenced Lockhart to death *in absentia*, along with Reilly, and banned both from ever returning. At home, he was suspected of having Bolshevik sympathies but, following the account of his perilous time in Russia and eventual release from a Kremlin jail, he became something of a celebrity before accepting the post of commercial secretary of the British legation in Prague. Three years later, he left his post and moved into finance, joining the new Central European Bank. Four years after that, he became a London journalist writing for Lord Beaverbrook's *Evening Standard*. Throughout the thirties, he began to publish autobiography and fiction, while dealing with debts and drinking. During the Second World War, he was director-general of an effort to coordinate British propaganda against the Axis powers, also rejoining the Foreign Service, working in political intelligence. In 1943 he was knighted. At war's end, he continued to write, lecture, and broadcast for the BBC.

But Lockhart's life was always tumultuous. Preceding his Russian adventures was a voyage to Malaysia in 1908 at twenty-one to work on a rubber plantation owned by two uncles. He sentimentally recalled the experience in Chapter Two of *Memoirs of a British Agent* which begins with "no journey will ever give me the same enchantment as that first voyage to Singapore" (Memoirs 7). The "kaleidoscope of ... haunting landscapes" was unforgettable. Remembered as a "pageant," these moments formed his introduction to a world of remarkable color etched with "saffron-tinted sunsets" (Memoirs 7). The romantic descriptive French writer, traveler, and novelist Pierre Loti, who focused on exotic Polynesian and Oriental life, was an early Lockhart favorite, Lockhart adopting Loti's style. In his recall of Singapore and the Malayan Peninsula, he celebrates not only the beauty of an orchard in the Malayan jungle—more beautiful than "the breast of the most beautiful woman"—but how the warmth of the tropical sun became "a necessity to my physical existence and a stimulant to my mind" (Memoirs 8).

Unsurprisingly, he fell in love with a Malaysian woman, Amai. He was twenty-three and convinced her that life with him was preferable to that with a minor Malaysian royal. The affair set a pattern: youthful disregard of convention in pursuit of a woman leading to initial success but then disapproval by senior figures and acquiescence to their demands. In fact, only a severe case of malaria, forcing Lockhart to recover in Japan, prevented further infatuations and life in

Malaya. As his memoir recounts, he continued his recovery with his family in Scotland and then, at his father's urging, applied to the Foreign Office, where after seemingly endless oral and written exams, he was admitted and ranked number one on the test papers. His facility with languages meant he already spoke French and German and had an early interest in Russian.

Overriding the conventional narrative of *Memoirs of a British Agent*, overshadowing the drama of politics, social unrest, shooting, and rioting, is another Lockhart love affair, this time with Moura Budberg. A remarkable woman, she was possibly a spy, who had three notable relationships: the first with Lockhart, the second with Maxim Gorky, and the third with H.G. Wells.[4] Known then as Moura Budberg, she was formally known as Baroness Maria Ignatievna Zakrevskaya Benckendorff, using the name of her first husband. Budberg was the name of her second. Born in the Ukraine, she was the daughter of a wealthy landowner and Russian senator under the Tsars. She was educated in England and married the Estonian Ivan Alexandrovich von Benckendorff in 1911 in London. He called himself a "count." At the time, he was at the Russian Embassy in London. Unofficially, she was a "countess." He took Moura with him when he went to Berlin as the Russian embassy secretary. After the revolution, the family, now with two children, returned to Petrograd but when the count went back to Estonia, peasant revolutionaries murdered him. A few years later, Moura married (a marriage strictly of convenience) the Estonian Baron Nikolai Budberg whose family was in the Tsarist military and bureaucracy. From Nikolai she became "baroness" but divorced him after a year.[5]

When he first met the 26-year-old Moura during his last frantic week in Petrograd before he fled to Moscow in the company of Trotsky, Lockhart wrote that she is "a Russian of the Russians, she had a lofty disregard for all the pettiness of life and a courage which was proof against all cowardice." Strikingly, "where she loved, there was her world, and her philosophy of life had made her mistress of all the consequences" (Memoirs 243, 244).

Initially, Lockhart spent little time with her, distracted by his own importance and the government upheavals, despite finding her a woman of immense attraction. Their romance would come later, although he always seemed to be in her company as when she gave a luncheon party for his Naval Attaché in Petrograd, "almost the last care-free hour we were to spend in Russia" (Memoirs 245). Ironically, the guest of honor was Captain Cromie who would die defending the Embassy in Petrograd when a band of Cheka agents burst in. He managed to kill one intruder but was shot at the top of a staircase. All the remaining British officials were arrested.[6] The day after the party, before the storming of the Embassy, Lockhart and a small group traveled with Trotsky on his train to Moscow. When the train stopped at Liuban, Trotsky, recently appointed Minister for War, invited Lockhart to dine in the station restaurant. He sat on Trotsky's right, his assistant Captain Hicks on his left while huge crowds stared at the ensemble (Memoirs 245). The next day, they arrived in Moscow making the Elite Hotel their headquarters. They found Moscow unexpectedly gay, partly because the Congress of Soviets had ratified, to the horror of the British, peace with Germany, the so-called Brest-Litovsk Treaty (Memoirs 246, 247).

But the arrival of a new German Ambassador in Moscow caused discomfort, if not embarrassment, for Lockhart and his delegation. Britain was still at war with Germany. The Bolsheviks were amused, playing the groups off one another (Memoir 268–9). Since neither the Allies nor the Germans could make up their minds on a policy toward Russia, Bolshevik diplomacy had the advantage. One day, when Lockhart and the Germans were together waiting at the Bolshevik Foreign Office, they turned their backs on each other and stared out the windows or read the papers (269). Hausschild, the German First Secretary, attempted to befriend Lockhart; he failed.

Lockhart had originally gone to Russia in January 1912 engaged: after meeting the beautiful Australian Jean Haselwood Turner two weeks before his departure at a farewell house party, he pursued her and won her over. They would marry when he returned later that year on leave, an act he describes as disingenuous, since he had no money and hardly any prospects. His wife grew up in luxury, while diplomacy paid poorly and life in Russia was strenuous at best (Memoirs 76–7). But soon, Lockhart (age 25) and his new wife (age 21) were in Moscow where he was Vice Consul, his first formal posting. To earn extra income, he wrote occasional pieces under a pseudonym for the British press, so-called "sketches of Russian life." At the time, he considered himself an incomplete blend of Lockhart caution and Macgregor recklessness, possibly recalling his time in Malaya.

In Moscow as a socially adept junior intelligence officer, he made friends among the intelligentsia, politicians, and even businessmen. He also found Russian society informal and unofficial with the English believing the Russians good natured but also "immoral savages" given to improper behavior. It was normal for a society woman to lunch every Sunday with her three husbands, two ex and one current. Such tolerance and understanding were beyond the range of the West: "English wives … held up their hands in pious horror" but such behavior would soon justify Lockhart's own subsequent love affair with a married Russian, while he himself remained attached to his Australia wife

(Memoirs 67). However, the appointment of a proper Consul General, Charles Clive Bayley, unable to speak French, German, or Russian, brought a new formality to the consular office, although Lockhart admired and absorbed Bayley's administrative know-how. But at the outbreak of the First World War, Lockhart experienced a personal tragedy: a daughter was stillborn, although his wife survived. He was devastated.

The winter of 1914–15 was difficult. His wife's slow recovery led to shattered nerves and the necessity of a Russian sanatorium. It did not help, and he found the expense trying, while his time was entirely absorbed by the war and the Consul General's constant reliance on him for political intelligence (Memoirs 101–2). But a visit by the writer Hugh Walpole, displaying an enthusiasm for all things Russian, was uplifting. After leaving Lockhart and his wife, Walpole went to the front as a Red Cross orderly. "Russia got the best out of him," Lockhart remarks, noting that Walpole's actions at the front produced two novels, *The Dark Forest* and, from his experience in Petrograd, *The Secret City* (Memoirs 102–3). Through Walpole, Lockhart met Gorky and during this time, January 1915, he also finished reading *War and Peace* in Russian. But Moscow continued to live only "on stories and rumors" becoming a "cesspool of rumors of pro-German intrigues in high places" (Memoirs 104).

By the spring of 1915, Lockhart was in charge of the Consulate; Bayley, Consul-General, had to return to England for an operation. He would be gone two-and-a-half months, followed by a new post in New York; to his surprise, Lockhart would become the Acting Consul General on the recommendation of the British Ambassador to Russia, Sir George Buchanan (Memoirs 125). At the time, Russia and Moscow were restless with defeat and stalemate characterizing their supposed advance against Germany. The Russian population resented what they thought was the alleged pro-German policy of the government. Industrial unrest and political anger characterized reports Lockhart supplied to the British Ambassador in Petrograd.

By June 10, three days of anti-German riots broke out in Moscow. The leading piano store in Moscow, with Bechsteins and Blüthners, was destroyed, the instruments burning in a giant bonfire. By the fall, Warsaw had capitulated to the Germans and the outlook was bleak. The Tsar's dissolution of the Duma brought initial support but his refusal to accept any reforms demanded by the people did not help. Yet diplomatic and social life continued with Lockhart and his wife attending as many as six events a week and hosting their own reception once a week where, at one point, Sasha Kropotkin (instrumental in Maugham's

Russian adventures) argued with a Countess over the lack of a martial spirit in Petrograd (Memoirs 130).

Despite the occasional official visit of British naval officers and diplomats, the tone of Moscow life remained pessimistic, but it was a depression distinct from Petrograd in that it was free from "malevolent pacifism." By contrast, Moscow was "prepared to fight to the end" (Memoirs 147). The spring of 1916 put additional strain on Lockhart, and he and his wife took a short vacation. On his return, he found that a new fatalism overtook the Russians. And the English received only damning praise: the diplomat Sergey Sazonoff, at one time the Russian Minister of Foreign Affairs, declared that "the whole art of diplomacy is to mask one's intentions. And that is where the English excel" (Memoirs 157). Lockhart then comments on the revolution, partly justifying the removal of the Tsar and ascent of the Bolsheviks by explaining that the revolution took place because "the patience of the Russian people broke down under a system of unparalleled inefficiency and corruption" (Memoirs 171).

But what Lockhart does *not* report is a breakdown in his personal life: he had a mistress. His private life was disintegrating in tandem with that of the public (Memoirs 191–2). In his *Memoirs*, Lockhart details his Moscow affair, ironically referring to it as a "minor tragedy." Some months before, he had begun an "attachment to a Russian Jewess—whom I met casually at the theater. I had made myself talked about"—never a good thing for a diplomat (Memoirs 191). She was subsequently identified as "Madame Vermelle" and likely French.[7] The Ambassador, Sir George Buchanan, hearing of the adventure from his wife in England, summoned Lockhart to the Embassy in Petrograd. They talked, and he shared with Lockhart his own early flirtation, mixing British obedience and Russian reality stating that "real happiness consisted in resisting temptations which one was bound to regret later." Don't ruin your career by carrying on with a "passing infatuation due to war strain," he muttered. The conventions of government service had to be observed (Memoirs 191). Duty and war must take precedent; put your country before self-indulgence. Lockhart returned to Moscow and made "the grand renunciation" but it lasted only three weeks. The Ambassador heard more and ordered him to return to England at once for "rest" (Memoirs 191).

There was no scandal. Lockhart left Russia explaining that overwork exhausted him and was able to depart without any publicity. His Moscow friends were sympathetic: "to such of the public as thought about me I was a martyr to duty" (Memoirs 192). But he feared the recall and that he may never return. He left more as a culprit than martyr when he departed Moscow in early September 1917, arriving in London six weeks before the Bolshevik Revolution, crossing paths in Bergen with his replacement, Sir Oliver Wardrop, an elderly diplomat. "The Foreign Office were taking no more chances with youth," he writes (Memoirs 195.). Lockhart's wife accompanied him on his return.

In London, the press wanted his opinion of the Kerensky-Korniloff clash. He dashed off a newspaper article which appeared anonymously claiming General Korniloff, with his White Army, would fail, contrary to London's view. With his 25 guinea payment, he went to Scotland to fish and refresh, returning to London two weeks after the Bolshevik Revolution. But among politicians and diplomats, he declared that Lenin would last; the country would not revert to Tsarism and Russia would be out of the war (Memoirs 197). Few listened and even fewer believed that England should take the Russian peace proposals for Germany seriously and aim at achieving an anti-German peace in Russia. Despite his controversial views, by December 21, 1917, after various high-level meetings, including with the War Cabinet, Lloyd George personally appointed Lockhart as a special commissioner to establish unofficial contact with the Bolsheviks but to do so with tact and care. He was to return (Memoirs 199–200).

Back in Moscow (but without his wife), a new round of diplomacy would follow but hampered by Lockhart not having an official appointment as a representative of the British government. Relations with the Bolsheviks had to be unofficial. This made Lockhart not a spy but an unofficial emissary of Britain. But before leaving for Russia, secret arrangements were hammered out in a Lyons tea shop in the Strand: Maxim Litvinoff (present), then living in exile in London with his English wife, would become the unofficial Soviet Ambassador to London, while Lockhart (also present) would have an analogous position in Russia. Both were given co-equal diplomatic privileges including the use of diplomatic codes and the right to use diplomatic couriers (Memoirs 201–2).

Lockhart's first task was to acquire introductions to Lenin and Trotsky. Litvinoff immediately wrote a letter to Trotsky while at the tea shop praising Lockhart as trustworthy and valuable to the Bolshevik cause (Memoirs 201; McDonald 44). A third party, Theodore Rothstein, a Russian journalist also present and informally negotiating for the Russians, assisted in working out further arrangements with Litvinoff. Lockhart called the entire meeting "a kind of intellectual cricket" (Memoirs 202). But Sir George Buchanan, the Ambassador, was unexpectedly recalled to London in January 1918 with no one to replace him. On his arrival in Russia, Lockhart was suddenly the top British diplomat in the country.

But a new challenge emerged: Lockhart's romance with Moura Budberg, the possible double agent. They became attached, remaining together "until we were parted by the armed force of the Bolsheviks" (Memoirs 269). They had written regularly during his absence from Russia, and she soon joined Lockhart's delegation in Moscow staying with him at his apartment. On first seeing her, his passion was renewed. But politics quickly intervened: implicated in the so-called "Lenin Plot" (or "Lockhart Plot") and imprisoned, Lockhart suggests in his *Memoirs* that he should have resigned and left Russia earlier but he did not: he would not leave Moura (Memoirs 288). He also admits that he lacked the moral courage to resign and oppose his government's policies, while others believed that he was pro-Bolshevik, even if he was prepared to assist the Allies in their possible invasion.

Lockhart's special knowledge of the Russian situation was both a plus and a minus in terms of his reputation (Memoirs 289). He understood that the Bolsheviks had power, organization, and capabilities. He knew that loyal Russians, even provided with ammunition and supplies, would never overthrow the Bolsheviks. But he was caught in the middle. Despite supporting intervention on behalf of the White Russians, the interventionists felt he was still pro-Bolshevik, while the Bolsheviks believed he was the incarnation of a counter-revolutionary (Memoirs 289). He was equally unpopular in London for upholding beliefs few supported.

In the midst of the political and military maneuvering, Moura left Moscow to visit her home in Estonia but communication and travel were limited. He was sure he would not see her before he had to leave the country because the unstable Russian situation was becoming dangerous. But she suddenly called him from Petrograd after an arduous six-day return trip: she was coming to Moscow. But assassinations and threats disrupted Lockhart's movements and on August 4 Moscow learned of the Allied invasion at Archangel and Vladivostok. Confusion and fear were everywhere and his consulate raided (Memoirs 309).

Lockhart provides an explicit account of the political situation and how the Germans, as well as the Americans, quickly deserted the Bolsheviks. But he was hopeful that the invading allies, later to be joined by the Americans and Canadians, would succeed with their coup, led by Tsarist Captain Georgi Chaplin working with General Poole, which started on August 2, 1918. He did not believe, however, that he, or the Allies, could persuade Russia to renew its war with Germany. However, by August 10, 1918, Russia achieved a naval victory at Archangel and resisted the invading forces. The anti-Bolshevik movement collapsed, while the majority of Russians remained apathetic but the misadventure galvanized the Bolsheviks who, according to Lockhart, gained "a cheap victory" (Memoirs 311).

## ii

The backdrop to all of these maneuverings was love, although the reasons for Moura's attachment to Lockhart were complex. While emotions played a part, there were other causes promoted by rumors that she may have been spying in the Ukraine for the Bolsheviks during her separation from Lockhart, although her journey to Yendel in Estonia was to see her children. But his attachment to her made her an ideal informant for the Cheka, the Bolshevik security force tasked to eliminate counter-revolutionaries. Her romance may have been a cover for spying on Lockhart and his mission. Her will to survive had likely trumped her love for Lockhart providing her, through the British legation, an elevated status and Cheka protection. Originally from a semi-aristocratic class, she could have easily become a Bolshevik target without Cheka intervention (McDonald 118). The new government termed her class "former people," those who lost their lands and assets. And new regulations meant that even owners of safe deposit boxes, for example, were compelled to turn over their contents to the state (McDonald 119).

Moura returned to Petrograd to be with her ill and elderly mother. But conditions worsened, economically and domestically. One senior Cheka officer outlined a new practice: when pursuing counter-revolutionaries, don't look for evidence that they acted against Soviet state but determine their class, often by examining their hands. Soft and uncalloused, they were bourgeoise; rough and cut, they were the proletariat. Arrest the former, protect the latter (McDonald 120). But in some fashion, Moura avoided eviction, arrest, or interrogation, despite her known closeness to the British missions in Petrograd and Moscow which the Cheka believed to be centers of subversive activity.

Soon, Lockhart had to leave his quarters at the Elite Hotel; it was being requisitioned by the Council of Russian Trades Unions. Diplomatic activities moved to an office building. But domestically, he was able to return to his old apartment on the fifth floor at 19 Khlebnyy pereulok. Lockhart and Moura moved in on August 3; his aide Hicks moved in with them but that weekend details of a coup attempt led by a Tsarist Captain Georgi Chaplin with Allied support (French and British troops) on August 2 at Archangel reached them. When the news reached Moscow, it galvanized Bolshevik support and put the British diplomats in jeopardy.

At the same time, Lockhart was discussing an attempt to bring down the Bolshevik's from within, considering a possible rebellion among restless and unhappy Latvian regiments working at the Kremlin (McDonald 121). But did Captain Cromie in Petrograd actually send these emissaries and had he written the letter that accompanied two visitors supposedly from Latvia? Moura was one of two to vouch for their authenticity but could she be trusted as espionage now mixed with diplomacy and propaganda? Could Lockhart be sure of anything during these uncertain times? And what was the role of the unreliable double agent Sidney Reilly? Russian-born, he worked for both Scotland Yard and the British secret service, able to infiltrate various White Russian organizations. Reilly suggested the Latvians arrest Lenin and Trotsky, something Lockhart rejected. During all these proposed acts, Lockhart's apartment and consulate was under Cheka surveillance. Ironically, it was later shown that both Latvian envoys were Cheka agents trying to dupe Lockhart (McDonald 129).

Cheka armed guards soon surrounded the Consulate, the leader bursting in on a meeting between Wardrop, Lockhart, and Hicks. All were to be arrested but Lockhart produced a pass signed by Trotsky for himself and Hicks. Wardrop announced that Chicherin, a senior Cheka official, had promised that consuls would not be subject to arrest. The three were then held under guard but the staff arrested. A similar situation occurred at their mission headquarters at Bolshaya Lubyanka street. There were also raids and arrests at the French Consulate; soon, similar diplomatic violations and arrests were reported in Petrograd. A new "oppressive tension" descended on the city. The Bolsheviks were frightened by events in the north, while new efforts of a Latvian mutiny resurfaced with Lockhart's supposed involvement (McDonald 125, 127). The times were treacherous.

Escape to Finland seemed Lockhart's only workable plan but the attempted assassination of Lenin in Moscow by Dora Kaplan on August 30, 1918, as he left the Mikhelson armament's factory, meant Lockhart's arrest along with Hicks and Moura by Cheka agents at 3:30 a.m. Implicitly, Lockhart appeared to be involved.[8] He was taken to the Lubyanka No. 11, headquarters of the Moscow Cheka (Memories 317 ff). Interrogated over the Lenin shooting and a pass he had given to the deceptive Latvian officers to identify them to General Poole, commander of Allied forces in Archangel, Lockhart sought the privilege of diplomatic immunity; it was discarded (McDonald 139). And then a woman (Maria Fride) appeared at Lockhart's now Cheka-occupied apartment; arrested, she carried sensitive documents outlining the movement of Red Army regiments on the front lines, material obtained by the woman's brother who was in the intelligence section of the Commissariat for Military Affairs. He was arrested; the Cheka now had a full picture of the Allies' spy network, implicating Lockhart.

But could there be a link between Dora Kaplan, who shot Lenin, and Lockhart? Yakov Peters, deputy head of the Cheka, decided to place Kaplan in Lockhart's cell. They had no exchange; he did not know her but guessed that Kaplan was sent to implicate him. She was taken out and Lockhart and his aide Hicks unexpectedly freed through the intervention of Commissar G.V. Chicherin. But on their return to their apartment, they learned that Moura had now been taken off by the Cheka. Peters, in charge, believed Moura, who accompanied Lockhart to multiple meetings as his "interpreter" (although he spoke fluent Russian), shared information with him and that she had collaborated with several important Allied spies. Additionally, Peters thought she was also a German agent during the war, backed up by information from the French *Sûreté* (Carr 239–40). She was unquestionably a double agent, spying for the Soviets *and* the Germans; she had to be detained. On top of that, she was pregnant but miscarried during Lockhart's later arrest and Kremlin imprisonment (McDonald 128, 143–4, 153).

After his first detention and then release and within days of Moura's original arrest, Lockhart visited an official at the Foreign Office demanding her release. On that Tuesday, September 3, 1918, the press gave an overblown and misleading account of the so-called "Lockhart Plot," plus the attempt to murder both Lenin and Trotsky, set up a military dictatorship in Moscow, and reduce the populations of Moscow and Petrograd by starvation after blowing up railway bridges (Memoirs 321–2). The source of this information was supposedly the Latvian emissaries who had visited Lockhart seeking funds for the false insurrection plot. The paper even claimed Lockhart was arrested at a conspirators' meeting, while Cromie's death in Petrograd was described as self-defense by Bolshevik agents returning his fire. "Anglo-French Bandits" was the headline (Memoirs 322). It was a dangerous period; the Bolsheviks shot seven hundred political opponents in reprisal for the threat of a government overthrow as the so-called Red Terror began (Memoirs 89).

Undeterred by excuses at the Foreign Office in pursuit of Moura's freedom, Lockhart went directly to Lubyanka (a former insurance company's headquarters) and asked to see Peters (who had an English wife), telling him the conspiracy story was fake and he knew it. Moura was innocent; free her. Peters said he would consider the request. He then told Lockhart that he had a warrant for *his* arrest, possibly because he was the paymaster for Sidney Reilly who likely had a role in the Lenin plot. Lockhart was immediately rearrested on September 4, 1918, and imprisoned for the next month.

His memoir gives details, from the size of his examination room to the furniture in his cell. The first five days he hardly slept because the lights were never turned off. Peters regularly interrogated him at midnight, although at one point he brought him two books: H.G. Well's *Mr. Britling Sees It Through* and Lenin's *State and Revolution*. Lockhart also had copies of *Izvestia* with accounts of workmen's committees demanding his trial and execution. And he knew that if the injured Lenin died, he would be executed. But Lenin recovered and Lockhart was transferred to a prison apartment in the Kremlin, normally home to the most unfortunate prisoners. He was sent there on September 8 only to find he had a roommate: one of the Latvians who was supposedly his accomplice (Memoirs 327, 329). They exchanged no words as hope for Lockhart's release dwindled: he was accused of espionage, sabotage, and implicitly the proposed murder of both Lenin and Trotsky.

He soon learned that Britain had arrested Litvinoff as reprisal for the death of Captain Cromie and Lockhart's detention. But Georgy Chicherin, Commissar for Foreign Affairs, suggested that an exchange was possible if it included other arrested Russians in France and England. Lockhart continued to plead for Moura's release. Peters then visited to say Moura was free (although how this happened is unclear) but he would likely be sent to the Revolutionary Tribunal for trial. If he cooperated, he could have better food, a visit from Moura, and new clothes. That afternoon he had the items and a long letter from her. Soon, his daily routine included exercise for two hours a day, decent meals, and daily reading, mostly history, from Carlyle's *French Revolution* and Thucydides, to a history of the Seven Years' War, Macaulay's *Life and Letters*, and Kipling's *Captains Courageous* (Memoirs 332). He was permitted to walk about the Kremlin walls, a place rarely seen by outsiders, noting that his previous interviews with Lenin, Trotsky, Chicherin, and other Commissars always took place outside the Kremlin. But its reputation remained: few prisoners who entered ever left alive.

Imprisoned, daily supplies from Moura still arrived, including a fountain pen and several notebooks. But even though a possible amnesty might occur if England made peace with Russia, nothing happened other than meeting other prisoners such as Lieutenant Sablin, a former Soviet Commander who was caught for his part in a *coup d'etat* in July (Memoir 301). Russia still believed England, with its aborted invasion in Archangel, was, nevertheless, plotting a war against the revolution, with Lockhart the principal agent. And then, on September 22, Moura, escorted by Peters, arrived in his cell. It was Peters' thirty-second birthday and he liked to give gifts. This was his to Lockhart (Memoirs 336). Moura used the occasion to clandestinely slip a note to Lockhart in his copy of Carlyle's *French Revolution*. It read: "Say nothing—all will be well" (Memoirs 337). The next day Peters returned with the Swedish Consul-General to confirm that Lockhart was healthy. But stories in the press condemning him continued. He was again denounced as the "arch-criminal of diplomacy" who deserved his solitary confinement despite the fact that he opposed intervention from the beginning, although the public read the opposite (Memoirs 338).

When Peters told him he would be freed in three days, the Cheka deputy head quietly asked if Lockhart would take a packet to his wife in London (Memoirs 339). He agreed, appreciating what Peters did in freeing Moura, although without a sense of what she needed to do to gain his privileges. She never alluded to it. Alone at last with Moura after Peters left his cell/apartment, Lockhart learned she had been in the women's prison, the Butirky, well provisioned through the efforts of Wardwell, the head of the American Red Cross in Russia.

But Peters' post-Revolutionary future was dark; he later divorced his English wife and remarried, but lost the trust of Stalin who in 1937 accused him of being a Latvian nationalist, not a Bolshevik internationalist. By then, Stalin had read Lockhart's memoir and underlined passages, including where Peters said signing death warrants caused him physical pain. Arrested and interrogated, Peters eventually confessed to all charges, even that he had been an English agent. He was either then shot by the NKVD or killed by the Germans in 1942 when they overran his prison camp.[9]

Fear that Lockhart himself would be shot remained until Lenin recovered and supposedly said "Stop the Terror." Then a scheme to exchange Lockhart and others for Litvinoff and additional Bolsheviks in England was proposed. But the British were hesitant, not trusting the Bolsheviks. They insisted Lockhart had to be released first. But Lockhart knew the Bolsheviks cared more about their image and prestige than Litvinoff and should be taken at their word. Cabinet advisors persuaded Balfour to let Litvinoff leave London at the same time Lockhart left Moscow. Balfour agreed despite opposition from his cabinet counsellors as the Swedes and Norwegians took formal charge of the negotiations (Memoirs 341). Moura was with Lockhart at the Kremlin both days before he was released, packing his belongings, on October 1, 1918.

Ironically, while preparing to be set free, Lockhart didn't want to leave. Peters had, in fact, suggested he stay along with Moura: "I gave it more consideration than the English reader may imagine," he writes (Memoirs 343). But he knew he could never become a Bolshevik in such a corrupt government and had official obligations to England. He agonized over leaving Moura, knowing also that it would be almost impossible for her to come to England with him. And there was a further complication: he was still married to Jean and Moura had yet to divorce her husband, Djon Benckendorff, although a year later he would be killed on his estate in Estonia.

Finally released through a falsified and misleading report prepared by Peters on Lockhart's espionage activities (it placed all blame on Colonel Fride, whose sister arrived at Lockhart's apartment with secret documents), Lockhart departed by train from Moscow after two nights at his ransacked apartment. Moura saw him off, talking with him about everything but themselves (Memoirs 345). But delays were constant and Litvinoff and fifty-four Russian prisoners had not yet arrived at Bergen. Lockhart spent three days waiting at the Finnish border. But before he left, one of his final acts was to provide an illegal British passport for Evgenia Shelyepina, Trotsky's secretary. She was to marry Arthur Ransome which she did in England in 1924.

But what of Moura, left behind? In the memoir, Lockhart blandly says she was wonderful and, despite being ill, made no complaints: "she accepted the parting with Russian fatalism" (Memoirs 343). This core statement of Russian love does not reflect her adventurous and duplicitous nature in pursuit of the expedient and self-protective. Nor does it suggest his likely disappointment that even when she had a chance to see him in England—at a later date, when she was in Finland—she chose, instead, to return to Russia, after a visit to Estonia to initiate a divorce from her second husband. She had not heard from Lockhart for some time believing he had lost interest in her, recalling Maurice Magre's "Avilir," a favorite poem of Lockhart's which summarizes elements of Russian love: "I have a profound urge to demean that which I love …. / I know by the sight of her tears that her suffering is great / And despite all that, I affect to doubt. / With careful cruelty I seek out / Her errors, her faults, her weakness / And in so doing, crumple and tear her affection" (McDonald 176). Love breeds pain, not joy; I prove my love by suffering.

Private and public circumstances limited the love of Lockhart and Moura, although Lockhart remained devoted, some suggesting that he maintained his involvement because she represented the Old Russia Lockhart long admired. But could she be trusted? When she first appeared with Peters in Lockhart's Kremlin cell, they walked in holding hands (Carr 259). What did it mean? Lockhart thought *he* might have gotten *her* released but some believe it is was the reverse: her broadly distributed sexual favors may have influenced Peters (Carr 258–9). A tip that the Soviets had copies of the British secret codes caused further suspicion and she might have even had something to do with the death of her husband, Djon Benckendorff, in Estonia (Carr 259; McDonald 180). The

Bolsheviks disliked nobility, so Moura might have been co-opted by the Soviets to spy to ensure her own safety.

Moura always claimed she was not a double agent, although new details surfaced after the Russian Civil War tying her to Stalin and as a lover of Genrikh Yagoda, deputy chairman of OGPU, the successor to the Cheka (Carr 259). In that position, she enjoyed certain privileges to enter and leave the USSR. She befriended Stalin in the 1930s, although by then she was also involved with Gorky and H.G. Wells. In Paris in the 1930s, she also briefly resumed her affair with Lockhart, meeting in semi-hidden Russian cafes. But as a result of her involvement with Wells and a life in London, she decided to become a British citizen. She died at eighty-two in Italy in 1974 having written the filmscripts for *Three Sisters* directed by Laurence Olivier and *The Sea Gull* directed by Sidney Lumet. She also translated Gorky's *The Life of a Useless Man* (1908) in 1971.

In an argument, Moura once criticized Lockhart as "a little clever, but not clever enough; a little strong, but not strong enough; a little weak, but not weak enough" (Memoirs 347; cf. Diaries I 59). She may have been right. Shortcomings and weaknesses, not virtues, characterize his behavior. He was almost paralyzed by his indecisions, becoming a passive Russian Romantic hero duplicating a series of hesitant Russian lovers—Onegin or Oblomov quickly come to mind, or the heroes of Turgenev where separation and loss dominate romance.

Lockhart did not dispute his submissive label, although he did offer protection and a possible English escape for Moura should she choose. But he left her not because of an individual decision but a sense of duty to the Foreign Office and Britain. In a melancholic final sentence to his memoirs, he writes that while his physical body was going forward, permitted at last to enter Finland, his "thoughts were back in Moscow and in the country which I was leaving, probably forever" (Memoirs 348). One recalls Paul Klee's painting *Angelus Novus*, showing an angel rushing away from some force with his face turned toward the past, while his body travels forward. A storm from Paradise "propels him into the future to which his back is turned while the pile of debris before him grows skyward."[10]

Lockhart ended his affair with Moura by necessity, although it later briefly rekindled. Their meeting records another moment in the trajectory of Russian love, although given her behavior, it's uncertain if she was using the relationship to further her own social and political advantage or genuinely felt love for Lockhart. In the film version of their story, she needed to be rescued but in Lockhart's account, he seems to be ensnared by her allure, echoing Turgenev whose hero Bazarov in *Fathers and Sons* remarks to his young friend Arkady that "you can never get beyond refined submission or refined indignation, and that's no good."[11] At the end of Lockhart's autobiography, at dawn on May 25, 1918, after a birthday celebration, he and Moura romantically drive out to the iconic Sparrow Hills "to watch the sun rise over the Kremlin. It came up like an angry ball of fire heralding destruction"—but they watch and do not act (Memoirs 280). The Hills would become the setting of Chapter 31 of Mikhail Bulgakov's important *The Master and Margarita*, the novel confirming Lockhart's belief that "manuscripts don't burn."[12]

Seven years later, Lockhart renewed contact with Moura, writing about her as he finishes Benjamin Constant's novel *Adolphe* (1816) and comments on the hero as a man unable to break with a woman, partly out of pity and partly out of vanity. "The shoe fits myself," he writes. The moral, he explains, is that "it is more cruel to the woman one pities not to break and to go on torturing her than to break once and for all." But a letter from Moura reignites his feelings: "she is a big-minded and a big-hearted woman," he claims (Diaries I 145). He sees her when she visits London in January 1932 and then again in October. The following year, she returns while he is under increased stress because of his wife's illness (he would not divorce her for adultery until 1938) and his need to work sixteen hours a day in Fleet Street and write books to earn a living (Diaries I 259).

Moura appears again in 1934, just before he departs for an American lecture tour. In 1935, he includes her in a luncheon for Somerset Maugham and again in 1937, both times in the company of H.G. Wells (Diaries I 320, 379). In a sense, he could not, and did not, want to rid himself of her, although in his 1934 work *Retreat from Glory*, as he is about to take a new post in Prague, he writes that although

> I had some knocks [in Russia] … I was still resilient as a tennis-ball …. Russia was behind me, and I was learning to store it away in a back recess of my mind.[13]

This is not entirely correct.

Earlier in his account, he writes that Moura "had been everything to me," proud of the way they had flouted all conventions "sharing our dangers and our pleasures" (Retreat 5). Prone to dramatic statements, Lockhart writes that "had this cataclysm of our arrest not intervened, I think I would have stayed in Russia for ever" (Retreat 5). Essentially, Lockhart could not give up Moura even as his criticisms mounted, even during her involvement with Gorky and then H.G. Wells. Despite his "unofficial romance," recorded in the archives of the Foreign Office which would harm his advancement, he was unable to renounce her (Retreat 6). This meant unpleasant explanations to wider circles including his wife, parents, and grandmother, who was his principal financial supporter. With understatement, Lockhart writes that "I could expect little joy from my homecoming," recalling that once in Moscow, a Foreign Office messenger violently denounced him as a Bolshevik (Retreat 6, 7)!

Cut off for months from communicating with Moura after his deportation, they had at first regularly corresponded through the offices of various foreign governments with embassies still in Russia. For weeks, he adds, her letters "were the mainstay of my existence" (Retreat 43). But as Russia became shut off from the world, communication became more difficult. Her letters ceased when the last foreign mission was withdrawn. "Even her fate was unknown to me. And as I tried to put Russia out of my mind, so, too, I tried to forget Moura" (Retreat 43). But "she had left a wound in my heart …," although this was more lip-service than accurate. He wanted to live in the present and Prague, his next appointment, "was a new world to conquer" (Retreat 43).

But even in Prague, Moura haunts him, ironically through his attempt to produce an evening of Russian ballet and gipsy music at the legation with a distinguished audience. It was a hit and soon other groups of Russian dancers sought him out for performances. But he melodramatically writes that when he renewed sentimental memories of his Russian past, "these plaintive minor melodies were at once a mirror of my own wrecked ambitions and a link with Moura" (Retreat 155). Images of the Kremlin projected by the moon on the Moscow river competed with memories of the quiet sleigh traffic. A longing to return to "that Russia which an Englishman either hates or can never forget" overtook him (Retreat 156).[14]

In 1923, in a state of semi-depression, Lockhart looked back and noted that his official career in Russia "had been meteoric and hectic. My romance with Moura had been flung in the face of the world," but "it had been excused and glossed over on the score of youth and of the revolutionary atmosphere of Russia" (Retreat 222). But after four years in Prague and in debt, he withdrew to London and sought new advances; he turned to banking. And then, unexpectedly, on July 29, 1924, he received a call from Vienna: it was Moura, who had escaped from Russia. It had been four years since they last communicated. He then recounts their affair as if it was about to happen (Retreat 233–4). Within days he meets her in Vienna, admitting that she looked older but she was still herself and that "her mind, her genius, her control were wonderful" (Retreat 235). His former assistant, Will Hicks, now head of the Cunard office in Vienna, arranged their reunion.

Lockhart provides a summary of Moura's life since they separated: she had been in prison, attempted to escape, been released, and tried to flee to Finland.

She then met Gorky who had given her literary work and made her his secretary and literary agent. She obtained a foreign passport and went back to Estonia where her former home stood, although the land had been confiscated. She remained, educating her two children, earning money by translating Russian books into English, including most of Gorky's writing (Retreat 236). To Lockhart, it was a tale of "fortitude in adversity" (Retreat 236). He felt his own narrative over the past six years was weak by comparison and turning thirty-seven an unwelcomed change. Moura returned with him to Prague from Vienna, speaking Russian the entire journey, a journey of remembrances. They parted on their arrival.

The impact of their meeting was to romantically recall their dramatic time in Moscow. He hoped she would encourage him to take up their life together again, although he was still filled with self-doubt about his ability to restart their affair, Russian love struggling to reassert itself through action (Retreat 240, 237). But she had announced that it would be a mistake. Hicks, his Russian wife, Moura, and Lockhart—all four suffered from the Revolution and "looked on the state of Europe with profound pessimism" (Retreat 238).

It is not until early 1937 that the topic of divorce appears. That February, Lockhart's wife, Jean, asked for a divorce to marry Loudon McLean (Diaries I 365). What disturbed Lockhart the most was the way she had been broadcasting the breakup to friends and the bills she left unpaid, plus the items she had taken from their home (Diaries I 368). In a state of despair, he went to Harrod's to order £35 of furniture and household items to replace what she secured. The divorce would become final in early 1938.

In the midst of these troubles, Lockhart lunches with Moura again who continues to pass on information such as the arrival of a worried Alexei Tolstoy, in London for a Congress of Friendship with the USSR but convinced he's being followed by a Cheka agent (Diaries I 369). She continued her role as a go-between during the Second World War, Lockhart repeatedly seeing her as she provided information on politicians and developments in Europe plus the occasional scandal (see Diaries II 121, 149 206). But by 1944, he writes that she's becoming expensive to feed "or, rather, to water. Today, she drank only beer with luncheon but she had an aperitif of three double gins at eight shillings apiece and with her coffee a double brandy at twelve shillings" (Diaries II, 348)!

In *The Two Revolutions: An Eye-witness Study of Russia 1917* (1967), Lockhart again reviews the Revolution, now divided into three sections: "The Historical Background," "The War and the March Revolution," and "The Triumph of Bolshevism." In a series of concise chapters, he offers candid remarks on the Revolution from the end of the Tsar to the rise of Lenin offering insight and commentary: "If the country was unanimous in its desire to be rid of Tsarism, it was hopelessly divided in its intentions for the future."[15] He also added color, noting that under the Provisional Government, "every street corner and square in Petrograd and Moscow was like a speaker's stand in Hyde Park;" "then was born the passion of the Russian Communist for interminable speeches" (79). Absent, however, are any comments or references to Moura or his romance.

The Lockhart/Moura story shows Russian love from different, often conflicting angles, not only from contrasting political points of view but from the perspectives of control, espionage, trust, and betrayal. It extends the unrequited love theme seen throughout the literature into the world of political intelligence against the backdrop of revolution, death, and international conflict. In this romance, contingency is all, Moura telling Lockhart that events and actions are always of the moment. Act or they are gone (Retreat 239).

In this narrative of Russian love, there is an almost non-stop social and political circumnavigation of emotion from the West to the East and the reverse; the journey never ceases. But even as Lockhart leaves Russia and Moura moves on, love remains. Further encounters in Vienna, Prague, or London confirm their unfulfilled longings circumscribed by his sustained marriage (at least until 1938) and her sudden widowhood. For Lockhart, Nezhdanov's comment in Turgenev's *Virgin Soil* seems apt: "I could not simplify myself."[16]

## Notes

1. R. H. Bruce Lockhart, *Memoirs of a British Agent* (London: Macmillan, 1934), 199–201. Hereafter Memoirs. For general information on his life, see "Sir Robert Bruce Lockhart, Ex-Diplomat, Is Dead," *New York Times,* February 28, 1970. https://www.nytimes.com/1970/02/28/archives/sir-robert-bruce-lockhart-exdiplomat-is-dead-moscow-envoy.html.
2. For a detailed account of the plot and backdoor negotiations, see Barnes Carr, *The Lenin Plot: The Unknown Story of America's War Against Russia* (New York: Pegasus Books, 2020), 125–33, 155–6, 228–30 and *passim*. Hereafter Carr. For a life of Reilly, see Benny Morris, *Sidney Reilly, Master Spy* (New Haven: Yale University Press, 2022).
3. The Bolsheviks appointed Litvinov Soviet Ambassador to London but if Lockhart was to be granted official diplomatic privileges without official recognition by the British Government, England would make the same concession to Litvinoff (Memoirs 201). He would later become Soviet Foreign Minister.

4   St. Petersburg became Petrograd in 1914. The former name was considered to be too German. It became Leningrad after Lenin's death in 1924. It reverted to St. Petersburg after a referendum in 1991. In his memoir, Lockhart persists in using St. Petersburg, even though the city's name had changed.

Following the revolution and October coup, Moura was removed from her Petrograd apartment by a Bolshevik housing committee. She moved in, with her title and a few clothes, with a former family cook and began to renew her acquaintance with Lockhart. She also maintained certain habits such as using a British accent when speaking Russian and translating idioms literally into Russian from English or French. She would soon move in with Lockhart and his assistant, Captain William Hicks, in Moscow and be in his apartment the night both were arrested by Pavel Malkov, a Chekist and Kremlin Commandant, and two of his aides.

Her association with Gorky began in the 1930s as his secretary, became a romance and lasted until she became involved with H.G. Wells and followed him to England. In the summer of 1935 in England, she refused to transfer Gorky's archive to Moscow but a visitor from the Soviet Union pressured her by showing a letter supposedly from Gorky. He wanted to see her before he died but she must bring the archive which he had actually wanted to be sent to Pushkin House in Leningrad as early as 1926, although it should now go to Moscow. Stalin would provide a special train car for her at the border. She consulted Lockhart who told her to cooperate, otherwise the papers would be taken by force (Berberova 240).

For more details, see Nina Berberova, *Moura, The Dangerous Life of the Baroness Budberg*, tr. Marian Schwartz and Richard D. Sylvester (New York: New York Review Books, 2005), 64–5 and *passim*. Hereafter Berberova. The actress Kay Francis played Moura in the 1934 film based on Lockhart's book, *British Agent* directed by Michael Curtiz who would go on to direct *Casablanca* in 1942 and *Mission to Moscow* in 1943. Ironically, in the late 1930s, and in London with H.G. Wells, Moura would become the personal assistant of the film producer Alexander Korda and even wrote several film scripts.

5   Carr 238–9; Lockhart, *The Diaries of Sir Robert Bruce Lockhart, Vol.1 1915–1938*, ed. Kenneth Young (London: Macmillan, 1973), 40, ftnt. 2. Hereafter Diaries I.

6   Lockhart, Memoirs 321; Deborah McDonald and Jeremy Dronfield, *A Very Dangerous Woman: The Lives, Loves and Lies of Russia's Most Seductive Spy* (London: Oneworld, 2015), 134–5. Hereafter McDonald.

7   See Lockhart, *The Diaries*, 30; Carr 126.

Carr cites further details suggesting that Lockhart's mistress might be Alisa Vermelle, wife of Dr. Samuil Vermelle, a Communist Party member and in charge of a center for restorative medicine. Lockhart may have also been asked to leave because she might have had ties to the Bolsheviks, making Moura a threat to British security because of her affair with the youthful Lockhart (Carr 127).

8   See Semion Lyandres, "The 1918 Attempt on the Life of Lenin: A New Look at the Evidence," *Slavic Review* 48.3 (1989): 432–48. The morning of the attempt on Lenin, August 30, 1918, Moisei Uritsky, head of the Petrograd Cheka, was killed on his way to his office. The event intensified efforts to discover and destroy all counter-revolutionaries.

9   Jonathan Schneer, *The Lockhart Plot, Love, Betrayal, Assassination and Counter-Revolution in Lenin's Russia* (Oxford: Oxford University Press, 2020), 261. Hereafter Schneer.

10  Walter Benjamin, "Theses on the Philosophy of History," *Illuminations*, ed. Hannah Arendt (New York: Schocken, 1969), 257–8. Lockhart provides details of the prisoner swap and the arduous journey to Finland in his *Memoirs*, 345–8.

11  Turgenev, *Fathers and Sons*, tr. Constance Garnett (New York: P.F. Collier & Son, 1917) Ch. XXVI par. 43. https://www.bartleby.com/319/2/26.html. Also see Irving Howe, "Turgenev: The Virtues of Hesitation," *Hudson Review* 8.4 (1956) with reference to Turgenev and the "politics of hesitation" (Howe 551).

12  Mikhail Bulgakov, *The Master and Margarita*, tr. Richard Pevear and Larissa Volokhonsky (New York: Penguin, 2001), 287. Offsetting the well-known phrase "manuscripts don't burn" is the Master's remark that if "there are no papers, there's no person" (290).

    Lockhart's diary contains anecdotes and incidents, often reporting on various dinners, occasionally with wit. At one point, he records a tea at Oxford where Vivian Jackson told the story of a don who complained that his lectures were not as well attended as they had been twenty years earlier: "'And I know it's not my fault because they are the same lectures'" he exclaimed (Diaries I 289). Lockhart also records Moura's literary opinions, largely gossip (Lockhart, *Diaries Vol. II, 1939–1965* [London: Macmillan, 1980], 672–4). Hereafter Diaries II. The date of his last entry for her in his published diaries is March 7, 1951. Lockhart died in 1970, Moura in 1974.

13  Bruce Lockhart, *Retreat from Glory* (London: Putnam, 1934), 43. Hereafter Retreat.

14  An incident in Prague echoes his Russian feelings. When he escorted a ballerina to hear the Russian gypsy singer Nastia Poliakova, the dancer was so moved that she presented a broach she was wearing to Nastia as a thank you: "it was very Russian, very emotional and completely natural," Lockhart wrote (Retreat 157).

15  Lockhart, *The Two Revolutions: An Eye-Witness Study of Russia 1917* (London: Bodley Head, 1967), 79.

16  Turgenev, *Virgin Soil*, Ch. XXXVII, Project Gutenberg. https://www.gutenberg.org/files/2466/2466-h/2466-h.htm#link2H_4_0040.

# 3

# Jane Ellen Harrison: In Love with Language

*"I had no expectation of finding in the Russian language a new birth and a new life."*

Jane Ellen Harrison, *Aspects, Aorists and The Classical Tripos*, 1919

*She loved Russia, loved it like a human being.*

D.S. Mirsky, "Jane Harrison and Russia," 1930

In *Russia and the Russian Verb* (1915), the classicist and Cambridge scholar Jane Ellen Harrison announced that a language consistently revealed the psychology and culture of its people. Languages, she believed, unconsciously expressed a people's philosophy of life. But despite growing up surrounded by Russia, and teaching Russian at Cambridge for three years, Harrison didn't begin to learn the language until her sixties in Paris. At first a reluctant student of the country and its culture—she visited only once—the discovery of its language ignited a new passion.[1]

Harrison's enthusiasm for Russia began late in her career but came at a critical time, as Robert Ackerman has suggested: the outbreak of the First World War meant the loss of her scholarly work and friends but it regained momentum with her discovery of Russian and its nuances understood as signposts and embodiments of a culture. In 1915, in "an attempt to teach English to Russian emigres, she began the language in earnest [and] stopped all work on classics," Ackerman writes.[2] Importantly, her later promotion of Russian was instrumental in the creation and sustaining the idea of Russia in England and beyond in the early twentieth century, displaying another form of Russian love: linguistic.

Harrison had no doubt that language, specifically Russian, could be a lover. "If I could have my life over again," she wrote at age seventy-five, "I would devote it not to art or literature, but to language" which "reflects and interprets and makes bearable life; only it is a wider, because more subconscious, life."³ Her deep love of Russia occurred for a set of complex reasons, not least her belief that it might create a society of social worth and equality. At one point, she even described herself as a "philosophical Radical with a dash of the Bolshevik."⁴ The emotional appeal of Russian was political as much as cultural, symbolized by the "dreaded Aspects of the Russian verb" which for her became delights that furnished "a clue to the reading of the Russian soul."⁵ Aspects of the Russian verb allow for a richer life projected on the country: "immediately what we get from Russia is the impulse to live in the living fact, rather than outside it, to look to process, *durée* rather than to achievement" (Russ 12). Grammatical tense is the key to action which is living.

This was part of a developing popular interest in Russian best seen in Baedeker's 1914 guide to Russia formally titled *Russia, with Teheran, Port Arthur and Peking, Handbook for Travellers with 40 Maps and 78 Plans* with its companion volume, *Manual of the Russian Language with Vocabulary and List of Phrases*. Paragraph two of the "Introduction" to the guide directs travelers to become acquainted with the language for ease of travel: learn at least the Russian alphabet, Baedeker urges, suggesting the *Manual* with its "useful vocabularies, common phrases and the grammatical rules [is] necessary for the construction of simple sentences."⁶

In a May 1928 letter, Hope Mirrlees, her former student and companion, wrote that Harrison's "whole heart was given to Russia." As early as 1914, she imagined a school of Russian at her Cambridge college, Newnham, adding that "it would be impossible to exaggerate how important to her in the last ten years of her life both emotionally and intellectually were the Russian language and literature and people and thought" (in Stewart 174–5). In November 1914, Harrison writes that "nothing has made me so happy as the 'aspects' of Russian verbs since I first had sight of the Greek particles. I just weep for joy" (in Stewart 156). A December 1920 letter tells of her excitement entertaining a "live Bolshevik bear," who had just married the daughter of the College nurse. He "might have been Dostoevsky—a pure Slav type, sunken cheeks, fanatical dreamy eyes and talking only Russian and Persian" (in Stewart 175). She understood every word but two, admitting that "Russians do go to my head, and make me feel how common we all are—but I do wish they wouldn't have such confusing names." She also inquired when it would be possible to visit Russia: "[I] wanted to see both old & new Russia before I died" (in Stewart 175). The answer of the Russian gentleman was that as a private traveler it would not be safe but if she came as a guest of the Bolsheviks, she would have no worries.

Compounding her attachment was the significance she attached to the Russian bear. "The most human looking of beasts" became her totem, symbolizing the unity of "living nature, the essential identity of man and beast" (Mirsky 10). She also found in Russia a primitiveness expressed in religion. But the decisive moment in her love of Russia, Mirsky writes, was her study of Russian. Her attachment to the language was passionate. Language offered to her a "wider life," unifying the human condition. She also believed in the value of the group, the people, expressed clearly in *Ancient Art and Ritual*, the earliest of her works to give Russia prominence (Mirsky 11–12). For her, the social function and character of art were elementary.

Importantly, Harrison's early explanation of language plays into her conception and treatment of Russian. Borrowing ideas from the anthropologist A. E. Crawley's *Idea of the Soul*, she rejects the idea that language began with nouns and the names of things, preferring the idea of beginning with whole sentences, holophrases, where subject and object are submerged in a situation. The holophrase expresses relations not ideas but over time it disintegrates into a subject and verb.[7] There is a certain return to the body in a recreation of a matriarchal past. The ego may be the enemy; character is collective. Harrison then substitutes a collective emotional experience as the source of a Hellenic spirituality revising an Olympian hierarchy (Carp 179). She found in the matriarchal religious practices the origins of Greek civilization related to the goddess Themis.[8]

Her love for the language was partly because she found in the imperfective aspect of Russian the philosophical *durée* of Bergson, "the thing lived." *La durée*, duration, is the time of one's inner subjective experience or lived, rather than observed, time (as with a watch or clock). She then asks in *Russia and the Russian Verb* whether the perfective is "the aspect of intellect, of the thing thought rather than the thing lived; of the mental net, in which, M. Bergson tells us, our mechanizing minds and brains have caught the living universe?"[9] For Harrison language was an entrance to not only philosophy but epistemology, the lived and imagined experience. This relates to Russian love in that the feelings expressed by the lovers pit *la durée* against objective time. The former, connected to human agency, always influenced by subjective and specific memoires of the past, shaped an anticipation of the future. *La durée* distorts but also intensifies one's feelings, the very nature of Russian love defined by painful self-incrimination as much as an attenuated happiness.

Russian writers, Harrison believed, sought the *durée*, its authors not judging any sinners but sympathizing with them. A writer like Dostoevsky does not approve of crime but neither does he disapprove of it: "he has not got there yet, he is living into it, understanding through feeling" and "it is this living into things that [a] new generation demands" (Russ 10). This Russia has to offer she claimed in a 1915 talk to the Heretics Society (restated in *Russia and the Russian Verb* [10–11]), and carried over to the last paragraph of *Aspects, Aorists*. There she explains that "the Russian stands for the complexity and concreteness of life—felt whole, unanalyzed, unjudged" (Aspects 16).

By contrast, the aorist is "the momentary action that may be compared to a point, and the action that goes on, the present and imperfect that may be compared to a line" (Russ 7). The word originates in the ancient Greek *aóristos*, indefinite, and refers to a class of verb forms that portray an undefined situation but in a perfective aspect referring to past events. The aorist was the unmarked form of the verb in contrast to the imperfective aspect which referred to an ongoing or repeated situation. The perfect referred to a situation with a continuing relevance. The aorist indicative expresses things that happen in general without asserting a time. This complemented Harrison's preference for the primitive, ritualistic, and emotional as more authentic than the developed or reasoned. Framing the cognitive appeal of Russia for her was the emotional.[10]

Harrison's Russia was a mental as much as a historical/linguistic construct contributing to early twentieth-century conceptions of the country. This is clear in the full title of *Russia and the Russian Verb: A Contribution to the Psychology of the Russian People*. The title suggests the importance of Russian as a cultural barometer. Her understanding of Russian, psychologically, socially, historically, and personally derived from her ethnographic studies and understanding of Greek and Latin and determination to study origins. Archaeology, rather than philology, was her principal interest as Robert Ackerman reports (Ackerman 211, 223–4).

Mythography, she then claims, will soon become part of advanced classical scholarship, supplanted in her own studies by anthropology (Ackerman 224). As she revealingly notes, "Reason has little use for the imperfective, but emotion, sympathy, hungers after it," although Russian has not escaped "the impulse to be perfective" (Russ 9–10). But such perfectiveness "leaves, for the Russian, an aching void" which, to move from language to action, may partly explain the persistence of longing in Russian love and the need for it to fail (Russ 10). "The Russian hungers for *durée* …. he suffers the perfective; [but] he desires, he needs, the imperfective" (Russ 10). This is the paradox of Russian love expressed linguistically. Love may be the goal but it will always be unfulfilled—but only that way does he or she know they are in love.

The epitome of Harrison's valuation of Russian is her claim that it should be admitted as a subject for the Classical Tripos at Cambridge alongside Greek. This radical idea, expressed in *Aspects, Aorists and the Classical Tripos* (1919), became the avenue to a humanistic education: "An accurate knowledge of the Russian and Greek languages together with an intimate understanding of the two civilizations should furnish a humanistic education at once broad and thorough" she believed (in Mirsky 14). But the civilization she admires, Mirsky explains, is distorted, that of nineteenth-century Russia without the Tsars but one of the "intelligentsia and intellgentsiafied gentry, of the peasants, and to a certain extent of the Orthodox Church" (Mirsky 14).

Furthermore, the "bedrock of Russian folklore that she identified in the Russian language, with its dominance of 'aspect' over tense and of 'imperfective' over 'perfective'" became for her a revelation parallel to the discovery of Bergson's *durée* (Mirsky 14–15). In clear language, she explains that "the imperfective has internal time but no time order; it may be past, present, or future .... the perfective is of the accomplished act .... the imperfective is of *non*-accomplishment, of process" (Mirsky 15).[11] These elements of the language offer an understanding of Russian love and make it possible, she writes, to "live *into* the future and the past" (Mirsky 15). Appropriately, Harrison explains, the first "glimmer of the beauty and significance of the Russian aspects came to me over the Russian verb 'to seek'" (Russ 8). She never gave up seeking.

ii

Harrison begins her *Reminiscences of a Student's Life* (Hogarth Press, 1925) by declaring that Moscow was almost the first word she ever heard, although with a touch of humor she explains it was a dog most likely so named to honor the Crimean War. But when she learned that Moscow was a "cathedral city," and not a dog, "my universe rocked with Einsteinian relativity." But in those days, Russia was "a strange, inhuman Russia of Tzars and Siberia" (Reminis 312).

But Russia grew in her imagination and became the focus of her later studies, recognizing, as she explained in a letter to her friend the classicist Gilbert Murray, that

> what ever wild beast Russia makes of herself she still cares more than any other nation for things of the spirit and that is priceless (though as you say dangerous) .... we literary cusses owe enormously to her. Just now I am feeling

it inwardly in learning Russian: the words even seem like Greek to seek for the things of the spirit.[12]

Harrison's father, a lumber merchant, had done business there; two nephews studied the language and visited as early as 1811. She grew up surrounded by Russia but her only trip to the country, in September 1886, was to study Greek vases excavated by Kertsch then at the Hermitage in St. Petersburg.[13] Her single-minded focus was the vases; she saw little of St. Petersburg or Russia but would later write, when her passion for Russia matured, that she was foolish

> to leave Russia without knowing it! I might so easily have made the pilgrimage to Tolstoy; I might even have seen Dostoevsky. It has been all my life my besetting sin that I could only see one thing at a time. I was blinded by over-focus .... never now shall I see Moscow and Kiev, cities of my dreams.
>
> (Robinson 84)

Although Harrison's physical encounter with Russia was limited, she was one of the most influential promoters of Russian language in the first three decades of the twentieth century, teaching, lecturing, and translating Russian culture for the English. Two of her finest students, in whom she imbued a love of Russia, were Hope Mirrlees (who matriculated from Newnham College in 1910 after studying with Harrison) and Virginia Woolf, who met Harrison in 1904.[14]

In brief, having been passed over at graduation from Newnham College for a classical lectureship—she had received a top second on the Classics Tripos, an eight-day affair that left examiners divided (some felt she should receive a First)—she taught briefly at Oxford High School before moving to London in 1880 to first teach in another high school plus lecture on Greek art while studying classical archaeology at the British Museum, developing her focus on mythology expressed as art (Robinson 53; Beard 54–5). The lectures were part of a University Extension program. Her method was the examination of objects often through photographs with interpretation, method, and argument her priorities. Her goal was to show how visual imagery was part of the cultural and religious history of the classical world. In addition to her lectures, she conducted private classes at her apartment at 45D Colville Gardens where, according to an interview in the *Pall Mall Gazette* of 1891, "the very air breathed antiquity" (Beard 101).

During this period, the 1880s and 1890s, Harrison also became fluent in German and traveled to the continent, especially the museums. Illustrations soon became her trademark in her writing, borrowed from her lecturing. She based her arguments mostly on things, classical objects not words, becoming fundamentally an "archaeologist rather than philologist" (Ackerman 218). The analysis of sculpture and vases was always via images. In Mary Beard's words, she was an "historian of images" (Beard 106).

Her activities as a student at Cambridge was a prelude to her academic and social success. At Newnham, she distinguished herself by hosting a series of eminent visitors: Turgenev ("Dare I ask him to speak just a word or two of Russian?"), Ruskin, Gladstone (who came to her rooms), and then George Eliot who, when visiting her rooms, remarked of her recent redecoration using William Morris wallpaper that "Your paper makes a beautiful background for your face" (Remins 327). Her last distinguished guest, years later, was the Crown Prince of Japan. In London, she would meet Robert Browning, Herbert Spencer, Walter Pater, and even Henry James. Tennyson was also an acquaintance, although she admits that he was "intensely English, and therefore not at his best as a conscious thinker" (Remins 328). Burne-Jones was another friend.

She spent fifteen years in London where she lectured in the city and provinces. She needed the funds: "being one of a family of twelve, my fortune was slender, and social life is costly" (Remins 335). Yet she regretted "those lecturing years," even if she was "voluble and had instant success." It was "mentally demoralizing," despite the crowds that came to hear her speak becoming a celebrity classicist and archaeologist. Her lectures on Greek art, using lantern slides and plaster casts, supposedly brought some 1,600 attendees in Glasgow, she once boasted (Remins 335; Beard 55-6). She was a popular speaker and records an anecdote from a lecture she gave at Winchester College. When a Master asked a student if he had liked the lecture, he replied, "Not the lecture … but I liked the lady; she was like a beautiful green beetle" (Remins 331). "Every lecture was a drama," stated the noted classicist and translator Francis Cornford, although some critics felt it was sensationalism at a high pitch. She even included sound effects, as well as dark lighting and "power dressing" (Beard 55, 58).

But she had a talent to translate antiquity into plain language, publishing a highly popular volume entitled *Ancient Art and Ritual* (1913) in the "Home University Library" series initiated by Oxford to make classical scholarship accessible to the general public. Such a move did not gain the approval of the patriarchs of classical studies, even if *Ancient Art and Ritual* derived from her scholarly *Themis* (1912). Her work seemed to simplify the connection between ritual and art, while confirming the reputation of a lively, engaged personality rediscovering antiquity for an interested community in theatrical ways.

While she continued to lecture professionally, she sought an academic appointment, applying for the Yates Chair of Classical Archaeology at University College London in 1880. Despite support from international scholars, she lost, the election widely reported in the press. Two members of the appointments committee even signed a document stating that it was "undesirable that any teaching in University College should be conducted by a woman" (Beard 62). But she was able to teach classics at Cambridge where she was finally offered a Research Fellowship at Newnham in 1898 and where she would stay for the next twenty-five years; by then, she had achieved an international reputation in classical scholarship turning increasingly to anthropology as a new approach to Greek art.

This method was evident as early as her first major work, the *Prolegomena to the Study of Greek Religion* (1903) where she differentiated between matriarchal rituals and Homeric, patriarchal rituals. The former had a crucial role at seasonal festivals; the latter did not. She also explored new archaeological discoveries indicating the primacy of Dionysian worship; her scholarship also offered new understandings of powerful female archetypes in Greek religious practice and drama. In *Themis: A Study of the Social Origins of Greek Religion* (1912) she linked Dionysian rituals and the Dionysian dithyramb or song with the beginnings of Greek theater.[15] In her "Reminiscences," she writes that "art in some sense springs out of religion; and between them is a connecting link, a bridge and that bridge is ritual." But surprisingly, she next writes that "on that bridge, emotionally, I halt" (Reminis 343).

It is ritual alone that moves her, partly because she senses that a ritual procession "seems to me like life, like *durée*, itself, caught and fixed before me" (Reminis 343). She also criticized art as mimesis, arguing that art is the outpouring of energy, its mainspring not the wish to copy Nature but the "desire … to utter, to give out a strongly felt emotion or desire."[16] This becomes language, the formation into words of an original emotive experience. Language, particularly Russian, relives these moments as words express a sense of community and participation. Art and ritual, she would write, "do not seek to copy a fact, but to reproduce, to re-enact an emotion" (Ritual 47). Art (and language) represents life and its emotions but "cut loose from immediate action." Offering a modernist perspective, she writes that "the end of art is in itself" (Ritual 135).[17] These views shape her understanding of the social/anthropological origins of Russian.

Interestingly, in her candid voice she challenges Professor Gilbert Murray's assertion that she never did an "hour's really hard work." Her riposte: "I think he forgets that I have learnt the Russian declensions, which is more than he ever did." But he may be right, she continues:

> I never work in the sense of attacking a subject against the grain, tooth and nail .... the Russian verb "to learn" takes the dative, which seems so odd till you find out that it is from the same root as "to get used to." When you learn[,] you "get yourself used to" a thing. That is worth a whole treatise of pedagogy. And it explained to me my own processes. One reads round a subject, soaks oneself in it and then one's personal responsibility is over; something stirs and ferments ... and you know you have to write a book.
>
> (Remnis 335)

Importantly, although she found men attractive and supposedly refused at least one offer of marriage, she felt confident that being alone worked: "By what miracle I escaped marriage, I do not know, for all my life long I fell in love .... I do not doubt that I lost much, but I am quite sure I gained more" (Reminis 345). From 1923 to 1925, living in Paris with Hope Mirrlees, she met and knew many Russians including Aleksey Remizov and the religious philosopher Lev Shestov. By 1924, she was "a leading figure in the networks of Russian emigres scattered throughout London and Paris."[18] This occurred partly through Prince Mirsky first met in Paris in the winter of 1923–4. He was an aristocratic intellectual who quickly admired Harrison. Leonard Woolf described him as cultivated but that he also possessed "that air of profound pessimism which seemed to be characteristic of intellectual Russians, both within and without the pages of Dostoevsky" (in Robinson 269).

When Mirsky was in Paris, Harrison made sure he met an expanding circle of Russian émigrés, the most eminent Shestov. Mirsky, in turn, put Harrison and Mirrlees in touch with the Russian modernist Aleksey Remizov and Marina Tsvetaeva. Inspired by Mirsky and Remizov, the two English women decided to translate the seventeenth-century orthodox Russian priest Avvakum's autobiography; Mirsky would supply the preface. Harrison's increasing identity with Russia took new form (Reminis 314).

Harrison went to Paris in 1914 to see her French doctor who was treating her for angina and to escape England, then under German bombardment. On a second visit in the spring, she and Mirrlees discovered L'École Orientale where they taught Russian not far from the Hotel de l'Élysée where they were staying. They joined a second-year class, beyond their proficiency. Three times a week they were taught by a M. Boyer, the other three days by a Russian woman who gave them oral practice using colored pictures. Her classmates were several pawnbrokers, an Abbé, a French suffragette, and others (Robinson 265). Ironically, Mirrlees would receive a Diploma in Russian from the school; Harrison did not bother with the credentials. This was an ironic reversal: Mirrlees had left Newnham without taking the Tripos exams, displaying a dilettantish attitude toward her studies (Robinson 281, 235).

But from the start, Russian captivated Harrison, partly because the language made use of the aspects of the verb to distinguish between performing an action and seeing an action take place. In addition to the language classes, she studied M. André Mazon's *Emplois de Aspects du verbe Russe*, an advanced text that confirmed her views on aspect linked to a broader cultural pattern (Russ 13). And she returned to the idea of "seeking," Mazon concluding that "the tendency 'to see and to evoke' … is the essential tendency of the Russian imagination" (Russ 14). Russian for her contained the "thing lived," the *durée* of Bergson, which must take precedence over the thing thought. But ironically, she was learning Russian through French.

By 1919, Harrison returned to Cambridge to teach Russian and as her confidence grew, publishing with Mirrlees and the assistance of Prince Mirsky and Rezimov, a translation of Archpriest Avvakum's autobiography, *The Life of the Archpriest Avvakum by Himself* (London: Hogarth Press, 1924). Two years later was a collection of Russian fairytales, *The Book of the Bear: Being Twenty-one Tales Newly Translated from the Russian* (London: Nonesuch Press, 1926), also with Mirrlees.

*The Life of the Archpriest*, appearing in 1924, the year Lenin died and St. Petersburg was renamed Leningrad, begins with a lengthy Preface by Mirsky. He argues that Avvakum is important in the history of Russian literature because his work is the only text of significance between the Old Russian *Lay of Igor* in the twelfth century and the "first expressions of modern poetry" in the later eighteenth. Old Russian, he adds, knew no imaginative literature. What literature existed was utilitarian and mainly ecclesiastic but Avvakum was "unlike his predecessors" largely because he created "a literary language of his own" from "the spoken language of his time."[19]

Such a colloquial language would have appealed to Harrison plus, as Mirsky points out, "Avvakum's Russian, archaic in detail, is essentially the same as the spoken Russian of to-day" (Avvakum 27). Yet his use of everyday language is precisely what makes him modern, suggesting that Russian writers of today have more to learn from him than any nineteenth-century Russian author (Avvakum 27-8). Turgenev and Tolstoy seem academic by comparison. He ends with a surprising reference to Proust, suggesting that both are difficult in their first few pages, citing sources and quotations.[20]

Coinciding with her interest in Russian was Harrison's interest in bears. She received her first in 1906 when teddy-bears first became popular (Robinson 238). She admired bears for their slow gait, preference for silence, and love of space. In a letter written during an intensely hot July day, she wrote that "it was always the dream of my childhood to sit upon an iceberg with a bear" (in Stewart 5). The psychological equation of Russia as a bear was imaginatively real to her, partly as an echo of her father's Russian travels and partly because of British cartoons which repeatedly depicted Russia as a bear.

In "Reminiscences," she reports on a dream which occurred on a night soon after the Russian Revolution, although earlier she recalled the discovery of a small stone figure of a bear in a rubbish pile among fragments at the Acropolis Museum on her first trip to Athens. She recovered the female figure and provides context related to the *arkteia*, a bear-service in the precinct of Artemis Brauraonia, adding that "no well-born Athenian would marry a girl unless she had accomplished her *bear-service*" (Remins 338). She then cites a line from *Lysistrata* by Aristophanes where the chorus of women chant that they were bears at the Brauronian festival. She then mentions the importance of the bear to the American Apaches (Remins 338). This sense of the bear myth is coincident with her ideas of a Russian bear; the animal, of course, a metaphor for the country.

The bear dream, shortly after the revolution, tells of a great ancient forest. In cleared round space, she sees huge bears "softly dancing. I somehow knew that I had come to teach them to dance the Grand Chain in the Lancers, a square dance now obsolete. I was not the least afraid, only very glad and proud." But they will not form a circle and hold hands: they "shuffled away, courteously waving their paws, intent on their own mysterious doings." But she also realized these "doings" were greater than the Grand Chain and that "it was for me to learn, not to teach. I woke up crying, in an ecstasy of humility" (Reminis 341). "That may stand for what Russia has meant to me," she concludes, a large, mysterious entity from which she is to learn its language and culture. But it was not the literature and great writers that drew her to Russia: "it was just the Russian language" (Reminisc 341).

However, in a late letter, she comically describes seeing sixteen polar bears perform in Paris, although they were not that talented, acting more like the independent figures in her dream she reports in her *Reminiscences*, "for when the trainer-man tried to make them do their stunts they just shambled past him & went nosing about their own business."[21]

If she could live her life over, Harrison continues, she would devote it not to art or literature but to language. "Life itself may hit one hard, but always, always one can take sanctuary in language" (Reminis 341). And, one wants to add, bears. It is hardly surprising that a photo taken of Mirrlees and Harrison in Paris's Tuileries garden in 1915 should include a toy bear held by Mirrlees. Harrison sent the photo/postcard to Gilbert Murray in July 1915 (see Beard 136–7). Several years later when she met Prince Mirsky, she wrote to Gilbert Murray that "I have lost my aged heart to a Bear Prince—why did I not meet him 50 years ago when I cld [sic] have clamoured to be his princess." He, in turn, acknowledged her importance to him when he dedicated the first volume of his *History of Russian Literature* to her.[22]

*The Book of the Bear* contains twenty-one tales translated by Harrison and Mirrlees with color woodcut prints by Ray Garnett, actually Rachell Marshal, wife of David Garnett. She, too, had traveled to Russia before the war. Harrison's interest in bears was, of course, longstanding, noting in her "Reminiscences" that the Russian sled she had allowed only one individual to ride: "Thank God it held only one, so I could dream undisturbed of steppes and Siberia and bears and wolves" (Reminis 312). The book originated in Paris where she retired in 1922 joining Mirrlees. The city had become the center of a "Russia Abroad" movement composed of displaced intellectuals and Russian aristocrats (or pseudo-aristocrats) after the 1917 revolution.[23]

In 1923, Harrison was invited to participate in an annual series of August colloquia convened by Paul Desjardins at his manor home at Pontigny in Burgundy. This was an honor, a recognition of belonging in a European intellectual circle. The theme of the 1923 meeting was, appropriate for Harrison given her youthful mind, "Perpetual Youth." Many of the discussions dealt with reuniting Europe after the war and eradicating nationalist isolation. Earlier, in 1914, in "Epilogue on the War: Peace with Patriotism," Harrison had looked to Russia to counter the polarizing nationalism that led to war.

Pontigny ushered Harrison into the "Russia Abroad" sphere. In a August 29, 1923 letter, she thrillingly notes that she sits between Heinrich Mann and "my adored Russian philosopher Shestov—so I am content" (Stewart 191). The émigré philosopher Lev Shestov had come to the attention of the French public through an article on Dostoevsky in a February 1922 issue of *La Nouvelle Revue Française* (NRF). Gide thought well of the piece and invited him to his own lectures on Dostoevsky. Shestov was on the faculty of University of Paris, the

Russian section of the Sorbonne, where he taught Dostoevsky. Through Shestov, it is likely she met the Russian Aleksey Remizov who figures importantly in *The Book of the Bear*.[24]

Preceding the preface to *The Book of the Bear* is the dedication: "TO THE / GREAT / BEAR," Prince Mirsky. The preface, written by both translators, emphasizes the bear in Russian folklore which in the mid-nineteenth century and beyond became a symbol of a devouring Russia embodying the Empire. But as a British Library text recently noted introducing *The Book of the Bear*, "in 1926, the Russian Bear first spoke English."[25] But the effort of Harrison and Mirrlees might be understood not only as an attempt to translate a set of folk tales but something political: an effort to assuage the devouring bear by showing its prominence in a range of Russian folk and fairytales where the bears, while still a threat, are also gentle figures and a surprise, as in Tolstoy's "The Bear Prince" included in the collection. The book itself mixes historical and modern fairy tales and genres: poetry, prose, and at one point music as in the "Bear's Lullaby." Contributors range from Tolstoy and Remizov to anonymous authors. And as a prelude to the volume, the preface ends with this celebratory sentence: "Remizov's bear dies of grief but before he does so, he thunders and lightens in the sky and shakes the great forest to its foundations."[26]

Harrison soon wrote (in Russian) to Remizov inviting him to tea on March 9, 1924, repeating the invitation a month later with the promise of Prince Mirsky, who became the second Russian to collaborate on the translations of both the autobiography of Avvakum and the bear collection. And as Harrison facilitated Mirsky's entrée into the "Russia Abroad" group in Paris, he in turn facilitated Harrison's into Bloomsbury.[27] She and Mirrlees even took a house in Mecklenburg Square, the heart of Bloomsbury. Mirsky was also Harrison's guide into Russian literature; she partly edited volume one of his *A History of Russian Literature* (1928). In return, and in recognition of their friendship, he dedicated the work to her. Soon Remizov, Shestov, and Mirsky formed a valuable troika of Russian writers and thinkers who aided Harrison and Mirrlees in translating first the Avvakum text and then *The Book of the Bear*. Remizov, in particular, played an important role in translating the Old Russian text (Schwinn-Smith 126). And while she often reported to Mirsky on their progress, he advanced the proposal with the Woolfs. Aesthetically, the translation goals of Mirsky and Remizov were similar: colloquial speech. Mirsky would write the introduction to the Avvakum text arguing for its modernity because of its reliance on everyday speech.

Leonard and Virginia Woolf first met Mirsky in Harrison's Paris apartment in March 1924, Leonard Woolf commenting that he was like "one of those unpredictable nineteenth-century Russian aristocrats" one meets in Turgenev or Tolstoy.[28] Internally, he was thoroughly Russian: "Prince Mirsky would have found himself spiritually at home in *The Possessed* or *The Idiot*" (L. Woolf 24). Externally, he energetically took part in Parisian cultural life. He also became a regular at the Woolfs' in London until he fatefully returned to Russia in 1932.

Empathy with Russian peasant culture and magic qualities of pagan belief were important for Harrison's work not only on bears but on her reformulation of Russian culture. Its primitive origins should not be forgotten, she believed. In theoretical terms, Harrison's mythologized image of Russia—entwined with deeply personal overtones—articulates her own sense of displacement into the space that enables creativity and transcendence. The dream of bears invokes Harrison's definition of the Dionysian dithyramb as a leaping, inspired dance and her understanding of pantomimic dancing as "a ritual bridge 'between actual life and those representations of life that we call art.'"[29]

### iii

Harrison admired Russian writers, especially Turgenev, Tolstoy, and Dostoevsky, although she was more "frightened" than elated by the last two (Reminis. 341). She particularly resented their "probing potency," citing the end of *The Brothers Karamazov* and the scene between Dimitri Karamazov and Grushenka which had a poignancy that passed "the limits of the permissible in art" (Reminis 341). She refers most likely to Grushenka sharing the guilt of the murder of Fyodor with Dmitri.

Headstrong and independent, she had been encouraged to become the mistress of Fyodor at the same time as Dmitri falls in love with her, a source of antagonism between the father and son. But she is manipulative and cannot make a decision about her lovers until the very end, after the murder of Fyodor. Such intemperate and willful behavior was likely brought on by being jilted earlier in her life by a Polish officer. Her behavior makes her, in Dmitri's eyes, the "queen of impudence" and therefore irresistible.[30] He recognizes that beauty can be "a terrible and awful thing …. mysterious as well as terrible." It can also arouse sexual desires but at the same time inspire noble and elevated thoughts. Or, to use his imagery, unite insects and angels, the insect stirring up "a tempest in your blood" caused by "sensual lust," in contrast to the angels who are self-sacrificial (BK 131). Paradox is all: "though I'm full of low desires, and love what's low, I'm not dishonorable" (BK 133).

Russian love, characteristically suspended and hesitant, has at the end of *The Brothers Karamazov* become painful, all-consuming, and emotionally dangerous—hence Harrison's own withdrawal from its emotional intimacy. Suffering caused by, impeded by, or withheld by love may be one of the strongest qualities of Russian love linked to the idea of transformation through suffering as experienced by Dmitri in jail and Grushenka through her illness. Knowledge and even love come through suffering, a religious as well as psychological concept that may bring salvation for the self. This is also Russian justice: not to punish but to reform. Law and love unite in the lawyer Fetyukovitch's address to the jury in Book XII although, ironically of course, Dmitri is found guilty.

One further text favored by Harrison, one that contains the essential qualities of Russia and Russian love, is Goncharov's *Oblomov*. Harrison spends pages discussing the novel in *Aspects* in a section Mirsky praises as the most "brilliant criticism of the Russian novel I know of" (Mirsky 16). In the behavior of Oblomov, she finds characteristics that were indisputably Russian. The term *Oblomovhina* can now be found "in any Russian dictionary and it means the imperfective state incarnate" (Aspects 27). Her eye is again on significant detail. Of Oblomov's dressing gown she writes that it's easy to get into but almost impossible to get out of: "it haunts the book like an Ibsen symbol. It stands for the impossibility of being 'well-groomed' physically, mentally" (Aspects 27).

Most importantly, Harrison philosophizes on the Russian character:

> The Russian does not judge, does not moralize, nor does he sentimentalize. In his imperfective way he lives into his subject till he almost ceases to be artist—so intense is his realization. He feels the thing so closely, so fully, that he has no need to pump up emotion and relive it in imagination just for the "sake of sensation."
>
> (Aspects 31)

This leads to a further observation at the core of Russian love:

> It is part of the great spiritual riches of the Russian that, because he sees or rather feels things living from the inside (imperfective) he sees or rather feels things *whole* (asyndeta). It is a corollary from his living into things, for life *is duree* unanalyzed, undistributed. These *asyndeta*, these bits of life so closely bound together that they refuse conjunctions, are countless in Russian, specially in epic and peasant Russian.
>
> (Aspects 32)

Living in the moment is key to understanding both Russia and its languages and emanates from Harrison's dual study of the language and literature expressing a deeply felt love restated in the final paragraph of the *Aspects* pamphlet: "Immediately what we get from Russia, is the impulse to live in the living fact rather than outside it, to look to process, *durée*, rather than to achievement" (Mirsky 16). This must apply to morality which she says is "the vice of the perfective; it is the judging of an act by its results" which can be tabulated. This in turn becomes "the stuff of which codes and strong government are made" but "the Russian stands for the complexity and concreteness of life—felt whole, unanalyzed, unjudged, lived into …." (Mirsky 16). The goal is to "live in the living fact" (in Mirsky 16).

## iv

Despite a thirty-two-year difference, Woolf and Harrison became close, Woolf reading all four of Harrison's key classical texts on the beginnings of the Olympian gods: *Prolegomena to the Study of Greek Religion*, 1903; *Themis: A Study of the Social Origins of Greek Religion*, 1912; *Ancient Art and Ritual*, 1913; and *Epilegomena to the Study of Greek Religion*, 1921. Woolf also owned Harrison's *Aspects, Aorists and the Classical Tripos* (1919), an expansion of *Russia and the Russian Verb* (that same year, the Hogarth Press published Hope Mirrlees' 600-line *Paris: A Poem*).[31] She also had a copy of *Alpha and Omega*, Harrison's essays. Woolf was excited to meet her in 1904 and visited her in Cambridge, London, and Paris. Not only was she a renowned classicist who published and lectured on Greek art and archaeology but she smoked a pipe on the steps of the Parthenon (Mills 8).

The Hogarth Press published Harrison's and Hope Mirrlees's translation of Avvakum in 1924 and Harrison's *Reminiscences* in 1925. There is a tribute to her in *A Room of One's Own* and she's cited again in Woolf's "The Intellectual Status of Women." In many ways she was a role model and mentor. Complicating the picture, however, is Woolf's distaste for Hope Mirrlees. Jealously might have been at play, Woolf commenting at one point that she knows "Greek and Russian better than I do French" (in Carpentier 172). But Woolf remained close to Harrison, taking tea with her a month before her death.

A sentence by Virginia Woolf two days after Harrison's passing epitomizes the remarkable, cultural life of Jane Harrison and her love affair with Russian.

Crossing a graveyard behind Mecklenburg Street, where Harrison died on April 15, 1928, Woolf met a distraught Hope Mirrlees: "we kissed by Cromwell's [grand] daughter's grave, where Shelley used to walk, for Jane's death." Woolf, Cromwell, Shelley, Mirrlees, and Jane Harrison—*la durée* triumphant.[32]

# Notes

1. Harrison's prodigious ability with languages resulted in knowledge of three Romance, three Scandinavian, three Oriental, and five dead languages plus German and Russian. See *Aspects, Aorists and the Classical Tripos* (Cambridge: Cambridge University Press, 1919), 6. Hereafter *Aspects*. She did not, however, qualify as a *Diplomée* in Russian like her former student and companion, Hope Mirrlees. Nevertheless, she was an enthusiastic instructor. See Jesse Stewart, *Jane Ellen Harrison, A Portrait in Letters* (London: Merlin Press, 1959), 172. Hereafter Stewart.

    On Harrison's teaching method, see 173.
2. Robert Ackerman, "Jane Ellen Harrison: The Early Work," *The Myth and Ritual School: J.G. Frazer and the Cambridge Ritualists* (New York: Routledge, 2002), 217–18. Hereafter Ackerman. Hellenic primitivism and classical archaeology would become her specialties.
3. Jane Ellen Harrison, "Reminiscences of a Student's Life," *Arion: A Journal of Humanities and the Classics* 4.2 (1965): 341. Hereafter Reminis. The entire work runs from 312–46 and reproduces the 1925 Hogarth Press Edition.
4. Prince D.S. Mirsky, *Jane Harrison and Russia* (Cambridge: Heffer & Son, 1930), 5. Hereafter Mirsky. This was the second Jane Harrison Memorial Lecture given in 1929. Gilbert Murray gave the first.
5. Harrison, *Russia and the Russian Verb, A Contribution to the Psychology of the Russian People* (Cambridge: W. Heffer & Sons, Ltd., 1915), 3. Hereafter Russ.

    As early as 1915, she assisted Professor Elsie Butler, at Newnham and waiting to join a Scottish hospital unit in Russia, learn the language. Within two weeks Butler could read Turgenev. Harrison's method was "grammatically formal" but it got down to roots (Stewart 173).
6. Karl Baedeker, *Russia, Handbook for Travelers* (Leipzig: Karl Baedeker, Publisher, 1914), xiii. A few pages later, Baedeker comments on the "despondent slackness" of the people which often leads to "disorder, and the waste of time." This "pessimistic outlook" finds expression in the word "nitchevó" translated as "it doesn't matter" (Baedeker xlii). He then suggests that Russian literature reflects a "dreamy and melancholy outlook on life" also seen in their "national songs and music" (Baedeker xlii).

7   Martha C. Carpentier, *Ritual, Myth, and the Modernist Text, the Influence of Jane Ellen Harrison on Joyce, Eliot and Woolf* (London: Routledge, 1998), 177. Hereafter Carpentier.
8   Carpentier makes this distinction clear in a discussion of *To the Lighthouse* and the differences between Mrs. Ramsay and her husband. See Carpentier 180–1.
9   Harrison, *Russia and the Russian Verb, A Contribution to the Psychology of the Russian People* (Cambridge: W. Heffer & Sons, Ltd., 1915), 8. Hereafter Russ. In 1891, Bergson married a cousin of Proust's whose work is shaped by *la durée* which shows how *la durée* expands and contracts regardless of objective time. A dual time is at work: the lived time, *la durée*, and an objective time different in each volume of *In Search of Lost Time*. Some volumes cover years, others just a few days, yet they are all roughly the same length.
10  Harrison, *Aspects, Aorists and the Classical Tripos*, 3.
11  Jessie Stewart, in *Jane Ellen Harrison, A Portrait in Letters*, writes that Aspects is "a feature of primitive languages, are in Russian two forms of the verb, *imperfective*, implying a continuing process, a thing not accomplished—and *perfective*, a thing definitely finished off; the relation of an open hand to a closed fist, 'to seek' and 'to find.'" Psychologically, Harrison sees in the imperfective "the imaginative tendency to live in the living fact rather than outside it." Stewart 172.
12  Harrison in Marilyn Schwinn-Smith, "'Bergsonian Poetics' and the Beast: Jane Harrison's Translations from the Russian," *Translation and Literature* 20.3 (Autumn 2011): 319. Hereafter Schwinn-Smith.
13  Annabel Robinson, *The Life and Work of Jane Ellen Harrison* (Oxford: Oxford University Press, 2002), 15, 84. Hereafter Robinson. Harrision traveled to Russia with her cousin Marian Harrison.
   An antidote to Robinson and other semi-pious celebrations of Harrison is Mary Beard, *The Invention of Jane Harrison* (Cambridge: Harvard University Press, 2000). Hereafter Beard. In her forthright manner, Beard opens with "Jane Ellen Harrison changed the way we think about the ancient Greeks" followed by "she infuriated the academic establishment … with her uncompromising refusal to play the submissive part" (Beard xi). Beard, in a work that focuses principally on Harrison's London years, also claims that "things done" not "things said" always took precedence for Harrison (Beard 7).
14  Note must also be taken of Eugénie (Sellers) Strong, a student of Harrison's, who went on to a distinguished career as a classicist becoming Assistant Director of the British School in Rome. She and Harrison were close friends and colleagues; at a certain point, Sellers acted as Harrison's business manager and secretary, even selling tickets to the lectures which formed the basis of Harrison's early books including *Introductory Studies in Greek Art* (1885) which reached its fifth edition by 1902. See Beard *passim* but especially 63–84.

15 On Harrison's development of powerful female archetypes and its impact on early modernist writing, see Carpentier 43–8, 51–5 and *passim*. Carpentier summarizes Harrison's progress as moving from archaeology and art to primitive rituals and then the religious impulse in psychology and modern life, adding that in her representation of female archetypes she "evaded patriarchal binarisms" (46, 57).
16 Harrison, *Ancient Art and Ritual* (London: William and Norgate, 1913), 26. Hereafter Ritual.
17 Samuel Beckett wrote in his early essay on Joyce's *Finnegans Wake* that "his writing is not *about* something; *it is that something itself.*" Beckett, "Dante ... Bruno. Vico. Joyce," *Our Exagmination Round His Factification* (1929; New York: New Directions, 1972), 14.
18 Jean Mills, "The Writer, the Prince and the Scholar," *Leonard and Virginia Woolf, The Hogarth Press and the Networks of Modernism*, ed. Helen Southworth (Edinburgh: Edinburgh University Press, 2010), 150.
19 D.S. Mirsky, "Preface," *The Life of the Archpriest Avvakum by Himself*, tr. Jane Harrison and Hope Mirrlees (1924; London: The Hogarth Press, 1963), 25–6.
20 Avvakum, burned at the stake in 1681 for his orthodoxy in dogma and ritual, had a connection to Mirsky: his own great great aunts were disciples who suffered persecution. When a copy of the translation was returned to Mirsky, who had sent it to Russia for review, it was marked "forbidden" (Stewart 174).
21 Harrison to Mirsky in Sandra J. Peacock, *Jane Ellen Harrison, The Mask and the Self* (New Haven: Yale University Press,1988), 231. She also saw them as a lifeline, writing "'oh those bears I should have been dead long ago but for them, bless them'" (232).
22 G.S. Smith, *D.S. Mirsky, A Russian-English Life, 1890–1939* (Oxford: Oxford University Press, 2000), 98. Hereafter Smith. Also useful on the Harrison/Mirsky association and *The Book of the Bear* is Francesca Wade, *Square Haunting: Five Writers in London between the Wars* (London: Duggan Books, 2020), 182–9.
23 On the overall topic of Russian diasporic communities with special attention to Paris, see Faith Hillis, *Utopia's Discontents, Russian émigrés and the quest for freedom 1830s-1930s* (Oxford: Oxford University Press, 2021).
24 Useful on these developments is Marilyn Schwinn-Smith, "Bears in Bloomsbury: Jane Ellen Harrison and Russia," *Virginia Woolf: Three Centenary Celebrations*, ed. Maria Candida Zamith and Luisa Flora (Porto: Faculdade de Letras da Universidade do Porto, 2007), 124–5.
25 Katya Rogatchevskaia, "British Intellectuals and Russian Bears," *European Studies Blog*, August 4, 2021. Prompting comment on *The Book of the Bear* was the British Library's exhibition entitled "Paddington: The Story of a Bear." https://blogs.bl.uk/european/2021/08/british-intellectuals-and-russian-bears.html.

The metaphor of Russia as a bear has a long history originating in folk tales. For a more recent reading of the metaphor, see Victor Madeira, *Britannia and the Bear: The Anglo-Russian Intelligence Wars 1917–1929* (Woodbridge, Suffolk: Boydell Press, 2016).

26  Jane Harrison and Hope Mirrlees, "Preface," *The Book of the Bear* (London: Nonesuch Press, 1926), xii.

27  Harrison and Mirrlees also offered financial advice and assistance to their Russian friends. At one point, Harrison send Mirsky a check for £60 to underwrite a new journal he would edit (Schwinn-Smith 136).

28  Leonard Woolf, *Downhill All the Way, An Autobiography of the Years 1919–1939* (London: Hogarth Press, 1967), 23–4.

29  Alexandra Smith, "Jane Harrison as an Interpreter of Russian Culture in the 1910s-1920s," *A People Passing Rude: British Responses to Russian Culture*, ed. Anthony Cross (London: Open Book Publishers, 2012), 182. https://books.openedition.org/obp/1580?lang=en.

The Harrison quote is from *Ancient Art and Ritual* (1913) 28.

30  Dostoevsky, *The Brothers Karamazov*, tr. Constance Garnett (New York: Lowell Press, 1900), 193. Here after BK. Project Gutenberg. https://www.gutenberg.org/files/28054/old/28054-pdf.pdf.

31  Ironically, Woolf did not initially think well of Mirrlees, noting in her diary for November 23, 1920 that she "has been for the weekend—over-dressed, over elaborate, scented, extravagant, yet with thick nose, thick ankles; a little unrefined, I mean." Yet she adds "I like her very much & think her very clever." Virginia Woolf, *Diary of Virginia Woolf*, vol. II, ed. Anne Olivier Bell (New York: Harcourt Brace Jovanovich, 1978), 75. November 23, 1920.

32  In Robinson 305.

# 4

# William Gerhardie: Flattery Is Not Enough

## or

## War de Luxe

"Played tennis this afternoon, love, then a bath, and afterwards witnessed a revolution."

William Gerhardie, "Diary" in *Memoirs of a Polyglot* (1931)[1]

William Gerhardie's jaunty tone belies the seriousness with which he experienced the Russian Revolution, his treatment of love, and his survival. In *Memoirs of a Polyglot* he goes on to explain that the remark about love relates to "the willing wife of some Russian officer unknown to me."[2] His insouciance was notorious as was his attitude toward women with whom he had numerous affairs. He candidly thought they should be beautiful but not necessarily think. But contradicting his dismissive view and belief that women had no talent, especially as writers, is his sustained correspondence with Katherine Mansfield, Edith Wharton, and Rosamond Lehmann. Ironically, the author of the accepted, standard biography of Gerhardie is also woman. Nevertheless, his nonchalant attitude toward women and war remains characteristic of his view of love and danger: "when it came I was not really interested in the Revolution, but was writing a war comedy entitled 'The Khaki Armlet; or Why Clarence Left Home'" (MP 122).

Gerhardie was never not in love; romance framed his life. Young girls, single women, married women, widows, prostitutes, or even female colleagues were all opportunities. Women in passing, whether on a street or in the countryside, held appeal and he was rarely incapable of meeting them. Sex was his rallying cry: "morally, everything is better for being ventilated, especially sex, which thrives on suppression" (MP 118). True love, he believed, was only a chimera. The genuine artist, he claimed, "hunger[s] for the love of women, beyond the capacity of a single woman to satisfy" (MP 328). He incorporates Proust who claimed that it is not to beings we "must attach ourselves … but ideas," which included polyamorousness and pleasure (MP 329). Typical of his encounters is this passage: going to meet "again a rather beautiful young [married] woman," who had "found the experiment unsatisfying romantically." She "was ready for an adventure with a poet." The German word *Dichter*, he quickly explains, means novelist *and* poet (MP 208).

Women for Gerhardie are only types and stereotypes to be conquered. In Greenwich Village during a US lecture tour, he met a fascinating girl "lying like a lioness on a couch" who read "out loud from Schopenhauer and later put some of his theories into practice" (MP 366). New York women reporters inquired about his views of love and sex and "would sometimes allow me to cut short the theory by a practical illustration" (MP 366–7). But two women might have made him "lastingly happy": Katherine Mansfield (whom he knew only through letters but who had found a publisher for his first novel, *Futility*) and a German woman fifteen years older, the daughter of a colleague of Einstein, whom he met in Innsbruck. "Unhappily married," he discovered her to be mentally stimulating but she mistook their common "ecstasy" of shared ideas, discovered in literature and nature, for love. "I was fascinated only by her mind," he defensively explains (MP 303).

Women were always a surprise to Gerhardie, as well as their husbands. An amiable Viennese discovering that his young wife was "with me in a situation that admitted of no doubt …. seemed not at all displeased" by his behavior, nor objected to his going off with her for a weekend (MP 208). One night at dinner in New York

> I found myself sitting beside a very-good-looking young woman, whose name I was trying to wheedle out of her, while she was trying to find out who I was.
> (MP 368)

He discovers she is the married daughter of the millionaire Otto Kahn from whom he sought financing for a play in New York. But his efforts comically fail despite his later intrusion on a family dinner (MP 369–70).

Comedy, however, buffers his misogynistic views, romantic ambitions, and observations of the Russian Revolution. Two young girls in a family of ten thought every time a distant uncle, a retired general, visited, they had to stand at attention, click their heels, and bow stiffly (MP 206). Another mistress, who confuses him with her former, now dead, paramour, wishes he would play the role of the deceased lover. Admitting that "posing as a dead man" was not simple, "I did not become alive till, a year hence, my own passion for her was dead" (MP 207). He then translates his humor to the transport of his father's ashes in an urn in his haversack, imagining that a traveling cemetery, following one about, would be easier. From Innsbruck to Vienna he carried out his duty, rationalizing the action in this manner:

> From now on my father, reduced to a few ashes in a zinc receptacle, began to travel furiously all over Europe. He had, poor man, wished to do so when still alive and confined to his [wheel]chair. Now he covered mile after mile with a vengeance.
>
> (Memoirs 221)

For Gerhardie, comedy is a constant part of tragedy.

## ii

Born in St. Petersburg in 1895 and educated in Russia and England, William Gerhardie (originally Gerharidi) was the son of a successful British expatriate industrialist educated in four languages: Russian and German at school, English and French (with a nanny) at home. His first school, modeled on the German system, stressed math and natural sciences.

The mill owned by his father thrived and soon a new and elegant home with marble staircases and a ballroom plus a chef was built overlooking the Neva adjacent to the factory in St. Petersburg.[3] The 1905 revolution, however, meant Cossacks, a workers' revolt, and a family flight to Finland initiating a lifetime of Russian exits and entrances. They returned and until the revolution of 1917 lived elegantly, the father importing the first, difficult to drive, motor car to St. Petersburg. Their dacha, visited every summer, was in the seaside town of Sestroretsk. Their visible status and prosperity offered them a highspot in the Anglo-Russian hierarchy of St. Petersburg society (Davies 27). At fourteen, he began an autobiography largely in Russian, while an early adolescent infatuation led to the writing of his first novel at sixteen. Following his Russian education at a secondary school, Gerhardie's father explained to his son that a life in commerce was intended and he would be off to London where he went with his mother in the fall of 1913.[4] But St. Petersburg would overshadow all, recalling in 1953 that for him it was "a city of broad thoroughfares, immense squares, wide bridges, lunatic dreams" (Gerhardie in Davies 4).

In London, he soon found the free range of talk and the ability to explore the city intoxicating despite classes at Kensington College, a commercial school. By June he had completed a program in Pitman's shorthand; that month the Archduke of Austria was assassinated. Germany soon declared war on Russia; England, days later, declared war on Germany and Gerhardie, who had gone to St. Petersburg for the summer, could not return to England. He became a clerk in his father's office until he was able to re-enter his English school. He was twenty with new literary ambitions (Davies 45). But with the war on, he tried to enlist which he eventually succeeded in doing after he left the desultory commercial school and spent some time writing silent film scripts.

In November 1915, he joined the Scots Greys, the Tsar of Russia their colonel-in-chief. But he was an unfocused soldier, more interested in reading than playing cards or drilling. He soon requested a transfer, spent a short amount of time in Dublin and was then seconded, as a Russian-speaking officer, to teach Bulgarian which he soon learned (Davies 51–2). But his final order changed and he was sent to St. Petersburg, but not without a sword required, he was told, if he wanted to be taken seriously as an officer in Russia (Davies 52). In January 1917, he returned to an anarchic (and renamed) Petrograd with family life overturned because of economic calamities and a stroke suffered by his father (Davies 53–7). He went to the British Embassy daily and worked for Major Alfred Knox, the admirable and impressive military attaché who was to liaise between the Russian and British military (Davies 57–8).

As the Revolution began, Gerhardie put hope in Kerensky and the provisional government, while his brother Victor, now running the factory, did not. Gerhardie portrays much of the violence that followed in *Futility* in the "Intervening in Siberia" section. Passages in *Memoirs of a Polyglot*, his autobiography, also refer to the experience of the Revolution. Ironically, the Bolshevik headquarters, housing Lenin and Trotsky, was directly opposite the British Embassy on the other side of Neva, the former home of the ballet star Mathilde Kshesinskaya. Few at first took them seriously, and certainly not a new battalion of women soldiers loyal to Kerensky. But events soon deteriorated and by November, the Gerhardie family departed from the Finland Station for the last time (Davies 62). Later that day the cruiser *Aurora* shelled the Winter Palace. Kerensy escaped in a car flying the American flag.

But life in Petrograd continued even with the revolution: Gerhardie and his oldest sister, Rose, known as Rosie (she had married a Russian, Leonya), went together to the ballet and he went to a local brothel, as well as to the home of a young Jewish woman (now married) who had been his teenage infatuation. But at one point, he glimpsed her hateful attitude toward his British uniform. At that moment, he realized that love was subjective and transferable, revising his understanding of Russian love, "the recognition that our love does not belong to the being who inspired it" (Davies 65; MP 111).

In the year following the Revolution, the British Embassy began to evacuate, Gerhardie one of the last to depart. In March 1918, he and the staff left, escorted by train to the Finnish border, but skirmishes occurred and they abandoned the train for sleds, crossing into Finland waving a Union Jack and a white flag (Davies 67). On his return to England, he trained recruits while monitoring his family, all of whom had escaped to England. At the end of the war, however, the Allies still maintained a military mission in Siberia, supposedly protecting supplies from the Germans and maintaining the Trans-Siberia railroad, although the actual purpose was to manage the White Army to unseat the Reds, the Bolsheviks. Vladivostok became the headquarters of the Allied forces, needing further protection given the volatile and unstable political situation in the country.

Major Knox was then appointed the British military representative for Siberia in June 1918 and selected Gerhardie, then in England, as his aide. Gerhardie was suddenly responsible for provisioning the expedition, starting with additional staff and ending with blankets, foodstuffs, and rifles. The journey began with a crossing to the United States, landing in New York which he found fascinating and his presence appealing: in one city, he was thought to be the Prince of Wales. The group then journeyed to Vancouver and Victoria, B.C., boarding a ship to Yokohama. During the voyage, he began to work on what would be *Futility*, while his current experiences would form the opening of his second novel, *The Polyglots*. Nine days after they departed Yokohama, they arrived at Vladivostok, a multilingual city mixing Allied servicemen, ex-Tsarist officers "in grey greatcoats lined with scarlet silk," Russian soldiers, foreign consuls, businessmen, Chinese merchants, Cossacks, and ex-prisoners of war (Davies 75). But administrative work had to be done and under Knox's command, Gerhardie kept busy but when not busy socializing.

Politics, of course, intervened, the corruption of the Whites making allegiance difficult. Many in the interventionist forces were sympathetic to the Bolsheviks despite the supposed neutrality of the Allied forces (Davies 78–9). Gerhardie, with characteristic comedy, saw the event as "a series of comic opera attempts to wipe out the Russian revolution … an adventure in futility."[5] Neutrality was the pretense but feelings were different while actions resulted in farce. In a notebook, Gerhardie describes the futile attempt of Siberians to give themselves up. They ran toward the Bolsheviks who thought they were attacking and retreated. The Siberians had to run further and faster after the Bolsheviks to surrender (in D 79).

Although he did not fight, Gerhardie witnessed brutality, the result of executions and battles. Compassion and detachment coexisted. He came under fire several times. But his diary contains numerous *louche* entries mixing sport, love, and war. Disturbingly, in the midst of the corruption and crime, half of the people still starved. Yet comedy persisted: on a trip to Harbin, a Russian town in Chinese territory, in search of sheepskin coats ordered by Knox, he turned up nothing; a few weeks later, Knox wrote to say it was not coats but hats he had ordered. Nonetheless, he was able to enjoy the women of Harbin: "every other girl was passable; every third, good-looking; every fourth, a beauty" (Davies 81). But despite the dangers, there was monotony, although years later he would describe in detail the dances, dinners, concerts, and clouds of political unrest—and the women. Knox himself would remark that one Russian woman was worth ten Russian men (Davies 85). And it was back in Vladivostok where Gerhardie remet Nina and her sisters, the foundation of *Futility*.

During his Siberian excursion, Gerhardie found Russian love. In Vladivostok, he became involved with Lina Goldstein, a voluptuous and dark-haired woman who for many years after would send him photographs of herself with provocative messages. Ten years later, she appeared in London with her husband still seeking him out (Davies 86). But the three sisters of Vladivostok—Nina, Sonia, and Vera in the novel—took precedent, although they have not been biographically or conclusively identified (Davies 86). Gerhardie transforms them, however, into the three Bursanov sisters of *Futility*. Nina was his infatuation and although biographical details are fleeting, she was apparently flighty, charming and innocently provocative (Davies 86). Michael Holroyd, who spearheaded the re-issue of Gerhardie's work in the 1970s, claims that Gerhardie's captivating Nina is largely based on "a Russian girl he met and fell painfully in love with at a dance on board a battle ship in Siberia." Gerhardie reports this in *Memoirs of a Polyglot*, his autobiography.[6] But cavalierly dismissing the adventure, Gerhardie writes that "I think the only good Siberia has done to me is that it has taught me to foxtrot, which I enjoy thoroughly" (in Davies 88).

Gerhardie and love remain an intriguing subject, his biographer writing at one point that "ever amorous, [he] became passionately involved with an Italian countess … and also with her younger sister" (Davies 197). The sentence suggests something of Gerhardie's romantic inclinations, energy, and actions. Like Algernon Moncrieff in *The Importance of Being Earnest*, or des Esseintes in Huysmans' *A rebours*, posturing and love joined hands. Rarely could he resist a woman.

Vain about his appearance, he was tall and fair with penciled, dark eyebrows, he would even adopt the Edwardian habit, shared with T. S. Eliot, of powdering his face white (Davies 198). Fastidious behavior defines his movements, always using a clean handkerchief to wipe door handles. But he was obsessed with sexual conquests, one of his fantasies being sex in a taxi between Marble Arch and Paddington Station. When it did eventually happen, he claimed to the startled porter on seeing the disheveled couple on their arrival, "No, thank you, don't want a porter!" (Davies 200).

But as the outcome of the Russian civil war remained obscure, the Allied mission seemed more and more fruitless. The interventionists became unpopular, especially among the Russians. At last, the Allies agreed to withdraw. By February 1918 most had left, although Gerhardie and Knox remained until April but were unable to return through Soviet Russia. A train took them through Manchuria to Peking and then Nanking and Shanghai where Gerhardie surprisingly encountered Nina and her family but was met with indifference. They fought and he peremptorily left. He then sailed heartbroken to Hong Kong. From there, he went on, via Singapore and Colombo, to Port Said and Cairo writing what would be *Futility* and sightseeing. He returned to England to find a disconsolate family lacking an income and deciding to leave London for Bolton in Lancashire to be near their daughter, Dolly. Clara, the mother, opened a small dress shop. His father, afflicted by his stroke, did little; his old intimidating personality vanished. And Gerhardie? To Oxford and university: just before his twenty-fifth birthday, he went up with a draft of his first novel in hand.[7]

The young, battle-experienced, Russian-speaking Gerhardi made an unusual impression on his fellow students, especially his first-year roommate John Rothenstein, son of the well-known painter William Rothenstein:

> Gerhardi had the characteristic Russian urge to talk constantly about his fundamental beliefs and the most intimate aspects of his personal conduct. But his talk had nothing of the characteristic Russian idealism and largeness; it was as though conversations from Tolstoy, Turgenev and Dostoievski were parodied by some cynical member of the Goncourt circle. But Gerhardi carried his cynicism gaily; few people I have ever known have an acuter sense of the absurd.
>
> (Davies 110)

And it was Rothenstein who, in frustration in trying to title Gerhardie's novel, said in dismay "'Hell—I give up. Call it futility,' and stomped off" (Davies 100).

Rejection notices soon piled up; Hugh Walpole and Arnold Bennett were unable to help. He then thought of Katherine Mansfield and wrote to her. After some time, she replied with compliments and assisted in locating a publisher (Davies 112–14). Among changes, however, she suggested the removal of many Russian phrases to slightly streamline the text.[8] Through their extended correspondence, she also thought it might be "the moment for a book on tchehov," adding that people understand him very little.[9] He followed her suggestion and in 1923 published the first study of Chekhov in any language other than Russian; it appeared a few months after Mansfield's death. Publication of *Futility* in June 1922 coincided with his Oxford examinations in modern literature with a concentration in Russian (Davies 115).

*Futility* is a satire of Russian love presented with relief and sadness. The hero, a young English officer named Andrei Andreiech, in pursuit of love (or so he thinks it's love), journeys from London back to Vladivostok via Port Said, Colombo, Hong Kong, Shanghai, and Peking to find that his admired Nina remains as uncommitted as ever. Her only sign of affection is the naming of her canary after him. She then leaves for Europe. Liberated, he realizes he does not love her. This is a mini, almost satiric *Liebestod*, the term referencing Isolde's song over Tristan's body at the end of Wagner's opera and used by the narrator as the first line of the final section of the novel titled "Nina." It ironically underscores the love as death theme, the consummation of love in death.

But Gerhardie uses it comically: "was she *à moi*, or wasn't she? Well, was she? She was. She wasn't. Oh—how the hell could I know" Andrei asks (F 181). But his return to Vladivostok only brings his dismissal. All she can say is that he has a speck of soot on his nose (F 193). His response is equally comical and detached: "I was late in the season with my love—perhaps too late. Tristan became a thing alien and remote, and I felt that I was singing in an altogether different opera" (F 194). In the final pages, Nina and her sisters depart for Shanghai, Andrei wistfully going to the dock to see the ship off not in terms of a romantic departure but as a ship leaving a dock piled with barrels, pipes, rusting wire, and machinery. The anti-romantic departure in "dull, dirty water," without even smoke from the steamer visible on the horizon, ends the novel. The English/Russian lover parodies Russian love.

*Futility* was the novel Edith Wharton enjoyed when traveling from Victoria Station to Paris. She wrote him a note of praise but he admits in his memoir that he had not heard of her and believed she might be "a lovely flapper polishing off her French at a Paris finishing school" (MP 199). But he quickly discovered her work, wrote an acceptable reply, and soon received an invitation to visit her at Hyères where he immediately disrupted the plumbing when he flushed bread and butter down the toilet. And after spending a day with her in her garden, he failed to recognize her at dinner because she was without her garden hat. He repeatedly but politely kept asking when would the hostess arrive only to be told "*I* am the hostess" (MP 201).

Finally, there was disagreement over the pronunciation of his name. Wharton asked if it was with a hard or soft "g." He said soft and she instantly dropped the "h" in the middle calling him Mr. Gerardy. He protested and she told him he couldn't have it both ways. A soft "g" with the "h" in the middle was a philological impossibility. He comically resolved the dispute by claiming that he would pronounce his name "Jerhardy" on Mondays, Wednesdays, and Fridays; "Gherhardy" on Tuesdays, Thursdays, and Saturdays; "but on Sunday, which is the day of rest, let it be 'Jeerady'" (MP 202).

The Chekhovian themes of *Futility* and narrative of Vladivostok made it a success. In the novel, characters repeatedly seek purpose similar to Irina in *The Three Sisters* who complains that she and her sisters have no sense of work: that is why "we are not happy and look at life so gloomily." Nikolai Vasilievich in *Futility* also repeats that he wants to act—"We ought to *do* things. I want *to* do things"—but that does not happen.[10] He prefers to sit and worry. He is part of a social class that cannot keep up with change and is incapable of reacting to the disintegration of their life. The family turmoil and muddle parallel that of the public which Uncle Kostia summarizes as an "ethical confusion" where "the blind habitually resort to bloodshed as a means of straightening it out." "More confusion" is the only result tinged with melancholy (F 79).[11]

*The Polyglots* (1925) continued Gerhardie's satire of Russian love, partly using material not included in *Futility* beginning with the narrator's repeatedly postponed marriage to Sylvia. She eventually marries a bore but her mother prevents the consummation of the match, while the hero, a young writer, manages to sleep with her on the wedding night. They then go off together to Europe, leaving the husband behind. This overturns conventional ideas of marriage, commitment, love, and even sex parallel to the unconventional trope of Russian love described as an unfinished romance.

The novel turns everything into comedy à la a French farce, while echoing Chekhov who in his notebook wrote that love is either a remnant of something degenerating, something which once has been immense, or... a particle of what will in the future develop into something immense; but in the present it is unsatisfying; it gives much less than one expects.[12]

"Unsatisfying" in the present is the keynote. Offsetting this is Proust's enigmatic quote cited by Gerhardie in his autobiography, *Memoirs of a Polyglot*: "A woman we desire, by causing us to suffer, draws out of us a series of feelings differently profound..." (MP 169). To process these often contradictory feelings, Gerhardie wrote the comical first sentence of *Futility*: "And then it struck me that the only thing to do was to fit all this into a book" (F 15).

A young woman Gerhardie met in Westbourne Grove in June 1918, just before he headed to Siberia, became the basis for Sylvia, a key figure in *The Polyglots*. On his return in 1920, he resumed the relationship while at Oxford, although she was not his cousin and had not been to the Orient as presented in the novel. She was Irish and lived in London with her sister (MP 166–7). In typical style, he also wrote love letters to a Nina while involved with "Sylvia," adding, dismissively, that neither woman had much to say (MP 167). His sexism was unbounded, explaining that he won Nina via a Gogolesque story about a man who cut off his nose while shaving (MP 167). "A woman does not fully exercise our spirit," he states, "unless she be attractive enough for us to desire her and so stupid that her ways must seem to us inscrutable. Intelligent women only attract men more stupid than themselves" (MP 168–9). Chauvinistically, he writes that poets and writers prefer women of physical beauty, those with "fragrant simplicity" mixing "the naïve and natural" (MP 168).

In Gerhardie, domestic and political dramas are always at play. Part of the comedy and satire of Russian love is that when Andrei meets the Bursanov family in *Futility*, his response to their romantic and financial problems is to diagram their domestic politics showing who should marry whom and how to satisfy the various financial and marital demands (F 56–8). He matches himself, the practical British-Sino figure, with Nina, the naïve, or at least innocent, figure who might also be the possible future of Russia (Nina responds with mockery when later told of this). He also suggests new pairings: Nikolai and his wife Magda become divorced; Nikolai marries Fanny giving her the respectability she deserves, while he permits the young Zena to live with them. Andrei and Nina marry.

Andrei undertakes this reordering in the novel as a "worthy mission" as he works to "arbitrate; to *settle* things" (F 59). But Nina again deflates his purpose: what business is it of yours, she asks? She makes fun of him, while all react to the reordering of their lives in frustration turning everything into farce. For example, Nikolai, the father, thinks the chart Andrei has prepared is tactless and makes fun of his family; as a consequence, he rips up both the chart and diagram (F 61). Andrei reacts by telling Nina everyone is no more than a laughable character from Chekhov and he will write a new *Three Sisters* using the family as its improbable characters, telling them, in exasperation,

> don't you silly people realize how utterly laughable you all are?... Can't you see yourselves?.... What's there to prevent some mean, unscrupulous scribbler, who cares less for people than for his art, from writing you up?
>
> (F 62)

With comic confidence, the narrator then declares "I feel I am almost capable of doing it myself." Of course, he does (F 62).

The moment also allows Andrei/Gerhardie a chance to explain that the trouble with "modern literature" is that "no fiction is good fiction unless it is true to life, and yet no life is worth relating unless it be a life out of the ordinary; and then it seems improbable like fiction" (F 62). He then dramatically leaves, hoping Nina will stop him. She does not, which is a good thing since his horse, Professor Metchnikoff, moves only backwards, not forward. His exit is itself a parody of a romantic departure.

Matching this energetic love play, however, is a sense of Chekhovian resignation, expressed in reaction to the war and love. But the Chekhovian irony is that entanglements are never resolved. Andrei Andreiech's four-year pursuit of Nina, to whom he is supposedly engaged, remains inconclusive. Love hasn't evaporated; it's just been suspended.

From Chekhov, subject of his 1923 study, Gerhardie developed a unique sense of fiction, favoring impartiality rather than plots of intense moral purpose as in Tolstoy. "To Chehov [sic] literature is life made intelligible by the discovery of form" Gerhardie writes of the dramatist, a writer who sees "life in the aggregate: which aspect, in truth, is his form."[13] Gerhardie here parallels Woolf and her ideas in "Modern Fiction" when he writes that in Chekhov "life is more complex, fluid and elusive ... than we had privately suspected to be told by others, much less to see in print."[14]

This view extends to his sense of structure, as the novelist/narrator of *Resurrection* explains: "My books are built up, not like a house, brick by brick, but like a body, cell by cell simultaneously, in all directions."[15] Of *Futility*, he later said that the plot of the book is the recognition that "there is no plot in real life!"[16] As Fanny Ivanovna, mistress of Nikolai Bursanov, exclaims, "we waited for an explosion. But it never came …. Life drags on: a series of compromises" (F 220–1). Literature needs form but life has none.

The repetitious or aggregate sense of order explains Gerhardie's reliance on juxtaposition and contrast without a seeming build-up of action. But it also explains the strength of his writing and its energetic presentation of character that may at first seem at odds with one another. But in *Futility*, he is able to mesh three plot lines: the social-political (Russia in turmoil), the familial (the confusions and complexity of the Bursanov family), and the personal (the desire and hopes of the protagonist, Andrei Andreiech).

But love disrupts these actions on multiple levels. Early in *Futility* it is the affair between Fanny Ivanova and Nikolai Vasilievich, the latter separated from his wife. The two meet in Basle and fall in love but the consequences of a divorce—Nikolai would be unable to see his children—force them into a common-law relationship. This is an introduction to the complications and compromises (and disappointments) of love in the novel where the longing for marriage never disappears: "in my secret heart I wanted his divorce so much," Fanny confides to Andrei. But the children must come first (F 31). But after eleven years, love has unraveled: the 53-year-old Nikolai now wants to marry a girl of seventeen, a classmate of his daughter Sonia. "It is love, this time, *real* love," he tells Fanny, emphasizing its powerful, romantic hold on a man who, even if married to Zena, ironically believes he can return nightly to Fanny and his daughters (F 33, 35). Love is here satirized and intensified by the belief that Nikolai's investment in Siberian goldmines has made, or might make him, rich. Like love, they are a fraud but one everyone pursues (F 40).

Compounding the confusion is that Nikolai's actual wife is living with a former actor turned unsuccessful dentist, Eisenstein. But she plans to leave him as the plot turns into a low-key French farce à la Molière or Feydeau. Andrei, in fact, compares the action of one evening to a "three-act soul-shattering melodrama. It was to be a night of bells and sobs" (F 45). At one point, there is direct reference to their proposed affairs (outlined by Andrei) as a farce which reaches comical proportions when Nikolai's seventeen-year-old wife-to-be proposes new relief from his multiple financial burdens: "we should commit suicide together" (F 61, 52, 65). Farcically topping this is Zina's Uncle Kostia who is a writer but at middle age has yet to publish a single line (F 53). History and philosophy are his specialties, and he spends his days supposedly thinking, but never communicating, to anyone—yet everyone believes he is clever (F 53–4). This is a marvelous parody of a scholar and another illusion in the play.

Life for the Bursanovs remains muddled: Nikolai, in pursuit of his anticipated youthful wife, has fled his family responsibilities only to enter new ones with Zina's family (F 55), while Andrei believes he can help. Another twist is that it soon becomes known that Nikolai would *not* lose the children through a divorce. He only uses that as an excuse to avoid marrying Fanny (F 48). But when Andrei encounters Magda, Nikolai's wife, he learns that *she* now wants to marry an Austrian named Cecedek. She is running away from Eisenstein, the dentist. In this novel, one repeatedly runs *from*, rather than *to*, love, which will occur in the final chapter with Nina departing for Shanghai while Andrei revels in his new freedom, not loss: "I longed to see the end of it, to know that they had gone" (F 204). He repeatedly visits the wharf to be sure their ship has left, until at twilight it had, with only dirty remnants of the sea left to wash up to the pier. Here, Gerhardie overturns the trope of Russian love: no longer genuine longing for the absent lover but relief that she was gone.

Love postponed or erased is the fate of Andrei and Nina, her actions becoming more willful and prolonged so that, at the end of the novel, separation, not union triumphs. Love becomes the embodiment of misplaced hope, the characters, like those in Chekhov cited by the narrator, "born on the line of demarcation between comedy and tragedy" (Beasley 423; F 18). In Gerhardie, his Chekhovian narrator confronts a Dostoevskian world of disappointment and reversal (Beasley 425). And as the novel proceeds, literary allusions increase, from Oscar Wilde and, of course, Chekhov to Gogol (F 52), all shields to protect one from the emotions of love.

*Futility*, however, also takes note of the Russian Revolution expressed through Gerhardie's tone of wonder and disbelief as all the groups sought to put down each other (F 74–5). Seconded to Petrograd and the British Embassy, Andrei watches the change as crowds of tumultuous soldiers and civilians "alike walked aimlessly rifle slung over the shoulder" (F 75). There were drunkards in the streets but "all seemed drunk with the revolution." Shots were occasionally heard "while the law courts had gone up in flames" (F 75–6). In this, the second part of the novel, history, politics, and revolution step forward but casually, while the Bursanovs and romance recede. The three sisters remain the same, although Fanny has married an elderly Russian gentleman of German extraction (F 77). With a touch of boredom, Fanny asks, "who *wants* the revolution" (F 78)?

Stasis seems to reign: the sisters, "always sitting in the same positions, perched on sundry chairs and sofas," don't move (F 80). The seasons would shift but not their positions with Fanny cogently expressing a central Chekhovian tenet: "how tiring this is …. to be always waiting to begin to *live*" (F 80). When will that splendid life begin? Anticipating a Beckettian malaise, all the characters wait but they are not sure for what: "there's got to be something, somewhere, sometime," they lament (F81). But there is only "indefinite waiting for indefinite things" (F 82). Money has also dried up. All Nikolai does is borrow and increase his debt. Their life (and the text) itself intensifies its Chekhovian dimension.

But Chapter IV of Part II is the morning of the Revolution, cold with drizzling snow, Uncle Kostia assuring others that the revolution was more than what the Bolsheviks bargained for. Honor and bloodshed pointlessly mix. But while the political revolution bypasses the Bursanovs, a domestic revolution begins: Nikolai's bookkeeper had been falsifying the books and robbing him—yet he does not let him go (F 84).

Part III of the novel, "Intervening in Siberia," is the longest and shifts the focus from romance to "a series of comic opera attempts to wipe out the Russian revolution" (F 91). The experience was "an adventure in futility" but also offers a marvelous sense of being alive according to the energetic narrator (F 91). The text narrates the futile attempts of the British and the Americans in Vladivostok to overturn the Bolsheviks. A comedy of errors follows, including the unexpected discovery of Nikolai and his three daughters in the city plus every immediate and distant family member. They are following him because they need his financial support (F 93). And his Siberian gold mines? Taken over by the workers and the government (F 95–8). Only a proper distracting ball relieves the dismal family prospects; the gold mines and love prove to be only illusions (F107–9).

*Futility*, the epitome of the tragicomic, was rejected by a series of publishers before Katherine Mansfield, ill in a Swiss sanitorium, read it and managed to place it with a publisher. She told Gerhardie that "it is a living thing. What I mean by that is, it is warm; one can put it down and it goes on breathing" (Davies 113).

Read and praised by H.G. Wells in 1923 in the *Adelphi*, Edith Wharton also soon became a fan and wrote to Gerhardie that it was the best thing she read about Russia since *Oblomov*. But as Frank Kermode observed, while "*Futility* is a Russian novel," it is actually "Chekhov naturalized," focusing on three Russian sisters (K 312). Anticipating Kermode's remark was the effort of American publishers to promote the book: it was sold in theaters during Russian performances of *Three Sisters* by the touring Moscow Arts Players. Many in the audience believed that the Chekhov was no more than a dramatized version of the novel (Davies 122).

*Futility* expands, inverts, examines, upholds, satirizes, and respects the ideal and practice of Russian love, part of its appeal. The roundelay of lovers, married and not, challenges the idea of Russian love as focusing on a single lover as seen in Turgenev or even Tolstoy. And what makes it all acceptable and even enjoyable is Gerhardie's comic tone mixing irony with pathos. The unfocussed lives of these characters, especially the three sisters, create a tragicomedy that revises our ideas of what Russian love is, which becomes as much as an inconvenience as an ideal.

*Futility* clearly deflates Russian love. When the protagonist persists in pronouncing his love to Nina late in the novel, she rebuffs him, but in a distracting, non-emotional manner. He then tells her it's taken him three months to return to Vladivostok to see her: "I have been three months on the way … three months. Good god, Nina travelling *three months* to come and see you—and there!" She comically replies that "It was an unusually long journey. You must have been moving very slowly." Frustrated, he responds:

> "There!" I went on protestingly, "I chuck Oxford, come all the way to Vladivostok, spend three months on the journey—because—because I love you, and you—"
> "You have a speck of soot on your nose," she remarked.
>
> (F 193)

All Nina can do to honor his affection is to name her canary after him (F 193).

And love? In fragmented conversations it is pushed aside as the narrator overhears Nikolai tell Fanny of his feelings for Zina: "I thought that I had loved, I *had* loved *you*, Fanny, but this is the love that comes once only, to which you yield gloriously" (F 130). But a statement midway in the novel, also by Nikolai, more accurately expresses the revisionist treatment of Russian love: "it is easier to hope knowing that one will be disappointed, than not hope at all" (F 86). This jaded view contradicts the excitement, optimism, and commitment to love seen in Turgenev's *First Love* or Chekhov's "The Kiss," or even his "Little Game."

In the spectrum of Russian love and Anglo-Russian writers, Gerhardie steps away from the conventional representation of the love situation and offers angles of satire and even parody against the backdrop of farce which, he claims, comes about "in the proper constitutional way, through a string of human motives" (F 119). His unique origins may have encouraged this distant view, recognizing that social status was one of those motives, confirmed by the comic and competitive efforts of the entire Bursanov family to have coupés (sleeping rooms or couchettes) for their train journey to Omsk, another farcical situation (F 119–20).

But Gerhardie did not strictly give up on love, although his commitment to Russian love had disappeared by 1936 when he published *Of Mortal Love*, a novel about loneliness, something he was experiencing himself (Davies 301). *Of Mortal Love* was a "simple love story" of an aspiring composer's love for the unhappily married Dinah, unable to decide what to do, although a casual love affair becomes real love (Davies 305). Gerhardie himself described the book as a fresh treatment of "love-lore" and how love moves from the erotic to the imaginative; of love becoming unselfish; of love becoming something transfigured (in Davies 305). Gerhardie is the model for the hero, Walter, while Dinah is the young Vera Boys, the most beautiful woman in London, according to Lord Beaverbrook.

Boys and Gerhardie met at the theater and soon began a relationship. She was spirited, spontaneous, and vulnerable (Davies 272). One of her goals was to appear in celebrity magazines which she apparently did. Gerhardie's affair with her, however, led to the husband suing for divorce, citing Gerhardie as co-respondent. Gerhardie, worried about the costs of defending such a suit (he always had money difficulties), prevaricated in going forward, despite being tracked by the husband's detective. But the threat was mitigated in a late Edwardian manner when Boys invited her husband to her flat and seduced him. The divorce went ahead but was uncontested, although Gerhardie remained a co-respondent, but Boys, previously deeply committed to Gerhardie, began to find another man more appealing. This only intensified Gerhardie's feelings for her and he redoubled his efforts to win her back. He did not, while she blamed his sense of delay for the failure played out in *Of Mortal Love*:

> "I thought we'd get married."
> "Its too late now. You should have thought of it before."
> "I did."
> "Well, if you did you kept it to yourself."
>
> (OML 191)

In a gesture of self-respect, Gerhardie would actually visit Boys to tell her he no longer cared for her and that he longed for another (imaginary) woman.

But in the midst of his social entanglements, Gerhardie remained enmeshed with Russia largely through family, attempting to get his older sister Rosie out. Stalin's purges were by now (1935) underway. Gerhardie wrote to his acquaintance Gorky to intervene; he forwarded his letter of appeal to the Soviet State Press who transferred 960 roubles to Rosie for the Russian translation of *The Polyglots*. With that she could pay the fee for an exit permit.

He then wrote to H.G. Wells enclosing a copy of his novel *Resurrection* and asking if Wells might send a word to Stalin. He could not and did not since he had criticized the dictator. But with further Foreign Office interventions, Rosie was allowed to leave for England; he hadn't seen her for fourteen years. And Vera Boys? She became a secretary for Lord Beaverbrook and advisor on women's dress and cookery. But she also became the model for Dinah in *Of Mortal Love*.

By the time her divorce was settled, Vera Boys had lost interest in Gerhardie, much like the love affairs in his fiction which are always whimsical, temporal, and undependable. There is almost a fear of traditional Russian love, overpowering, all-consuming but also, in the end, disappointing. In the novel, Dinah is capricious, elusive, vain, mercurial (like Nina in *Futility*), while Walter is uncertain and vacillates. His infatuation remains sustained more by what she represents rather than who she is. But her own efforts to plot her life go wrong, parallel to Walter's efforts to succeed. Expressing why love in Gerhardie fails, Walter realizes that love always has a hidden dimension:

> There was her unknown life of which he had merely seen the face, the dear familiar hieroglyphics he knew so well but could not read—the voucher, faithful and exact, for her unknown life.
>
> (OML 289)

The imagery is fascinating, mixing the external with the internal, the obvious with the unseen linked to the economics of love where a "voucher" is no guarantee of a return on one's emotional investment. Love has become a wall he cannot climb. He understands that he cannot know her, "could never know her, however much he listened to her and stared at her" which may be the condition of this revised idea of Russian love: the recognition that full possession is impossible and that it is futile to secure it. Paradoxically, Walter sees through what has become the hoax of love, a certain knowledge or awareness often unknown or protected from Russian lovers.

Old love fades, even when the narrator explains that "now that she had been deeply hurt herself she began to feel a growing tenderness for him whom she had hurt." Walter feels, however, that she was becoming what he feared she would be if they were married: "an intension of himself, of his anxieties," no longer a "toy of passion" but one "who leaned on him for support." He loved her because she was "young, and beautiful and foolish" but humiliated by another admirer (OML 231). Walter now disguises his feelings, becoming gruff, believing it "best to clear the system of filmy self-pity" because "fatal love … [can be] diagnosed as a form … of temporary insanity" (OML 232).

But there is always comedy; late in the novel Dinah laments that all the men she gets engaged to die: "Howard Blundon, Mark Stropher. Isn't it awful? I wonder who next? I hope it's me: I'm *so* depressed" (OML 284). For respite, she calls Rex Ottercove, modeled on Beaverbrook, who is always at ease, largely because he has "£100,000 a year" (OML 284). But at the end, diphtheria isolates Dinah from everyone. When Walter is permitted at last to see her in hospital, she is disheveled, thin and without allure, reminding him of Marguerite in the prison scene from *Faust* (OML 295). Finally moved to a private hospital, she acts like a young society matron with her visitors, including her three suitors: Walter, Jim, and Eric. But even as she makes a slow recovery and Walter suggests a trip to Italy and marriage, Dinah vacillates (as Walter had) and can't decide among her three admirers (OML 303). And then she dies, almost before the eyes of the three men, now dazed and surprised. Three weeks after her cremation, while walking about the city on a Saturday night, Walter is able at last to see her whole in a vision. But he also realizes that love is random, without permanence and entirely mortal (OML 321).

In the novel, Russia has receded, consisting only of interspersed references to life after the revolution often through figures who managed to leave, with one or two eager to return. A reference to Diaghilev's Russian ballet, however, does appear (OML 299). But Russia, while it may have fashioned the past of various characters, no longer has agency. But it did for Gerhardie, expressed in *The Romanovs* (1939), a dramatic 542-page history of their rise and fall, and *God's Fifth Column* (1981), his incomplete history of the period 1890–1940. It contains chapters on Chekhov, Tolstoy, Tchaikovsky, and several on Lenin. Occasionally, there are odd pairings: Chapter 26 is "Nicholas II, Lenin, Oscar Wilde," a combination continued in Chapter 28, "Singing Captives." Other chapters focus on "The Spirit of Modern Russia," with a further oddity: Chapter 92, "Hitler and Gertrude Stein." Anecdotally prolonging his Russian identity was his daily lunch from Admiral Volkoff's Russian Restaurant, a short distance from his London flat (Davies 274). But Russia would not leave him alone.

During the war, having turned down a job with British Intelligence, he was offered work at the BBC who planned to start broadcasting to Russia. But no Russian section was formed; instead, he adapted and edited English news for broadcasts to Czechoslovakia. His knowledge of the language was limited so he merely distorted his Russian so it might resemble Czech, a typical Gerhardie gesture (Davies 335).

In the meantime, his brother Victor had moved from Russia to Finland while his sister Rosie, married to a Russian, had remained (Davies 209–10). Clara, their mother, visited Rosie in Russia in late 1928 and sought to remove her from Russia to Finland for medical treatment. She received a one month permit in August 1929. Gerhardie then urged her to defect to England but she would not, although she sent one of her children with Clara to England when she (Rosie) had to return to Leningrad. But as conditions deteriorated for her and her family, plagued by illness and lack of proper work, Gerhardie sent provisions and money *c.* 1931–2 until she did obtain a permit to leave Russia for England, arriving in March 1935 (Davies 212, 266). But England soon lost its allure and she missed her husband who remained behind. England was dull and she found no work. Despite its poverty and uncertain, Russia, with its free medicine—her daughter Galina was disabled and required constant attention—still appealed. Seven months after Rosie's arrival, she returned.

In February 1938, however, the secret police stormed her apartment and arrested her husband without stating a crime. Rosie was distraught. Gerhardie responded by writing letters and making phone calls to free her husband and herself from Russia. G.B. Shaw could do little, the Foreign Office less; the British Ambassador in Moscow feared that any intervention might mean Rosie's internal exile which was proposed at one point. She was allowed to stay in Leningrad by good luck (Davies 318–19). But in the midst of this, Gerhardie could not himself renounce Russia or his own past and agreed to a suggestion in the fall of 1937 to write a history of the Romanovs, largely because he could secure a £500 advance as noted above. This would be published in 1939 in the United States and 1940 in England.

*The Romanovs* opens with "An Historical Credo" where he criticizes the abstract in historical writing which overlooks or even discards the individual. History, he argues, must be "*morally* accurate—accurate in the relation of what has been done to what has been suffered," arguing that the historian's own point of view or personality must be present and to eliminate the "bloated solemnity" of historical presentation.[17] His own style mixes the dramatic with the abstract and detailed:

> The Romanov genius indeed has never been political, having in the space of three hundred years evolved nothing more constitutional than absolute monarchy tempered by assassination. Nicholas was pushed not merely off the throne, but out of life.
>
> (Romanovs 32)

Narrating the collapse of Russian absolutism is his goal told through the Romanovs' rise and fall.

And Rosie? She and her daughter survived the siege of Leningrad and eventually settled in a communal apartment in the postwar city, although her husband had died in an Arctic labor camp (Davies 360). Rosie lived on until 1969.

But Vera Boys lingered. As late as 1972, when she was sixty-five and about to marry for the fourth time, she called Gerhardie to renew their relationship. He declined. He also declined an offer from the *Daily Telegraph* to visit Russia and write a series of articles, although he needed the funds. He chose not to revisit the world of his youth and its illusions; the visit might also endanger Rosie who had returned to Russia in October 1935 to join her imprisoned husband, Leonya (Davies 370).

The status of Russian love for Gerhardie alternates between the deadly serious and marvellously playful which in the end becomes a modernist form of engagement and disengagement. A late conversation in *Futility* captures the tone. Meeting Nina accidentally in a Vladivostok street, Andrei straightforwardly asks:

> "Will you marry me?"
> "No." She shook her head. "I am tired of you."
> "I know that," I replied, and walked silently beside her.
> "If I were really tired of you I wouldn't tell you."
> "Then why do you tell me?" I took it up hungering for something positive, however, small.
> "I don't always say what I think" was the answer.
> She walked on.
> "We are leaving in any case," she said. (F 199)

Happiness may lie in "grounding the soul in the optics of contemplative love" but emotional reality and disillusionment habitually come along to shatter the moment.[18] Contradiction defines the above exchange with the departure of the Bursanovs both imminent and anticlimactic. The action, which should be *fortissimo*, is *diminuendo*. This also becomes the fate of Russian love, diminished, receding, and fading, at least in the eyes of an Anglo-Russian writer. The Bursanov family departs for Shanghai; the lady and love vanish.

In his "Imaginary Letters," originally titled "Letters from Petrograd," Wyndham Lewis wrote that "The Russian factor is quite curious in this game. It is really, much more than the other countries, a theater to itself, carrying on a play of quite a different description." Gerhardie regularly attended such performances from the moment of his St. Petersburg birth and could not, or did not, ever want to leave the theater.[19]

## Notes

1. An earlier version of this laconic sentence is "Played tennis in the afternoon; then had a woman; then a bath, and afterwards witnessed a revolution." Gerhardie in Davies 80.
2. William Gerhardie, *Memoirs of a Polyglot* (1931; London: Robin Clark, 1990), 142. Hereafter MP. The tone reminds one of Kafka's well-known diary entry of August 2, 1914: "Germany has declared war on Russia. Went swimming in the afternoon."
3. Dido Davies, *William Gerhardie, A Biography* (Oxford: Oxford University Press, 1990), 25–7. Hereafter Davies.
4. There are broad parallels with Vladimir Nabokov born four years after Gerhardie in St. Petersburg. He was also multilingual and began to write at an early age. Like Gerhardie, he was also educated in England, although as an exile. The October Revolution caused both families to leave Russia, although Gerhardie's returned until 1918. Nabokov received his degree in French and Russian literature from Cambridge. Gerhardie went to Oxford. Several critics have suggested that Nabokov used Gerhardie's study of Chekhov for his lectures on literature. Both Nabokov and Gerhardie died in the same month and year: Nabokov in Montreux on July 2, 1977, Gerhardie on July 15 in London. One was acclaimed, the other forgotten.

   For general similarities, see Davies 21–2. Gerhardie declined to meet Nabokov in London in 1937 when the latter was to read from *Despair* and his autobiography (Davies 312).
5. William Gerhardie, *Futility, A Novel on Russian Themes*. Preface Michael Holroyd (1922; London: Macdonald, 1971), 91. Hereafter F.
6. Michael Holroyd, "Preface," *Futility* (London: Macdonald, 1971), 10. Gerhardie, *Memoirs of a Polyglot*, 150, 167–8.
7. For details on his Oxford life and how he spoke English with Russian intonations, see Davies 93–101. His early efforts at finding a publisher for *Futility* are also retold.
8. On the Wharton/Gerhardie relationship see Gladys Mary Coles, "Katherine Mansfield and W. Gerhardie," *Contemporary Review* 229 (1976): 32–40 and Randall Craig, "Edith Wharton and William Gerhardie," *Journal of Modern Literature* 16.4 (1990): 597–614.
9. Mansfield in Coles 35. In another note, she explains that "The Garden Party," praised by Gerhardie, attempts to convey "the diversity of life and how we try to fit in everything, Death included." Life is not ordered, nor even segregated into compartments; events do all happen at once: "it is inevitable. And it seems to me there is beauty in that inevitability." Mansfield in Coles 37.
10. Chekhov, *The Three Sisters*, tr. Stark Young (New York: Samuel French, 1941), 26. Gerhardie, *Futility*, 78.

11 For criticism stressing the Chekhovian elements of the novel, see Hena Maes-Jelinek, "William Gerhardie," *Criticism of Society in the English Novel between the Wars* (Liège: Presses universitaires de Liège, 1970), 283–300.
12 Chekhov in Frank Kermode, "On William Gerhardie," *The Uses of Error* (Cambridge: Harvard University Press, 1991), 313. Hereafter Kermode.
13 Gerhardie, *Anton Chekhov A Critical Study* (London: Cobden-Sanderson, 1923), 58.
14 Gerhardie, *Chekhov,* 106–8, 14; also see Rebecca Beasley, *Russomania, Russian Culture and the Creation of British Modernism, 1881–1922* (Oxford: Oxford University Press, 2020), 418–19. Hereafter Beasley.
15 Gerhardie, *Resurrection* (London: Cassell, 1934), 25.
16 Gerhardie to his parents in Davies, *William Gerhardie,* 119.
17 Gerhardie, *The Romanovs, Evocation of the Past as a Mirror for the Present* (London: Rich & Cowan, 1940), 20–1. Hereafter, Romanovs.

   Despite the size of the work, Gerhardie maintains a strong sense of structure. At the end of Chapter XXVIII (p. 510), his final sentence reads "the sequel is known from the opening chapter of this narrative, and it only remains to tell of the final pilgrimage to Siberia and the end" (Romanov 510). Dramatic irony rules buttressed by introspection. After his sensitive description of the execution of Nicholas II and his family, Gerhardie becomes philosophical in an attempt to understand why such acts occur, leaving the reader at the end puzzling over the insoluble future (Romanovs 530–2).
18 Gerhardie, "Bibliographical Note" in Randall Craig, "The Early Fiction of William Gerhardie," *Novel* 15.3 (1982): 256.
19 Wyndham Lewis, "Petrograd Letters," published in the *Little Review* as "Imaginary Letters." Qtd. in Beasley 427.

## *Interlude*: Edmund Wilson: In Love with Lenin

"Break down the walls of the present."

Edmund Wilson, *Axel's Castle* (1931)

Edmund Wilson's declaration at the end of *Axel's Castle*, his study of literary modernism, provides an introduction to his 1940 study on the writing and acting of history, *To the Finland Station*. The work begins with Michelet and ends with Lenin at the moment of his triumphal 1917 return to the Finland Station in Petrograd. It is a work variously described as novelistic, inaccurate, and immensely readable, but it is also a love story, focusing on Lenin, Wilson's personal life, and the relation of historical practice to the meaning of history—with several additional romances thrown in.

Trotsky offers a prelude. In his *History of the Russian Revolution*, he asks what would have happened if Lenin had not managed to return to Russia in April 1917?

> Is it possible… to say confidently that the party without him would have found its road? We would by no means make bold to say that… a disorientated and split party might have let slip the revolutionary opportunity for many years.[1]

In a letter to economist and sociologist Yevgeni Preobrazhensky, Trotsky had also written that "You know better than I do that had Lenin not managed to come to Petrograd in April 1917, the October Revolution would not have taken place."[2] And Wilson would likely not have had a story.

*To the Finland Station* follows a narrative arc climaxing with Lenin's return while detailing the emergence of revolutionary socialism and its fate in Europe and Russia. This occurs against the background of Russian love and love for Russia, while Wilson adds several Russian love stories of his own: Marx's love for Jenny von Westphalen and Lenin's for Nadézhda Krúpskaya, but also his attachment to Inessa Fédorovna Armand. These are the starting points but Wilson also incorporates his own romantic Russian encounters, underscored by the trope of unfulfilled Russian love with Lenin and Wilson at the center. What begins as Lenin's fulfilling marriage with Krúpyskaya, for example, becomes a complicated relation since Lenin also had a long and even more satisfying relationship with his mistress, Inessa Armand. *To the Finland Station* begins as the history of an idea but quickly becomes a romance.[3]

More concretely and directly, Wilson concentrates on Lenin as an idealized hero in a work that contextualizes his life before the revolution begins and climaxes at the anteroom of action, the Finland Station. In fact, Lenin is the very center of the book which becomes almost a remaking of the Communist leader. Wilson's inscription of a copy of the book to Nabokov made this absolutely clear. It reads "to Vladimir Nabokov in the hope that this may make him think better of Lenin."[4] As part of the narrative, and to provide authenticity for the project, Wilson marks his own romantic adventures during his 1935 Russian trip which includes a visit to Ulyanovsk, Lenin's early home.[5] The undercarriage of *To the Finland Station* is the role and performance of the individual in the drama of history which has a distinct plot according to both Marx and Wilson. Actions in the Marxist universe have a purpose.

But other love affairs catch Wilson's attention, notably Marx and his wife Jenny von Westphalen, a political activist who devoted herself to Marx and the promotion of his ideas. Their life of poverty, despite her aristocratic origins (Marx himself was an educated Prussian), tested both their commitments to marriage and ideology. They had seven children, although only three daughters lived to maturity; two of them later committed suicide. Marx also had a son he did not claim with the long-serving family housekeeper Helene Demuth, buried in the Marx plot in Highgate Cemetery in London.

Jenny became secretly engaged to Marx in Berlin at age twenty-two; he was eighteen. On their honeymoon in 1843, Marx brought forty-five books to study, fashioning two of his principal ideas: religion was the opium of the people and that only the proletariat could emancipate society. Over time, Marx became the headlight of Communism but it was a relentless struggle.[6] Marx had been expelled from country after country and ended up as a refugee with his family in damp and unwelcoming London in 1849. But Lenin, seconded by Engels, is Wilson's pivot to shift the theme from politics to romance, the engine of the story, anticipated by a novelistic style supported by metaphor.

As Wilson describes it, love for Lenin was a test of physical and moral courage. Isolated and exiled to Siberia, and demoralized by the recent suicides of friends like the Marxist N. E. Fedoséyev, Lenin had encouraged the companionship and support of the radical Nadezhda Krúpskaya, whom he married, even though the radical youth of his party despised marriage as a bourgeoise institution. On principle, they opposed legal marriage but Lenin and Krúpskaya did so because only if married could she legitimately remain with him.

The daughter of a former military governor in Poland, Krúpskaya became a governess and graduated from a small woman's college in St. Petersburg. She taught geography in a workers' Sunday school and joined a Marxist reading circle and shortly after became a Marxist. She met Lenin in 1894 when, in Wilson's colorful language, he was new to St. Petersburg, spending his time "walking the streets looking for Marxists" (Station 442). They soon worked together on various projects in an effort to improve workers' conditions.

Wilson writes dramatically, contrasting dazzling and dark St. Petersburg with its gold-and-white opera houses, low and dirty wooden buildings of the poor in conflict with the majestic golden spire atop the Admiralty tower (Station 442). Krúpskaya would help the Marxist cause by dressing as a working-class woman and visiting the factory barracks to witness and report on the desperate conditions. Soon, she and others would distribute Lenin's leaflets prepared for the Union of Struggle. But Lenin and Krúpskaya were soon arrested and exiled. But despite his isolation, Lenin still managed to communicate with his comrades, often in milk out of inkstands molded from bread that he could swallow if a guard passed by (Station 443). And despite the "side-trackings, hardships, and distraction," he continued to write his Marxist study of capitalism in Russia (Wilson 443). Even in prison, he obtained blue books and statistics and managed to work in libraries when he had leave to move from one prison to another.

In another Wilsonian detail adding color to Lenin's life, we learn that sometimes it would take a year-and-a-half for his texts to arrive. And in letters to his family, Lenin would describe how by "figuring on the dates of departure of the mails, calculating the delay from the spring torrents, testing out the speed of the express trains," he succeeded in engineering a correspondence that "kept him in touch with the West" to convince outsiders to turn "rapidly into a group of outlaws who exercise the most admirable qualities in outwitting and subverting society" (Station 443–4). He was able to enter the lives of others "with a peculiarly sensitive sympathy" (Station 445). Lenin captured Wilson's imagination.

Wilson then spends pages on the compatible relationship between Lenin and his wife, Wilson relying on her memoirs which he had with him. Together, the two skated, translated, and espoused Marxism, once explaining to a storekeeper that he was a parasite of the capitalist system. Lenin often gave the peasants free legal advice and drew up a new program for the Social Democratic Party, despite an additional year at the end of his three years of exile, living under surveillance in Ufá. Interspersed with this semi-idyllic, detailed account, Wilson describes the threats to the Social Democrats. By 1902, however, Lenin was in Munich publishing a new paper, *The Spark*, with the assistance of Krúpskaya; in 1902 he also published *What is to be Done?* in Stuttgart. Wilson then interjects a useful comment: "All the writing of Lenin is functional; it is all aimed at accomplishing an immediate purpose" before presenting a stylistic analysis of his writing practice (Station 448–9). Supplementing this is the impact of his speaking. Wilson is impressed, bordering on adulation, adding that "like almost all educated Russians, he loved music and literature" (Station 450). But Wilson neglects Lenin's emerging relationship and dependency on another woman, Inessa Armand, preferring to keep it hidden as he did with his own affairs.

Only in Wilson's 1971 "Introduction" to a new edition do we learn about Armand and that she was the daughter of a Scottish mother and French opera singer. Born in Paris, Armand had been taken to Russia by her grandmother after her father died; she became a governess to children of a Franco-Russian industrialist whose son she married. Together, they opened a school for peasant children. By 1902, however, she left her husband to live with his younger brother who shared many of her radical views. She also soon joined the illegal Russian Social Democratic Labour party. In 1907, she was arrested and sentenced to two years of internal exile but escaped after one year and left Russia for Paris where she met Lenin in 1909, soon becoming a Bolshevik and his disciple. By 1911, she became secretary to the committee established to coordinate Bolshevik groups in Europe. Returning to Russia in 1912, she was again arrested but later released. She left Russia illegally and went to live with Lenin and Krúpskaya in Galicia.

Armand's fluency in five languages, musicianship, and contributions at party meetings soon made her indispensable. By 1910, she and Lenin developed a serious relationship; a lengthy correspondence began, although Soviet historiography often suppressed their intimate connection. Her linguistic skills meant she accompanied Lenin to numerous international conferences and congresses.[7] At one point, Krúpskaya offered to resign from the marriage, a marriage she called a *mariage blanc* because of Armand. Lenin wanted her to stay, more for appearance than love. Krúpskaya, along with Armand, was part of the group that accompanied Lenin in the sealed train through Germany to the Finland Station arriving to revolutionary acclaim.[8]

Armand, one recent biographer declared, was "arguably the most powerful woman in post-revolutionary Moscow."⁹ She had five children in her open marriage with her husband, one of the children with his brother with whom she lived. She was vivacious, an excellent pianist, and was jailed three times. With her auburn hair, green eyes, and mastery of Leninist thought, she became Lenin's confidante, organizer, translator, and, on certain occasions, even spoke for him when he could not be present. As his marriage with Krúpskaya deteriorated—she became physically unappealing and politically uninformed—personal attachment evaporated, although they united in the revolutionary cause (Pearson 92). From roughly 1911 until 1916, she tolerated Armand in Lenin's life, although the sexual partnership between the two likely ended sometime in 1914 (Pearson 92-3, 116).

Lenin, however, was unable to escape the trope of Russian love, supposedly breaking off their affair in 1914—it was too difficult and he did not want the public embarrassment of divorcing his wife—but he remained deeply in love with Armand until her death in 1920. He did, however, demand the return of his passionate letters to her. Several have suggested that Armand had a daughter with Lenin. She was a determined woman devoted to Lenin and his ideas, although Wilson is hesitant to allow her much agency, citing an acquaintance to offer this critical remark: she was "pedantic and one hundred percent Bolshevik in the way she dressed (always in the same sever style)" in his "Introduction" (Station xiv). But she became a test of Lenin's personal philosophy whereby he subordinated his private life to the political and revolutionary cause. Nevertheless, his biographer Tamás Krausz refers to Inessa Armand as the "emotional gift of a lifetime" for Lenin (Krausz 466 ft.nt. 175; 55).

Lenin's relationships with Krúpskaya and Inessa occurred simultaneously and for a few months in the autumn of 1915 in Sörenberg, not far from Bern, all three lived uncomfortably with each other.¹⁰ Krúpskaya knew of Lenin's affair, although Lenin had difficulty with Inessa's argument for free love which he articulated as she prepared a pamphlet on the subject: "Kisses without love" are meaningless she argued, an idea she articulated in an unpublished pamphlet she was preparing for working-class women on love and family. In a letter criticizing free love—it is "a bourgeois, not a proletarian demand"—Lenin made clear that love is not what you "*subjectively* mean by this. The thing is the *objective logic* of class relations in affairs of love." This, not subjective desires, was for Lenin the true measure of affection, eliminating hurt, misunderstanding and emotion, although he himself could not remove such feelings in his relation with Armand (Krasuz 63-4; Pearson 127-8).¹¹

But Armand is strangely absent from Wilson's account, perhaps in an effort to prolong the image of heroic Lenin having no other interest other than political change, although she strenuously worked in the winter of 1915–16 to promote Lenin as a leader, generating enthusiasm for Lenin among Parisian socialists. Later, in October 1917, he turned to her to aid his safe passage from Zurich to Petrograd, either through England or, failing that, assuming a fake identity, using a Russian or Swiss passport.[12] A complicated solution meant a sealed train provided by the enemy across Germany, realizing it would be in their interests to have radical groups return to Russia to overthrow the Provisional Government (Merridale 139). Lenin was uncertain; it might be a trick and drew up a list of conditions including no passport controls (Merridale 141). The Germans continued to hope that the returning Bolsheviks would dismember Russia who would then make peace with Germany. Wilson includes none of this intrigue.

At Lenin's request, Armand joined him and his party totaling thirty-two on the train from Zurich across Germany to Petrograd. Following the October Revolution, she headed the Moscow Economic Council and was an executive member of the Moscow Soviet. She also became an activist for women's rights including the right to abortion and divorce. But she died at age forty-six from cholera and became the first woman to be buried next to the Kremlin walls.[13] Only in his 1971 "Introduction" does Wilson take note of her.

Wilson's realization that Lenin had a mistress while also being married likely vindicated his own actions and attitudes. He often found marriage a restraint but had time for various affairs—some suggest two dozen. Even at the end of his life and married, he had two dates with two different women the week he died.[14] Like Lenin, he was peremptory, demanding, cold, and preferred to lecture rather than listen.

Disregarding the purges and trials overtaking Russia during his 1935 visit, Wilson offers a *corrigendum* to his celebration of Lenin thirty-one years after *To the Finland Station* appeared. But years later Wilson revises, if not retracts, his intense romance with the leader, acknowledging his too positive view. The 1971 "Introduction" to the 1972 reprint of *To the Finland Station* (appearing the year Wilson died) records this change, although he earlier had begun to have second thoughts about his praise of Lenin.

The first sentence of the "Introduction" begins with an apology: "It is all too easy to idealize a social upheaval which takes place in some other country than one's own" (Station v). This is naïve, and he claims that American socialists and liberals were naïve and did not realize that "the new Russia must contain a good deal of the old Russia: censorship, secret police ... an all-powerful and brutal autocracy" (Station v).

In his defense of his breakup with Lenin and, indeed, with Russia, Wilson claims he had no premonition that the Soviet Union would become a "hideous tyranny" (Station v). His account should, therefore, be read only as an account of what the radicals thought they were doing, not what happened. After acknowledging his neglect of French post-revolutionary writers, and that he has little to add on Marx and Engels, Wilson does admit that his portrait of Lenin had been too sympathetic, presenting him heroically. But he claims Trotsky, too, wrote of Lenin in a "vein of eulogy almost equal ... to that of Plato on Socrates" (Station vii–viii). But his (Wilson's) view was further limited because he had access only to censored or government approved documents; only recently have new papers revealed Lenin's more "disagreeable" side (Station viii).

Wilson becomes a lover spurned as he reports that Lenin favored only those who agreed with him. Wilson then quotes Pyotr Struve, a former Marxist exiled to Paris where he became a critic of Russian Communism, who explained that being close to Lenin was no assurance of support. *Cassant* [brittle] best conveys Lenin's character, Struve writes, adding there was something "intolerably plebeian and at the same time something lifeless and repulsively cold" in him (Station viii).[15] Using extensive statements by Struve, Wilson presents his own statement of defense: Lenin remained an enigma, unknown even to those closest to him. Wilson was misled as a lover but still maintains his allegiance. Lenin's brusqueness and cruelty were bound up with his "love of power" (Station ix). Testimony from others confirms this view used by Wilson as if he were presenting an affidavit justifying his romantic breakup, much like Lenin seeking evidence for his (unsuccessful) breakup with Armand. Wilson's "Introduction," in fact, becomes a repeated collection of criticisms of Lenin citing writers and politicians dropped or rejected by Lenin. The love affair, like so many others in Russian literature, was over.[16]

But there was another love Wilson identifies in *To the Finland Station*: that of Engels and his mistress Mary Burns. Wilson writes empathetically about Engels as a young, curious, and unrestrained student of industrialization sent by his father to Manchester. Wilson then describes Engel's early love affair with Burns, an Irish factory girl who worked in the textile factory established by his father named Ermen & Engels. Burns had recently been promoted to operate a new machine labeled a "self-actor," a spinning machine that processed wool automatically. The name was revealing given her own independent character. She rejected Engels' offer to relieve her of work but allowed him to set her and her sister up in Salford, a Manchester suburb, surrounded by woods and fields. Engels then began a double life: factories and business during the day, the Burns sisters at night. While they settled in a natural surrounding, he worked on his book exposing the brutality of factory life which appeared in 1845 in German as *The Condition of The Working Class in England* (Station 159).

Wilson never forgoes detail in his account, reporting how the poor of Manchester nourished themselves on flour "mixed with gypsum and cocoa mixed with dirt" (Station 160). Women worked relentlessly in the factories and often became prostitutes. But Wilson soon broadens Engels's perspective relating it to the conception of the individual in modern society as "helpless, sterile and selfish" (Station 162). After meeting Marx in Cologne in 1842, Engels returned to Barmen, Germany to work further in the family business and where he had contracted an engagement with a woman of his own class before he left for Manchester. He felt obligated to the family firm but the situation became untenable. He could not become a bourgeois "working against the proletariat" and renounced his work and his engagement (Station 176).

He soon began to preach communism upsetting his father and remet Marx in Paris in 1844. But the police were soon after him; he left Germany in 1845 to join Marx in Brussels where Marx presented his general economic theory: in Wilson's words, history was "a succession of struggles between an exploiting and exploited class," the outcome of the "methods of production" (Station 184). But life for Engels and Marx, both in Paris, soon deteriorated, accelerated by a cholera epidemic and the failure of the 1848 revolution. The French police warned Marx, who was using an alias, that he would soon be exiled from Paris and sent to Brittany. He chose refuge in England. He wanted Engels and Mary to join him, although there was social friction: Jenny Marx refused to meet Mary because she lived with Engels out of wedlock (Station 209).

While Marx and family spent six years on Dean Street in run-down Soho, Engels returned to the factory in Manchester in the autumn of 1850; their revolution was on pause. Engels maintained his arrangement with Mary, visiting her in the woods while keeping a bachelor apartment in the city (Station 248). But contradictions emerged: gifted a horse by his father, he soon joined a fox hunting set, while Marx was destitute in London, although he sent him minor remittances. At one point, the Marxes pawned their children's shoes and Marx's winter coat (Station 256). But Wilson sympathizes with Marx: "where he dominated, he was able to love" and shut down his habit of cynical jokes and off-color language when he knew he was in control (Station 258). But a perpetual challenge remained: how could a communist who set himself against "the whole complex of society [exist] while trying to live in it without being of it" (Station 261)? The paradox became vivid in Marx's reaction to the unexpected death of Mary from an apoplectic stroke on January 7, 1863.

Marx's letter in response began with his surprise and shock but then goes on to complain about his own economic difficulties and inability to gain a loan in London. If only it had been my mother instead of Mary who died he writes, neglecting to mention anything personal about Engels' state of mind or how much he has helped him (Station 297). Engels had been for years supplying Marx with an allowance which he always exceeded. Engels had also been writing Marx's articles, while Marx collected the payments. Even when Engels persuaded Marx to write the articles in German, they still required Engels' editing. Earlier, in 1857, Engels broke down from the extra work, the contradictions between his communist views and the aims of his commercial life growing.

But Marx did not let up, as Wilson in his drama emphasizes. The amiable Engels faced the sarcastic and satiric Marx who repeatedly needed more and more money. Engels, hurt by Marx's cold response to Mary's death, and without even a notice from Jenny acknowledging his loss, meant the breakdown of their friendship. It took Engels five days to respond to what he called Marx's "frigid attitude" (Station 301). While others expressed sympathy, he writes, you did not. He then addresses the money question, explaining that he cannot afford more. Ten days later, Marx apologizes but then points out he will have to end the education of his daughters who will become seamstresses. Feeling guilty, Engels sends him £100 which he actually did not have. Marx then generates further distance by replacing any concern for Engels after Mary's death with inquiries about machinery and further complaints about his health.

A few months after Mary's death, Engels began to emerge from his depression, reconnecting with Marx, while living now with Mary's sister, Lizzy. Wilson justifies this renewed equanimity by writing that "it is the triumph of Marx's greatness over the maddening defects of his character as well as of Engels' capacity for sympathy ... even when he received so little in return" (Station 304). Their behavior renewed their friendship. No less a reader than Nabokov praised this section, responding to it as modulated melodrama. The examination of the letters which hurt Engels, he writes, is "beautifully shrewd ... the clumsy attempts of a boorish person trying to atone for a gaffe and making it still worse. The book is so entertaining that I could not stop it, let alone stop myself" he adds.[17]

The doubleness of Lenin's, and earlier even Engel's life, projects Wilson's own behavior in narrating the story of all three key figures: Marx having a son with the house keeper Helene Demuth, Engels sustaining a loving relationship with an unmarried factory worker, and Lenin attached to Armand. Such adventures corroborated Wilson's own behavior who, while married, carried on multiple affairs. When Wilson writes that Mary, an Irish patriot, fed Engels's "revolutionary enthusiasm at the same time that she served him as guide to the infernal abysses of the city," he may be protecting but also expressing his own inner thoughts as he restlessly searched for a proper companion (Station 159).

Abstractly, and more broadly, Wilson outlines another love affair, that with history presented as a meaningful plot supported by dramatic characters, incidents, and orchestrated scenes. Supplementing his love of Lenin and qualified praise of Marx is Wilson's love of Russian ideas, if not ideology. Romance in its emotional sense takes a back seat to a discovery of ideological identities where the figures instinctively realize that they will work together to fulfill their platforms and policies. Wilson makes this clear when discussing other examples of romance emerging from the political identities notable in the marriages of Marx and Lenin. Both men found women who shared their platforms and may have been models for Wilson. At the time of his Russian trip, Wilson was single (or rather between marriages) but on his return, while writing and polishing *To the Finland Station*, he was romancing the young Mary McCarthy whom he would marry in 1938, although it did not turn out to be the romance he anticipated. Only his fourth marriage to a half-Russian woman, Elena Mumm Thornton, would come close to the partnership he desired.

## ii

Before detailing his travels in his book, Wilson praises Russia, led by Lenin, as the "moral top of the world."[18] He first heard of Lenin in 1917 and the revolution in newspapers at Southampton at the embarkment of his army unit.[19] Soon after, speaking to a Russian couple, he perceived Lenin not as a historical hero but an important contemporary. In his journal, Wilson proudly announces that "I'm on my way to Leningrad with a biography of Lenin and a Russian grammar" (Thirties 524).

Wilson's journal, published as *The Thirties* (1980), is an expanded form of entries that first appeared in *Travels in Two Democracies* (1936) and then, with further expansion and commentary, in *Red, Black, Blond and Olive* (1956). They report on his meetings, reactions, and impressions of the country visited at what he would later claim was "the most liberal period ever known in Soviet Russia.

Visitors from abroad were welcome for the valuat [script] they had to spend" but were closely watched, although

> contact with the West was encouraged. The political terror had already begun with the first trials of Stalin's opponents; but the writers were still being urged to avail themselves, from bourgeois culture, of whatever it had to offer them.
>
> (Thirties 522)

Lenin's victories, beginning with his 1917 return and revolution, appealed to the young American journalist eager to see the new society. And although the Stalinist trials began, Wilson excludes that terror from his journey in search of the great socialist experiment armed, at the outset of his journey, with idealized thoughts of a socialist dream (Thirties 524).[20] He also overlooked the hanging of Lenin's older brother, his own internal banishment, and then admission to university contingent on constant surveillance. Wilson also overlooks Lenin's internal anger expressed through later class hatred and formation of such organizations as the secret police. Nabokov explained Wilson's omissions by writing that "your concept of pre-Soviet Russia, of her history and social development came to you through a pro-Soviet prism."[21]

Dismayed with the Americanization of London, Wilson was thrilled to be on a Soviet steamer chugging down the Thames and the feeling of "a new country, a new life, the loosening up from the English atmosphere in the atmosphere of the Soviets." Enthusiasm and expectations mark the outset of the journey. In the evening, he read Nadezhda Krúpskaya's memoirs, drawing on her chronicle throughout *To the Finland Station* (Thirties 527). On board, two Americans who long lived in Russia helped him pronounce the Russian alphabet. And details soon catch his eye like the small writing desks at either end of the saloon with the hammer and sickle etched on the inkwells (Thirties 528). In fact, detail textures his work, in many ways emulating Turgenev or Tolstoy.[22]

He also begins to sense parallel identities between Americans and Russians, closer to each other than to the English: "we, like them [the Russians], have had a new deal from the old Europe; they are still fixed in their old hierarchy, maintaining their differences from each other" (Thirties 530). During the trip, he studies Lenin, one day asked by a boy of nine if he thought Lenin was a good man (Thirties 531). In response to comments by an insensitive English woman on the ship about Russia, he refers her to *The Possessed* and soon hears an old waltz from *The Cherry Orchard* on the radio (Thirties 532).

Finland then suddenly appears: awe inspiring, "the bleak clear top of the world" he writes (Thirties 533). In anticipation of his arrival in Russia he tries to discuss Pushkin with his fellow travelers but to no avail. On May 23, 1935, he arrives at Leningrad, greeted by long waits since the boat docked earlier than expected and officials were not ready. The Intourist sign he sees at breakfast is appropriate: "An old Russian custom: to wait" (Thirties 534). But Leningrad quickly becomes a swirl of activity from a performance of *Otello*, to walking in a room at the opera with a statue of Lenin, his hand extended, "as if he were at once giving the worker what they had made and opening out the future to humanity to make whatever they could conceive" (Thirties 535). Back at his hotel, he meets his New York friend Muriel Draper ("a parlor Bolshevik" [Thirties 263]) and the English wife of Soviet foreign minister Litvinov, the writer and translator Ivy Litvinov.

In his expanded journal narrative *Travels in Two Democracies*, Wilson writes that "the first impression of Leningrad is absolutely dreamlike and dazing." But critically, he comments that it was impossible for him to imagine what Russia and the Russians were like until you are there. And one can have had no experience of socialism: "it is probably impossible for an American—it was impossible for me at any rate—to Imagine Russia correctly." It is definitely not the United States plus the ideal of socialism (Two 162).

These direct, immediate reactions are unmediated by the themes or even structure he would provide six years later in *To the Finland Station* ending with Lenin's arrival in Petrograd, as it was then called, on April 16, 1917, a moment when, in highly metaphorical language, for the "first time in the human exploit the key of a philosophy of history was to fit an historical lock" (Station 546). "The imagination for history has been transferred to practical politics" and is preoccupied with the present Wilson celebrates (Station 528). But despite the anticipation and lead-up to Lenin's arrival, the Lenin section of the text is only ninety-eight pages out of 554 in the 1972 edition or 17.6 percent.

Wilson's comments in *Travels in Two Democracies* provide more context than his journal notes offering more evaluation and criticism. He remarks on the large scale of the city, which he calls St. Petersburg (although the official name was Leningrad when he entered, so named from 1924–1991) but is disturbed by the crowds, mostly silent and grimy and monotonous, inhabiting a city of wide boulevards that "seem the thoroughfares of an empire" (Two 163).

St. Petersburg is Wilson's entrance to Russian life; he is a sightseer visiting, among other things, the Museum of the Revolution where a tableau shows an official with an album of suspects before him open to photographs of Lenin and his wife. Another shows young people, idealists, and university students, forced to live out "whole lives of thought, political organization, prison, before they are out of their twenties."[23] He also visits the Peter Paul Fortress. The value of what he sees, however, often originates from "the imaginative re-creation of what he has read about the object before him" (Paul 119). He sees best what he has imagined, a process that provides the literary thrust and form of To the Finland Station.

Moscow is next but he worries over the gap between Leninist ideals and Stalinist facts. Nevertheless, he is a keen observer of city life, noting that Moscow lacks a special smell, largely because it is kept so clean.

> But it is also partly due to the absence of so many things that have smells: foliage… and perfumes; restaurants cooking rich foods and bars serving pungent liquor… incense in the churches, and the fumes of private motor-cars and taxis.
> (Two 197)

A visit to the Park of Culture and Rest hides what he already knows: class exclusion. He furthermore objects to the glorification of Stalin but believes it has nothing to do with Marxism (Red Black 241–3). The contrast is with his hero Lenin: "Lenin was irreverent toward himself in the sense that he took himself seriously only as the agent of his cause. He cared nothing about power for its own sake; nothing about admiration" (Red Black 245). But this is its own form of hero worship on Wilson's part, overlooking the coming gulag or the Lenin who wrote a telegram saying "SHOOT MORE PROFESSORS."[24] He also neglects the massacre of the Kronstadt sailors on Lenin's orders or Stalin's intense December 1934 response to the assassination of Kirov.

Wilson defensively suggests that the brutality of the Tsars could not disappear overnight and should not be considered a product of socialism.[25] But as his biographer defensively writes, "had Wilson any idea of what was happening, he could not have completed Finland Station as planned" (Dabney 211). Wilson, nonetheless, wrote in 1956 that "I present here without apology this sympathetic account of the Soviet Union in 1935" (Red Black 378). Nevertheless, he could not stop himself from celebrating Lenin as an icon, commenting on those who passed through Lenin's tomb under the Kremlin wall, knowing that Lenin "was one of them" and that "from their sluggish plasm" he summoned up triumphs "to which he thought himself but a guidepost," claiming little or no self-aggrandizement (Red Black 377). Wilson's Moscow guide was Irina Grynberg, a lawyer, and ironically the sister of Roman Grynberg, a New York businessman and friend of Wilson's after the Second World War.

One other explanation of Wilson's attachment to Russia is its parallel to America. In *Travels in Two Democracies*—the title itself is misleading since Russia was hardly a democracy—he writes that

> our period of pioneering was more like the present period in Russia which is preoccupied with settling new country, constructing new industrial plants and developing natural resources, than like anything else that has happened in Europe; and the American and the Russian, who have both left the old system behind, feel a natural sympathy with one another.
>
> (Two 161)

He then offers this grandiose declaration: "The Soviet Union stands in relation to the rest of the world today very much as the United States stood for a century after the Revolution," a statement displaying the affinity between liberal/radical aspirations on the American left in the 1930s and the supposed accomplishments of the Soviet Union (Two 161–2; cf. Red Black 378–9).

Wilson repeatedly celebrated Russian intellectuals and was jealous of the place of the Russian writer and literature in Russian society, overlooking the danger and persecution of Akhmatova or Mandelstam or even the fate of D. S. Mirsky, arrested as a spy in 1937 and sent to the Gulag where he died in a labor camp in June 1939. Wilson's early views were the opposite, writing in *Two Democracies* while in Odessa that he felt the Soviet Union "with all its old slowness and debris … was the only guarantee in Europe against another receding tide of civilization …. I felt that it was safer here" (Two 304). But his heroes were "political idealists in the populist-Marxist tradition" (Remnick 183), his Lenin an aesthetic object, especially when he describes him in his tomb at the end of *Two Democracies*. Lenin, too, invented the terror and the camps.

Wilson's love affair with Lenin stalls and never leaves the Finland Station, at least not for thirty-one years when, in his new "Introduction" to the work, he admits his blindness, although in 1936 he saw Russia as a world of "extraordinary heroism" (Two 319). He supports the claim with vivid examples of individuals whose lives have been radically remade and that "one is made to feel the terrible seriousness of what is being done … and the terrible cost which it requires" (Two 320). In the Soviet Union, he repeats, you feel "that you are at the moral top of the world" (Two 321).

Wilson concludes *Two Democracies* with a vivid description of those lining up in Red Square to visit Lenin's Tomb. And here, his hero-worshipping attains new heights: even in death, Lenin looks like a leader as Wilson compares his death mask to that supposedly of Shakespeare (Two 321–2). Wilson's apostrophe of Lenin presents him as "a scientist whose study is humanity, the poet whose material is not images but the water and salt of human beings" (Two 322). It is also a face that seems to transcend being Russian, the entire section a prelude to his admiration of Lenin in *To the Finland Station* six years later, although it differs from his view of Lenin in *Red, Black, Blond, and Olive* (1956), where he calls him a "shriveling shell of flesh" (Red Black 377).

## iii

Wilson's earliest interest in Russia likely began at Princeton with Christian Gauss who introduced him to Russian literature. Gauss praised the Russians, writes Wilson, for "their sober art of implication."[26] *The Brothers Karamazov* became important for its contrasting lives of spirituality and brutality. After nearly two years in the US Army in a hospital unit, Wilson returned to New York in July 1919 reading Chekhov and more Dostoevsky and was able to see the Moscow Art Theater who visited the city in 1923. Shaping his Russian sensibility was his use of understatement without losing the atmosphere of an idea but at the same time valuing the intensity, completeness, and depth of Russian writing.

Wilson had been seriously considering Marxism since 1930 when he began to research what would become *American Jitters: The Year of the Slump* (1932), twenty-nine representative episodes of capitalistic society under strain between October 1930 and October 1931. He went to the Ford factory in Detroit, then witnessed rural poverty and miners' strikes in Kentucky, as well as the Scottsboro trial in Tennessee. Scenes of class and "muted fury" greeted him creating a sense of new opportunities to right social wrongs (Remnick 181). His account of the Depression, traveling coast to coast between 1930 and 1934, offered graphic reports of nationwide suffering, of protests and struggle, focusing in part on the Harland County coal strike. American society had become a machine that was running down.

He also began to sense that beauty and harshness link together. He managed to even incorporate ideas from an essay on Dostoevsky in a monologue on literature in *I Thought of Daisy* (1929) where he essentially shows that the discords of life, even the brutalities of life, reveal if not confirm the importance of literature.[27] Genuine artistic creation must include horror as he made clear in an essay on *Philoctetes* by Sophocles published in *The Wound and The Bow* (1941).

Wilson actually began *To the Finland Station* before he went to Russia, publishing the first chapters on Michelet in *The New Republic* in August 1932. In October that year a piece on Marxist history appeared. By January 1933, his essay on Trotsky was published in *The New Republic*; by August, "Art, the Proletariat and Marx." In August of 1934, "To the Finland Station I," the first of six essays with that title, was published in *The New Republic*, all in advance of his visit. Following his return, there was another series with titles like "First days in Moscow," "London to Leningrad," "Stalin Ikon," and "Russian Paradoxes," all in 1936. In 1937, it was "Marxism and Literature" in the *Partisan Review*. Increasingly, essays on Marxism emerged in 1939 and 1940 until the completed book appeared with its full title: *To the Finland Station, A Study in the Writing and Acting of History* in September 1940. Acting, however, is ambivalent: it can mean the enacting of history, the application of history to events or the opposite, used in a theatrical sense, the performance or imitation of history. Wilson uses the term in both ways.

But before that, Wilson sensed the excitement of Lenin's return asking Christian Gauss in 1934 about Lenin's dramatic arrival: "have you read any accounts of the extraordinary scene that occurred? It marked dramatically the first occasion that a trained Marxist had been able to come in and take hold of a major crisis."[28] Wilson seized the moment to recreate the enthusiasm and reaction to Lenin's appearance, something the leader himself had not anticipated.

Wilson went to Russia in May 1935, aided by a Guggenheim Fellowship six months after the Kirov assassination and six years after the slaughter of the Kulaks. He followed visits by Shaw, Lincoln Steffens and Dos Passos, dismissing later accounts such as Gide's critique, *Return from the USSR* (1937). He overlooked several points cited by Dos Passos in a Christmas 1934 letter to him listing its horrors including the exile of Trotsky, massacres in the Crimea, and persecution of the Social Revolutionaries (Lett. 182). Wilson's heroes were political idealists, neglecting the demonization of Akhmatova or Mandelstam while transforming Lenin into an appealing, artistic object. He questions the glorification of Stalin but with humor and irony:

> Stalin goes to bed every morning at 4. This is precisely what I do myself; but, although it is admirable for writing, I am not sure it is so good for administrative work. I should think the projects they draw up would tend to become works of the imagination.
>
> (Two 192)

Mary McCarthy astutely complained that it was a mistake for Wilson "to like Lenin but that was the only way he could believe in the Russian Revolution."[29] In his new 1972 preface, Wilson admits his shortcomings, writing that one "cannot be surprised that he [Lenin] gave offense and did not show himself so benevolent as I perhaps tend to make him" (Station xii). Earlier, in a 1958 Postscript to *The American Earthquake*, he acknowledged that the optimism of the Soviet experiment distorted his sense of later atrocities. An imagined utopianism needed correction.

But certain aspects of the Russians did disturb him: their disorganization, unreliability, disregard of punctuality, and unpredictable behavior confirmed by his stay in an Odessa hospital with its bugs, flies, and garbage in bathrooms (Two ca. 285 ff). He became exasperated with the country writing that "we think in America that Kansas is flat, but you have to go to Russia to know how flat the earth can be" (Two 278). Earlier, on his last night in St. Petersburg, Wilson attended a production of Tchaikovsky's opera *The Queen of Spades* directed by Meyerhold which rewrote the libretto to emphasize its menacing features. Afterwards, he went to bed "full of vodka and Pushkin," imagining characters from the opera and then the city with Dostoevsky's uneasy characters

> roaming the bridges in the half-day of night… the great unintegrated city which in itself seemed to make no meaning, in which the individual had to make his own meaning.
>
> (Two 178)

This unreal city he analogizes to America at its start, a provincial, incomplete civilization. But in such places, we are free to think "the long, long thoughts of the poem" and explore our inner purpose he explains (Two 178).

As early as 1932, Wilson wrote to his friend the writer John Peale Bishop with a reading list clarifying his ideas on Marxism, suggesting that he had studied the three core writers: Marx, Lenin, and Trotsky, beginning with Trotsky's *Literature and Revolution* (1928), "an extraordinary and unique piece of literary criticism." Then, the *Communist Manifesto* and Marx's *Eighteenth Brumaire*. And if you can't "swallow the abstracts of Das Kapital … at least read the historical," telling Bishop that

> The point is that the literature of Marxism is not really a body of dogma… though Communism itself—the Third International that is—has some of the characteristics of a secular church: it corresponds more or less to the literature of the Enlightenment before the French and American Revolutions, and people

of our own time can no more afford to be ignorant of it than people of the eighteenth century could of Voltaire and Montesquieu and Rousseau.

(Lett 227)

Here, Wilson blends literature, liberalism, and history, reading history as literature as he considers a fuller engagement with Russian character and thought.

In the next paragraph of this September 20, 1932, letter, he jumps to Dostoevsky saying that he read Stavrogin's confession cut from *The Possessed* and believes that "great damage was done to the book when Dostoevsky was forced to leave it out" (Lett. 227). In November that year, he tells Christian Gauss that he's been rereading Michelet's history after dropping it several years earlier at the same time he begins to define his own sense of Marxism (Lett. 229).

To Paul Elmer More he explains that "the point I was trying to make—not writing at that time as a Marxist—"

was that the liberal bourgeoisie had better bestir itself if they didn't want the Marxist catastrophe to occur. Today I should say in the light of events that Marx's prophecies were correct.

(Lett 230)

Our own ruling class cannot resist inertia "and greed to which their money and power have exposed them" (Lett. 230).

A year later he thanks the poet Phelps Putnam for his praise of his articles about Marx, adding that "I'm gong to rewrite it later on for a book, I think. I've been made not a little uneasy by the activities of the Marxist literary guys" (Lett. 232). The confluence of writing history, literary criticism, and a critique of Marxism resulted in *To The Finland Station*. In his Journal for the spring of 1934, Wilson writes that at some point

it occurred to me that nobody had every presented in intelligible human terms the development of Marxism and other phases of the modern idea of history. I saw the possibilities of a narrative which would quite get away from the pedantic frame of theory.

(Thirties 298)

He also admitted that it would take him away from his main interest, fiction, but he was soon applying novelistic and dramatic methods to the proposed text which has its heroes, failures, confrontations, and an exhilarating narrative structure. It does not, however, experiment: there are no flashbacks, repetitions, reconsiderations, or parallel actions, just a steady historical progress to an end announced in the title.³⁰

Buttressing his story would be five months in the Soviet Union experiencing the same material conditions of many Russians. But one may argue that in the face of Stalin's atrocities, Wilson defended, or perhaps masked, his support through reliance on the literary devices he employed to construct his narrative of Lenin's triumphant return at which point the story ends not with immediate acceptance of Lenin's rhetoric but the anticlimax of his return with Krúpskaya to their family apartment where they found a banner over their beds: the last words of *The Communist Manifesto*: "Workers of the World Unite!" In his text, Wilson turns Lenin into an author, not "an architect of power," while Wilson himself becomes a "historian of motive and behavior."³¹

Initially prompting the book was the desire to write a history of socialism measured by its key figures culminating in Lenin to show how certain ideas take shape through individuals. It was a pattern he sought and narratively told. The consequences mattered less.

Many, of course, had preceded him to Russia in the post-Revolution period, including Lincoln Steffens (1919), Isadore Duncan (1921–4), W. E. B. Dubois (1926), Theodore Dreiser (1927), John Dewey (1926), Dos Passos (1928), and Waldo Frank (1931).³² Between 1935 and 1937 additional visitors included Brecht, Sydney and Beatrice Webb, Paul Robeson, Frank Lloyd Wright, Antoine de Saint Exupéry, and Romain Rolland. But few provided a context for the journey as clearly as Wilson who joined the parade, eager to pursue the fate of an idea—socialism. He would do so through the lives of its key figures, excited by the cultural pre-eminence of Russian politicians and writers transferred to his biographical history of an idea.

By July 11, 1934, Wilson could present a reasonably firm outline of his book to George Soule, editor of *The New Republic*: it would deal with

> the development of the modern conception of history from the first attempts to apply scientific methods to the study of human affairs in the past… to the recent more or less successful effort to determine the course of events in the present.
>
> (Lett 246)

His ambitious plan had already taken shape: he offers Soule sections dealing with Vico, Michelet, Renan, Taine, and the French Revolution. They could appear as installments, collectively totaling 15,000 words. The next section would deal with Marx and Engels and the third with the Russians. "My idea," he explains, "is not to write a complete account, but to present the development of the organic conception and scientific study of history through a number of key figures, with the background amply filled in" (Lett. 246). It's worth doing, he explains, because "Marxism often gets dissociated from the French revolutionary tradition it grew out of" (Lett. 246). In the letter, he also announces the title: *To the Finland Station*. Before he embarked for Russia, the book had been fully plotted.

On July 28, 1934, Wilson sends Soule the first section explaining that it hangs on Michelet, the second on Marx and Engels and the third on Lenin and Trotsky. He then lists the subheadings duplicated in the Table of Contents of the finished book. He then outlines how the essays might be altered to fit the space limitations of the *New Republic*. In a note of August 10, 1934, he provides a memorandum for the advertising department concerning its promotion and offers details on subheadings and the heads on each installment adding *To the Finland Station I*. This will ensure that the reader knows he/she is heading to a larger idea.

On August 31, 1934, Wilson explains to Christian Gauss the importance of the title, noting that the scene—and Wilson conceived of the book in terms of scenes—was "the first occasion that a trained Marxist had been able to come in and take hold of a major crisis" (Lett 248). In another letter, this time to Malcolm Cowley at the *New Republic*, Wilson refines his ideas, explaining that his problem in the first section is "to present the non-Marxist French Revolutionary bourgeois writers from the point of view of my own Marxist lights and yet give an illusion of how the world looked to them …. Marx's discoveries are precisely a part of my story"; I must not give them away too early he adds (Lett. 249). The Paris Commune, he states, was a pivotal point in the intellectual careers of those he treats in the first section because they were all trying to escape it. Later, he shows it was to become the pivotal point in the opposite way of thinking and practice of the Marxists (Lett. 249).

Two days after, writing again from Provincetown, MA, Wilson explains to Gauss that he's not offering "a literary history or even a history of the study of history" (Lett 249). If it were, the space given to the different men at the opening would change: "my treatment of these French writers will have to justify itself artistically in relation to the whole scheme. The purpose of this first section is to show the dying out of the bourgeois revolutionary tradition as a prelude to presenting the rise of Marxism" (Lett. 249). To disarm bourgeois liberal objections to the Marxists by reviewing liberal attitudes exemplified by these French writers is his goal—and to show this in relation to their fear of social class socialism. The impact of the Commune cannot be overstated. For the bourgeois writers, the Commune was a scandal, but to the Marxists before the revolution it is "the pivotal event on which their historical thinking turns" (Lett. 249–50). These are among his clearest statements on the purpose of the book.

The key point is that *before* Wilson went to Russia in May 1935, he had a clear and definite idea of his book, both its structure and certainly its content.

Less reportorial and factual than *Travels in Two Democracies*, more literary and analytical, *To the Finland Station* develops the trope of drama in its treatment of society, change, history, and leadership. Characters are always on stage.

Michelet's claim at twenty-two that "we are all more or less romantics," cited by Wilson on page 11, becomes the entry point for Wilson's method which treats love as political and politics as love (Station 11). Recreating social history through romantic imagery—"the cloud shapes of legend lift"—with an emphasis on accomplishment, not failure, lend a propulsion to the text that culminates with not an end but a beginning: Lenin's arrival (Station 4). The rhetoric is vivid, semi-poetic, and casual but always with a romantic undercurrent. Everyday idioms abound—Vico is "a crank"; Lenin, in his effort to implement Marxism itself, "had really to reload the weapons that had been hung up by Marx and Engels after the campaign of 1848" (Station 3, 453).[33] But, as he explains when writing about Michelet, he was interested in "remarkable individuals as representatives of movements and groups" (Station 11).

Wilson the novelist interferes with Wilson the historian. Commenting on the steady rays of Vico's insight, he says it is "almost as if we were looking out on the landscape of the Mediterranean itself—we see the fogs that obscure the horizons of the remote reaches of time recede" (Station 4). The syntax, imagery, and rhythm are poetic as are his chapter titles mixing individual action with concepts: "Michelet Tries to Live His History"; "Marx and Engels: Grinding the Lens"; "Karl Marx Dies at His Desk"; "Lenin: The Great Headmaster"; "Lenin at the Finland Station." Even incidents blend the romantic with the lyrical, adding details to humanize the experience: "they had loaded themselves with books, but never read them. At night they fell right into bed" he writes of Lenin and Krúpskaya when they retreat to the mountains in 1904. Earlier, he records that when Marx published the last issue of *Neue Rheinische Zeitung* it was entirely printed in red (Station 471, 202).

A sense of theater runs throughout and what appears to be a lack of imagination on Lenin's part is actually only the transfer of imagination to history and then to practical politics; hence, his preoccupation with the present. And this conception of the present has proven to be a great imaginative influence on the age, "a world-view which gives life a meaning in which every man is assigned a place." This is monumental. Even Stalin, Wilson writes, had a part in Lenin's drama. The "bandit-politician who started on the road to power with a few Marxist texts in his head, thought for a time he was a character in Lenin," as if Lenin was a play (Station 528–9). From dramatic scenes constructed with realistic details such as the state of the actual Finland Station towards the end of the narrative, to the construction of individual confrontations, Lenin was a character on the stage of history constructed by Wilson. Even when criticizing Lenin's failure to "elaborate a social philosophy or to give much thought to prefigure the future," he created theater (Station 528).

But Wilson is not above his own self-criticism, interrupting his chapter on Marx and Engels, for example, to explain that readers must not be misled by his "spotlighting method" highlighting individual figures and the belief that great ideas only come from singular great men. There are sources obscure and less well-known that are crucial: "all the agitators, the politicians, the newspaper writers, the pamphlets, the conversations, ... the implications of conduct deriving from inarticulate or half-conscious thoughts, the implications of unthinking instincts" (Station 166–7). In *Red, Black, Blond and Olive*, he brackets his own self-criticism that he soft-pedaled the class stratification that was "already well advanced" in Russia (Red Black 223).

It is important, he explains, to interrupt his narrative to fill in the background of early nineteenth-century thought out of which grew Marx and Engels. In short, context is essential as seen in Wilson's treatment of Lenin's family, the Ulyánovs, drawing parallels to the family of New Englanders focused on "plain living and high-thinking" (Station 411). He also provides an extensive description of their home and area in Simbrísk with such detail as the books on the bookshelves (Station 412–17). But metaphor has its place, mostly when Wilson advances abstract ideas, later writing that it would be tedious to trace in detail "the stages which Lenin steered his followers through the rocks and shoals of revolutionary politics" (Station 453). On the same page he offers this overall assessment: "The theoretical side of Lenin is, in a sense, not serious; it is the instinct for dealing with the reality of the definite political situation which attains in him the point of genius" (Station 453).

Throughout his work, Krúpskaya is Wilson's companion as well as Lenin's. Through her memoir, she offers Wilson insight into Lenin's ideas and actions, becoming another woman Wilson admires.

Wilson includes his own self-dramatizing reaction to history in his story: "let us note the crudity of the psychological motivation which underlies the worldview of Marx"; let us not deal with the question of the primitive past "since Marx gave it but little attention in his writings and since I cannot find that even Engels made very much effort to fit it into the dialectical theory of history" (Station 351, 355).[34] This habit engages the reader with his text, while creating a narrative self-consciousness aware of the shortcomings of the very text he is fashioning. There is a meta-textual dimension to the work, part of the "Acting of History" in the title and its focus on personalities. "To approach Lenin ... through his writings," he declares, "is not to understand him at all" (Station 453).

But what of love? Does it reflect the paradigm of Russian love outlined in earlier chapters? To answer, one needs to contextualize Wilson's own view of love at the time he began his visit. Wilson went to Russia as a widower but in Russia, romance and women were never far away. Becoming an unexpected widower—his wife Margaret Canby unexpectedly died in a California car crash—he initiated several liaisons in New York (with Louise Connor and Elizabeth Waugh plus interludes with the less educated Anna) before he left; after his return from Russia, he would soon pursue and marry Mary McCarthy seventeen years his junior. But Wilson did not hesitate from engaging in various Russian intrigues.

On the voyage to Russia, Wilson quickly makes overtures to the Russian stewardesses on board who all seem to wear heels; in a patronizing tone, he writes they are "very amiable and accommodating, these little blond girls." And the one who at midnight turned off the lights in the saloon and took away the phonograph "made gestures when I offered to go that I could stay, making cunning little sounds like the language of mice" (Thirties 529). Later, when he visits Lenin's family home in Ulyanovsk, he overnights at a cheap hotel where he meets and attempts to seduce a *blondínka* who makes the beds. In the afternoon after a small tour of the town, he returns to find her and writes that "a great liking for this blond girl began to warm me—the kind of liking that sometimes arises ... in the presence of the sweet Russian blend of sensitivity with candid simplicity" (Red Black 311).

Wilson then provides details of her hair and eyes, even listing her name, Clavdia. Twenty-one but with a thick figure, he still found her attractive and responsive to his overtures, or so he thought, admiring in her a kind of "sudden flurry of animation, volatile, emphatic, smiling," characteristic of certain Russian women who display what he calls "gusts of animation" (Red Black 311–12, 314). But in the midst of their awkwardly playing checkers, he notes that when the odds were against her, "she would begin throwing away all her pieces," something peculiarly Russian (Red Black 312). There was nothing in-between. It was all or nothing. They hold hands but nothing further happens, although she does ask him to feel her muscles (Red Black 315–16). Further "petting" leads nowhere, so while waiting for a boat to arrive at 2.30 a.m., "I thought I would sit up and read Lenin till the boat got in" (Red Black 316, 317).

The moment he boards, however, he spots a pretty woman in second class, "small, with lively dark eyes" and a striking way of doing her hair. He later sees her swimming using "a very feminine breast stroke" he finds irresistible (Red Black 319). Meeting a newly wed couple on the ship, they ask him if they had love in America. They had been influenced by the official policy of encouraging domestic affections and implying that at least, while vacationing, "genuine love" was a benefit but "possible only in a socialist society—conferred by Comrade Stalin on the inhabitants of the Soviet Union" (Red Black 320).

Sex surrounds Wilson everywhere in Russia. Earlier during his stay in St. Petersburg he finds himself at the Marínsky Opera House in the director's room with New York critic Harold Clurman, the composer Shostakovich, and a "Leningrad woman intellectual," a psychologist who is translating Mark Twain. She's unattractive but has intense eyes and "in spite of her flat shoes, has a distinct even strong, sex appeal. Yet I ask myself, where am I?" (Red Black 185).

The encounter in the flop house, however, is a chance to offer some additional comments about Russia: "nothing except hours of work ever begins or ends in Russia. Their time behaves so differently from ours" he writes, offering a parallel to the imperfective aspect of their verbs which represent a continuing action and the norm (Red Black 313). He also records that when you meet someone in Russia, they ask you where you work, not where you live. They also avoid the explicit, preferring innuendo or allusion. But wildness and sadness seem to coexist (Red Black 314, 315). Wilson's Russia neatly divides itself: one is either like Oblomov, filled with indolence, or Stavrogin, "possessed by some passionate purpose" (Red Black 188). Some remain in bed all morning "trying to make up their minds whether or not to get up," while others immediately rise because of a demonstration to enact a determined goal (Red Black 187–8).

But even when ill, women still appeal. While in in Kiev and beginning to feel ill (scarlet fever would hospitalize him in Odessa), he walks through a park above the Dnieper river, commenting that the people look happy and that "the women were extremely good-looking …. they had immensely big broad bodies, but small well-shaped hands and feet, and faces that were, surprisingly not fat." They also talked in low voices and as twilight fell, it all began "to seem like some pleasant but faint phantasmagoria which merged with the vagueness of my fever" (Two 278). And even when taken by ambulance to an Odessa hospital, he cannot resist writing that he was met by a young doctor and "by a blond girl, one of the most beautiful I had yet seen." And after a shower and being wrapped in blankets, he lay on a stretcher on the hospital floor "a long time regarding the blond girl's feet …. she had unbuttoned the straps of her shoes" (Two 285). Even infants he finds attractive, mentioning that a baby girl "seemed to have come into the world with a fully developed feminine beauty and a feminine self-consciousness about it" (Two 300).

When his Intourist interpreter arrives as his health improves, a thin "washed out girl with eyeglasses" from Odessa, he asks her why Russians were so "wonderful in the theatre?" "Because they feel things more deeply" she answers (Two 301). But balancing her plainness was the "handsome brunette Komsomolka" who visited every afternoon and promoted standard Communist ideas. But she was a dreadful nurse (Two 301). Another temptation, however, is a "Mediterranean-looking girl" who was a bacteriological researcher who took her experiments seriously. She could also speak French and struck him as mature and sensible, "full of vitality" (Two 302). Wilson's eye never stopped wandering.

In the words of his editor Leon Edel, although Wilson no longer kept detailed "Casanovaesque records of his adventures," his "sexual activity did not flag in the Russian environment" (Thirties 523). His health, however, required quarantine for a month-and-a-half in Odessa when he became part of an epidemic of scarlatina. Kidney problems further delayed his return. But throughout his journey, his interest in Russian woman never flagged; it is perhaps no surprise that his fourth and final wife, Elena M. Thornton, was half-Russian.

But Lenin was the consistent focus of Wilson's intellectual, political, and even emotional attachment evident in his language and defense of the Communist leader. At one point in the *Finland Station*, he writes that Lenin "implacable as he was as a fighter, was essentially a good-natured man" (Station 469). His "revilings are the routine of Marxist controversy: [but] there is no malice in them" he protectively adds (Station 469). But other readers such as Nabokov saw things differently: "your criticism of Marxism is so ferocious that you kick out the Marxism stool from under the feet of Lenin, who is left dangling in midair" (N-W Lett. 31–2).

Wilson had high aims when he began his work, telling Gauss that it would be an account of the "dying out of the bourgeois revolutionary tradition as a prelude to presenting the rise of Marxism" (Lett. 249). But the final text, with its literary devices and stylized writing, becomes a personal story of relationships including that of Wilson's with Lenin, going beyond concerns with social class and political change to become a Russian love story echoing disappointment after disappointment.

The analogy might be to the narrator of Dostoevsky's "White Nights" who, after many nights of sympathy with the distressed Nastenka, mysteriously met on a St. Petersburg bridge, finally confesses his love to her, while simultaneously declaring he must go away. She tells him he must stay but then, at the end, they unexpectedly encounter her former suitor who has reappeared after a year. She rushes to him and rejects the narrator while still professing her love for him. This is a quintessential act of Russian love. Devastated and in despair, the narrator cries out with a rhetorical flourish, while shielding his dismay, "My God, a whole moment of happiness! Is that too little for the whole of a man's life?"[35] Wilson may have felt the same.

## Notes

1 Trotsky, *The History of the Russian Revolution*, tr. Max Eastman (Chicago: Haymarket Books, 2017), 238. Also see Trotsky, *The History of the Russian Revolution*, Vol. 1 Ch. 16. https://www.marxists.org/archive/trotsky/1930/hrr/ch16.htm.
2 Trotsky letter cited in David Caute, *Isaac and Isaiah: The Covert Punishment of a Cold War Heretic* (New Haven: Yale University Press, 2013), 84.
3 For a broad discussion of the novelistic and romantic elements of the text, see Louis Menand, "The Historical Romance," *New Yorker,* March 24, 2003. https://www.newyorker.com/magazine/2003/03/24/the-historical-romance. This became the basis for Menand's "Foreword" to the 2003 re-issue of the book published by New York Review Books Classics with a toppled Lenin on the cover. The essay addresses issues of historiography, as much as Wilson's writing.
4 Wilson to Nabokov in 1940. See Brian Boyd, *Vladimir Nabokov, The American Years* (Princeton: Princeton University Press, 1991), 20.
5 Details appear in *To the Finland Station*, expanded later in *Red, Black, Blond and Olive*.

   Edmund Wilson, *To the Finland Station, A Study in the Writing and Acting of History*, new introduction (New York: Farrar Straus and Giroux, 1972), 413–16. Hereafter Station. It originally appeared in September 1940.

   *Red, Black, Blond and Olive, Studies in Four Civilizations: Zuni, Haiti, Soviet Russia, Israel* (London: W.H. Allen, 1956). Hereafter Red Black. An earlier description appears in Ch. V. of *Travels in Two Democracies* (1936). Wilson's itinerary was, roughly, Leningrad, Moscow, a trip down the Volga, a stop at Ulyanovsk and then by way of Stalingrad, Rostov-on-the-Don and Kiev to Odessa where he caught scarlet fever requiring a stay for six weeks in the Hospital for Contagious Diseases.
6 On the Marx marriage, see Mary Gabriel, *Love and Capital: Karl and Jenny Marx and the Birth of a Revolution* (Boston: Little Brown and Co., 2012).

7   See Tamás Krausz, *Reconstructing Lenin, an Intellectual Biography*, tr. Bálint Bethlenfalvy with Mario Fenyo (New York: Monthly Review Press, 2015), 61–4. Also see 466 ftnt. 175.
8   For a less dramatic arrival, see John Dos Passos, "Finland Station" in his "Russian Visa," *In All Countries, Travel Books and Other Writings 1916–1941* (New York: Library of America, 2003), 283. Dos Passos visited Russia in 1928 and spent two months in Moscow. *In All Countries* appeared in 1934. In the same essay he writes that walking about Leningrad felt like "walking around in the burntout crater of a volcano" (Passos 292).
9   Michael Pearson, *Inessa, Lenin's Mistress* (London: Duckworth, 2001), ix. Hereafter Pearson.
10  There is a parallel with Ezra Pound who, with his wife Dorothy, moved in with his long-term mistress Olga Rudge in her small home during the shelling of Rapallo during the Second World War.
11  Lenin, "To Inessa Armand," Letter from Berne. January 17, 1915. https://www.marxists.org/archive/lenin/works/1915/jan/17.htm.
12  Catherine Merridale, *Lenin on the Train* (London: Penguin, 2017), 133. Hereafter Merridale.
13  She is thought to be the heroine of Alexandra Kollontai's 1923 novel, *A Great Love*. The author knew both Lenin and Armand. Useful on her life is Ralph Carter Elwood, "Lenin's Correspondence with Inessa Armand," *The Slavonic and East European Review* 65.2 (April 1987): 218–35 and Elwood, *Inessa Armand: Revolutionary and Feminist* (Cambridge: Cambridge University Press, 1992).
14  On this topic see David Castronovo and Janet Groth, *Critic in Love, A Romantic Biography of Edmund Wilson* (Berkeley: Shoemaker Hoard, 2005), 179 and *passim*.
15  Struve was also the editor of *Russian Thought* (*Russkaya Mysi*), a liberal paper, who rejected Andrey Bely's important novel *Petersburg* (first published in 1913) because he thought it parodied the intelligentsia.
16  A line from Turgenev's first novel, *Rudin*, may summarize Wilson's encounter with Lenin: Lezhnev tells Alexandra Pavlovna that often "'you tell a woman something out of simple conviction and she can't be content until she's thought up some superficial, irrelevant reason why you should have said that and not something else.'" Lenin appears to have acted in that way, corrupting allegiances between himself and colleagues, and, by extension, Wilson. Turgenev, *Rudin*, tr. Richard Freeborn (London: Penguin, 1975), 93.
17  Nabokov to Wilson February 23, 1948 in *The Nabokov-Wilson Letters*, ed. Simon Karlinksy (New York: Harper & Row, 1979), 33. Hereafter N-W Lett.
18  Wilson, *Travels in Two Democracies* (New York: Harcourt Brace and Company, 1936), 321. Hereafter Two. The Soviets were not pleased with his criticisms and he was told he would never be granted another visa. See

Dabney, *Edmund Wilson, A Life in Literature* (New York: Farrar, Straus and Giroux, 2005), 217.

19  Wilson, "Journey to the Soviet Union, 1935," *The Thirties, from Notebooks and Diaries of the Period*, ed. Leon Edel (New York: Farrar, Straus and Giroux, 1980), 524. Hereafter Thirties.

20  Wilson, like Dreiser, Dos Passos, and Sherwood Anderson, voted for the Communist candidate for president in 1932, William Z. Foster. He even held a reception for Foster in his apartment. In a letter to Theodore Dreiser he explained his support: "The Communist Party alone is working to educate and organize the classes dispossessed by the present system…." See Wilson in Jeffrey Meyers, *Edmund Wilson, A Biography* (Boston: Houghton Mifflin, 1995), 150.

21  Nabokov to Wilson February 23, 1948, N-W Lett 195.

Nabokov earlier told Wilson in a December 1940 letter that his portrait of Lenin was incomplete and that "not even the magic of your style has made me like him." You have "faithfully and fatally followed" the official biographies. Eight years later, Nabokov offered a more stinging rebuke: when improved information and "inescapable facts dampened your enthusiasm… you somehow did not bother to check your preconceived notions in regard to old Russia, while on the other hand, the glamor of Lenin's reign retained for you the emotional iridescence which your optimism, ideals and youth had provided." N-W Lett. 33, 195.

22  See Turgenev, "Diary of a Superfluous Man," *First Love and Other Stories*, tr. Richard Freeborn (Oxford: Oxford World's Classics, 2008), 36, 41, 54; Tolstoy, *War and Peace*, tr. Louise and Aylmer Maude, rev. Amy Mandelker (Oxford: Oxford World's Classics, 2010) Book One, Part Three, Ch. 16, pp. 296–9 when Prince Andrei witnesses a battle and is himself injured. A sentence from Book Two Part One reads "In the room next their bedroom there was a confusion of sabres, satchels, sabretaches, open portmanteaus, and dirty boots. Two freshly cleaned pairs with spurs had just been placed by the wall" (320). A late example from Book Three, Part Three, Chapter 18 is the description of Pierre taking down one of Bazdeev's manuscripts (933) or from Ch. 25, Count Rastopchin accosting Kutuzov, who is on a bench near the Yauza bridge, "toying with his whip in the sand" (959).

23  Wilson in Sherman Paul, *Edmund Wilson, A Study of Literary Vocation in Our Time* (Urbana: University of Illinois Press, 1965), 119. Hereafter Paul.

24  David Remnick, "Wilson and Soviet Russia, A Roundtable," *Edmund Wilson, Centennial Observations*, ed. Lewis M. Dabney (Princeton: Princeton University Press, 1997), 184. Hereafter Remnick.

25  Lewis M. Dabney, *Edmund Wilson, A Life in Literature* (New York: Farrar, Straus and Giroux, 2005), 201–2. Hereafter Dabney.

26  Helen Muchnic, "Edmund Wilson's Russian Involvement," *An Edmund Wilson Celebration*, ed. John Wain (Oxford: Phaidon, 1978), 86. Hereafter Muchnic.

The essay considers Wilson's view of the major Russian writers from his published criticism with an emphasis on Pushkin, Turgenev, and Pasternak. Wilson and Muchnic were friends.

27 The essay was "Meditations on Dostoevsky," *The New Republic* 56 (October 24, 1928), 274–6. See Wilson, *I Thought of Daisy* (Iowa City: University of Iowa Press, 2001), 143–50.

28 Edmund Wilson, *Letters on Literature and Politics 1912–1972*, ed. Elena Wilson, intro. Daniel Aaron and Foreword Leon Edel (New York: Farrar, Straus and Giroux, 1977), 248. Hereafter Letts.

29 Mary McCarthy to Lewis M. Dabney, 1984 in Dabney 287.

30 In reviewing the book in the *Partisan Review* of November-December 1940, the art critic Meyer Schapiro described how Wilson's portraits "impose themselves by their concreteness, finesse and sympathy… like the great fictional characters of literature." It is a work that focuses on personality. See Schapiro, "The Revolutionary Personality," *Partisan Review* Nov.-Dec. 1940: 467. Also in Morris Dickstein, "Edmund Wilson: Three Phases," *Edmund Wilson, Centennial Observations*, ed. Lewis M. Dabney (Princeton: Princeton University Press, 1997), 23.

Helpful in understanding Wilson's approach is Max Eastman's *Artists in Uniform* (1934) which defended the intelligentsia of Russia, which became something of a tradition. Eastman's view was that the decline of the Soviet Union was the result of Marx, not Lenin. Wilson developed a similar argument. See Paul Berman, "Wilson and Soviet Russia, A Roundtable," *Edmund Wilson, Centennial Observations*, ed. Lewis M. Dabney (Princeton: Princeton University Press, 1997), 200.

But in his accounts, Wilson was never one to skip a comic anecdote. Describing how Sergei Alymov, futurist poet, songwriter, and drinker, was locked in an apartment to sober up, friends would "sometime lower a bottle down to him from [a] window above." He was a "Russian with ineradicable sorrow in his soul" (Thirties 562).

31 David Remnick 201. Also see Morris Dickstein, "Edmund Wilson: Three Phases," *Edmund Wilson, Centennial Observations*, ed. Lewis M. Dabney (Princeton: Princeton University Press, 1997), 23.

32 Among texts recording these visits are Dreiser's *Russian Diary*, Dewey's series of articles on education in the *New Republic* and Waldo Frank's *Dawn in Russia, The Record of a Journey*. Helpful is Lewis S. Feuer, "American Travelers to the Soviet Union 1917–32: The Formation of a New Deal Ideology," *American Quarterly* 14.2 (1962): 119–49.

The mid-1930s was the peak of foreign tourism to Russia before the war with approximately 1,500 visitors per year. There was also an influx of "celebrity tourists." Sheila Fitzpatrick, "Foreign Visitors Observed: Moscow Visitors in the 1930s Under the Gaze of their Soviet Guides," *Russian History* 35.17 (2008): 218–19.

Among the colorful characters in Russia was Ruth Epperson Kennel, a 34-year-old American expatriate living in Moscow who became Dreiser's private secretary, translator, companion and lover during his October 1927 visit. Others were Big Bill Haywood, American labor militant and Anna Louise Strong, to be expelled from the Soviet Union as a spy.

33  A further example is this sentence on Bakunin mixing high and low diction: "Bakunin knocked around for some years between Sweden, Italy and Switzerland, subsisting on borrowed money and on the patronage of a Russian princess; associating himself with revolutionary movements and trying to cook up movements of his own" (Station 319).

34  Wilson has a useful complaint about dialectical materialism in *The Thirties* writing that there is a "curious effect of trying to cut off the past and starting with dialectical materialism—they are now trying to relieve this impoverishment by bringing back the culture of their tradition: Ostrovsky and Chekhov, Pushkin, pictures of Pushkin all over, right beside Engels and Marx—candy with Pushkin on the box." He then writes "they have been whitewashing everything, and the foreigners are usually covered with whitewash and brushing each other off. The Russians seem to know how to avoid it" (Thirties 558).

35  Dostoevsky, "White Nights," *White Nights and Other Stories*, tr. Constance Garnett (New York: Grove Press, 1960), 56.

As a further correction, Wilson published *A Window on Russia* the same year *To the Finland Station* was reissued, also the year Wilson died, 1972. In it, he calmly writes that "the Russian purges, as news, are now an old story." He now roots his Russia in the moment, the post-Stalinist moment, and to ensure his change of view and authenticity of his new understanding, not only dedicates *A Window on Russia* to his half-Russian wife but acknowledges that he owes to her and her Russian family and friends "a great debt." Lenin makes less than ten cameo appearances. Wilson, *A Window on Russia* (New York: Farrar, Straus and Giroux, 1972), 252, [i].

# 5

# H.G. Wells: Triangles

The focus on love and H.G. Wells in this chapter unavoidably includes Bruce Lockhart and Maxim Gorky, all three united by the *femme fatale* Moura Budberg. A possible spy, political prisoner, and romantic deceiver, who mixed with diplomats, writers, politicians, journalists, and nobility, she was intriguing, intelligent, and instrumental in revising the drama of Russian love. The story of Wells is her story which shifts the narrative from sincerity to betrayal.

H.G. Wells's friendship with Maxim Gorky forms the backdrop. They met in 1906 at a banquet in the United States when Wells, in fact, defended Gorky's arrival in New York with his then mistress, the actress Maria Andreeva of the Moscow Art Theater. They met again in London in 1907 when Gorky was there for the Fifth Congress of the Communist Party. In 1914, Wells made a brief trip to Russia and encountered Moura socially, although he wouldn't remember it but he did recall attending a session of the State Duma at the Tauride Palace, shocked to see a portrait of Nicholas II hanging in the chamber.[1]

But as Gorky's translator/secretary and occasional lover, Moura becomes a pivotal figure in the story of Russian love. She began to work for him in 1919, the widowed daughter of a Russian nobleman whose husband, Johann von Benckendorff, a high-ranking Czarist diplomat, was shot in 1918, murdered by peasants on his estate in Estonia (where, in fact, Wells would complete his *Experiment in Autobiography* in 1934). She herself would later be arrested on suspicion of being a spy for the British when she worked with the acting British Consul General in Petrograd and then special agent for the British government in Russia, the British diplomat Bruce Lockhart with whom she also had a relationship.

To recap, Lockhart had first arrived in Russia in 1912 and was at the British Consulate in Moscow (the embassy was in Petrograd). The next year he met Gorky; by then, he already knew Stanislavsky and the owner of the popular cabaret theater named The Bat, owned by Kikita Baliev. The mayor of Moscow,

Mikhail Chelnokov, also became a friend. A return to England in 1913 meant a marriage but also a reposting to Moscow as Consul General. But involvement with a mistress meant another return to England until the fall of the Provisional Government. He returned to Russia one more time in January 1918 with the goal of preventing Russia from signing a peace treaty with Germany but a truce had been signed a month before.

He had returned to Petrograd as a special diplomatic agent to get a sense of the Bolshevik government and its plans. He was thirty-one and more or less in charge of the embassy, the ambassador having returned to England in ill-health. Moura had been stopping by the embassy for weeks to see old friends from London where she had been with Count Benckendorff before his posting to Berlin. She saw Lockhart on his third day in Petrograd and made an impression elaborated by Lockhart in his *Memoirs of a British Agent*:

> A Russian of the Russians, she had a lofty disregard for all the pettiness of life and courage which was proof against all cowardice. Her vitality, due perhaps to an iron constitution, was immense and invigorated everyone with whom she came in contact. Where she loved, there was her world, and her philosophy of life had made her mistress of all the consequences. She was an aristocrat. She could have been a Communist.... I found her a woman of great attraction whose conversation brightened my daily life.[2]

She hosted a small birthday party for Captain Cromie, military attaché at the embassy at Lockhart's apartment. The carefree evening lingered in Lockhart's mind. But as the war intensified and the Bolsheviks announced that Moscow would become the new capital, delegations prepared to depart. Lockhart remained and began an affair with Moura, while maintaining a skeleton British presence in both Petrograd and Moscow, befriending Trotsky as well as Lenin (Berb 25).

By April 1918, Moura joined Lockhart in Moscow at the consular apartments; he offered a romantic description of their reunion in *Memoirs of a British Agent*. She was never to leave "until we were parted by the armed force of the Bolsheviks" (Mem 269). Ironically, England had not yet recognized Bolshevik Russia. The politics intensified when Britain joined the Allies for an invasion via Archangel and Vladivostok to support the White, not Red, Russians, although Lockhart opposed the action believing that the British should join the Bolsheviks to defeat the Germans. He spent his last night in Moscow before fleeing to Vologda on May 27, 1919, at the Strelna café and then going out to Sparrow Hills with Moura. He returned on May 31 to a city now under martial law. Soon, civil war broke out in Siberia, the Red Army was mobilized, and his efforts turned to escape.

But he did not want to leave, nor leave Moura who had moved into the apartment Lockhart shared with Hicks, an officer from the titular embassy near the Arbat. That summer she told Lockhart she had to go to her home in Revel in Estonia to see her children, cut off from them since the fall of 1917. But would her papers allow her to travel and cross? There was no train service, he later learned, and the area was under German control. She had disappeared for two weeks and could not travel to Revel (Berb 43–5). Was she on a spy mission, was she meeting another lover? No clear answers emerged, and then events in July and August accelerated the danger and their anticipated separation.

Deceptions, intrigues, and then the attempted assassination of Lenin meant the unexpected arrest of Lockhart in his apartment on September 1, 1918, at 3:30 a.m. Reports are confusing: Hicks was there and probably Moura, although several accounts fail to report her. He and Hicks were taken to Cheka headquarters on Lubyanka Square, Moura to another prison (Breb 60–9). By morning, the two men were freed but not Moura. On September 3 *Izvestia* printed a full account of a supposed Anglo-French conspiracy led by Lockhart and the French Consul General where more than a million rubles were supposedly spent in attempted bribes. His own efforts to locate and free Moura led to his rearrest.[3]

But there were suspicions. When Peters told Lockhart all the British cipher codes had been obtained by the Bolsheviks, Moura was a suspect. Her two-week disappearance when she was supposed to visit her children was another mystery. Her arrest and then release during the attempt to kill Lenin was a further mystery, her freedom occurring without the influence of Lockhart. Later, she claimed to be pregnant with Lockhart's child but then had a miscarriage.[4] Several thought her a Soviet spy within the British Embassy and that her arrest was a cover-up.

But after Lockhart's forced return to England, Moura, lost and unsure of her future in 1919, began to pursue Gorky beginning with his publishing effort, Universal Literature. Moura went to the publishing company to meet the translator Kornei Chukovsky: she had heard he needed assistance for translations of Galsworthy's novels and Wilde's fairy tales. Lacking idiomatic Russian, Chukovsky nonetheless found office work for her and managed to get her a ration card (Berb 99). Early that summer he took her to meet Gorky where she discovered a chaotic home with women, children, assistants, and papers everywhere. His wife, the actress Andreeva, also lived at No.5 Kronverk Prospect but so, too, did his mistress Vavara Tikhonova and various children Gorky adopted.[5]

Moura soon made herself part of the household by performing a myriad set of duties and soon moved into his large apartment, quickly becoming indispensable, filing his manuscripts, reviewing his mail, organizing his reading, preparing materials for the day's work, while typing and translating foreign texts as Gorky needed them (Berb 106). She even took over household responsibilities directing the servants, Gorky calling her "a woman of iron" (Berb 115). During this period, she had a brief marriage of convenience to Baron Nikolai von Budberg (January 1922) to restore her Estonian citizenship and passport but left him within months, going first to London before returning to Gorky, then in exile in Italy.

But even with Gorky she was under suspicion. Zinoviev, Chairman of the Petrograd Soviet after the revolution, became an enemy of Gorky. A principal collaborator of Lenin's, he stood third in line after Trotsky. But he also distrusted Moura, convinced she was a British agent and at one time organized a search of Gorky's apartment with special attention to Moura's room.

Wells renewed his friendship with Moura in 1920 when he visited Russia to study the new economy and society, and reconnect with Gorky. By then, she had become Gorky's private secretary and he asked her to act as Wells's interpreter and guide about Petrograd and when he traveled to Moscow to meet Lenin; they also began a casual affair, their difference in height not an issue: she was nearly six feet tall, while he was approximately four-and-a-half inches shorter.

At the time, Wells had something of reputation as a lady's man, mixing marriage with short- and long-term relationships. While married to his first wife, his cousin Isabel Wells, he had a short affair with Ethel Kingsmill before leaving his wife in 1893 to begin a more sustained relation with his former student "Jane," born Amy Catherine Robbins, whom he married in 1895. He had two sons with her but other affairs meant other children: Anna Jane was his daughter with Amber Reeves (1908–9), while Anthony West was a son with Rebecca West (1913–24). A long series of other women interrupted his more permanent associations; stopping and starting again was typical. His relationship with Moura began in 1920, paused, and then restarted in 1928/9 and more-or-less lasted until his death in 1946.[6]

In 1929 Moura and Wells met again in Berlin and she then pursued him to England when she decided that for political reasons she could not return to Russia with Gorky. Within a few years, Wells would repeatedly ask her to marry but she refused.[7] When he asked her to accompany him on his third visit to Russia in 1934, she also declined, claiming it would be too dangerous. But he later learned that she had secretly visited Gorky a few months before; deceitful acts were part of her nature. Volume two of his autobiography, *H.G. Wells in Love, Postscript to an Experiment in Autobiography*, describes their confrontation over her secret trip. Speculation continued that she was a double agent spying on Wells and others.[8]

Her entanglement with Wells, however, did not prevent her from swiftly returning to Moscow from London to be at Gorky's bedside when he died on June 18, 1936, at his villa Leninskie Gorki outside of Moscow. Her entry into Russia was not even stamped in her passport. At first, Wells was not told of the trip, nor did he know that Moura was receiving Gorky's foreign royalties under a power of attorney. Even Stalin visited the declining Gorky whose death remains suspicious.[9] The estimated crowd at Gorky's funeral in Red Square was 800,000. André Gide spoke; Stalin and Molotov were pallbearers. The body was cremated and the ashes placed in the Kremlin wall.

But to return to 1920, Wells had telegraphed Gorky that he would be visiting to see the new Russia. But Gorky explained there were no hotels operating in Petrograd; staff had been mobilized to fight the Germans. Why not stay with him? He had a twelve-room apartment at 23 Kronverksky Prospekt. Wells accepted and arrived with his son Gip; what was to be a few days became two weeks. Among events was a House of Arts dinner in his honor where Moura acted as his interpreter. She also became his guide. But when not attending meetings, the Hermitage, churches, or Smolny (Bolshevik headquarters), he sat with Gorky in his study, Moura between them, discussing education, the life of nations, technology, and world peace (Berb. 118).

A well-known studio photo from Petrograd in 1920 shows Wells on the left in profile, Gorky seated above smiling at Wells with this left arm pointed in Wells' direction and a slyly smiling Moura, the only figure looking directly at the camera, the only individual aware of and confidently challenging the viewer mixing allure with self-assurance (WLove 144a). In Wells's autobiography—this section written in 1934—Wells does not hesitate to celebrate Moura and her "commanding distinction" while describing her less attractive personal habits, including her rapid eating and love of drinking resulting in a heavy frame. She smokes too much but she is always a presence and cannot be overlooked, he adds (WLove 162). A "bravery of bearing" and "the quiet assurance of her pose" compel people to approach her, her Tartar cheekbones giving her "an expression of amiable serenity, even when she is really in a thoroughly bad temper" (WLove 162). She is always self-possessed; the camera cannot do her justice, Wells believes.

When Wells met her in 1920 in Gorky's Petrograd flat, she wore a khaki British army raincoat and a shabby black dress but had "magnificence": she stuck her hands in the coat and at twenty-seven "seemed not simply to brave the world but disposed to order it about" (WLove 163). She became his official translator and he immediately fell in love with her, convincing her one night to flit "noiselessly through the crowded apartments in Gorky's flat to my embraces. I believed she loved me and I believed every word she said to me" (WLove 164).

Nevertheless, he unwillingly recognized her "insincerities," although he did not identify her lies: Did she spend six months in prison? Had she been sentenced to be shot? Why was she paroled (WLove 164)? He does not investigate, believing what she says. Most importantly, he realizes that "she thinks like a Russian; copiously, windingly and with that flavour of philosophical pretentiousness of Russian discourse, beginning nowhere in particular and emerging at a foregone conclusion." Her mind is active and "shrewdly penetrating. It is silk, not steel." She is a "creature of impulse" (WLove 165).

Berberova reports that Wells began to confide in Moura, mostly about his distress over the condition of Petrograd and the loss of its culture. He recalled earlier meetings with her, as early as a ball at the home of the Russian Ambassador to England nine years before (Berb 120). And now, a connection had formed. He went on to Moscow and a meeting with Lenin, after which he traveled back to Petrograd, joined Gorky again at Kronverk, and toured the city, including the Commission for Improving Living Conditions for Academics, always in the company of Moura. At a farewell dinner, he promised to stop at her home in Tallinn, the capital of Estonia, to see her children and report back. And that very night, Wells entered *her* bedroom. The move from conversation, to exile, to sex is less conjecture than action (Berb. 123). In the morning, Wells left and Moura prepared to take her own surreptitious journey to Estonia.

One result of Wells's trip was *Russia in the Shadows* (1921), a pessimistic account of the destruction of Petrograd and the downfall of Russia and its culture. The widespread end of social order and administrative efficiency overshadows the revolution he writes. Everything has broken down and people live in a "camouflage of realities" without "proper food or clothes."[10] Eleven black-and-white photos document places and people. But with chapter titles like "Petersburg in Collapse," "Drift and Salvage," and "The Dreamer in the Kremlin," his point of view is clear. And when he achieves his goal of interviewing Lenin, he conveys his disappointment and pervasive sense of a constantly controlled conversation.

At his desk, he reports, Lenin's feet could scarcely touch the ground and, despite his excellent English, a Mr. Rothstein chaperoned the dialog.

Uncharacteristically, Lenin did not lecture Wells who came expecting "to struggle with a doctrinaire Marxist." That was not the case. Two motifs shaped their conversation: What do you think you are making of Russia (Wells to Lenin) and then, why hasn't the social revolution started in England (Lenin to Wells)?[11] Lenin's failure to answer left Wells with a sense of the unpreparedness of Marxist thought: "they do not know what to do" (Shadows 156). For Wells, the "dark crystal of Russia" remained a puzzle which seeks a balance: "The Bolshevik Government is inexperienced and incapable to an extreme degree; it has had phases of violence and cruelty; but it is on the whole honest," although the "impression of a vast irreparable breakdown" is written everywhere on the great "Eastern wall of Europe."[12]

Moura left Russia in December but was quickly arrested since it was illegal to leave the country without proper documents. Gorky rushed to the Cheka headquarters in Petrograd. A cable to Moscow led to her release with official permission to leave. She traveled in January 1921. Gorky was also encouraged to leave for health reasons, a move endorsed by Lenin. But when Moura arrived in Tallinn, she was immediately arrested, taken to a cell and then interrogated as a Soviet spy (Breb 127–8). Earlier, as part of Lockhart's household, she was supposedly working for British intelligence and later, in the 1930s, having emigrated to England, she was said to be a German spy. A rumor even circulated that she slept with Kaiser Wilhelm when Benckendorff was secretary at the Russian embassy in Berlin just before the First World War.

When news of her imminent arrival in Estonia reached the brother and sister of her late husband, a week before her arrival, they petitioned the Estonian Supreme Court to have her immediately deported and prevented from seeing her children. She soon had a lawyer and the injunction was lifted. She made a written promise not to leave Estonia. She was told she could likely stay three months, that she would be followed, and that she should find asylum somewhere (Berb 129–30). She spent two weeks with her children and saw no one else during the three-month period. But the Benckendorff family would soon stop supporting her children.

In early June, a lawyer returned to visit her with a tall "assistant." It was Baron Nikolai Budberg, poor but with status, marriageable but eager to leave Estonia (supposedly, he once shot himself out of boredom). If she married him, she could reclaim her Estonia citizenship and be able to travel with an Estonian passport (Berb 133). He was several years younger than Moura but was without a profession or career. In the meantime, she heard that Gorky was not well and not writing but trying to generate international support for the starving people of Russia. He was also preparing to leave for Berlin. He did in mid-October traveling first to Helsinki; Moura received a special visa to visit him. In a letter a month after they met, Gorky wrote the artist and costume designer Valentina Khodasevich from Berlin that Moura has become even sweeter than before and

> as ever, she knows everything and is interested in everything. A superlative person! She wants to marry some baron but we're protesting vociferously. Let the baron pick himself another fantasy! This one is ours!
>
> (in Bereb. 140–1)

Gorky went on to Berlin and then a sanatorium in the Black Forest. In January 1922, Moura married Baron Budberg (although she had told Gorky she had married in the fall of 1921, another falsehood). In December 1921, she told him she would soon be there to see him but did not appear. On the wedding evening, her new husband departed for Berlin; she stayed behind a few days preparing to visit Gorky.

During this period, she was also writing to Lockhart as she had been doing for several years. He did not reply. Nor did Wells. And then she secretly went to London, although neither Lockhart or Wells was there. After obtaining some new clothes and seeing some friends, she returned to Estonia but did not see Gorky on her return journey. She was beginning to wear well-made suits from England and a man's watch on her wrist but still possessed a captivating, "feline smile" and mystery (Berb. 166).

It was not until June 1922 that she visited Gorky, then in Berlin, and joined his household, stabilizing her role and their relationship by the summer. She and Gorky reunited, although his coughing and illness (tuberculosis) did not abate. But her role expanded to mistress of the house as well as secretary, interpreter, and literary agent, all the while alternating between Saarow and the Black Forest (Berb 173). She then had a new assignment: translating Gorky's *The Judge* into English for a possible UK/US production. It was deemed not suitable, however, in its first draft and despite revisions was never produced.

By 1923, however, Moura was becoming bored and worked to ship the baron (with his gambling debts) to Argentina, and pursue her mantra, "survival." The baron left, only to disembark in Antwerp or Cherbourg and return, demanding a notarized letter confirming financial support. He got it and left and she never saw him again. By March 1923, Gorky was off to recover in Sorento, while Moura dealt with publication and translation rights in Germany (Berb 183). But her allegiance to Gorky was faltering, having met Lockhart three times in the past year.

But what of Wells? Beginning in 1924, Moura saw him from time-to-time in London, but there was competition from Lockhart located by Moura in Prague where he had been working since 1920, first as part of the English mission as a commercial attaché and then as a director of the Anglo-Austrian Bank. But Lockhart was indecisive about restarting with Moura and did not tell her that he had separated from his wife, that he had had an affair with an actress from the Moscow Art Theater in 1923, or that he was currently involved with Lady Rosslyn (Berb. 191). She, in turn, misled him about the number of her translations of Gorky and the supposed income she was receiving (Berb 191).

By March 1925, however, Gorky began to think of returning to Russia, an economic as much as political decision. His European and North American readership was falling and his journal *Beseda* was not allowed in Russia. He needed funds. By 1928, he acted, preceded by the sale of his collection of jade figurines at Sotheby's in London.[13]

Accelerating the decision to return was a raid on Gorky's villa by Italian police. They principally searched Moura's room taking some manuscripts and correspondence. Gorky was furious and contacted the Soviet ambassador in Rome. Appropriate apologies, even from Mussolini, were offered. The papers were returned. During this period, which involved a temporary move to Posillipo, west of Naples, Gorky began his four-volume novel *The Life of Klim Samgin*, dedicated to Maria Ignatievna Zakrevskaya, Moura's birth name. Once completed, he thought he would return to Russia but he and Moura realized that she could not for political reasons.

One result of a search of her room in Il Sorito, the Sorrento villa, was that on her next trip to Estonia she was arrested at the Italian/Austrian border. She was held and her luggage searched. When released, a great many of her papers were missing. Having notified Gorky, he again contacted the Soviet Ambassador but this time there was no action. But her reputation became more complicated: in Moscow she was once considered a secret agent of England; in Estonia, a Soviet spy. Russian émigrés in France believed she was working for Germany, while in England it was thought she was an agent of the Soviets. In 1924, Yakov Peters, associate Cheka head, believed she was a German spy who also worked for the Cheka. Mussolini's government was confused but convinced she was not to be trusted. Lockhart would later confirm that she provided him with "extensive information" about Russian emigration and developments in Eastern Europe becoming an informant and back-channel source for visible and invisible Soviet activities (Berb 202). She and Lockhart would meet every three or four months in a Central or Eastern Europe capital.

When Lockhart showed Moura parts of his *Memoir of a British Agent* before publication, she became upset but not because of the intimations of spying. In his diary for June 18, 1932, he wrote that she wanted revisions which would present her in a more formal manner, calling her not Moura but Mme Benckendorff throughout. She has turned into a "Victorian spinster …. Therefore, either the full love story or nothing. This will be very difficult" but "she is the only person who has the right to demand an alteration." Three days later, he writes, "dined with Moura at the Eiffel Tower" (Lockhart, Diaries I, 220, 221). The memoir did appear with adjustments and two years after became the successful international film *British Agent*, directed by Michael Curtiz (later to direct *Casablanca*). It stressed the revolution, conspiracies, prison, and a love affair between Lockhart and Moura.[14]

Lockhart took Moura to a London screening of the film but to his surprise, no one else was there (Berb 208). At the end, they parted on the street but she still provided him with details of Russian political and cultural life: she had details on André Gide's trip to the Soviet Union and Alexei Tolstoy's to London as well as gossip (see Berb 210–14). One diary entry by Lockhart notes that Moura and Wells are seeing each other but they "squabble violently … about Russia and foreign politics" (Berb. 212). Another sentence from his November 17, 1932, diary entry summarizes the complications of Russian love: "she is going with H.G. [Wells] to Paris and then goes to Sorrento to Gorky" (Berb. 213). For her, love has few, if any, personal or geographical boundaries, combining the behavior of a coquette with Matta Hari.

But again, what was Wells's state of mind? How did he react and did he become romantically embroiled with her again? Or did he never leave her, at least emotionally? It appears that by 1927/8 the two were again entangled. Wells had broken up with Rebecca West in the mid-1920s and was living with the determined, demanding Odette Keun in the south of France. He was sixty and she was thirty-eight. He was committed to building a home on the Riviera in Grasse; she was determined to perfect her social skills. But when told that he had slept with Moura, she went into a rage and threatened to kill herself. Such behavior only drove him further to Moura, who, realizing that by 1928 her relationship with Gorky was ending, recognized that her only salvation would be some form of semi-permanent connection with Wells. Establishing herself in England would be her remedy in the face of Gorky's return to Russia, politics now shaping love.

In June 1928, Moura applied for a British visa, ostensibly to escort an adopted daughter to a London secretarial school. It was declined because she was thought to be a security risk. Gorky then asked her to accompany him to Russia should he return. She said no and moved to Berlin, looking after Gorky's literary work, notably translations. In the spring of 1929, Wells went to Berlin to lecture. She had a note handed to him. She would be there. Their romance restarted as Wells outlines in *H.G. Wells in Love*. To him, she always had an "unquestionable attraction, and unless she is the greatest actress in the world, I have something of the same un-analysable magic for her" (141). Of course, self-deception operated on both sides.

At the time, Wells was also widening his vision, writing about biology, economics, and the natural sciences. But by 1931, Wells and Moura were appearing in the papers. By 1933 (the year Gorky officially returned to Russia), he met Moura in Dubrovnik for a session of the International PEN Club, and they were inseparable. But he was also breaking up with Odette which meant the loss of his French home. Odette took her revenge by publishing a reminiscence of her life with Wells, a tell-all of a failed man, a *parvenu*. Four years later, in *Apropos of Dolores,* he gained his revenge.

In May 1933, Wells returned to London, while Moura went on to Istanbul to see Gorky before his final return to Russia. In July 1933, Moura also told Wells that she was pregnant. He was sixty-seven; she was forty-eight. But was it true or a cover-up allowing her to disappear to Europe for two weeks? At the time, abortions in Great Britain were illegal; only in Russia were they permitted.[15] And rumors continued to swirl that she was actually a Soviet spy, something she was pointedly accused of by Rebecca West, Wells's former lover, information which was passed on to MI5 (McD 318–9).

In 1934, Wells decided he had to meet Stalin, so arranged to return to Russia and interview him for *The New Statesman*. He had just met Roosevelt who was quick and flexible in this thinking but he found Stalin dogmatic: "His was not a free impulsive brain nor a scientifically organized brain; it was a trained Leninist-Marxist brain." Nevertheless, he left after his nearly three-hour meeting with a positive impression of the Soviet leader, referring to him as "fair, candid and honest."[16] Gorky was similarly uncommunicative except for the Soviet rhetoric.

Wells ended the trip in Estonian with Moura and they returned to London together where her apartment was just steps from his. She had become a consultant and assistant to the director Alexander Korda and J. Arthur Rank. Movies with Russian subjects were fashionable, and she assisted with all aspects of production, becoming an advisor on Russian matters. But she was also still acting as Gorky's literary agent, now attempting to get his plays produced. She also continued to circulate in the proper émigré circles which included Kerensky, the three Benenson sisters from St. Petersburg (the youngest, Manya Harai, would become one of the early English translators of *Doctor Zhivago*), and the wife of the Polish ambassador.

Moura also still visited Gorky, one of their last encounters focusing on his archive which he wanted kept in Pushkin House in Leningrad. But the large number of letters was problematic: revolutionaries, dissidents, and émigrés made up a good portion of the correspondence. Confusion as to where it should go and who would protect the material followed with the final decision that Moura should guard them. In April, she left Sorrento for London with a suitcase of materials, keeping the papers for two years, refusing requests to send them on to Moscow. Then a threat: if she wanted to see Gorky before he died, she and the papers had to return to Moscow. There would be private train car for her once she reached the Russian border. Lockhart agreed that she had to go, otherwise the papers would be taken by force (Berb 240). In June 1936, she returned with Gorky's archive. He had asked Stalin for permission for her to return in order to see him before he died, although this is a subject of some dispute; she kept the trip a secret. Stalin, however, may have used some of the material in the letters as preparation for the Moscow Show Trials. Ironically, the Sorrento suitcase arrived in Moscow but Gorky never saw it (Berb 247–8, 250–1).[17]

## ii

*"The sincere falseness, the bluff of love-making"*
H.G. Wells, *H.G. Wells in Love* (1984)

Moura's relationship with Lockhart and Wells has a cynical side: Russian women were often sent to Paris or London to attach themselves to prominent writers or cultural figures as a way for Moscow to keep the men under surveillance and Stalin's influence, while preventing their criticism of his policies or actions. For example, the Russian wife of Romain Rolland, Maria Kudasheva, who at just over thirty married him at age sixty-eight, surrounded him with her Soviet friends and convinced him to visit Moscow as a Nobel Prize winner (Berb. 241). This may have actually been Moura's agenda with Wells, even after she settled with him in London, greeting well-wishers (who included Shaw, Sydney and Beatrice Webb, J.B. Priestly, and Lady Diana Cooper) at his seventieth birthday at a PEN club reception at the Savoy. Wells had become president of International PEN, although from the early 1930s to the 1950s, according to

Berberova, Moura was instrumental in barring Russian émigré writers from membership. She did try to bring Soviet writers into the organization, however, but that failed (Berb. 255–6 nt.1).

And then, a caricature of Russian love. Wells had for some time been trying to convince Moura to marry but she decided to play a practical joke on him and his friends who were also urging her to marry. She sent out invitations to an engagement or possibly wedding banquet. The guests arrived at the gala at the Quo Vadis restaurant in Soho in November 1933 (Anthony West, Wells's son via Rebecca West, claims it was 1935). But when the guests—including Max Beerbohm, Maurice Baring, Harold Nicolson, Lady Cunard, Enid Bagnold, David Low, and others—congratulated Moura, she said to several it's not going to happen. He only thinks I am going to marry him. They did appear arm-in-arm, however, until at one moment she announced to all that it was a joke and the event only marked their open liaison. We never did get married, nor plan to, Moura proclaimed to all. Wells was surprised and, in some versions of the event, supposedly proposed to her in front of the guests. He was rebuffed (Sherborne 211; Berb. 257). For Wells, he believed that the prank and his declaration might have embarrassed Moura into accepting his marriage proposal, while distracting him from his repeated worries over death, illness, the impending war, and destructive weapons.

Wells had actually suggested marriage as early as 1932, writing that he was prepared to do anything and overlook anything to "make Moura mine" (WLove 169). She repeatedly refused: marriage was not necessary, she argued. Yet after the PEN conference in Austria, he willingly introduced her as the woman he wished to marry. But his objectivity gave way to his imagination, although that was soon to burst when he discovered her secret trip to see the ailing Gorky. The former Moura of "free uninquisitive intimacy" had vanished. They wounded each other by failing to follow through with their announced love (WLove 171).

Following the pseudo-engagement dinner, the party went to Wells's flat in Bickenhall Mansions for a concert that never took place, despite rows of rented gilded chairs. Another sham, although the couple did go off to Sussex for a supposed honeymoon. The charade was then complete, although afterward, Wells continued to live alone with his daughter-in-law who acted as secretary and housekeeper (McD. 262–3).

The Quo Vadis dinner became a parody of love, a simultaneous celebration and denial of romance. Yet the two stuck together, although by 1934, when she did not want to accompany him to the States, he became impatient and wrote to a friend that he intended to break up with her: "I can't stand any more of this semi-detached life." She travels too much and "for all I know is a drug trafficker or a spy or any fantastic thing" (McD 264).

After his return, he planned another visit to Moscow and asked her again to join him. Too dangerous, she replied. She said she would go to Estonia. But after his interview with Stalin, he went to see Gorky where an interpreter casually mentioned that Moura had just been to see Gorky the week before; Gorky confirmed the visit (McD 265). Wells was devastated and felt betrayed. He then canceled tickets for their journey from Estonia to England and made a codicil to his will, cutting her out. He wanted to cancel the Estonia leg of the trip but also wanted to see her; she met him at the Tallinn airport.

She explained that her trip to Gorky was impromptu and arranged while she was in Estonia. They quarreled, made love, and seemingly reconciled but while he couldn't believe her, he could not part from her either. Russian love again at play. They were unable to separate (McD 266). His suspicions and jealousies met her defensiveness. Yet they continued on, although the relationship did not prevent him from having an affair with an American widow met in France who reminded him of Moura, the tall, dark, and charming Constance Coolidge (McD 267). But paradoxically, the intensity of Russian love between Moura and Wells increased.

Ultimatums, however, met with objections, his demands with rejections. She ignored his pronouncements on how they should live together, preferring only to end up with him in bed (WLove 195). She did not return his latchkey to Chiltern Court, although when he moved to Hanover Terrance and made no provision for her to stay there, he still gave her a key (WLove 195–6). He knew that he could never be done with her which he explained via an astronomical metaphor: we are like "double stars that rotate about each other but never coalesce. Our very looseness now averts a conclusive rupture" followed by this passage on love:

> It is absurd to say I am still in love. And yet I love—after a fashion. I doubt if we love each other very much, continuously and steadily. We still have phases of intense companionship and satisfaction with each other. And pride and ownership.
>
> (WLove 196)

Love that is not love is here. He wanted to separate but could not.

In a subsequent passage, Wells tries to justify his ambiguous portrait of Moura explaining that there was a profound difference between an intricate Russian, capable of blanking out anything in her memory she does not like, and that of a mind accustomed to intellectual consistency. It is also a statement of my own unreasonable monstrous demands for a Lover-Shadow.

(WLove 197)

He then tries to rationalize this through a world view of relationships and his need for someone to match the "color" of his own mind.

However, in a further passage from the autobiography, he explains that he truly loved only three women before revealing a set of misogynist views. The three he loved are his first wife, his second, and Moura. Rebecca West was a question mark. In a condescending and patronizing manner, he exposes an unflattering, egotistical attitude toward love and physical relations:

I had one great storm of intensely physical sexual passion and desire with Amber Reeves. Beyond that, all these women I have kissed, solicited, embraced and lived with, have never entered intimately and deeply into my emotional life. I have liked them, found them pretty, exciting, amusing, flattering to the secret rakish braggart in my composition. I was jealous of them as one is jealous in a partnership… and my impression is that I got nothing better than I gave. I was loved as I loved.

(WLove 60–1; cf. 161)

Moura, however, rebelled, resisting control or even compatibility. She was an individual and had her own life of intrigue and suspicions marked by sudden disappearances and reappearances. Wells admits that by the summer of 1935 they had lost "the sincere falseness, the bluff of love-making" which is the truth of Russian love and why it largely ends in disappointment (WLove 198). One is in love with love, not with a person. This is the "tragic significance of love" Rudin describes in Turgenev's early novel, defining Russian romance as a play with two acts: the first is expectation, illusion, possibility, and often misunderstanding. The second is reality, deflation, and disappointment often plagued by social, political, or even geographical excuses.[18]

How did it end for Wells and Moura? Unhappily. It's a Russian love story framed by an expression of Moura's used in a parting letter of August 1924 after leaving Lockhart remet in Prague: "all I wanted was to have an illusion to live for" (in McD 228). Illusion, coupled with deceit, appears to have defined her life. In the summer of 1935, she proposed a new and colorful narrative to Wells which started in 1916 when the Germans caught her spying for Russia. She then reversed the situation explaining that she spied on the Russians for the Germans. Since that period, she told Wells, she waffled between governments that needed her services, contacts, and access to power and individuals to whom she felt obligated.

At one point the Italians, French, and British security services were examining her correspondence, friendships, and movements. The *Deuxième Bureau* was also monitoring the gossip among the many Russian émigrés in Paris to learn more about her. For her, morality did not enter the equation, only survival. Yet her own grown daughter disputed the full story and its many shadows, although one feature was persistent: that she pretended to spy for Germany while working for the Russians (McD 237, 270–1).

Juggling was her principal skill. In 1928, for example, as Gorky renewed his connections with Soviet Russia, she handled all his business affairs, while maintaining their romantic relationship but also pursuing H.G. Wells, who was himself juggling love relationships: the affair with Rebecca West had ended, his second wife Jill was ill and would soon die, while he was already involved with Odette Keun on the French Riviera. That would eventually break up while Moura pursued him, realizing that a safer life with Wells in England would stabilize her nomadic and at times dangerous life in Eastern Europe. As a backstop, she also attempted to renew her relationship with Lockhart. Again, her motives were self-preservation and protection.

Russian love became her operative mode, a world of promise and illusion supposedly removing hesitation, indecision, and social reality. But it could not control the emotions: "I was already very tired of Odette in 1928; I rediscovered Moura in 1929," Wells writes, although he says he did not become Moura's "open and professed lover until 1933," adding that "we were lovers but in conspiracy" (WLove 141). "Conspiracy" is apt, a term that virtually defines all of Moura's life.

But as Moura continued with her deceptive behavior, losing Wells's trust, he still could not end their union, stating in a 1936 letter to her that "there is an irrational gravitation between us" (WLove 196; McD 272). When he moved into a new home at 13 Hanover Terrace, Regent's Park, he gave her a key. In his *Experiment in Autobiography*, he admits his own failure to act and understand himself, mixing rationalization with self-justification claiming that he "now loved Moura more than I did any other woman" (WLove 143; 142ff). After their Berlin meeting, he settled a £200 annuity on her but when she came to England, he explained that he still wanted to keep Odette in the South of France, that he and Moura must not have a child but that, in turn, he would not expect her to remain faithful. Her enigmatic reply was "As you will. If I happen to be faithful to you that is my own affair" (WLove 143). Of course, the open relationship did not work and he dropped all pretense to allowing Moura to be "free," although he sensed they both enjoyed their adventurous behavior with vivid and intense encounters (WLove 145). But in 1936, he published *The Anatomy of Frustration*, supposedly a critique of the work of William Steele; more accurately, it was about himself.

Moura and Wells lived separate lives in London but traveled and vacationed together which always caused friction. And her views were as complex as they were changeable, telling Gorky on October 23, 1925, that she had loved him in Russia and during their time at Saarow but then gradually realized that "I was no longer in love with you. I love you but I was not in love," a distinction and condition that has shadowed and even defined Russian love (McD 231). Love mattered; the person less so. *To be in love meant more than the object of that love—and this is the secret of Russian love*. Rapture, not just a feeling of care, was needed, as Moura sought a love "that gives everything, but demands nothing" (McD 231–2). Moura's candor was typical if irregular; she had trouble with the truth even when telling it.[19]

Did she remain Gorky's lover? The answer is unclear but suggestive. He kept a plaster cast of her hand on his desk (WLove 168). Her words and subsequent letters to him led to disagreements and a possible severance of their union, even though he stated he loved her; complicating matters was a supposed new lover of Moura, a young Italian only known as "R" (McD 233).[20] During this period, the fall of 1926, she also perfunctorily divorced Baron Budberg. Nevertheless, she struggled to repair the damage with Gorky, as she would later do with Wells. For a while it worked. But secrets persisted, secrets Gorky and Wells did not want to know (WLove 167–8).

Reluctantly, Wells finally renounced the idea of marriage between himself and Moura, although they remained together through June 1935 when he wrote this section of his autobiography (WLove 199). Citing "Life Sentence," a short story by Rebecca West because it conveys a similar attitude toward marriage, he declared that "I don't want to go about with a woman who has to be explained" and Moura required a great deal of explaining (WLove 199). By the time he returned from a 1936 trip to America and she unexpectedly met him on his arrival at Waterloo, he finally realized that his obsession with her was over (WL 208–9).

But not entirely. He dedicated his 1936 novella *The Croquet Player* to her and, as he writes in a neutral style at the end of *Wells in Love*, "Moura and I will certainly stick together in our peculiar detached way" (WLove 216). He wrote that on the eve of his seventieth birthday, September 21, 1936. Moura was with him in Stockholm when war was declared on Germany, on September 3, 1939, making their return to England problematic (WLove 223). But during a fall 1940 lecture tour of America, on how it was necessary for Britain, Russia, and the United States to unite for the common goal of world peace, he managed to have a "last flare of cheerful sensuality. I loved it" (WLove 224). He was seventy-four and found another new woman or several. Yet Moura did not disappear: at the very end of his second autobiographical volume, he notes that she has become "like a Vatican cherub, three times life-size but still delightful, an ample woman" (WLove 227).[21]

But the paradox of Russian love remained, taking shape in a final question Moura posed to Wells: "why do you always *reason* about love and misjudge me so" (WLove 210)? Joy and misfortune unite.

## Notes

1  But Vladimir Nabokov remembered Wells. Nabokov's father was a journalist and liberal politician and Wells came to the Nabokov home in St. Petersburg for dinner. See Michael Sherborne, *H.G. Wells, Another Kind of Life* (London: Peter Owen, 2010), 222; Brian Boyd, *Vladimir Nabokov, The Russian Years* (Princeton University Press, 1990), 178. One of Nabokov's favorite novels was Wells's *The Passionate Friends* read as a teenager (Boyd 91).

   Part of Well's Russian trip appears in his 1915 novel, *The Research Magnificent*.

2  Nina Berberova, *Moura, The Dangerous Life of the Baroness Budberg*, tr. Marian Schwartz and Richard D. Sylvester (New York: New York Review Books, 2005), 21. Hereafter Berb; R.H. Bruce Lockhart, *Memoirs of a British Agent* (1932; London: Macmillan, 1974), 243–4. Hereafter Mem.

3  A play about Lockhart and his supposed "Lenin Plot," Nikolai Pogodin's *Enemy Vortext* (1953; film 1956), slandered Lockhart as a vulgar spy.

4  Michael Sherborne, *H.G. Wells, Another Kind of Life* (London: Peter Owen, 2010), 258. Hereafter Sherborne.

5  For Gorky on women, see Berb 114–15.

6  Additional affairs occurred with Rosamund Bland, 1907; Elizbeth von Arnin, 1910–13; Margaret Sanger, 1920; Hedwig Gatterenigg, 1924; Dorothy Petrie, 1924 (likely); Odette Keun, 1924–32 (she wouldn't let him go!) and Constance Coolidge, 1935, an American heiress. The list is incomplete.

7  Wells, *H.G. Wells in Love, Postscript to an Experiment in Autobiography*, ed. G.P. Wells (London: Faber & Faber, 1984), 169–74. Hereafter WLove.

   Vera Shamina and Maria Kozyreva, "Russia Revisited," *The Reception of H.G. Wells in Europe*, ed. Patrick Parrinder and James S. Partington (London: Bloomsbury, 2013), 59.

8  Wells, *H.G. Wells in Love, Postscript* 164–5, 170–82, 193–6. Andrea Lynn, *Shadow Lovers: The Last Affairs of H.G. Wells* (Boulder CO: Westview, 2001), 174–91; Deborah McDonald and Jeremy Dronfield, *A Very Dangerous Woman: The Lives,*

Loves and Lies of Russia's Most Seductive Spy (London: Oneworld Publications, 2015), *passim*.

9   McDonald, *A Very Dangerous Woman*, 277, 279. Hereafter McD.
10  Wells, *Russia in the Shadows* (New York: George H. Doran, 1921), 16, 17.
11  Wells, *Russia in the Shadows* (New York: George H. Doran, 1921), 154–5. Hereafter Shadows. At times, Wells is clearly theatrical in his presentation of the leader. Discussing how agricultural production was no longer peasant based, "at the mention of the peasant Lenin's head came nearer to mine; his manner became confidential. As if after all the peasant *might* overhear" (Shadows 160). The extent of Wells's criticism reaches its height in his final chapter, "The Envoy."
12  Wells, Shadows, 159, 174, 17, 179.
13  For the fascinating story of Gorky's collection and how he obtained it, see Berb 194–6.
14  The story of its production is surprisingly simple. At Lord Beaverbrook's home one evening—Lockhart at the time had become one of his journalists—he met Samuel Goldwyn who asked "When will your book be finished?" "As soon as I have leave to complete it," he replied. Beaverbrook quickly gave him a leave to finish and shortly after its successful publication, production was underway. Elena Moura (Kay Francis) is the *femme fatale*, Steven Locke (Trevor Howard) the Lockhart character. The screenplay is by Laird Doyle and Roland Perwee.
15  On the pregnancy and abortion question, see McDonald and Dronfield, *A Very Dangerous Woman*, 260–1. Hereafter McD.
16  Wells in "H.G. Wells Interviews Joseph Stalin in 1934," *Open Culture*, April 23, 2014. https://www.openculture.com/2014/04/h-g-wells-interviews-joseph-stalin-in-1934.html. Wells met Stalin on July 23, 1934.

    For a valuable analysis of their meeting, see Malcolm Cowley, "H.G. Wells' Interview with Stalin Helped Change the Fundamental Principles of Liberalism," *The New Republic*, April 23, 1935. https://newrepublic.com/article/119904/review-hg-wells-interview-joseph-stalin.
17  Other Russian archives in Europe were subject to destruction or theft. Trotsky's archive in Paris was burned; Gorky's was transported by Moura to Moscow after Stalin supposedly made a deal with Gorky; Kerensky's was stolen from his Passy apartment in the 16th arrondissement of Paris (Berb 252).
18  Ivan Turgenev, *Rudin*, tr. Richard Freeborn (London: Penguin, 1975), 89. Chekhov's *Uncle Vanya* is a primary example with thwarted love and disappointment unravelling hope.
19  This phrase appeared in a January 22, 1989, story in the *New York Times Magazine* on Robert C. McFarlane, former National Security Advisor to President Ronald Reagan.

20 Wells reports that she had six lovers: Arthur Engelhardt, a youthful Estonian fling; Baron Benckendorf, a marriage of social convenience and status; Lockhart, British diplomat; Baron Budberg, a marriage of political expediency; an Italian lover in Sorrento and himself. There were likely more (WLove 168.)

21 With a touch of wit, he adds that "My pancreas has not been all that it should be; nor has Moura" (WLove 210). She was, however, in-and-out of his house at Hanover Terrace during his final illness until his death on August 13, 1946.

# 6

# Virginia Woolf: The Sound of Russian Love

*I prefer it when it's Russians who make you suffer.*

Lucien Descaves, *La Colonne* (1901)

Virginia Woolf's Russian love affair was with Russian literature, dance, and sound prompted by Dostoevsky, Turgenev, Serge Diaghilev, and V. I. Pudovkin. As far as we know, she had no actual Russian romance, although she developed close personal ties with the Russian émigré, translator, and writer S. S. Koteliansky and then, peripherally, with the Russian literary historian D. S. Mirsky. Three of the most popular Russian titles published by the Woolf's Hogarth Press involved Koteliansky: Gorky's *Reminiscences of Anton Chekhov, Alexander Kuprin and Ivan Bunin* (1921; translated by Koteliansky and Leonard Woolf); *The Note-Books of Anton Tchekov* (1921; also translated by Koteliansky and Leonard Woolf), and then Dostoevsky's *Stavrogin's Confession* (1922; translated by Koteliansky and Woolf).[1] Framing her romance with Russia was Russian writing, dance, and then film.

Woolf's appetite for matters Russian began early, not only in reviews that appeared in the *Times Literary Supplement* beginning in 1917, but as early as 1904 when she read a translation of Tolstoy's stories.[2] On her honeymoon, she read *Crime and Punishment* in French, given to her by her new husband, Leonard. It became one of her favorite novels from one of her favorite authors, telling Lytton Strachey that Dostoevsky was the greatest writer ever born. Her sentiment echoed her sustained interest in matters Russian, part of the overall British interest in Russian music, art, and literature at the time. In 1929 she wrote that "I like talk of Russia, & war & great doings & famous people—If I don't see them I romanticise them."[3]

Leonard Woolf was largely the impetus, his political interests and concern for the Russian Revolution a factor in Virginia's sustained interest in Russian culture. Late in his life, Leonard still believed the revolution was "essential for the future of European civilization."[4] The 1917 Club, founded in December 1917 by Leonard Woolf and Oliver Strachey, was another manifestation of support for Russia. Political discussions dominated lunch, art and culture the afternoon teas. With Lytton Strachey, Virginia Woolf often joined Leonard at the gatherings. Earlier that same year Katherine Mansfield and John Middleton Murry had introduced Koteliansky (known as Kot), a Jewish Ukrainian émigré, to the Woolfs; Mansfield and Murry met him through D. H. Lawrence who met him in 1914 when Kot worked in London as a secretary and translator for the Russian Law Bureau.[5] By 1918, he was an occasional guest at the Woolfs, a figure Woolf always found intriguing: "He has some likeness to the Russians in literature," she believed.[6]

In 1919, Kot approached the Woolfs as possible publishers of Gorky's reminiscences of Tolstoy. Leonard was enthusiastic, Woolf less so but the idea coincided with Leonard's realization that their press must expand its list to maintain its viability and went ahead. The book was an unexpected success and soon broadened the range of the press which would, by 1924, include the works of Freud (Diment 131, 133).

Leonard Woolf and Kot became friends and he started Russian lessons with him; Woolf later joined in.[7] Kot, along with Jane Harrison, stimulated the interest of the Woolfs in studying Russian and then co-translating and publishing selected works of Russian writing. The *Life of Archpriest Avvakum* (1924), the forty-first imprint from the Hogarth Press, came to the Woolfs from Jane Harrison, by then a major figure in the network of Russian émigrés in London and Paris. They had earlier published her *Russia and the Russian Verb* (1915).

Another figure of importance, located through Harrison and her companion/protégé Hope Mirrlees, was Prince D. S. Mirsky, a pre-revolutionary aristocrat from St. Petersburg in exile in both Paris and London who became a translator, literary historian, and professor at the University of London. He met the Woolfs in Paris in 1924 and saw them on-and-off until he returned to Russia in September 1932, the year he joined the British Communist Party. The Woolfs, in fact, had tea with him at their home shortly before he returned. Virginia, in particular, sensed his unhappiness and anxiety over his going back as a patriotic gesture, ironically noting that Mirsky physically resembled Lenin.[8]

Mirsky's publishing was prodigious, his authoritative two volume *History of Russian Literature* appearing in 1926/7. Earlier, in 1924, he published a small anthology of Russian poetry and then two additional modest volumes, *Modern Russian Literature* (1925) and a *History of Russia* (1928). He also supplemented links between the Woolfs, Russia, and the Hogarth Press, initiated by Harrison and Kot. Notably, he wrote the "Preface" to *The Life of Archpriest Avvakum* (1925), considered to be the first autobiography in Russian, translated by Harrison and Mirrlees. A substantial correspondence between Leonard and Mirsky continued for roughly eight years, Leonard offering a vivid portrait of him in his autobiography noting that he had "that air of profound pessimism which seemed to be characteristic of intellectual Russians, both within and without the pages of Dostoevsky. Certainly, Mirsky would have found himself spiritually at home in *The Possessed* or *The Idiot*."[9]

But Russian politics were not central to Woolf whose views of the Russian Revolution were circumspect, writing in her diary for 1918 of her impatience with those who insisted on taking sides for or against the contending parties.[10] What she did know of the history came from the press, William Gerhardie's *Futility* (1922), and impressions from Maynard Keynes who visited in 1925 and whose *Short View of Russia* would appear the same year from the Hogarth Press. There were also letters from Vita Sackville-West writing from Moscow in 1927, but, essentially, she learned of Russian politics through Leonard and his circle. Her keen literary interests were pre-Revolutionary writers, notably Chekhov, Dostoevsky, Tolstoy, and Turgenev—reading their works between 1904 and 1917. But although she intermittently studied Russian, she was dependent on translators, critics, and publishers of Russian works. In February 1921, she began Russian lessons with Koteliansky, while also editing Kot's translations from Chekhov, Dostoevsky, and Tolstoy.[11]

Britain's sustained fascination with Russia had not abated, even by 1929.[12] For many, and Woolf in particular, this was a persistent attraction to the language, literature, and culture of the country manifested by its writers, artists, dancers, musicians, and filmmakers, whether through new translations of Dostoevsky or radical performances by the Ballets Russes. Woolf regularly attended performances of Diaghilev's company and concerts of Russian music. Her character Martin in *The Years* briskly tells a society girl he thought of three subjects to talk about: "Racing; the Russian ballet; and ... Ireland. Which interests you?"[13] Elements of Russian love blended with Russian culture throughout her writing.

Reading Dostoevsky signaled Woolf's early absorption with Russian writers which she summarized in her 1925 essay, "The Russian Point of View." Preceding this, however, were a series of early reviews of Dostoevsky and Tolstoy that began to appear regularly in the *Times Literary Supplement* with titles like "More Dostoevsky" (1917), "A Minor Dostoevsky" (1917), "Tchehov's Questions" (1918), "Dostoevsky in Cranford" (1919), "The Russian Background" (1919),

"Dostoevsky the Father" (1922), culminating in "The Russian Point of View" (1925).[14] The period of her most sustained Russian interest, 1917–22, coincided with her major narrative experiments: "The Mark on the Wall" (1917), "An Unwritten Novel" (1920), and *Jacob's Room* (1922).

*The Voyage Out* (1915), Woolf's first novel, has Rachel Vinrace plunge into a near Dostoevskyan state of unconsciousness at one point but her second, *Night and Day* (1919), records more outwardly her Russian fascination when two characters in Chapter 26 discuss Dostoevsky's *The Idiot* and Tolstoy's *War and Peace*. The slightly comic exchange highlights her broad awareness of Russian works. The speakers are Cassandra Otway, cousin of the protagonist Katharine Hilbery, and her fiancé William Rodway, a poet:

> Cassandra's voice rose high in its excitement.
> "You've not read *The Idiot*!" she exclaimed.
> "I've read *War and Peace*," William replied a little testily.
> "*War and Peace*!" she echoed, in a tone of derision.
> "I confess I don't understand the Russians."
> "Shake hands! Shake hands" boomed Uncle Aubrey from across the table.
> "Neither do I and I hazard the opinion that they don't themselves."[15]

Earlier, Katharine Hilbery ("in a fatalistic mood") begins Chapter 11 by quoting a passage from *The Idiot* on the process of discovery being the only way to identify happiness. It cannot be directly sought but comes only from one's immersion in life, she believes (N&D 138). As evidence, Woolf has her character then quote from the recent 1913 translation by Constant Garnett, specifically the last paragraph from the character Ippolit's document "My Essential Explanation" found in Part III, Chapter 5. It is there where the character announces that "it's life that matters, nothing but life—the process of discovering—the everlasting and perpetual process, not the discovery itself, at all."[16]

Two elements in Dostoevsky appealed to Woolf: his courage in addressing the deep questions of spirituality and existence, and his ability to convey a character's stream of thought, often jumbled, repetitious, and with ellipses and associative leaps. Expressing thought through discontinuous language she found absorbing (which she would later link to montage in Russian film). In "An Unpleasant Predicament," a short story by Dostoevsky in a volume entitled *An Honest Thief and Other Stories* reviewed by Woolf in 1919, the rambling thoughts of a civil servant, Ivan Ilyitch Pralinsky, illustrate a technique Woolf would soon imitate. Pralinsky, standing in front of the home of a junior clerk in his department, thinks:

What if he knew that at this very moment I, I his superior, his chief, am standing by his house listening to the music? Yes, really how would he feel? No, what would he feel if I suddenly walked in? H'm![17]

The extended interior monologue occurs without the intervention of the omniscient narrator who enters only at the end but earlier he outlines the very process Woolf would develop in texts like *Jacob's Room*, *Mrs. Dalloway*, and *The Waves*.

The narrator then explains that:

It is well known that whole trains of thought sometimes pass through our brains instantaneously as though they were sensations without being translated into human speech, still less into literary language. But we will try to translate these sensations of our hero's and present to the reader at least the kernel of them ... For many of our sensations when translated into ordinary language seem absolutely unreal. That is why they never find expression, though everyone has them.

(An Honest Thief 206)

The literary value Dostoevsky began to sense in his own epileptic seizures—"When such a nervous time came upon me formerly, I made use of it for writing," he once wrote—finds an echo in Woolf who told E. M. Forster "not that I haven't picked up something from my insanities and all the rest."[18] In her *Diary*, she wrote that "I believe these illnesses are ... partly mystical." Dostoevsky, conveying a similar theme, writes in *The Idiot* of Prince Myshkin just before he has a seizure that "suddenly in the midst of sadness, spiritual darkness and oppression, there seemed at moments a flash of flight in his brain ... and all his vital forces suddenly began working at their highest tension." Woolf read *The Idiot* as early as January 1915.[19]

The impact of Dostoevsky was strong, Woolf writing in a passage omitted from a later version of "Mr. Bennett and Mrs. Brown" that "after reading *Crime and Punishment* and *The Idiot*, how could any young novelist believe in 'characters' as the Victorians had painted them?" For figures like Raskolnikov, Myshkin, or Stavrogin, we "go down into them as we descend into some enormous cavern ... it is all dark, terrible and uncharted."[20] One of Woolf's unwritten but outlined essays, counterbalancing such darkness, was "The Russian Sense of Comedy, Dostoevsky & Comedy Altogether" (Rubenstein 39). Unsurprisingly, Dostoevsky appears in *The Waves*, where Bernard disavows any identity with him or even learning Russian.[21]

But other Russians appeared directly or indirectly in her work: Tolstoy in the dinner scene of *To the Lighthouse*, Sasha in *Orlando*, and Nicholas Pomjalovsky in *The Years*. She read *Anna Karenina* three times and in 1933 read through eleven volumes of Turgenev's fiction, as well as a biography, memoir, and set of letters for her essay "The Novels of Turgenev." That same year, she began her last novel, *The Years*.

Tolstoy made a particular impact, first reading *War and Peace* in 1910. As late as 1940 she still recorded her reaction to Tolstoy: "like touching an exposed electric wire ... his rugged short-cut mind—[is] to me the most, not sympathetic, but inspiring, rousing; genius in the raw" (Diary 5: 273). Her ambitions for *The Voyage Out* were Tolstoyan as she explained to Lytton Strachey: she "wanted to give the feelings of a vast tumult of life, as various and disorderly as possible" cut short by death but then resumed.[22]

One example of Woolf's incorporation of a Russian allusion is her use of a globe that appears in *War and Peace* when, late in the novel, Pierre dreams of a globe shown to him by his former teacher, "a living quivering ball, with no definite limits. Its whole surface consisted of drops, closely cohering together."[23] The ball is life, his teacher tells him. In *The Waves*, Bernard remarks that one should pretend that "life is a solid substance, shaped like a globe, which we turn about in our fingers" (Waves 210). A few pages later, however, he notes that "the crystal, the globe of life as one calls it, far from being hard and cold to the touch, has walls of thinnest air" (Waves 214). Woolf herself would confess that "my map of the world lacks rotundity" (Diary 3: 316), while the Russians always possessed circumference.

ii

Translation was another form of Russian immersion for Woolf and with Kot she translated Dostoevsky's *Stavrogin's Confession* and *The Plan of the Life of a Great Sinner* (Hogarth Press, 1922).[24] This was one of three collaborative translations she published with the Hogarth Press which did a further eleven Russian/English translations in concert with a growing Russian émigré population which saw the emergence of institutions like the Free Russian Library at 15 Whitechapel Road, London. Furthering the awareness of Russian culture, beyond the new translations by Constance Garnett and others at this time, were a series of new histories and studies that generated interest in the literature but were unmediated accounts of contemporary history. Among the works explaining the literary texts were Maurice Baring's *Landmarks in Russian Literature* (1910) and *Outline of Russian Literature* (1914), Jane Harrison's *Russia and the Russian Verb* (1915), and John Middleton Murry's study of Dostoevsky (1916). Edward Garnett's *Turgenev: A Study* appeared in 1917, Garnett the husband of Constance Garnett. A few years later, even J. M. Keynes would get into the act, publishing *A Short View of Russia* in 1925 with Woolf's Hogarth Press. Fascination with Russia was everywhere, multiplying on cultural, linguistic, and literary levels.[25]

The sensational Ballets Russes helped. Founded by Serge Diaghilev in Paris in 1909, they gave their first London performances in 1911 (the year of the first London production of *The Cherry Orchard*). Their impact was widely felt, *The Studio* magazine writing in 1914 that "art has danced to the strains of the Russian Ballet, leaving here and there lingering notes on dress fabrics, wallpapers and cushions."[26]

The original and unorthodox performances of the Ballets Russes, with scores by Stravinsky, Satie, Ravel, and others, projected a new set of modernist ideals. Additionally, the deliberate drive toward simplification of melody and harmony in music, led by Satie, Stravinsky, Milhaud, and Auric, paralleled the intensified attention to line and angle in the Ballets Russes productions which writers like Woolf and Mansfield, among others, would incorporate. Stravinsky, in particular, turned to the energy of Russian folklore with a kind of ritualistic power and primal violence in *The Firebird*, qualities that Woolf admired in Dostoevsky. The *Firebird*, *Petrushka*, and *Rite of Spring* radically broke with a Germanic orchestral tradition causing writers to readjust their modernist values. *The Firebird*, in fact, self-consciously invented Russian ballet not only with its Russian-sourced folk story but costumes, choreography, and music.[27]

Freed from restraining outfits, dancers could emphasize movement. As the choreographer Fokine noted of Ida Rubinstein dancing the role of Schéhérazade, "she awaits her fate in a pose without emotion. What powerful expression without movement" he added, a remark applicable to Woolf and her concentrated imagery free from rhetorical excess partly derived from Chekhov.[28] Nijinsky's choreography in particular demonstrated a formalist effort toward unity, the dancer/choreographer "working to express an idea through moving forms," a phrase equally apt for Woolf.[29] Commenting on *Le Sacre du printemps*, a reviewer noted that the "literalness of plot has gone; we do not rely on an unforeseen *denouement* to excite us; we look for the unfolding of an idea," a comment especially important for Woolf's evolving technique (in S. Jones 98–9).

The performances of the Ballets Russes, which combined Russian style with Parisian avant-garde music and art, became a laboratory of cultural experimentation which Woolf found engaging. The interconnected worlds of the visual and performing arts displayed by the ballet also elided the gap between culture and entertainment. The adaptation of a painterly style to a corporeal medium, with its kaleidoscope of color and pattern, became a projection of Woolf's own unfolding literary practice.[30]

The Russian dancers would not leave Woolf's imagination and various references to them occur throughout her writing. Discoursing on the importance of letters in *Jacob's Room*, for example, the narrator celebrates their usefulness for news and gossip, writing "have you heard the news? Life in the capital is gay" referring to "the Russian dancers."[31] Describing the site of Miss LaTrobe's pageant (a panorama of British history) in her final novel, *Between the Acts*, Woolf writes that "swallows darting seemed, by the regularity of the trees, to make a pattern, dancing, like the Russians, only not to music, but to the unheard rhythm of their own wild hearts."[32]

In addition to attending performances of the Ballets Russes, Virginia and Leonard attended the Russian section of Roger Fry's Second Post-Impressionist Exhibition of 1912. But beyond these manifestations of Russian literature, dance, and painting was film, a further catalyst for Woolf's sustained Russophilia.

Woolf had an early interest in film, publishing her essay "The Cinema" in June 1926, written at the same time she was grappling with *To the Lighthouse*. The emotive potential of moving spaces in film found echo in the "Time Passes" section of her novel. One critic, in fact, has suggested that "film theory of the twenties informed Woolf's critical and creative projects."[33] In April 1926, for example, just before her essay on cinema appeared, she told Vita Sackville-West that "my mind is all awash with various thoughts; my novel, you … the cinema; and so on" (Lett. 3: 254). But one can be more specific.

In Berlin in 1929, and in the company of Leonard, Vanessa Bell, Duncan Grant, Vita Sackville-West, her cousin Edward Sackville-West, and her husband Harold Nicolson, Woolf viewed V. I. Pudovkin's anti-imperial *Storm over Asia*, the first movie ever filmed in Mongolia.[34] Nicolson was then Councilor (First Secretary) at the British Embassy in Berlin. The Woolfs visited the city, essentially to allow Woolf to see Vita, from January 16 to 21, 1929. It was likely that Woolf was aware of the controversy surrounding the film since various journalists had reported on the work in the British press, notably *The Times*, which attacked the film as revolutionary on January 12, 1929, via a report from the paper's Berlin correspondent. *Close Up* ran a series of pieces countering the *Times* position.³⁵

Berlin at the time was a mecca for avant-garde film, especially Soviet film, restricted from screenings in England because of censorship. Film and psychoanalysis were also linked at this time, especially through the psychoanalyst Hanns Sachs, a member of Freud's circle. He contributed various articles to *Close Up*, one entitled "Film Psychology" which discussed the relationship between conscious and unconscious knowledge and their connection to dream and film. Kenneth Macpherson, co-funder of *Close Up*, remarked that "Berlin is one big movie, like an impossible dream."³⁶

Woolf may have already known of Pudovkin before seeing *Storm over Asia*. Publicity for an October 1928 showing of *Mother* by the Film Society may have been one source; another may have been the news of Pudovkin's February 3, 1929, lecture at the Film Society on "Types as Opposed to Actors." Copies of the talk, which explicated the techniques of montage, were sent to members. Leonard Woolf may have received one or perhaps Duncan Grant who was also an enthusiastic attendee, as was Eddy Sackville-West, Vita's cousin.³⁷

Ironically, Soviet audiences at this time had little patience with Russian avant-garde films. Experimental works were difficult to follow and few films of this style were ever box office successes. Soviet audiences went to films to be entertained, not for an education or exposure to art. Cross-cutting/montage was thought to be erratic and confusing.³⁸

A letter from Vanessa Bell to Roger Fry summarizes the intensity and impact of viewing Pudovkin's film in Berlin which was a spectacle showing masses of people filmed with a moving camera while incorporating his theory of editing: "The film seemed to me extraordinary—there were the most lovely pictures of odd Chinese types, very well done. I enjoyed it immensely." She thought others did as well but they were upset over whether or not it might have been an anti-British propaganda:

> No doubt it was—at least the feeblest part of it consisted of the flight of soldiers in British uniforms flying from Asiatics. Vita again enraged Leonard by asking him 6 times whether he thought they were meant for Englishmen—she and Harold both thought they weren't but managed to quarrel with each other all the same. This discussion went on & on, all standing in the melting snow .... Never have I spent such a thundery evening. As I was quite uninvolved however I got a good deal of amusement out of it.
>
> (January 19, 1929, in Bell 142)

So, apparently, did Woolf according to Quentin Bell. But the film may have had an aesthetic rather than political effect on Woolf.

Pudovkin confirmed several techniques on screen that Woolf had already attempted on the page. Following the Berlin trip, in fact, Woolf wrote in her *Diary* about her writing method in composing "Women & Fiction" (later *A Room of One's Own*) that it is "half talk half soliloquy" which allowed her "to get more onto the page than any how else. It made itself up & forced itself upon me … as I lay in bed after Berlin," noting that the thinking had been done "& the writing stiffly & unsatisfactorily 4 times before" (Diary 3: 221–2). "This way," she adds, "gives one freedom & lets one leap from back to back of one's thoughts" (Diary 3: 222). This—a form of montage seen in *Storm over Asia*—also has an important role in her next work of fiction, *The Waves*, although she was already conscious of the importance of sound as early as 1920 in her short story "An Unwritten Novel."[39] In her works, sound operates as a counterpoint to image.

The silent film *Storm over Asia* was an implicit attack on British imperialism in Asia, the story one of how a formerly unknown heir of Genghis Khan leads a revolt against the British overlords. At the end of the film, there was a small demonstration in the Berlin audience which might have been considered anti-British, wrote Quentin Bell.[40]

The creation of political awareness and a new ideology triumphs over the foreign forces. Pudovkin also emphasizes his characters as individuals with human emotions; in this, he differs from Eisenstein who used individuals only as symbols or types. *Storm over Asia* completed Pudovkin's trilogy of films in tribute to the Russian Revolution and Civil War: *Mother, The End of St. Petersburg*, and *Storm*. All three silent films relied on the central story, the growth of a revolutionary consciousness, although the arresting visual dimension of *Storm over Asia* almost overpowered its political message. Furthermore, long shots of the sky and steppe, with often silhouetted figures, alternating with close-up reaction shots, established an integrated but varied visual narrative.[41]

Not only the film but Pudovkin's own writings on film technique, especially sound, mattered to Woolf partly because they seemed to parallel many of her ideas of narrative, structure, and character presentation. His work *Pudovkin on Film Technique* first appeared in English in October 1929, the year he came to lecture in London (in February) at London's New Gallery Cinema for the Film Society.[42] Pudovkin was the first invited speaker, and it is possible Leonard and Virginia Woolf, given their affiliation with the society, attended or were at least aware of the talk. In November 1929, Eisenstein spoke, introducing his long-awaited film *Battleship Potemkin* (1925).

In his published collection, Pudovkin emphasizes the importance of light, noting that without light, "neither object nor human being nor anything else has existence on the film … light serves not only to develop the forms" but becomes part of the "expressive work." It should "enter as an organic component into the actor's work"; light can "eliminate much, emphasize much and bring out with such strength the expressive work of the actor" as it does repeatedly in *The Waves*.[43]

Of greater importance for Pudovkin, however, was sound, the coming revolution in cinema which he noted in a 1928 essay written with Eisenstein and Alexandrov. This was simultaneous with an overall pessimism in the Soviet film industry because of purges instituted by Stalin and a general sense that Soviet cinema had not achieved any of its social/political goals. Film at this time was also generally inaccessible to the public. Industrial needs meant that filmmakers and distributors had no government funds to import new equipment; and the advent of sound meant the need to replace old devices with new. It has even been suggested that the lack of enough cameras and film stock necessitated the use of canceled footage found in the cutting room which, when joined together, displayed its own jump cuts and out-of-sequence series. This created the montage repeatedly used in Soviet silent films. The radical effects produced when the sequence changed was startling and matched what Woolf was undertaking in an early work like *Jacob's Room* and then *The Waves*. A smuggled copy of D.W. Griffith's three-and-a-half-hour *Intolerance* (1916), with its four parallel story lines, led to constant rerunning and re-editing of the film at Lev Kuleshov's film workshop where Pudovkin studied.[44]

Eisenstein has predominated in the history of the montage, but he differs from Pudovkin. Both believed that editing, not plot, made a film, anticipating Woolf whose narrator in *Between the Acts* rhetorically asks "did the plot matter?" and answers "don't bother about the plot: the plot's nothing" (BA 82). Eisenstein believed montage was a way of creating dissonance, establishing a "jagged cinema of conflict."[45] Pudovkin was more lyrical, his cross-cuts enhancing rather than disrupting the narrative to create emotional effects. He also believed actors are affective not through their acting but context, by their relationship to exterior objects, something Woolf would develop in *Mrs. Dalloway* with the solo aircraft flying over London seen by Mrs. Dalloway and Septimus Smith or *To the Lighthouse* with Mrs. Ramsay's fruit bowl or Lily Briscoe's painting finished only on the last page.

Politics and film in Russia became an immediate union with the First All-Union Party Conference on Cinema Affairs held in March 1928, where the

Party argued that Soviet cinema was neither socially responsible nor fiscally sound. There were also not enough theaters to view films, as a polemic by a S. M. Krylov, entitled *Cinema Instead of Vodka*, made clear. The state's support and monopoly over vodka production needed to change to fund filmmaking and distribution. Subsidies, Krylov argued, must go to film, not vodka manufacture. Widespread illiteracy also made the reception of films difficult because most silent films required inter-titles. Criticism of film critics and the press followed, one speaker charging that the cadre of film critics was insufficiently communist, only two-thirds being Party members.[46] At issue was cinema as a propaganda weapon in the cultural and educational revolution with the hope that cinema revenue would exceed that of vodka. To achieve this, cinema was encouraged to follow the example of literature and become more proletarian.

Against this backdrop of turmoil and confusion came sound. Eisenstein, abroad from 1929 to 1932, ostensibly to study sound film, wrote to the central arts committee warning them that Soviet film exports would be non-existent if they continued to make only silent pictures. Sound was the future but remained a technical challenge and required much more pre-production preparation and a tighter script which limited the freedom of the director. Numbers reveal the difficulties in learning and producing sound production. In 1932 there were only forty sound films planned compared with eighty-five silent. In 1933, there were only 200 sound projectors in the country and 32,000 silent (Youngblood 222).

Montage was the hallmark of the silent film, a rapid and often unrealistic cutting style. But such cutting was impossible in the sound film: the ear is slower to understand than the eye. A sound film is also slower in tempo than a silent film. Nonetheless, Eisenstein and Pudovkin hoped to develop a sound montage, using sound for dramatic punctuation, as Woolf would soon do. The "talkies" were a literal description of early sound films emphasizing a new realism, although Eisenstein, Pudovkin, and Alexandrov, in their August 1928 "Statement on Sound," noted that the invention of sound was "double-edged": it will likely be exploited commercially and affect the impact of cutting (montage) because it increases inertia and reduces the "independent significance" of fragments. But if directed to the "*contrapuntal use* of sound vis-à-vis the visual arrangement of montage," new possibilities will occur. The new experiments must "*aim a sharp discord with the visual images*" because only through such contrast will a new "*orchestral counterpoint* of visual and sound images" occur.[47] Sound will unquestionably solve a variety of complex problems in the construction of image and meaning, they argue. Reprinted, the essay appeared as "The Sound Film: A Statement from USSR" in the October 1928 issue of the British film journal *Close Up*.

The new idea, applied by Woolf, was "contrapuntal sound," a new form of montage. The idea was that the first experimental use of sound "*must be directed along the line of its distinct non-synchronization with the visual images*" (in Youngblood 223). A parallel statement was that of Lev Kuleshov, Pudovkin's teacher, that "the essence of the cinema lies in composition, the alteration of sequences which have been shot."[48] In another essay, "On the Principle of Sound in Film," Pudovkin criticized the potential control of a film by sound but realized that sound was a "*new raw material for composition*," sound becoming a "stimulus that evokes definite and precise associations and then of combing this sound with a selected visual stimulus."[49] The statement from 1929 parallels Woolf and her treatment of sound and dialogue as elements of narrative. But a danger emerging in Soviet film and art was Eccentrism, the presentation of the irregular or aberrant or outlandish, unusually expressed in this statement:

>                    Paris, Berlin, London
>                          romanticism,
>                           stylisation,
>                            exoticism,
>                            archaism,
>                          reconstruction,
>                           restoration,
>                           the pulpit,
>                           the temple,
>                          the museum!
> Only our methods are indivisible and inevitable
>
>                                                    (in Taylor 147)

"Statement on Sound" appeared in *Close Up* and was immediately controversial. Montage, the authors write, operates through the "juxtaposition of fragments" but "*only the contrapuntal use* of sound vis-à-vis the visual fragment of montage will open up new possibilities for the development and perfection of montage" ("Statement on Sound" 141). Woolf will say almost exactly the same thing: expressing frustration with her drafts of *The Waves*, she writes in her *Diary* for February 1930, "Lord how I wonder if I shall pull this book off! It is a litter of fragments so far" (Diary 3: 287). Woolf implicitly absorbed these new ideas of form and sound in *The Waves* and *Between the Acts* where she expresses the idea of "thoughts without words" (BA 50). Not silence but sounds form the channels of communication. A sound, in fact, bisects individual words when Rev. Streatfield tries to speak but has his words severed by twelve planes flying in perfect formation overhead (BA 174). Post-Berlin and post-*Storm over Asia*, Woolf grasped what might it might be possible to do by transposing elements of film into fiction as sound gave voice to ideas.

Recovering from her Berlin trip, Woolf had just finished a draft of what would become *A Room of One's Own* and was anxious about finding a new form of narrative after she recovered from three weeks in bed and three weeks unable to write. In her *Diary* she states that:

> [O]ne ought perhaps to be forever finding new things to say … one ought to invent a fine narrative style … all the time I shall attack this angular shape in my mind. I think the Moths (if that is what I shall call it) will be very sharply cornered. I am not satisfied though with the frame … In old days books were so many sentences absolutely struck with an axe out of crystal: & now my mind is so impatient, so quick, in some way so desperate … I think I am bolder as a writer … I feel on the verge of some strenuous adventure.
>
> (March 1929, Diary 3: 219)

This is most evident in the lyrical sections preceding each unit in *The Waves*. As the sun traverses the sky, the images and intensity of light alters but so does *sound*, used for dramatic and rhythmic effect. A late section begins with "*the hard stone of the day was cracked and light poured through its splinters.*" Waves fell on the shore "*in one long concussion, like a wall falling*" (Waves 173). A field seems momentarily empty of action: "*There was no sound of cropping, and no sound of wheels, but only the sudden roar of the wind letting its sails fill and brushing the tops of the grasses*" (Waves 173–4). Throughout the novel, competing with the sound of nature is the sound of human voices. Bernard, in fact, notes that the tone of his voice has become middle-aged when he says "Hampton Court." He then remarks that "the words beat a gong in the space which I have so laboriously cleared with half a dozen telephone messages and post cards, give off ring after ring of sound, booming, sonorous" (Waves 175).[50]

Sound forms the landscape of *The Waves* as powerfully as image. And as Woolf writes, sound is life:

> There is a sound like the knocking of railway trucks in a siding. That is the happy concatenation of one event following another in our lives … must go, must sleep, must wake, must get up—sober, merciful word which we pretend to revile, which we press tight to our hearts, without which we should be undone. How we worship that sound like the knocking together of trucks in a siding!
>
> (Waves 195)

Earlier, Louis said "But listen ... to the world moving through abysses of infinite space. It roars," causing Bernard to respond with "Silence falls; silence falls ... but now listen; tick, tick; hoot, hoot; the world has hailed us back to it" (Waves 188). Sound restores us to life.

From Soviet silent films, Woolf witnessed cinematic rhythm and the spontaneous appearance of sounds and images she first used in "Kew Gardens" (1919). Emerging in her writing and drawn from cinema is a new "structure of feeling," the phrase used by Raymond Williams and suggesting the lived experience of the moment (in Kuo 183). This is often an interior instant where characters display a kind of associative logic that frees them from time and even space. Film theory of the twenties informed Woolf's critical and creative projects.

Woolf and the Russians is an absorbing subject involving dance, cinema, literature, translation, painting, and love that captivated her imagination and energy. In her fiction, strains of Russian love appear with heartbreak, disappointment, and unrealized love throughout. Love fails, or if it doesn't, love triangles cause it to rupture. And *The Idiot*, which she read in 1915 before she began *Night and Day*, is the prototype. Love triangles (a central trope of Russian love) appear in both creating a framework for ideas about politics *and* relationships. In *The Idiot*, Prince Myshkin's feelings for Aglaya and Nastasya remain unresolved. Ultimately, he chooses neither. At the end, Rogozhin murders Nastasya and Aglaya marries someone else; Myshkin suffers another breakdown. The triangle crumbles.

With a gender reversal, the triangle reappears in *Night and Day*. Katherine Hilbery faces a choice between two marriage partners: William Rodney, the conventional choice, and the artistic poet Ralph Denham whom she finally chooses, an individual respectful of her independence. She also realizes that happiness arrives through the process of living, the idea of Ippolit in his "Essential Explanation" from *The Idiot*.

*Mrs Dalloway* offers another, if attenuated, triangle: Clarissa Dalloway, Peter Walsh, and her husband, Richard Dalloway. A long-ago romance is now rekindled but it stalls. Mrs. Dalloway will remain Mrs. Dalloway and not run off with her earlier lover. But Peter rediscovers her lasting influence upon him and that in itself satisfies. Love of a slightly altered triangle appears in *To the Lighthouse*: that of Mr. Ramsay, Mrs. Ramsay, and Lily Briscoe who completes her relationship with both when she completes her painting with the final strokes on the final page of the novel in concert with Mr. Ramsay landing at the lighthouse. It is a moment of triumph, the union of space, time, and relations ten years after the death of Mrs. Ramsay. In *The Waves*, Woolf doubles the triangle, pushing the Russian trope further. The three major characters turn into six. Bernard annotates the process when he says "I am not one person; I am many people; I do not altogether know who I am—Jinny, Susan, Neville, Rhoda, or Louis" (Waves 165). In an earlier statement, he alludes to a novel by Dostoevsky whose name he forgets (Waves 150). It's *The Possessed;* even at this late stage in Woolf's writing, the Russians still appear, offering, in Bernard's words, "disillusioned clarity" (Waves 159).

Love in Woolf shadows that of the Russians: powerful but incomplete, magnetic but unfulfilled. Dostoevsky and others like Turgenev and Tolstoy importantly frame Woolf's writing, Roberta Rubenstein explaining that "Dostoevsky's inclusion of characters in *extremis* may have authorized Woolf in her own choice to depict emotional anguish," while confirming the validity of self-annihilation and madness for fiction (Rubenstein 47). The Russians infiltrated Woolf's writing, *Orlando* in many ways the capstone of their presence.

By the time of *Orlando* (1928), Woolf could take a playful view of her Russian infatuation, observing that in Russia "the sunsets are longer, the dawns less sudden, and sentences often left unfinished from doubt as to how best to end them."[51] But love can still create pain. Orlando's love for the Russian princess Sasha turns inside-out when he thinks she deceives him. For a moment he believes her protests and then reverses himself. Russian love is a constant twisting of unsettled feelings (OR 50–1). Woolf understood that the power of the Russian writers originated in "their deep sense of human suffering and their unwavering sympathy with it" ("The Russian View," Essays 2: 341–2). For English writers, this often became sentimentality; but for the Russians, the truth. Or as she remarked about Koteliansky, with the Russians there is always an immediacy that is simultaneously about love and the spirit: "he will begin," she notes in her *Diary*, "to explain his soul without preface," a quintessentially Russian practice (*Diary* January 1918).

## Notes

1   For a series of other Russian titles published by the Hogarth Press, see Galya Diment, *A Russian Jew of Bloomsbury, The Life and Times of Samuel Koteliansky* (Montreal: McGill-Queen's University Press, 2011), 134. Hereafter Diment.
2   It was Vol. II of the *Complete Works of Tolstoy* and in the Stephens family library. The stories included "A Landed Proprietor," "The Cossacks," and "Sevastopol," tr. and ed. Leo Wiener (London: Dent, 1904).

3   Woolf, *Diary of Virginia Woolf*, ed. Anne Olivier Bell, vol. 3 (New York: Harcourt Brace Jovanovich, 1977), 221 (April 13, 1929).
4   Victoria Glendinning, *Leonard Woolf, A Biography* (New York: Free Press, 2006), 192. Hereafter Glennd. For Leonard Woolf's political views of Russia, see Duncan Wilson, *Leonard Woolf, a Political Biography* (London: Hogarth Press, 1978).
5   On Koteliansky and the Hogarth Press and his work as a translator, see Laura Marcus, "The European Dimension of the Hogarth Press," *The Reception of Virginia Woolf in Europe*, ed. Mary Ann Caws and N. Luckhurst (London: Bloomsbury, 2002), 328–56; Claire Davison-Pégon, "Samuel Solomonovich Koteliansky and British Modernism," *Translation and Literature* 20 (2011): 334–47. For almost forty years, Kot lived in rooms once shared with Mansfield, Murry, and the painter Mark Gertler at 5 Acacia Road in St. Johns Wood close to Regents Park. See Diment 112–14.
6   Woolf, 18 January 1918, *Diary*, vol. 1, ed. Anne Olivier Bell (New York: Harcourt Brace Jovanovich, 1977), 108.
7   Leonard Woolf was one of the few Kot wanted to see when he was dying in 1955. He earlier sought him out amid the grim reports about the fate of German and European Jews during the Second World War (Diment 297).
8   On this topic and other connections with the Woolfs, see G. S. Smith, *D.S. Mirsky, A Russian-English Life, 1890–1939* (Oxford: Oxford University Press, 2000), 98, 99, 209–10. Mirsky emirated to Britain in 1920 and lectured in Russian literature at University College London from 1922 to 1932. Mirsky's return to Soviet Russia was not a success; he was arrested in 1937 and sent to a gulag labor camp where he died in June 1939.

   Edmund Wilson visited Mirsky in Russia in the summer of 1935 and twenty years later published a vivid account of their meeting in a dark and dank Moscow room in a large apartment complex on Gorky Street. See Wilson, "Comrade Prince," *Encounter* 5.1 (1955): 10–20. Wilson's analogy for Mirsky was Dostoevsky; Leonard Woolf had the same comparison but Pasternak thought Tolstoy more appropriate. See Smith, *Mirsky* 362 ftnt.79.
9   Leonard Woolf, *Autobiography II: 1911–1969* (Oxford: Oxford University Press, 1980), 202.
10  Woolf in Darya Protopopova, "Woolf and Russian Literature," *Virginia Woolf in Context*, ed. Bryony Randall and Jane Goldman (Cambridge: Cambridge University Press, 2012), 386.
11  For an overall, if brief, survey of Woolf's Russian interests, see Protopopova, "Woolf and Russian Literature," *Virginia Woolf in Context*, 386–97. Roberta Rubenstein's *Virginia Woolf and the Russian Point of View* (New York: Palgrave/Macmillan, 2009) provides a much fuller discussion.
12  On this topic, see Beasley, *Russomania*, and the earlier *Russia in Britain, 1880–1940*, ed. Rebecca Beasley and Philip Ross Bullock (Oxford: Oxford University Press, 2013).

13 Woolf, *The Years*, ed. Hermione Lee (Oxford: Oxford World's Classics, 2009), 239.
14 Among the books in the library of Virginia and Leonard Woolf at this time were Maxim Gorky, *Comrades* (1915); I. D. Levine, *The Russian Revolution* (1917); D. Bondar, *Bondar's Simplified Russian Method* (1918); J. Spargo, *Bolshevism* (1919); J. Reed, *Ten Days that Shook the World* (1919); B. Russell, *The Practice and Theory of Bolshevism* (1920); K. Marx, *The Civil War in France* (1921); and S. Aksakoff, *A Russian Gentleman* (1923). In April 1912, Leonard Woolf gave Virginia a copy of Constance Garnett's translation of *The Brothers Karamazov*. The inscription reads "To VS from LSW. April 1912." The following year he gave her *The Idiot*. See *Catalogue of Books from The Library of Leonard and Virginia Woolf* (Brighton: Holleyman & Treacher, 1975) *passim* for details.
15 Virginia Woolf, *Night and Day*, ed. Suzanne Raitt (Oxford: Oxford World's Classics, 2009), 366. Hereafter N&D.
16 Fyodor Dostoevsky, *The Idiot*, tr. Constance Garnett (1913; New York: Modern Library, 1935), 375. And one comes full circle: an early essay by Walter Benjamin is "Dostoevsky's The Idiot" (1917). See Benjamin, *Early Writings, 1910-1917*, tr. Howard Eland et al. (Cambridge: Harvard University Press, 2011), 275-80.
17 Fyodor Dostoevsky, *An Honest Thief and Other Stories*, 1919, tr. Constance Garnett (Westport, CT: Greenwood Press, 1975), 206. Hereafter *An Honest Thief*.
18 Dostoevsky in Roberta Rubenstein, *Virginia Woolf and the Russian Point of View* (New York: Palgrave/Macmillan, 2009), 27. Hereafter Rubenstein. Woolf, *Letters of Virginia Woolf*, vol. 2: 1912-1922, ed. Nigel Nicolson and Joanne Trautmann (New York: Harcourt Brace Jovanovich, 1976), 499.
19 Woolf, *Diary of Virginia Woolf*, ed. Anne Olivier Bell, vol. 3 (New York: Harcourt Brace Jovanovich, 1977), 287 (February 16, 1930). Dostoevsky, *The Idiot*, tr. Constance Garnett, 213-14; Woolf, *Diary*, vol. 1, ed. Bell (New York: Harcourt Brace Jovanovich, 1977), 10 (January 6, 1915).
20 Woolf, *The Essays of Virginia Woolf*, vol. 3, ed. Andrew McNeillie (New York: Harcourt Brace Jovanovich, 1988), 386.
21 Woolf, *The Waves*, ed. David Bradshaw (Oxford: Oxford World's Classics, 2015), 212, 155. Hereafter, *Waves*.
22 Woolf, *Letters*, vol. 2: 1912-1922, ed. Nigel Nicolson and Joanne Trautmann (New York: Harcourt Brace Jovanovich, 1976), 82.
23 Leo Tolstoy, *War and Peace*, tr. Constance Garnett (1904; New York: Modern Library, n.d.), 992.
24 For Woolf and Koteliansky's translations, see Virginia Woolf and S. S. Koteliansky, *Translations from the Russian*, introd. Laura Marcus, ed. Stuart N. Clarke (Southport: Virginia Woolf Society of Great Britain, 2006), 13-52; Rubenstein, *Virginia Woolf and the Russian Point of View* 232 nt. 13.

   Also important is Galya Diment, *A Russian Jew of Bloomsbury, The Life and Times of Samuel Koteliansky* (Montreal: McGill Queen's University Press, 2011).

Hereafter Diment. Additionally, see Darya Protopopova, *Virginia Woolf's Portraits of Russian Writers: Creating the Literary Other* (Newcastle upon Tyne: Cambridge Scholars Publishing, 2019).

25  An important summary of this interest is *Russia in Britain, 1880–1940, From Melodrama to Modernism*, ed. Rebecca Beasley and Philip Ross Bullock (Oxford: Oxford University Press, 2013). More recently is Beasley's *Russomania, Russian Culture and the Creation of British Modernism, 1881–1922* (Oxford: Oxford University Press, 2020).

26  In Mary E. Davis, *Ballets Russes Style: Diaghilev's Dancers and Paris Fashion* (London: Reaktion, 2010), 7.

27  Jennifer Homans, *Apollo's Angels, a History of Ballet* (London: Granta, 2010), 301. Also useful is Rupert Christiansen, *Diaghilev's Empire, How the Ballets Russes Enthralled the World* (London: Faber and Faber, 2022).

28  Michel Fokine, *Fokine: Memoirs of a Ballet Master*, tr. Vitale Fokine, ed. A Chujoy (Boston: Little, Brown & Co., 1961), 155.

29  In Susan Jones, *Literature, Modernism and Dance* (Oxford: Oxford University Press, 2013), 98. Hereafter S. Jones.

30  Combined with frequent concerts of Russian music, Russian culture was unavoidable in the British capital. Even the popular Promenade series reflected this. The 1914 season regularly included a performance of the Russian national anthem (Russia was an ally in the war), as well as the obligatory "God Save the King." By 1917, the Proms offered their first "Russian Night" (all Russian music) in more than a decade, Russia the only country so honored. See Philip Ross Bullock, "Tsar's Hall, Russian Music in London, 1895–1926," *Russia in Britain*, ed. Beasely and Bullock (Oxford: Oxford University Press, 2013), 113–28.

31  Woolf, *Jacob's Room*, ed. Kate Flint (Oxford: Oxford World's Classics, 2008), 125.

32  Woolf, *Between the Acts*, ed. Frank Kermode (Oxford: Oxford World's Classics, 2000), 59–60. Hereafter BA.

33  Leslie Kathleen Hankins, "'Across the Screen of My Brain,' Virginia Woolf's 'The Cinema' and Film Forums of the Twenties," *The Multiple Muses of Virginia Woolf*, ed. Diane F. Gillespie (Columbia, Missouri: University of Missouri Press, 1993), 148–79.

34  Quentin Bell, *Virginia Woolf, A Biography* (New York: Harcourt Brace Jovanovich, 1972), 142. Hereafter Bell.

35  See Leslie Kathleen Hankins, "Virginia Woolf and Film," *Edinburgh Companion to Virginia Woolf and the Arts*, ed. Maggie Humm (Edinburgh: Edinburgh University Press, 2010), 351–74.

36  For Macpherson on Berlin, see Marcus, *The Tenth Muse*, 333. For details on the film culture of Berlin at this time, see passages by Bryher and Stephen Spender in Marcus, *The Tenth Muse*, 329–32. H.D., in her article in the "Russian Film" issue of *Close Up* (September 1928), refers to viewing Russian films in Berlin the previous month.

37 The lecture was also published in the journal *Cinema* (February 6, 1929) and in an enlarged edition of Pudovkin's *Film Technique* published in English in 1933.
38 Susan Goodman et al., *The Power of Pictures, Early Soviet Photography, Early Soviet Film* (New York: Jewish Museum/ Yale Univeristy Press, 2015), 48. Also see Jay Leyda, *Kino, a History of the Russian and Soviet Film* (New York: Collier Books, 1960), 193–238, 244–60. One important feature Leyda points out is that almost every Soviet director of importance wrote frankly about their work, often against Soviet doctrine (Leyda 226).
39 Woolf, "An Unwritten Novel," *The Mark on the Wall and Other Short Fiction*, ed. David Bradshaw (Oxford: Oxford World's Classics, 2008), 18–29. See 26.
40 Laura Marcus, "The Tempo of Revolution, British Film Culture and Soviet Cinema in the 1920s," *Russia in Britain, 1880–1940, From Melodrama to Modernism*, ed. Rebecca Beasley and Philip Ross Bullock (Oxford: Oxford University Press, 2013), 225–40.
41 For a brief but insightful commentary on the film, see Louis Menashe, *Moscow Believes in Tears, Russia and Their Movies* (Washington: New Academia Publishing, 2010), 73–4.
42 Pudovkin wrote the book during the making of *Mother* (1926), a film stressing the pain of experience on the faces of characters. His previous films include *The Extraordinary Adventures of Mr. West in the Land of the Bolsheviks* (1924) and *The Mechanism of the Brain* (1926), a documentary recording Pavlov's work on conditioned reflexes. *Chess Fever* (1925) was a comedy made to coincide with a chess congress in Moscow that year. *The End of St. Petersburg* (1927) was a historical drama involving trade unions and industry.
43 V. I. Pudovkin, *Film Technique and Film Acting*, tr. Ivor Montagu, memorial ed. (London: Vision Press, 1958), 147.
44 On these early developments of the montage see Jonathan Jones, "The Silent Revolutionary," *The Guardian*, August 31, 2001; Denise J. Youngblood, *Soviet Cinema in the Silent Era 1918–1935* (Austin: University of Texas Press, 1991) and *Sound, Speech, Music in Soviet and Post-Soviet Cinema*, ed. Lilya Kaganovsky and Masha Salazkina (Bloomington: Indiana University Press, 2014).
45 Jonathan Jones, "The Silent Revolutionary," *The Guardian*, August 31, 2001. https://www.theguardian.com/film/2001/aug/31/artsfeatures1 [April 3, 2017].
46 Denise J. Youngblood, *Soviet Cinema in the Silent Era 1918–1935* (Austin: University of Texas Press, 1991), 157–9. Hereafter Youngblood.
47 S. M. Eisenstein, V. I. Pudovkin, and G. V. Alexandrov, "Statement on Sound," in Vsevolod Pudovkin, *Selected Essays*, ed. Richard Taylor, tr. Richard Taylor and Evgeni Filippov (London: Seagull Books, 2006), 139–42. Hereafter "Statement."

The essay appeared in Russian in August 1928. An English translation appeared as "The Sound Film, a Statement from USSR," in *Close Up*, October 1928: 10–13. Eisenstein drafted the first version, revised to incorporate additions by Pudovkin and Alexandrov.

48 Kuleshov in Richard Taylor, *The Politics of The Soviet Cinema 1917–1929* (Cambridge: Cambridge University Press, 1979), 136.
49 Pudovkin, "On the Principle of Sound in Film," *The Film Factory, Russian and Soviet Cinema in Documents 1896–1939*, ed. Richard Taylor and Ian Christie (Cambridge, MA: Harvard University Press, 1988), 264–7.
50 For an earlier example of sound and its relation to memory, see Mrs. Dalloway's recall of the squeak of the latch on the gate at Bourton while waiting for the furniture men to remove the doors for her party at the opening of *Mrs. Dalloway* (3).
51 Woolf, *Orlando,* ed. Rachel Bowlby (Oxford: Oxford World's Classics, 2008), 44–5. Hereafter OR.

## *Postscript*: Isaiah Berlin: From the Finland Station

*"Who can love in our time? Who can dare to love?"*

Turgenev, *Rudin*

The shortest and most intense experience of Russian love was that between Isaiah Berlin and Anna Akhmatova. It occurred one night in late November 1945 in Fontanny Dom (Fountain House) in Leningrad but lasted a lifetime. They spent one night together but it altered their lives, reasserting the experiential authenticity and validity of Russian love, a contest between passion and possession. But it also ended in separation as it did with Benjamin, Maugham, Lockhart, Gerhardie, Wilson, and Wells. Yet, it also validated the responses and emotions of those outsiders who intersected with Russian lives, society, and culture as the Riga-born, British-educated academic and diplomat Isaiah Berlin experienced in his encounter with the revered revolutionary poet whose work was thought to be subversive and forgotten, Anna Akhmatova.

Unable to publish anything substantial since 1925, Akhmatova maintained a "creative silence" until 1935/6 when she began to write again.[1] Yet at one time she was the leading figure of the St. Petersburg avant-garde poetry scene which often gathered at the Stray Dog Cafe. At 5' 11" with dark hair and pale green eyes, she was physically and poetically stunning with verse of strict meters, exact rhymes, simple syntax, and short sentences creating a kind of "cryptic simplicity" as she mastered "the public use of a private persona."[2] From the start to the finish of her career, Joseph Brodsky wrote, she was "perfectly clear and coherent."[3]

Her image, however, soon became one of tragedy: her first husband, Nikolai Gumilyov, had been executed by the secret police in 1921 for supposedly plotting against Lenin. A second marriage ended in divorce; while her third, a common-law marriage to the art critic Nikolay Punin, ended with his first arrest in 1935 (the year her son was also arrested [to be rearrested in 1938]) and then a second arrest and disappearance in 1949. He would die in the gulag in 1953. Interspersed among these years of terror were restrictions on her ability to publish, appear, or even live in either St. Petersburg, her home, or Moscow. Yet political oppression and domestic distress stimulated her poetic drive. Her Cassandra-like reputation, prophesizing a dark and painful future for Russia, defined her, yet she did not leave Soviet Russia but stayed on as poetic witness to its deprivations and horrors.[4]

During this period of persecution, she survived by working in the library of an agricultural institute, translating and publishing critical studies especially on Pushkin. She had little or no contact with fellow writers and none with Western poets or artists, although Osip Mandelstam and Pasternak were artistic colleagues. She was in fact with Mandelstam in 1934 when he was taken for his first interrogation. From that moment until his death in the gulag in December 1938, she supported the poet and his wife, Nadezhda, who had been sent to the Urals with him into internal exile.[5] His unstable mental condition meant a partial release but his forecast proved true: "Only in Russia is poetry respected—it gets people killed. Is there anywhere else where poetry is so common a motive for murder?" Earlier, Aleksandr Blok remarked that literature in Russia was a vital force: "nowhere else does Word become Life, nowhere [else] does it turn into bread or stone, as it does with us."[6]

Akhmatova understood this clearly. Not only had her first husband experienced such a death, but in March 1938 her son Lev was arrested and disappeared for seventeen months, a loss which absorbed her daily. She regularly joined lines of women at the Kresty Prison in Leningrad to learn of any news and it was there one day a woman who recognized her whispered, "Can you describe this?" "Yes" she answered, prepared to bear "poetic witness."[7] The incident forms "Instead of a Preface" to *Requiem*, her lengthy poetic cycle on Stalin's terror, the pages burned after each reading because they were too dangerous to keep. She had also suffered during the war, evacuated from Leningrad during its siege to Tashkent where she lived in a hostel for writers from 1941 to 1944. Nadezhda Mandelstam and Lydia Chukovskaya were with her. She gave readings in hospitals to wounded soldiers and was allowed to publish a censored *Selected Poems*. On her release in May 1944, she stopped in Moscow to give a reading. Her unsanctioned fame resulted in a standing ovation when she appeared on stage. Later, hearing of the event, an angered Stalin supposedly asked Andrey Zhdanov, Stalin's *apparatchik* for culture, "Who organized this ovation?" (Ignatieff 153).

But this is the poet who three years before her death in 1966 could still write:

Everything in Moscow is steeped in verses,
Riddled with rhyme.
Over us let stillness reign,
Let us each make a separate peace with rhyme,
Let silence be the secret sign
Of those among you who, like me,
Are joined in secret marriage.

(Complete Poems II: 701)[8]

Isaiah Berlin's life had taken a different path up to late 1945. Born in Riga in 1909, now capital of Latvia, he moved to Russia when he was six. In Petrograd in 1917, he witnessed both the Social Democratic Revolution and that of the Bolsheviks. Preceded by his father to make arrangements, the family arrived in England in February 1921 where Berlin began his education at St. Paul's School and then, starting in 1928, Corpus Christie College, Oxford. After graduation with a first in Classics, he decided to stay another year and read for Philosophy, Politics, and Economics for which he also received a first. He became a philosophy tutor at New College which he disliked; it was dull and he did not enjoy teaching. Encouraged, he sat a three-day fellowship exam for All Souls. To his surprise, if not shock, he was elected to the prestigious college in 1932, the first Jewish academic so honored; he was twenty-three.

Berlin would spend his entire career at Oxford, subsequently becoming Professor of Social and Political Theory and then the founding President of Wolfson College. During the war, he worked for the British government in New York and then Washington; and then as the war ended, he was seconded to the British Embassy in Moscow as First Secretary, accredited with a diplomatic passport. His role was to assess the new Soviet government and its ideology. Following the war, he returned to Oxford where he would soon become an establishment figure, knighted in 1957. His interest in Russian culture and politics never waned, writing, lecturing, and translating books and essays on Russian political thought throughout his career.

Berlin's 1945 visit to Russia was his first since his departure in 1921, at eleven; he would return again in 1956. The unexpected meeting with Akhmatova in November 1945 would have a lasting effect on both writers. He was also her first outside guest from the West in years, although they would not personally see each other again until 1965 when she came to Oxford to receive an honorary degree.

His 1945 trip also had family overtones: although relatives left behind in Riga were murdered by the Nazis, he had an uncle who had settled in Moscow after the Revolution. Berlin managed two brief visits with him, the second including a series of extended relatives.[9] He also met Pasternak, Sergei Eisenstein, and, of course, Akhmatova.

## ii

*"All Russian writers preach to the reader."*
Boris Pasternak to Berlin, *Personal Impressions*

The story of their meeting has been told many times. This is only a sketch: visiting a Leningrad bookstore after traveling from Moscow and checking in at the Astoria Hotel with Brenda Tripp, a chemist representing the British Council, Berlin headed to a bookshop. He was told books were cheaper in Leningrad than Moscow, largely because of the siege. In a shop, he accidentally met the critic Vladimir Orlov and casually asked about Akhmatova: he knew her reputation but not her work. Orlov asked if he would like to meet her. Unaware she lived nearby and even if she was alive, Berlin quickly said "Yes." Orlov called, and she agreed to meet at 3 p.m. He was thirty-six, she was fifty-six.

Her reputation and status in November 1945 linked dignity with sorrow, political condemnation with literary respect. Her poetry was known but secretly, as were the fates of her husband-lovers and son. Tragedy could not release her. In the 1930s, helping her get through these multiple upheavals was Vladimir Garshin, a married doctor and professor with strong artistic interests. They grew close; he was with her in August 1939 when she went to her son's Leningrad prison cell for the last time to give him a package before his internal exile (Reeder 223). Garshin then looked after her with food parcels and occasionally clothes while she lived with the Tomashevskys and slept on a couch in a hallway before she was evacuated to Tashkent during the siege. Garshin remained behind, becoming chief coroner for the city, but he suffered mentally from the horrific role and then from the sudden death of his wife who collapsed on the street in 1942. He learned of it only when he unexpectantly identified her body in a morgue. Shortly after, he proposed to Akhmatova; she accepted (Reeder 277–8). This was to be a bright new beginning.

In May 1944, permitted to return to Leningrad, she first stopped in Moscow to give a reading. Those who attended noted that she seemed both sadder and more profound because of the years of isolation and loneliness but excited at the prospect of marriage (Reeder 279). On her arrival in Leningrad, however, there was a change: Garshin had become disoriented from the thousands of deaths and the disaster of Leningrad and had had an affair with a female doctor whom he would shortly marry (or might have already married; details are unclear). Shocked at these developments, Akhmatova nonetheless displayed restraint, especially to friends, but was inwardly damaged. She only referred to the situation indirectly. It was in this emotional state that Berlin met her at Fountain House on November 25, 1945.[10]

Love triangles, however, surrounded her life at Fountain House: she moved into the apartment of the Punin family which had only four rooms with a shared kitchen and toilet. At various times it was home to Nikolay Punin, his first wife, and their daughter Irina with her small daughter. But there would also be Punin's third and current wife, Margarita. Later, Irina Punina's second husband moved in. Lev Gumilyov, Akhmatova's son, lived at the end of a long corridor until his arrest in 1938; after the war, he had a room of his own until his third arrest in 1949.[11]

For Akhmatova, Berlin would become the prototype of her "Guest from the Future" in *Poem without a Hero*, a work that would take her twenty-two years to complete.[12] But to meet with the provisional First Secretary of the British Embassy in Moscow was a risk. Nevertheless, she agreed and on the afternoon of November 25, 1945, it happened. Exacerbating the meeting, however, was another unexpected guest: Winston Churchill's son Randolph, in Russia as a journalist, who sought out Berlin because he needed a translator. Knowing only that he was at the Sheremetev Palace (a.k.a. Fountain House), Churchill roamed the courtyard shouting Berlin's name. Berlin rushed downstairs to quiet Churchill and left with him, only to then call Akhmatova to apologize and ask when he might see her again. Nine that evening, she told him. He returned and they spent the night discussing her admiration for Dostoevsky, criticism of Turgenev, and anger at Tolstoy for his treatment of Anna Karenina.[13] She spoke about her life and he likely revealed that he was in love with someone he met in the United States but from London (Patricia Douglas).

That night, Akhmatova recited portions of "Poem Without a Hero" as well as *Requiem*. He wanted to transcribe both works but she told them they would soon be printed in a volume the following February; she would send him a copy. She then described her loneliness and isolation: Leningrad was for her "nothing but a vast cemetery, the graveyard of her friends."[14] But the visit immediately raised suspicions, largely caused, Berlin thought, by Randolph Churchill's unplanned appearance. Rumors soon circulated that Churchill was part of a large delegation sent to convince Akhmatova to leave Russia and that Winston Churchill would send a special plane to take her to England.[15]

Berlin revisited Akhmatova again on January 5, 1945, just before departing from the Finland Station to return to England and then Washington. The result of this meeting was her cycle of poems, *Cinque*, which she composed between November 25, 1945, and January 11, 1946, a sign of the importance of Berlin's presence for her. The lines of one poem read:

> Sounds die away in the ether,
> And darkness overtakes the dusk.
> In a world become mute for all time,
> There are only two voices: yours and mine.[16]

Later, she would dedicate her "The Wild Rose Comes into Bloom" to Berlin, who would contact her again in the summer of 1956 wishing to meet. He was in Russia for a month with his new wife Aline. Akhmatova, then in Moscow, refused, fearing that it might mean the rearrest of her son who had recently been released from a prison camp. Their only contact was to be a phone call, a kind of non-meeting where among other things, she told him she had reread Chekhov and that "Ward No. 6" accurately described her situation and that of others (Berlin Conv. 79; Haight 168; Reeder 326–7).

The paradox and irony of their 1945/6 encounter was that while it caused her new troubles, it also gave her new energy to survive them and a new desire to write. She did not want to incite any fresh concerns, however, by meeting again. Here, the contradictions of Russian love reached beyond the individual into history. The timeless quality of their original meeting paradoxically made it unnecessary for them to remeet.[17] She writes:

> Of a non-meeting full of secrets
> The desolate splendors,
> The unspoken sentences,
> the words silent.
> This is love as absence but also presence. (Haight 170)

The last two poems of *Cinque*, written a week after Berlin's departure, highlight the intensity of their meeting:

> And what kind of hellish brew
> Did the January darkness bring us?

And what kind of invisible glow
Drove us out of our minds before dawn?

January 11, 1946 (Coll Poems II 239)

When asked by Berlin if she intended to compose a record of her literary life, she said that her poetry "was that, in particular the *Poem without a Hero*."[18]

Within days of his leaving, secret police arrived while she was out to install hidden microphones (Ignat. 164). An informant then suggested to the police that Berlin was a spy and had supposedly announced his love for the poet. As a result of continued surveillance and reports, the security service compiled nine-hundred pages on Akhmatova hidden in their Leningrad files (Ignat. 165). Nevertheless, after an April 1946 Moscow reading with Pasternak, the latter wrote to Berlin to say that every third word of hers was yours (Ignat. 165). But there were repercussions to the Berlin/Akhmatova meeting of 1945: in August, Andrei Zhdanov, secretary of the Central Committee responsible for ideology, authored a report condemning her and her work; on September 4, the Writers' Union expelled her, and shortly after, her new book of poems was pulped.

After 1946, she was unable to publish and became a target of multiple forms of literary and public abuse, often stressing that her poetry lacked any ideological content and was nothing more than reactionary, anti-Soviet tools (Haight 147). Poetry must become, according to the Soviet critic Viktor Pertsov, part of the nation's "work plan" (Haight 147). But in reaction to her exclusion from the literary world and loss of any income, Pasternak, on a Moscow visit, gave her 100 rubles. She repaid the money in 1953 when she received funds for her translations of Victor Hugo. The year before, Pasternak praised Akhmatova in a dedicatory poem writing that she was always a "source of precision and clarity" who constantly "strengthened him" (Haight 161).

In November 1949, her son Lev would be rearrested and remain in prison camps for almost seven years; he had originally been detained for seventeen months in March 1938. In 1949 he went first to the Lefortovo Prison in Moscow and eventually to Omsk. In response, Akhmatova burned her papers: the manuscripts of poems, notes, and letters—they were too incriminating. She went to Moscow every month to give Lev the allowed 100 rubles for prison goods, regularly traveling between the two cities. But she never lost her dignity, a dignity shaped by grief but managed by understated irony. When asked by a friend why her son was arrested, she replied "does there have to be a reason?" When asked by a doctor if the August 1946 Central Committee report condemning her had affected her heart and her art, she ironically replied, "I don't think so" (Reeder

307). Her entire life then focused on her son, soon transferred to Siberia. Every month she sent him a package.

Nikolai Punin, art critic, curator of the Hermitage and the Russian museum, and for fifteen years Akhmatova's common-law husband, was also rearrested (September 30, 1949), and would die in the camps in 1953 (Stalin, a few weeks later). His first arrest in October 1935 was reversed after Akhmatova's petition (partly written by Pasternak) reached Stalin (Reeder 202–3). The next day both her son (he, too, had been arrested) and Punin were released. The supposed cause of Punin's later rearrest was his comment that the thousands of portraits of Lenin were tasteless.

In an effort to protect her son, Akhmatova wrote a series of poems praising Stalin entitled "In Praise of Peace" (1950). To have done such a thing earlier would have betrayed herself but now she forfeited her vanity in an effort to save her son. He survived; poetry saved his life (Haight 159). In actuality, she did not believe these works were poetry and asked that they not be included in her collected poems. They were.

By 1956, the Soviet view of Akhmatova slowly shifted; she was called "a true Soviet patriot" who had rebuked all attempts by the western press to make use of her name: "The patriotic and courageous behavior of this fine, elderly poet after such a stern decree has called forth deep respect in writers' circles ..." (in Haight 163). But she could not jeopardize her position and possibly cause her son's rearrest by meeting Berlin during his 1956 visit. A phone call would suffice. But support grew for her and her rehabilitation at age sixty-seven. As public support increased, her son was released almost simultaneously (Haight 163). He was freed on May 14, 1956, and was formally exonerated by the Supreme Soviet on June 2, 1956. But relations between Akhmatova and her son became acrimonious; after one bitter argument, she suffered a heart attack. He moved out.

Although there was new scrutiny of her work by the security services in the late 1940s, after Khrushchev's 1956 speech to the Twentieth Party Congress, the beginning of the so-called "thaw," Akhmatova's name gradually reappeared. By 1959, poems by her were included in two anthologies: *Literary Moscow* and *Poetry Day*. A debate on the value of her poetry began and in 1958, her first post-Stalin collection appeared, *Poems*, with several translations; 25,000 copies were printed (Haight 172, 173). A critic in the *Literary Gazette* praised her work as "confessions of a daughter of the century who understood that solitude and isolation forces the artist into an impossibly difficult role" (Haight 173). In 1961, *Poems 1909–1960* appeared in an edition of 50,000 (Haight 173). Her patriotism, which overpowered any thought of emigration, brought her into the rank of Soviet poets (Haight 174).

In her later years, there were few official obstacles blocking the appearance of her writing. But she still believed that her meeting with Berlin affected her literary and political status. Strangely, Berlin expressed no guilt in this turn of events. Yet she knew contact with the West was a necessary but dangerous act: knowing beforehand that she would be questioned, she nevertheless agreed to see Berlin twice, first on November 25, 1945, and then on January 5, 1946. Knowing afterward that the meeting would be misunderstood by the authorities, she still wrote about it in *Cinque* and then *Sweetbrier in Blossom*, while adding his name by inference as the third dedicatee to "Poem without a Hero." Later, when meeting Berlin in June 1965 at Oxford for an honorary degree, she repeated her unfounded belief that their encounter infuriated Stalin and contributed to the Cold War (Caute 143; Reeder 497–8). Nevertheless, she held court at the Randolph Hotel greeting Russian visitors and reading from her verse into a tape recorder. She also visited Shakespeare's birthplace.

### iii

In *Cinque*, her short lyrical cycle, she captured the importance of Berlin's challenging visit which she later believed, given the xenophobic atmosphere of Stalin's government, was the cause of the Central Committee of the Communist Party's Resolution of August 14, 1946, which launched a campaign against her and her work and likely led to the rearrest of Lev Gumilyov, her son, and Punin in 1949. The resolution censured two magazines for publishing the ideologically harmful and apolitical works of Zoshchenko and Akhmatova but more importantly claimed that Akhmatova's writing represents "empty poetry lacking in ideals that is foreign to our people." Her poems are "saturated with the spirit of pessimism and degeneration." The *Star* and *Leningrad* magazines were complicit in publishing her "empty and apolitical poems" (in Haight 144).

Accused of being an Acmeist pursuing only the clarity of form and expression and promoting art for art's sake, disregarding the needs of the people and their socio-political life, Andrei Zhdanov's report for the Leningrad branch of the Union of Soviet Writers dismissed her work.[19] Her writing, he claimed, is the "portrait of a frantic little fine lady flitting between the boudoir and the chapel." Her spiritual world is one of doom, hopelessness, and mysticism "intermingled with eroticism." The report ended with the now infamous claim that she is "half nun, half harlot, or rather a harlot-nun whose sin is mixed with prayer" (in Haight 144). Her poetry poisons the young and is "alien to modern Soviet reality and cannot be tolerated" he concluded (Haight 145).

Expelled from the Union of Soviet Writers and her new book of poems destroyed, she became *persona non grata*, shunned by many. The August 14 attack and then expulsion were a complete surprise to her which she later attributed to her meeting with Berlin. But in Soviet comic style, she found about it accidentally when she unwrapped some salted herring done up in a newspaper which happened to have printed the resolution of the Central Committee (Haight 145).

The attack confirmed her belief that Stalin's Russia had not changed since the Terror of the 1930s and believed that she was singled out because of her meeting with a British diplomat, a foreigner, in her home. Her "nun-like" character, as Stalin had thought of her, evaporated and she soon believed there was a direct link between her meeting Berlin and the beginning of the Cold War. Nonetheless, the third dedication of "Poem without a Hero" implies an element of hope:

> He will not be a beloved husband to me
> But what we accomplish, he and I,
> Will disturb the Twentieth Century.
>
> (Complete Poems II: 407)

## iv

When Akhmatova and Berlin met again in Oxford in 1965, Akhmatova repeated to Berlin that Stalin had been enraged by their original meeting: "So our nun now receives visits from foreign spies" he supposedly said (Conv. 79). Ironically, Berlin never worked for any intelligence agency. But to Stalin, every foreigner was a spy. She felt they caused Stalin's fury and his repudiation of his work. But, she believed, the two also changed history which always had an uncanny way of finding her (Conv. 80). For example, when the bombing started during the siege of Leningrad, her friend Boris Tomashevsky went to bring her to the safety of the House of Writers. An air raid began as they scurried through the streets and the two ran for shelter into a courtyard and then down into a cellar. In the semi-darkness Tomashevsky realized they had unexpectedly returned to the Stray Dog, the infamous pre-Revolutionary cellar café (its heyday was roughly 1911–14) where she read, Mandelstam spoke, Mayakovsky held court and artistic happenings occurred nightly, whether it be Karsavina from the Ballets Russes dancing or the presence of Diaghilev, Marinetti, or Strauss. With a touch of historical irony, she calmly told Tomashevsky "it's always like this with me" (Reeder 258; cf Reeder 63–6).[20]

But despite her 1965 trip to Oxford and then Paris, she was adamant about returning to Russia and its repressive regime. It was the order of her country and she must follow: "with it she had lived, and with it she would die. This is what being a Russian meant" Berlin wrote (Conv. 80). A year after her Oxford visit, she died of heart failure at age seventy-six in Domodedovo, thirty-seven kilometers south of Moscow on the very day of Stalin's death thirteen years earlier (March 5, 1953).[21] But despite the tragedies and persecutions of her life, she never lost her dignity or nobility. She remained, in Berlin's words, "an unsurrendering human being."[22] While managing not once to criticize the Soviet regime, she still fulfilled Herzen's description of Russian literature: "one continuous indictment of Russian reality" (Conver. 83).

Standing as a testament to the importance of Berlin's visit are the lines from Part I, Chapter One of "Poem without a Hero" which partially read:

*The sound of steps, those that don't exist,*
*Across the shining parquetry,*
*And bluish cigar smoke.*
*And reflected in all of the mirrors*
*Is the man who didn't appear,*
*Who could not get into the hall.*
*He is no better than the others and no worse,*
*But he doesn't waft on Lethe's chill,*
*And his hand is warm.*
*The guest from the future! — Is it true*
*That he really will come to me,*
*Turning left at the bridge?*

(Coll. Poems II 417)

For Berlin, the impact of their meeting was different, allowing, if not encouraging him, to reconnect with pre-revolutionary Russia and reconsider concepts like liberty, freedom, and political thought, elements he would soon analyze not only in his political talks and essays but in revisions to his popular *Karl Marx: His Life and Environment* (1939; 1947). Further works that reasserted his Russian identity during this period are "The Hedgehog and the Fox," on Tolstoy (1953); "Four Weeks in the Soviet Union" (ca. 1956; pub. 1980); "Boris

Pasternak" (1958); "Tolstoy and Enlightenment" (1961); *Russian Thinkers* (1978); and "Conversations with Akhmatova and Pasternak" (1980). The encounter also prompted the revaluation of his ideas presented in "Historical Inevitability" (1954) and "Two Concepts of Liberty" (1958).[23] The encounter with Akhmatova triggered Berlin's re-evaluation of a world that persisted in complex forms. When he met her at No.44 for the first time on the afternoon of November 25, 1945, she—gray haired, dignified, and with unhurried gestures—rose to greet him. He bowed.[24]

On a personal and emotional level, the meeting also reignited passion. From his days at Oxford, Berlin enjoyed the company of women and began an early relationship with Rachel Walker (nicknamed Tips), a philosophy undergraduate he visited in Paris in 1935. While walking at the Paris zoo, she proposed marriage to him, although he was only twenty-six. "We went on aiming at each other, missing mostly with desperate gravity … I can't possibly marry her. She thinks I can," he wrote (Ignat 69). Earlier in Salzburg he had a repressed romance with Sheila Lynd, daughter of an Irish journalist. But he ended the romance with Rachel, which meant her descent into depression and occasional violence against her widowed mother. Hospitalization overtook a good portion of her life; Berlin accepted responsibility for the condition. According to Ignatieff, Rachel was his first serious emotional relationship and "it would be nearly ten years before he allowed himself another" (Ignat 69).

The next would be with Patricia Douglas from London, who he met in 1942 in Washington. Married, her husband was a POW in North Africa, but of little importance to her. Berlin found her marvelously attractive, and she admired clever men. She had actually enrolled at Radcliffe and was attending lectures at Harvard and studying the cello. She quickly invited him to her Cambridge apartment and he eagerly appeared; he was soon in love with her, meeting in Washington, New York, or Cambridge. But her unreliability undermined the romance. In almost a parody of Russian love, she declared herself his and then disappeared for months into another affair. By 1943, she had fallen in love with someone else, and Berlin became miserable.

In a caricature or echo of Russian love, Douglas had met and became involved with Jacques Abreu, a Franco-Cuban graduate student. In December 1943, all three attended *Oklahoma!* in New York, returning to a hotel where Patricia and Abreau's room was next to Berlin's. Throughout the night, he heard their sounds. The next morning, he left, taking the key with him which he kept for the rest of his life (Ignat 112). But the impact of Patricia lasted, partly through letters she sent him from Europe after D-Day suggesting a possible renewed love, letters that kept him on the string for another four years. Her husband had escaped and he returned. He, in turn, focused on his work gathering political intelligence at the British Embassy in Washington for the Foreign Office, the Cabinet, and even, on occasion, the Prime Minister. But time in Moscow at the end of the war and then in England was a constant in-and-out of a relationship with her (Ignat 209).

Berlin assuaged his feelings by translating Turgenev's *First Love*, assisted by a Shirley Morgan from the Foreign Office. He became a kind of curé to her and her adventures which ended with a marriage to the Marquis of Anglesey. Yet he was still emotionally involved with Patricia captured by the young hero in *First Love* whose deep attachment to a young woman becomes subverted when he finds that the woman is his father's mistress. Berlin dedicated the first edition of the translation to Patricia but then removed her name (printed as "To P de B"— Patricia de Bendern) from later editions. But he fell out of love with her when he pursued another married woman, the wife of an Oxford don, a woman with strong political opinions.

Sexually, the new woman was adventurous but it was he who initiated the affair, emotionally and perhaps even physically frustrated after his meeting with Akhmatova in Leningrad (Ignat 210). And in another aspect of Russian love, he told his new lover's husband twice that he was in love with his wife. The man ridiculed him: impossible! The affair continued for several years until Berlin began a newer relationship, shifting his affections to the unhappily married wife of another Oxford colleague. The woman was Aline Halban from an exiled half-Russian, half-French aristocratic Jewish banking and petroleum family from France. She was also an excellent golfer. Her husband, confronting Berlin, suggested an informal *ménage à trois*. Berlin knew it would not work. She divorced and he married her in 1956, becoming at once a husband and stepfather to her three sons (Ignat 211–19).

The purpose of this narrative of Berlin's love life is to provide perspective for his response to meeting Akhmatova, a blend of romance, resilience, and intellectual union. Had she been twenty years younger, and given Berlin's commitment to her and what she represented, the story might have been different. A passage from *Doctor Zhivago* summarizes the situation and that of the pattern of Russian love: "I don't think I could love you so much if you had nothing to complain of and nothing to regret. I don't like people who have never fallen or stumbled. Their virtue is lifeless and it isn't of much value. Life hasn't revealed its beauty to them."[25] This might be Berlin's superego speaking and realizing that to love is to fail. In a February 1946 letter, he spoke of his visit as "the most thrilling thing that has ever, I think, happened to me" (Ignat 164).

The visit, however, became controversial. Not only because the Russian security services believed Akhmatova was meeting with a British spy, but because Western media and Russian sources began to dramatize and fictionalize the encounter. Akhmatova became upset, aware of these fabrications often expressed through the memoirs of emigres who imagined incidents in her life and the nature of her encounter with Berlin. Georgy Ivanov's *Petersburg's Winters* was such a work filled with distorted facts. One complete misrepresentation was the claim that Vyacheslav Ivanov was credited with discovering her as a poet. There were also many false pictures of her relationship with her husband Gumilyov (Haight 177–8). It was falsely written that Gumilyov played a major role in her early poetry and that she dedicated much of her work to him. The reverse was the actual truth. So, too, the image presented by Sergey Makovsy, former editor of *Apollon* magazine where much of her early verse appeared. He was not, as he claimed, a close friend.

Émigré memoirs, she repeated, were notoriously unreliable. She furthermore believed that the private life of a poet was not essential to the appreciation of the work, although she continued to write about the lives of Mandelstam, Tsvetaeva, Gumilyov, Pasternak, and Berlin (Haight 178–9). Characteristically, perhaps, "Requiem" appeared in Munich in 1963 without her knowledge or consent. Subterfuge persisted.

Expanding the controversy in the West of his visit to Akhmatova, and especially offensive to Berlin, was an account by the American journalist Michael Straight appearing in the *New Republic* of August 24, 1953. Headed "To Our Readers," it was signed "M.S." and appeared on page 23. Straight's family, owners of the magazine, had appointed Straight as publisher. His narrative dramatizes Berlin's visit, and fictionalizes Akhmatova's words on Modigliani.[26]

Berlin unleashed a series of letters condemning the piece because Straight argued, on what was essentially gossip told to him by Berlin, that Akhmatova was rehabilitated because Stalin's daughter read several of her poems and asked her father what had happened to her?[27] A lengthy letter to Straight (who was actually a Communist spy recruited at Cambridge by Anthony Blunt) from Berlin challenges the authenticity of what Straight reported about this and his characterization of Modigliani. Berlin had, in fact, shared details of his meeting with Akhmatova when he met Straight at the Dartington summer school where he lectured on "The Beginnings of Russian Music." Straight misinterpreted them.

In a note to Arthur Schlesinger, Berlin complains that Straight's article makes him out to be "an unspeakable cad and liar" (Lett 486). His mistake, he admits, was talking to Straight about Akhmatova's security but now his reputation was paramount. He is also anxious that the Russian émigré press will reprint the fabricated story. Yet he still refers to his interview with Akhmatova as "one of the most moving experiences of my life" (Lett 387).

In a letter of August 27, 1953, to Straight, Berlin asks for a "*démenti*" (denial) and begins to list the errors, starting with where he met Akhmatova: Leningrad, not Moscow. He then emphasizes that the Stalin/rehabilitation story mixed gossip with anecdote and that he had no factual evidence for the action. But he did see a drawing of the poetess by Modigliani in her room but conveyed nothing of the painter nor its context which he, Straight, concocted (Lett 387–8). He then castigates American journalism, Straight in particular; he also feels embarrassed by those still alive who know Akhmatova and who will now think of him as "a liar and a vulgarian" (Lett 388). He is also ashamed to think that Akhmatova might someday see the article. "Madame A., besides being a poetess of genius," he writes, is "an exceedingly distinguished woman of great sensibility whose life has been a martyrdom for many years" adding that the sensitivity of her situation in Russia established limits as to what journalists anywhere might write about her (Lett 388).

Berlin concludes by reminding Straight of the dangers in the Soviet Union to all citizens who have contact with foreigners, especially citizens with "dubious adherence to Communism" (Lett 389). The appearance of the *New Republic* article will certainly "endanger the safety" of Madame A. who, after her brief rehabilitation, had been condemned seven years earlier by Andrei Zhdanov (Lett 389). "Your story makes things worse. And the blood seems to me on both our hands" (Lett 389). He then appeals to Straight to minimize what he had done in print. He feels humiliated by what happened, but privileges Madame A's safety above all else. He then includes a letter he wants printed in the next issue of *The New Republic* in which he denies the authenticity of the story regarding Stalin and Akhmatova, and disavows the details regarding Akhmatova and Modigliani. It appeared in the September 14, 1953 issue.[28]

In 1979, in a letter to his scholarly editor and bibliographer Henry Hardy, Berlin reveals his awareness of the Akhmatova/Berlin fable.

> I gather that there is a vast myth about Akhmatova in Russia, into which I enter, and many versions of why and when I saw her, and how often … so that whatever I write is likely to be controverted by someone. I shall have to be careful in declaring that memory may play one false but that in this case I do not think it has.

The general reference is to his essay titled "Meetings with Russian Writers in 1945."[29]

An example of the lingering controversy surrounding Berlin's visit is a 2009 publication in Russian from the Akhmatova Museum in St. Petersburg questioning Berlin's account of his visit and his motives. In reality, it argues, he visited the poet perhaps five times, not two, and that his first visit had been arranged in advance through figures in Moscow. It was not chance. He was unquestionably a spy.[30] The claims seem dubious at best.

Berlin was particularly sensitive to adverse criticism as the incident with Straight confirms. As he wrote in a note to Hardy, his great fear was not making a fool of himself but of being "guilty of blunders, or superficiality." Not a scholar by temperament, neither does he want to generalize without evidence: "I do not wish to be justifiably scorned—being laughed at I do not mind much."[31] But some details may never be known. Berlin even sought to refute his identity as the "guest from the future." Such an identity is mistaken, he wrote in 1996, the year before he died (Berlin in Hardy 165–6).

A better record of the encounter and its meaning for both Akhmatova and Berlin may be literature which sharpens our understanding of the nature of Russian love, mixing intensity with distress and disappointment. The second of the *Cinque* poems reads:

> In a world become mute for all time,
> There are only two voices: yours and mine.
> And to the almost bell-like sound
> Of the wind from invisible Lake Ladoga,
> That late-night dialogue turned into
> The delicate shimmer of interlaced rainbows.
> 20 December 1945

(Coll Poems II 237)

Hope, Vaclav Havel wrote, "is not the conviction that something will turn out well, but the certainty that something makes sense, regardless of how it turns out"— otherwise known as Russian love.[32]

# Notes

1   Ronald Hingley, *Nightingale Fever, Russian Poets in Revolution* (New York: Knopf, 1981), 109. Hereafter Hingley. Also see Amanda Haight, *Anna Akhmatova, A Poetic Pilgrimage* (New York: Oxford University Press, 1976), 80–96, 110–12. A 1939

history of Russian Literature in the twentieth century complained that Akhmatova had "'fenced herself off'" from the revolution and focused only on day-to-day life within the narrow confines of personal circumstances. Absent from her writing are the political and social problems of the day. See Haight 110.

Also helpful on Akhmatova's publishing career is Roberta Reeder, *Anna Akhmatova, Poet and Prophet* (New York: St. Martin's Press, 1994), 211–14; hereafter, Reeder. Also see Anna Akhmatova, *The Word that Causes Death's Defeat, Poems of Memory*, tr. and ed. Nancy K. Anderson (New Haven: Yale University Press, 2004). See Akhmatova, "publication," in the Index. This useful work also contains critical essays, biographical details, and commentary.

2  Barbara Heldt, *Terrible Perfection, Women and Russian Literature* (Bloomington: Indiana University Press, 1987), 124.

3  Joseph Brodsky, "Introduction," Anna Akhmatova, *Poems*, sel. and tr. Lyn Coffin (New York: W.W. Norton, 1983), xv. Stressing her non-experimental style, Brodsky adds that "she wanted her verse to maintain appearances ... without bending or inventing the rules." He then explains that Akhmatova sounds "so independent because from the very threshold she knew how to exploit the enemy" (xvi).

4  Osip Mandelstam, poet, actually applied the Cassandra image to Akhmatova. See Nadezhda Mandelstam, *Hope against Hope*, tr. Max Hayward (New York: Atheneum, 1970), 159.

5  Just after their arrival in Voronezh, Boris Pasternak received a phone call from Stalin, his only conversation with the dictator. Stalin wanted to know whether Mandelstam really was a talented poet. "He's a genius isn't he?" he is reputed to have asked Pasternak. See 187; Elaine Feinstein, *Anna of all the Russias, The Life of Anna Akhmatova* (London: Weidenfeld and Nicolson, 2005), 146.

At the end of his three years of exile, Mandelstam and his wife moved closer to Moscow but on a supposed holiday trip, he was re-arrested for "counter-revolutionary activities." In August 1938, he was sentenced to five years in correction camps and was sent to a transit camp near Vladivostok where he died from typhoid fever.

6  This is a colloquial rendering of a passage by Mandelstam in Nadezhda Mandelstam's *Hope against Hope*, tr. Max Hayward (1970; New York: Atheneum, 1983), 159. The actual translation offers something more formal: "'Poetry is respected only in this country—people are killed for it. There's no place where more people are killed for it'" (Ch. 35, 159).

Blok in Ronald Hingley, *Nightingale Fever, Russian Poets in Revolution* (New York: Knopf, 1981), 8.

7  Roberta Reeder, *Anna Akhmatova, Poet and Prophet* (New York: St. Martin's Press, 1994), 211–13; hereafter Reeder. Michael Ignatieff, *Isaiah Berlin, A Life* (Toronto: Viking, 1998), 153. Hereafter Ignat.

Nadezhda Mandelstam wrote that "they forget that everything here is secret even the way we breath." In Jessie Davies, *Anna of the all the Russias* (Liverpool: Lincoln Davies & Co., 1988), 99.

8   Akhmatova, *The Complete Poems of Anna Akhmatova*, II, tr. Judith Hemschemeyer, ed. Roberta Reeder (Somerville, MA: Zephyr Press, 1990), 701. Hereafter Complete Poems.

Lyn Coffin offers a more colloquial translation of this important verse:

> All of Moscow is soaked with verses,
> Skewered with meter time after time.
> Let wordlessness rule over us,
> Let us live apart from rhyme.
> Let muteness be the secret badge
> Of those with you who seem like me,
> And you unite in a secret marriage[.]

Akhamatova, *Poems*, tr. Lyn Coffin, intro. Joseph Brodsky (New York: Norton, 1983), 97.

9   David Caute, *Isaac & Isaiah: The Covert Punishment of a Cold War Heretic* (New Haven: Yale University Press, 2013), 134. Caute's Ch. 12 discusses Berlin and Akhmatova.

10  Her dilapidated room at Fountain House—no heat, no light, no glass—required immediate repair. Friends knew the proper people to renovate but glass was in short supply. However, the former deputy director of the Saltykov-Shchedrin State Public library raided the library's warehouse and used duplicates of portraits of writers, taking the glass from the frames for her apartment, commenting that "'I think they will forgive us'" (Reeder 282).

11  György Dalos, *The Guest from the Future, Anna Akhmatova and Isaiah Berlin*, tr. Antony Wood (London: John Murray, 1998), 27.

The Russian love triangle appeared frequently in life. Pasternak met Olga Ivinskaya in 1946 and she, younger than Pasternak, soon became his mistress and companion for the rest of his life, yet he never divorced his second wife. He split his time between two households. She was the apparent inspiration for Lara in *Doctor Zhivago* (Reeder 355).

12  Berlin actually disputed criticisms to smear such a designation. In a letter of April 4, 1996, to Henry Hardy, he summarized his efforts to refute any misidentification. Prompting the discussion was a 1995 article in *Voprosy literatury* No. 6: 57–85. See Henry Hardy, *In Search of Isaiah Berlin, A Literary Adventure* (London: I.B. Tauris, 2018), 165–6 and 278 notes. 29, 30, 32 and 33.

Earlier, in 1979, Berlin wrote to Hardy acknowledging the myths about his meeting and relationship with Akhmatova in Russia. Partly to counter this, he appended a long list of her poems that refer or allude to his meetings with her. It appears as the Appendix to "Meetings with Russian Writers in 1945 and 1956,"

*Personal Impressions*, ed. Henry Hardy, intro. Noel Annan (1980; London: Hogarth Press, 1981), 209–10. For a compressed summary of the impact of his visit to Akhmatova, see, in the same essay, 199.

13   Reeder, *Anna Akhmatova,* 287. Berlin also tells the story in greater detail in "Conversations with Akhmatova and Pasternak," *The Soviet Mind, Russian Culture under Communism*, ed. Henry Hardy (Washington: Brookings Institution Press, 2004), 71–3. The essay first appeared in 1980. Hereafter Conv.

    For further, elaborated details on his 1945 visit, see György Dalos, *The Guest from the Future, Anna Akhmatova and Isaiah Berlin*, tr. Antony Wood (London: John Murray, 1998), 32–40.

14   Berlin, "Anna Akhmatova: A Memoir," in Akhmatova, *Complete Poems*, II, tr. Judith Hemschemeyer, ed. Robert Reeder (Somerville, MA: Zephyr Press, 1990), 35.

15   Berlin, "Conversations with Akhmatova and Pasternak," *The Soviet Mind,* 72; Reeder 287.

16   Akhmatova, *The Complete Poems,* 237. For a general discussion of the volume and her poetry, see John Bayley, "Anna of All the Russias," *New York Review of Books*, May 13, 1993. https://www.nybooks.com/articles/1993/05/13/anna-of-all-the-russias/.

17   Haight 169. Berlin did re-meet Pasternak, however, who gave him a finished ts. of *Doctor Zhivago*. A first copy went to Sergio d'Angelo, a journalist and literary scout in Moscow for the young Italian publisher Giangiacomo Feltrinelli for publication abroad. For details see Paolo Mancosu, *Zhivago's Secret Journey from Typescript to Book* (Stanford: Hoover Institution Press, 2016).

18   Berlin, "Meetings with Russian Writers," *Personal Impressions,* 199.

19   Two lines from Valery Briusov (or Bryusov) state the Acmeist aesthetic clearly: "I love the trueness of straight lines / In dreams I like there to be a limit." "Books are more beautiful than roses!" he adds. See Briusov in Avril Pyman, *A History of Russian Symbolism* (Cambridge: Cambridge University Press, 1994), 165–6.

20   As early as 1912, her dignity mixed with sadness. She would enter with grandeur, pausing a moment to write her latest poem, and then proceed into the room, capturing everyone's attention but with something of the tragic suggested in Mandelstam's "Anna Akhmatova," a woman akin to Rachel in *Phaedra*. "'Half-turned, oh grief, / She gazed indifferent'" he wrote (Reeder 64).

21   In another touch of historical irony, she and Hitler were born in the same year, 1889, three months apart.

22   Berlin, "Anna Akhmatova: A Memoir," *Complete Poems of Anna Akhmatova*, II, tr. Judith Hemschemeyer, ed. Roberta Reeder, 43. The entire memoir, excerpted from "Meetings with Russian Writers in 1945 and 1956" in *Personal Impressions* (1980), runs from pp. 25–45.

23   A number of these pieces appear in Berlin, *The Soviet Mind* (2004), notably "A Visit to Leningrad," "Conversations with Akhmatova and Pasternak" (hereafter Conv.) and

"Soviet Russian Culture." There is also important material in his *Personal Impressions* (1980), mainly a longer version of "Meetings with Russian Writers in 1945 and 1956" from which "Conversations with Akhmatova and Pasternak" was extracted. As late as 1991, he would write of her as "an outstanding figure in the martyrology of her time." Berlin, "Foreword," Anatoly Nayman, *Remembering Anna Akhmatova*, intro. Joseph Brodsky, tr. Wendy Rosslyn (London: Peter Halban, 1991), vii.

24 Berlin, "Conversations with Akhmatova and Pasternak," SM 71. She was not alone; an academic friend was with her and was present when he returned at nine that evening but left just before midnight; Akhmatova then became more animated asking him about the composer Artur Lurie and Boris Anrep, a mosaicist who included an image of her at the entrance to the National Gallery in London. She then spoke of her life and the death of her first husband, the poet Gumilyov. She then offered to recite some of her poetry, prefaced by two cantos from Byron's *Don Juan*. She spoke from memory.

Poems from Gumilyov and Mandelstam followed. And then the unfinished *Poem without a Hero* before passages from *Requiem*. At 3 a.m. they ate potatoes, all she had. Afterward, a discussion of Russian literature, dismissing Chekhov because of the absence of heroes and martyrs, and criticism of *Anna Karenina* because Tolstoy allowed her to die. She worshipped Dostoevsky but despised Turgenev. Kafka was also for her a hero, as was Pushkin. And then Pasternak, to whom she was devoted. But like the poet/novelist, she would not abandon Russia.

These and additional details of their night together—he was only her second foreign visitor since the First World War—appear in "Conversations with Akhmatova and Pasternak," SM 73–9 (cf. "Meetings" 200). Interestingly, Berlin only briefly mentions his second visit on January 5, 1946, just before his departure from the Finland Station to London. She gave him a collection of her verse with a new poem inscribed on the flyleaf, one that would later form the second in the cycle entitled *Cinque*.

25 Boris Pasternak, *Doctor Zhivago*, tr. Manya Harari and Max Hayward, intro. John Bayley (1958; New York: Everyman, 1991), 422. Bayley remarks that "like most Russian novels, *Doctor Zhivago* has its didactic side" ("Introduction" xxvi).

26 Emphasizing the poverty of Modigliani at the time—Paris 1911—she supposedly told Berlin that when he "finished the picture he gave it to me for a loaf of bread and a bottle of wine." This was fabricated by Straight. See Straight passage in Berlin, *Enlightening, Letters 1946–1960*, ed. Henry Hardy and Jennifer Holmes with the assistance of Serena Moore (London: Chatto and Windus, 2009), 385. Hereafter Lett. Akhmatova admired the drawing selecting the 1911 drawing for the book jacket of *The Flight of Time* (1963), a compilation of her poetry. On the Akhmatova/Modigliani relationship in Paris in 1911, see "Modigliani and Akhmatova in Paris," tr. Nora Favorov, *Russian Life,* March 5, 2016. https://russianlife.com/the-russia-file/modigliani-and-akhmatova-in-paris/.

27 This was partially correct: Stalin remembered Akhmatova's work in February 1939 and asked a literary gathering where she was. Updated, he gave her permission to publish and, in the summer of 1940, Akhmatova's *From Six Books* appeared. A rumor suggested that it was allowed because Stalin's daughter admired her poetry. "Papa's gift to Svetlana" was the volume's popular nickname. The novelist Mikhail Sholokhov then suggested the collection be nominated for the Stalin Prize. Soviet critics warmed to her writing but several months later Stalin read the book and objected to the poem "Slander" thinking it was directed against his regime, unaware that it was written in 1922. The book was immediately withdrawn and he forbid her poetry from being printed (Reeder 229–30).

28 Berlin's letter appeared as "Madame Akhmatova," *New Republic* (September 14, 1953): 22–3. Also see Lett. 390.

29 Berlin in Henry Hardy, *In Search of Isaiah Berlin: A Literary Adventure* (London: Bloomsbury, 2020), 92. Hereafter Hardy.

30 Josephine Von Zitzewitz summarizes and challenges the account in "That's How It Was. New Theories about Anna Akhmatova and Isaiah Berlin," *TLS* (September 9, 2011) 14–15. Surprisingly, Henry Hardy, *In Search of Isaiah Berlin: A Literary Adventure* (London: Bloomsbury, 2020), does not outwardly reject the possibility of five visits, although Berlin insisted there were only two. See *In Search* 92, 95.

31 Berlin in Hardy, *In Search of Isaiah Berlin* 79.

32 Václav Havel, *Disturbing the Peace: A Conversation with Karel Hvizdala*, tr. Paul Wilson (New York: Knopf, 1990), 181.

# Bibliography

Ackerman, Robert. "Jane Ellen Harrison: The Early Work," *The Myth and Ritual School: J.G. Frazer and the Cambridge Ritualists*. New York: Routledge, 2002.

Akhmatova, Anna. *The Complete Poems of Anna Akhmatova*, II, tr. Judith Hemschemeyer, ed. Roberta Reeder. Somerville, MA: Zephyr Press, 1990.

Akhmatova, Anna. *Poems*, tr. Lyn Coffin, intro. Joseph Brodsky. New York: Norton, 1983.

Akhmatova, Anna. *The Word that Causes Death's Defeat, Poems of Memory*, tr. and ed. Nancy K. Anderson. New Haven: Yale University Press, 2004.

Baedeker, Karl. *Russia, Handbook for Travelers*. Leipzig: Karl Baedeker, Publisher, 1914.

Bayley, John. "Anna of All the Russias," *New York Review of Books*, 13 May 1993. https://www.nybooks.com/articles/1993/05/13/anna-of-all-the-russias/.

Beard, Mary. *The Invention of Jane Harrison*. Cambridge, MA: Harvard University Press, 2000.

Beasley, Rebecca. *Russomania, Russian Culture and the Creation of British Modernism, 1881-1992*. Oxford: Oxford University Press, 2020.

Beckett, Samuel. "Dante … Bruno. Vico. Joyce," *Our Exagmination Round His Factification*. 1929; New York: New Directions, 1972.

Bell, Quentin. *Virginia Woolf: A Biography*. New York: Harcourt Brace Jovanovich, 1972.

Benjamin, Walter. "Conversations on Love," *Early Writings 1910-1917*, tr. Howard Eiland *et al*. Cambridge: Harvard University Press, 2011.

Benjamin, Walter. "Dostoevsky's the Idiot," *Early Writings, 1910-1917*, tr. Howard Eland *et al*. Cambridge: Harvard University Press, 2011. 275-80.

Benjamin, Walter. "Erotic Education," *Early Writings, 1910-1917*, tr. Howard Eiland *et al*. Cambridge: Harvard University Press, 2011. 166-7.

Benjamin, Walter. "Moscow," *Reflections, Essays, Aphorisms, Autobiographical Writings*, tr. Edmund Jephcott, ed. Peter Demetz. New York: Schocken Books, 2007.

Benjamin, Walter. *Moscow Diary*, ed. Gary Smith, tr. Richard Sieburth. Cambridge: Harvard University Press, 1986.

Benjamin, Walter. *Moscow Diary*, tr. Wolfram Eilenberger in Eilenberger, *Time of the Magicians, Wittgenstein, Benjamin, Cassirer, Heidegger and the Decade that Reinvented Philosophy*, tr. Shaun Whiteside. New York: Penguin, 2020.

Benjamin, Walter. "On Love and Related Matters (A European Problem)," *Selected Writings*, vol. 1 1913-1926, ed. Marcus Bullock and Michael W. Jennings. Cambridge: Harvard University Press, 1996.

Benjamin, Walter. *One-Way Street and Other Writings*, intro. Susan Sontag, tr. Edmund Jephcott and Kingsley Shorter. London: NLB, 1979.

Benjamin, Walter. "Review of Gladkov's *Cement*," *Selected Writings*, vol. 2 1927–1934, tr. Rodney Livingstone *et al.*, ed. Michael W. Jennings, Howard Eiland, and Gary Smith. Cambridge: Harvard University Press, 1999.

Benjamin, Walter. "Theses on the Philosophy of History," *Illuminations*, ed. Hannah Arendt. New York: Schocken, 1969. 253–64.

Berberova, Nina. *Moura: The Dangerous Life of the Baroness Budberg*, tr. Marian Schwartz and Richard D. Sylvester. New York: New York Review Books, 2005.

Berlin, Isaiah. "Anna Akhmatova: A Memoir," in Akhmatova, *Complete Poems*, II, tr. Judith Hemschemeyer, ed. Robert Reeder. Somerville, MA: Zephyr Press, 1990.

Berlin, Isaiah. "Conversations with Akhmatova and Pasternak," *The Soviet Mind, Russian Culture under Communism*, ed. Henry Hardy. Washington: Brookings Institution Press, 2004.

Berlin, Isaiah. *Enlightening, Letters 1946–1960*, ed. Henry Hardy and Jennifer Holmes with the Assistance of Serena Moore. London: Chatto and Windus, 2009.

Berlin, Isaiah. "Foreword," Anatoly Nayman, *Remembering Anna Akhmatova*, intro. Joseph Brodsky, tr. Wendy Rosslyn. London: Peter Halban, 1991.

Berlin, Isaiah. "Madame Akhmatova," *New Republic* (September 14, 1953): 22–3.

Berlin, Isaiah. "Meetings with Russian Writers in 1945 and 1956," *Personal Impressions*, ed. Henry Hardy, intro. Noel Annan. London: Hogarth Press, 1981.

Berlin, Isaiah. *The Soviet Mind, Russian Culture under Communism*, ed. Henry Hardy, foreword by Strobe Talbott, glossary by Helen Rappaport. Washington: Brookings Institution Press, 2004.

Berman, Paul. "Wilson and Soviet Russia, a Roundtable," *Edmund Wilson, Centennial Observations*, ed. Lewis M. Dabney. Princeton: Princeton University Press, 1997.

Boyd, Brian. *Vladimir Nabokov: The American Years*. Princeton: Princeton University Press, 1991.

Boyd, Brian. *Vladimir Nabokov: The Russian Years*. Princeton: Princeton University Press, 1990.

Boym, Svetlana, "Loving in Bad Taste," *Sexuality and the Body in Russian Culture*, ed. Jane T. Costlow *et al.* Stanford: Stanford University Press, 1993.

Brinkmanis, Andris. "Introduction," Lācis and Benjamin, "Signals from Another World; Proletarian Theater as a Site for Education." https://www.documenta14.de/en/south/25225_signals_from_another_world_proletarian_theater_as_a_site_for_education_texts_by_asja_la_cis_and_walter_benjamin_with_an_introduction_by_andris_brinkmanis.

Brodsky, Joseph. "Introduction," Anna Akhmatova, *Poems*, sel. and tr. Lyn Coffin. New York: W.W. Norton, 1983.

Brower, Brock. "Bud McFarlane: Semper Fi," *New York Times*, January 22, 1989. https://www.nytimes.com/1989/01/22/magazine/bud-mcfarlane-semper-fi.html.

Bulgakov, Mikhail. *The Master and Margarita*, tr. Richard Pevear and Larissa Volokhonsky. New York: Penguin, 2001.

Bullock, Philip Ross. "Tsar's Hall, Russian Music in London, 1895–1926," *Russia in Britain*, ed. Beasely and Bullock. Oxford: Oxford University Press, 2013. 113–28.

Carpentier, Martha C. *Ritual, Myth, and the Modernist Text, the Influence of Jane Ellen Harrison on Joyce, Eliot and Woolf.* London: Routledge, 1998.

Carr, Barnes. *The Lenin Plot: The Unknown Story of America's War against Russia.* New York: Pegasus Books, 2020.

Castronovo, David and Janet Groth, *Critic in Love: A Romantic Biography of Edmund Wilson.* Berkeley: Shoemaker Hoard, 2005.

*Catalogue of Books from the Library of Leonard and Virginia Woolf.* Brighton: Holleyman & Treacher, 1975.

Caute, David. *Isaac and Isaiah: The Covert Punishment of a Cold War Heretic.* New Haven: Yale University Press, 2013.

Chekhov, Anton, "Concerning Love," *The Kiss and Other Stories*, tr. Ronald Wilks. London: Penguin, 1982. 145–53.

Chekhov, Anton. "The Kiss," tr. Ann Dunnigan, *Anton Chekhov's Selected Stories*, ed. Cathy Popkin. New York: Norton, 2014. 115–30.

Chekhov, Anton. "The Lady with the Little Dog," *Anton Chekhov's Selected Stories*, ed. Cathy Popkin, tr. Richard Pevear and Olga Volokhonsky. New York: Norton, 2014. 414–27.

Chekhov, Anton. "A Little Game," *Anton Chekhov's Selected Stories*, ed. Cathy Popkin, tr. Katherine Tiernan O'Connor. New York: Norton, 2014. 57–60.

Chekhov, Anton. *The Three Sisters*, tr. Stark Young. New York: Samuel French, 1941.

Cheever, John. "The Geometry of Love," *Collected Stories and Other Writings*. New York: Library of America, 2009.

Coles, Gladys Mary. "Katherine Mansfield and W. Gerhardie," *Contemporary Review* 229 (1976): 32–40.

Conrad, Joseph. *Under Western Eyes*, ed. Stephen Donovan, intro. Allan H. Simmons. London: Penguin, 2007.

Cowley, Malcolm. "H.G. Wells' Interview with Stalin Helped Change the Fundamental Principles of Liberalism," *The New Republic*, April 23, 1935. https://newrepublic.com/article/119904/review-hg-wells-interview-joseph-stalin.

Craig, Randall. "The Early Fiction of William Gerhardie," *Novel* 15.3 (1982): 240–56.

Craig, Randall. "Edith Wharton and William Gerhardie," *Journal of Modern Literature* 16.4 (1990): 597–614.

Dabney, Lewis M. *Edmund Wilson: A Life in Literature.* New York: Farrar, Straus and Giroux, 2005.

Dalos, György. *The Guest from the Future, Anna Akhmatova and Isaiah Berlin*, tr. Antony Wood. London: John Murray, 1998.

Davies, Dido. *William Gerhardie: A Biography.* Oxford: Oxford University Press, 1990.

Davies, Jesse. *Anna of all the Russians.* Liverpool: Lincoln Davies & Co., 1988.

Davis, Mary E. *Ballets Russes Style: Diaghilev's Dancers and Paris Fashion*. London: Reaktion, 2010.

Davison-Pégon, "Samuel Solomonovich Koteliansky and British Modernism," *Translation and Literature* 20 (2011): 334–47.

Dickstein, Morris. "Edmund Wilson: Three Phases," *Edmund Wilson, Centennial Observations*, ed. Lewis M. Dabney. Princeton: Princeton University Press, 1997.

Diment, Galya. *A Russian Jew of Bloomsbury: The Life and Times of Samuel Koteliansky*. Montreal: McGill-Queen's University Press, 2011.

Dos Passos, John. "Finland Station" in "Russian Visa," in *All Countries, Travel Books and Other Writings 1916–1941*. New York: Library of America, 2003.

Dostoevsky, Fyodor. *The Brothers Karamazov*, tr. Constance Garnett. New York: Lowell Press, 1900. Project Gutenberg. https://www.gutenberg.org/files/28054/old/28054-pdf.pdf.

Dostoevsky, Fyodor. *An Honest Thief and Other Stories*. 1919, tr. Constance Garnett. Westport, CT: Greenwood Press, 1975.

Dostoevsky, Fyodor. *The Idiot*, tr. Constance Garnett. 1913; New York: Modern Library, 1935.

Dostoevsky, Fyodor. *The Idiot*, tr. Richard Pevear and Larissa Volokhonsky. New York: Vintage, 2003.

Dostoevsky, Fyodor. "White Nights," *White Nights and Other Stories*, tr. Constance Garnett. New York: Grove Press, 1960.

Eiland, Howard and Michael W. Jennings, *Walter Benjamin: A Critical Life*. Cambridge: Harvard University Press, 2014.

Eilenberger, Wolfram. *Time of the Magicians, Wittgenstein, Benjamin, Cassirer, Heidegger and the Decade that Reinvented Philosophy*, tr. Shaun Whiteside. New York: Penguin, 2020.

Eliot, T.S. "Reflections on Vers Libre," *To Criticize the Critic and Other Writings*. New York: Farrar, Straus & Giroux, 1965.

Elwood, Ralph Carter. *Inessa Armand: Revolutionary and Feminist*. Cambridge: Cambridge University Press, 1992.

Elwood, Ralph Carter. "Lenin's Correspondence with Inessa Armand," *The Slavonic and East European Review* 65.2 (April 1987): 218–35.

Feinstein, Elaine. *Anna of All the Russias: The Life of Anna Akhmatova*. London: Weidenfeld and Nicolson, 2005.

Feuer, Lewis S. "American Travelers to the Soviet Union 1917–32: The Formation of a New Deal Ideology," *American Quarterly* 14.2 (1962): 119–49.

Fitzpatrick, Sheila. "Foreign Visitors Observed: Moscow Visitors in the 1930s under the Gaze of Their Soviet Guides," *Russian History* 35.17 (2008): 215–34.

Fokine, Michel. *Fokine: Memoirs of a Ballet Master*, tr. Vitale Fokine, ed. A. Chujoy. Boston: Little, Brown & Co., 1961.

Fox, Ralph. *The Novel and the People*, Preface Jeremy Hawthorn. London: Lawrence and Wishart, 1937.

Fox, Ralph. *Storming Heaven*. London: Constable, 1928.

Gabriel, Mary. *Love and Capital: Karl and Jenny Marx and the Birth of a Revolution*. Boston: Little Brown and Co., 2012.

Gerhardi, William. *Anton Chekov: A Critical Study*. London: Cobden-Sanderson, 1923.

Gerhardi, William. *Futility, a Novel on Russian Themes*. Preface Michael Holroyd. 1922; London: Macdonald, 1971.

Gerhardi, William. *Memoirs of a Polyglot*. 1933; London: Robin Clark, 1990.

Gerhardi, William. *Resurrection*. London: Cassell, 1934.

Gerhardi, William. *The Romanovs, Evocation of the Past as a Mirror for the Present*. London: Rich & Cowan, 1940.

Glendenning, Victoria. *Leonard Woolf: A Biography*. New York: Free Press, 2006.

Goncharov, Ivan. *Oblomov*, tr. Stephen Pearl. Richmond, Surrey: Alma Classics, 2015.

Goodman, Susan et al. *The Power of Pictures, Early Soviet Photography, Early Soviet Film*. New York: Jewish Museum/Yale University Press, 2015.

Groskop, Viv. "Surviving Unrequited Love with Ivan Turgenev," *Paris Review*, October 19, 2018. https://www.theparisreview.org/blog/2018/10/19/surviving-unrequited-love-with-ivan-turgenev/.

Haight, Amanda. *Anna Akhmatova: A Poetic Pilgrimage*. New York: Oxford University Press, 1976.

Hankins, Kathleen Leslie. "'Across the Screen of My Brain,' Virginia Woolf's 'The Cinema' and Film Forums of the Twenties," *The Multiple Muses of Virginia Woolf*, ed. Diane F. Gillespie. Columbia, Missouri: University of Missouri Press, 1993. 148–79.

Hankins, Kathleen Leslie. "Virginia Woolf and Film," *Edinburgh Companion to Virginia Woolf and the Arts*, ed. Maggie Humm. Edinburgh: Edinburgh University Press, 2010. 351–74.

Hardwick, Elizabeth, "Hedda Gabler," *Seduction and Betrayal: Women and Literature*. New York: Vintage, 1975.

Hardy, Henry. *In Search of Isaiah Berlin: A Literary Adventure*. London: I.B. Tauris, 2018.

Harrison, Jane Ellen. *Ancient Art and Ritual*. London: William and Norgate, 1913.

Harrison, Jane Ellen. *Aspects, Aorists and the Classical Tripos*. Cambridge: Cambridge University Press, 1919.

Harrison, Jane Ellen. *Introductory Studies in Greek Art*. London: Fisher Unwin, 1885.

Harrison, Jane Ellen. With Hope Mirrlees. "Preface," *The Book of the Bear*. London: Nonesuch Press, 1926.

Harrison, Jane Ellen. "Reminiscences of a Student's Life," *Arion: A Journal of Humanities and the Classics* 4.2 (1965): 312–46.

Harrison, Jane Ellen. *Russia and the Russian Verb, A Contribution to the Psychology of the Russian People*. Cambridge: W. Heffer & Sons, Ltd., 1915.

Hastings, Selina. *The Secret Lives of Somerset Maugham*. London: John Murray, 2009.

Havel, Václav. *Disturbing the Peace, A Conversation with Karel Hvizdala*, tr. Paul Wilson. New York: Knopf, 1990.

Heldt, Barbara. *Terrible Perfection: Women and Russian Literature*. Bloomington: Indiana University Press, 1987.
Hills, Faith. *Utopia's Discontents, Russian Émigrés and the Quest for Freedom 1830s-1930s*. Oxford: Oxford University Press, 2021.
Hingley, Ronald. *Nightingale Fever, Russian Poets in Revolution*. New York: Knopf, 1981.
Holroyd, Michael. "Preface," *Futility*. London: Macdonald, 1971.
Homans, Jennifer. *Apollo's Angels: A History of Ballet*. London: Granta, 2010.
Ignatieff, Michael. *A Life of Isaiah Berlin*. Toronto: Viking, 1998.
Ingram, Susan. "The Writing of Asja Lacis," *New German Critique* 86 (2002): 159–77.
Jeffreys-Jones, Rhodri. *American Espionage, from Secret Service to CIA*. New York: The Free Press, 1977.
Jones, Jonathan. "The Silent Revolutionary," *The Guardian*, August 31, 2001. https://www.theguardian.com/film/2001/aug/31/artsfeatures1.
Jones, Susan. *Literature, Modernism and Dance*. Oxford: Oxford University Press, 2013.
Kermode, Frank. "On William Gerhardie," *The Uses of Error*. Cambridge: Harvard University Press, 1991.
Krausz, Tamás. *Reconstructing Lenin, an Intellectual Biography*, tr. Bálint Bethlenfalvy with Mario Fenyo. New York: Monthly Review Press, 2015.
Kropotkin, Alexandra. *How to Cook and Eat in Russian*. New York: G. P. Putnam's Sons, 1947.
Lanser, Susan and Evelyn Torton Beck, "[Why] are there no Great Women Critics?" *The Prism of Sex: Essays in the Sociology of Knowledge*, ed. Beck and Julia A. Sherman. Madison, WI: University of Wisconsin Press, 1979.
Le Carré, John. *The Pigeon Tunnel, Stories from My Life*. New York: Viking, 2016.
Lenin, Vladimir. "To Inessa Armand," Letter from Berne, January 17, 1915. https://www.marxists.org/archive/lenin/works/1915/jan/17.htm.
Lewis, Wyndham. "Petrograd Letters," published in the *Little Review* as "Imaginary Letters," *Little Review* 4.1 (May 1917): 19–27.
Leyda, Jay. *Kino, A History of the Russian and Soviet Film*. New York: Collier Books, 1960.
Lockhart, R.H. Bruce. *The Diaries of Sir Robert Bruce Lockhart, Vol.1 1915–1938*, ed. Kenneth Young. London: Macmillan, 1973.
Lockhart, R.H. Bruce. *Diaries Vol. II, 1939–1965*. London: Macmillan, 1980.
Lockhart, R.H. Bruce. *Memoirs of a British Agent*. London: Macmillan, 1934.
Lockhart, R.H. Bruce. *Retreat from Glory*. London: Putnam, 1934.
Lockhart, R.H. Bruce. *The Two Revolutions: An Eye-witness Study of Russia 1917*. London: Bodley Head, 1967.
Lyandres, Semion. "The 1918 Attempt on the Life of Lenin: A New Look at the Evidence," *Slavic Review* 48.3 (1989): 432–48.
Lynn, Andrea. *Shadow Lovers: The Last Affairs of H.G. Wells*. Boulder, CO: Westview, 2001.
Maes-Jelinek, Hena. "William Gerhardie," *Criticism of Society in the English Novel between the Wars*. Liège: Presses universitaires de Liège, 1970. 283–300.

Mancosu, Paolo. *Zhivago's Secret Journey from Typescript to Book*. Stanford: Hoover Institution Press, 2016.

Mandelstam, Nadezhda. *Hope against Hope*, tr. Max Hayward. New York: Atheneum, 1970.

Marcus, Laura. "The European Dimension of the Hogarth Press," *The Reception of Virginia Woolf in Europe*, ed. Mary Ann Caws and N. Luckhurst. London: Bloomsbury, 2002. 328–56.

Marcus, Laura. "The Tempo of Revolution, British Film Culture and Soviet Cinema in the 1920s," *Russia in Britain, 1880–1940, From Melodrama to Modernism*, ed. Rebecca Beasley and Philip Ross Bullock. Oxford: Oxford University Press, 2013. 225–40.

Marcus, Laura. *The Tenth Muse, Writings about Cinema in the Modernist Period*. Oxford: Oxford University Press, 2007.

Marvell, Andrew. "The Definition of Love," *Norton Anthology of English Literature*, vol. 1, 7th ed., ed. M.H. Abrams. New York: Norton, 2000. 93.

Matich, Olga. *Erotic Utopia: The Decadent Imagination in Russia's Fin de Siècle*. Madison: University of Wisconsin Press, 2005.

Maugham, Somerset. *Ashenden*. London: Vintage, 2000.

Maugham, Somerset. *The Summing Up*. London: Heineman, 1938.

Maugham, Somerset. *A Writer's Notebook*. London: Vintage, 2001.

McDonough, Anna. "Love and Heartache in 19th century Russian Literature," *Emory Journal of Asian Studies* II Special Edition (April 2020). https://ejasonline.org/wp-content/uploads/2020/04/REALC_2020_McDonogh.pdf.

McDonald, Deborah and Jeremy Dronfield, *A Very Dangerous Woman: The Lives, Loves and Lies of Russia's Most Seductive Spy*. London: Oneworld, 2015.

Menand, Louis. "The Historical Romance," *New Yorker*, March 24, 2003. https://www.newyorker.com/magazine/2003/03/24/the-historical-romance.

Menashe, Louis. *Moscow Believes in Tears, Russia and Their Movies*. Washington: New Academia Publishing, 2010.

Merridale, Catherine. *Lenin on the Train*. London: Penguin, 2017.

Meyers, Jeffrey. *Edmund Wilson: A Biography*. Boston: Houghton Mifflin, 1995.

Mills, Jean. "The Writer, the Prince and the Scholar," *Leonard and Virginia Woolf: The Hogarth Press and the Networks of Modernism*, ed. Helen Southworth. Edinburgh: Edinburgh University Press, 2010.

Mirsky, Prince D.S. *A History of Russian Literature*. New York: Knopf, 1927.

Mirsky, Prince D.S. *Jane Harrison and Russia*. Cambridge: Heffer & Son, 1930.

Mirsky, Prince D.S. "Preface," *The Life of the Archpriest Avvakum by Himself*, tr. Jane Harrison and Hope Mirrlees. 1924; London: The Hogarth Press, 1963.

"Modigliani and Akhmatova in Paris," tr. Nora Favorov, *Russian Life*, March 5, 2016. https://russianlife.com/the-russia-file/modigliani-and-akhmatova-in-paris/.

Morgan, Ted. *Maugham*. New York: Simon and Schuster, 1980.

Morris, Benny. *Sidney Reilly, Master Spy*. New Haven: Yale University Press, 2022.

Muchnic, Helen. "Edmund Wilson's Russian Involvement," *An Edmund Wilson Celebration*, ed. John Wain. Oxford: Phaidon, 1978.

Nabokov, Vladimir. *The Nabokov-Wilson Letters*, ed. Simon Karlinksy. New York: Harper & Row, 1979.

Nadel, I.B. "Maugham and Woolf in Russia: *Ashenden* and *Orlando*," *Journal of English Language and Literature* 66.1 (2020): 23–43.

Nadel, I.B. "The Russian Woolf," *Modernist Cultures* 13 (2018): 546–67.

Pasternak, Boris. *Doctor Zhivago*, tr. Manya Harari and Max Hayward, intro. John Bayley. 1958; New York: Everyman, 1991.

Paul, Sherman. *Edmund Wilson: A Study of Literary Vocation in Our Time*. Urbana: University of Illinois Press, 1965.

Peacock, Sandra J. *Jane Ellen Harrison: The Mask and the Self*. New Haven: Yale University Press, 1988.

Pearson, Michael. *Inessa, Lenin's Mistress*. London: Duckworth, 2001.

Pinkham, Sophia, "Sofiya Tolstoy's Defense," *New Yorker*, October 21, 2014. https://www.newyorker.com/books/page-turner/sofiya-tolstoys-defense.

Popkin, Cathy, "Kiss and Tell," *Sexuality and the Body in Russian Culture*, ed. Jane T. Costlow *et al*. Stanford: Stanford University Press, 1993. 139–55.

Protopopova, Darya. "On the Principle of Sound in Film," *The Film Factory, Russian and Soviet Cinema in Documents 1896–1939*, ed. Richard Taylor and Ian Christie. Cambridge, MA: Harvard University Press, 1988.

Protopopova, Darya. *Selected Essays*, ed. Richard Taylor, tr. Richard Taylor and Evgeni Filippov. London: Seagull Books, 2006.

Protopopova, Darya. *Virginia Woolf's Portraits of Russian Writers: Creating the Literary Other*. Newcastle upon Tyne: Cambridge Scholars Publishing, 2019.

Protopopova, Darya. "Woolf and Russian literature," *Virginia Woolf in Context*, ed. Bryony Randall and Jane Goldman. Cambridge: Cambridge University Press, 2012.

Pudovkin, V.I. *Film Technique and Film Acting*, tr. Ivor Montagu, memorial ed. London: Vision Press, 1958.

Pushkin, Alexander. "Eugene Onegin," tr. Babette Deutsch, *Poems, Prose and Plays of Alexander Pushkin*, ed. Avrahm Yarmolinsky. New York: Modern Library, 1964.

"Pushkin's Death and Its Aftermath," British Library. https://www.bl.uk/onlinegallery/features/blackeuro/pushkindeath.html.

Pyman, Avril. *A History of Russian Symbolism*. Cambridge: Cambridge University Press, 1994.

Reeder, Roberta. *Anna Akhmatova, Poet and Prophet*. New York: St. Martin's Press, 1994.

Reinhold, Natalya. "Virginia Woolf's Russian Voyage Out," *Woolf Studies Annual* 9 (2003): 1–27.

Remnick, David. "Wilson and Soviet Russia, a Roundtable," *Edmund Wilson, Centennial Observations*, ed. Lewis M. Dabney. Princeton: Princeton University Press, 1997.

Robinson, Annabel. *The Life and Work of Jane Ellen Harrison*. Oxford: Oxford University Press, 2002.

Rogatchevskaia, Katya. "British Intellectuals and Russian Bears," *European Studies Blog*, August 4, 2021. https://blogs.bl.uk/european/2021/08/british-intellectuals-and-russian-bears.html.

Rubenstein, Roberta. *Virginia Woolf and the Russian Point of View*. New York: Palgrave/Macmillan, 2009.

*Russia in Britain, 1880–1940, From Melodrama to Modernism*, ed. Rebecca Beasley and Philip Ross Bullock. Oxford: Oxford University Press, 2013.

"Russian Princess Comes to Study US," *New York Times*, April 6, 1927. https://www.nytimes.com/1927/04/06/archives/russian-princess-comes-to-study-us-daughter-of-prince-kropotkin.html.

Rutten, Ellen. *Unattainable Bride Russia, Gendering Nation, State and Intelligentsia in Russian Intellectual Culture*. Evanston, IL: Northwestern University Press, 2010.

Schapiro, Meyer. "The Revolutionary Personality," *Partisan Review* 7.6 (November–December 1940): 466–79.

Schneer, Jonathan. *The Lockhart Plot, Love, Betrayal, Assassination and Counter-Revolution in Lenin's Russia*. Oxford: Oxford University Press, 2020.

Schwinn-Smith, Marilyn. "Bears in Bloomsbury: Jane Ellen Harrison and Russia," *Virginia Woolf: Three Centenary Celebrations*, ed. Maria Candida Zamith and Luisa Flora. Porto: Faculdade de Letras da Universidade do Porto, 2007. 119–44.

Schwinn-Smith, Marilyn. "'Bergsonian Poetics' and the Beast: Jane Harrison's Translations from the Russian," *Translation and Literature* 20.3 (Autumn 2011): 314–33.

Shamina, Vera and Maria Kozyreva, "Russia Revisited," *The Reception of H.G. Wells in Europe*, ed. Patrick Parrinder and James S. Partington. London: Bloomsbury, 2013.

Sherborne, Michael. *H.G. Wells, Another Kind of Life*. London: Peter Owen, 2010.

"Sir Robert Bruce Lockhart, Ex-Diplomat, Is Dead," *New York Times*, February 28, 1970. https://www.nytimes.com/1970/02/28/archives/sir-robert-bruce-lockhart-exdiplomat-is-dead-moscow-envoy.html.

Sisman, Adam. *John Le Carré: The Biography*. Toronto: Knopf, 2015.

Smith, Alexandra. "Jane Harrison as an Interpreter of Russian Culture in the 1910s-1920s," *A People Passing Rude: British Responses to Russian Culture*, ed. Anthony Cross. London: Open Book Publishers, 2012.

Smith, G.S. *D.S. Mirsky: A Russian-English Life, 1890–1939*. Oxford: Oxford University Press, 2000.

Sobol, Valeria. *Febris Erotica, Lovesickness in the Russian Literary Imagination*. Seattle: University of Washington Press, 2009.

Sontag, Susan. "Introduction," Benjamin, *One-Way Street and Other Writings*, tr. Edmund Jephcott and Kinsley Shorter. London: NLB, 1979.

Stewart, Jesse. *Jane Ellen Harrison: A Portrait in Letters*. London: Merlin Press, 1959.

Stewart, Megan. "Curbing Reliance on Abortion in Russia," *Human Rights Brief* 11.2 (2004): 51–54.

Stoppard, Tom. "Voyage," *The Coast of Utopia*. New York: Grove Press, 2007.

Taurens, Jānis. "Asja Lācis and Walter Benjamin: Translating Different Cities," *Canadian Review of Comparative Literature* 45.1 (March 2018): 18–27.

Taylor, Richard. *The Politics of the Soviet Cinema 1917–1929*. Cambridge: Cambridge University Press, 1979.

Tolstoy, Leo. *Anna Karenina*, tr. Richard Pevear and Larissa Volokhonsky. New York: Penguin, 2002.

Tolstoy, Leo. *Family Happiness*, tr. Louise and Aylmer Maude. Part I Ch. 2. http://www.magister.msk.ru/library/tolstoy/english/tolsl19e.htm.

Tolstoy, Leo. *The Kreutzer Sonata and Other Stories*, tr. Benjamin R. Tucker. Boston: Tucker Publisher, 1890. Project Gutenberg. https://www.gutenberg.org/files/689/689-h/689-h.htm#pref01.

Tolstoy, Leo. *The Kreutzer Sonata Variations*, tr. and ed. Michael Katz. New Haven: Yale University Press, 2014.

Tolstoy, Leo. *War and Peace*, tr. Constance Garnett. 1904; New York: Modern Library, n.d.

Tolstoy, Leo. *War and Peace*, tr. Louise and Aylmer Maude, rev. Amy Mandelker. Oxford: Oxford World's Classics, 2010.

Trotsky, Leon. *The History of the Russian Revolution*, tr. Max Eastman. Chicago: Haymarket Books, 2017.

Tsvetaeva, Marina "Diary" of 1919 in Boym, "Loving in Bad Taste," *Sexuality and the Body in Russian Culture*, ed. Jane T. Costlow et al. Stanford: Stanford University Press, 1993.

Turgenev, Ivan. "Asya," *Phantoms and Other Stories*, tr. Isabel F. Hapgood. New York: Scribner's Sons, 1904. 239–321.

Turgenev, Ivan. "A Correspondence," in V.S. Pritchett, "Introduction," *First Love*, tr. Isaiah Berlin. London: Penguin, 1978. 13.

Turgenev, Ivan. "A Correspondence, Letter VI," *The Diary of a Superfluous Man and Other Stories*, tr. Constance Garnett. Project Gutenberg. https://www.gutenberg.org/cache/epub/9615/pg9615.html.

Turgenev, Ivan. "Diary of a Superfluous Man," *First Love and Other Stories*, tr. Richard Freeborn. Oxford: Oxford World's Classics, 2008.

Turgenev, Ivan. *Fathers and Sons*, tr. Constance Garnett. New York: P.F. Collier & Son, 1917.

Turgenev, Ivan. *First Love*, tr. Isaiah Berlin. London: Penguin, 1978.

Turgenev, Ivan. *A Month in the Country*, tr. Richard Freeborn. Oxford: Oxford World's Classics, 1991.

Turgenev, Ivan. *Rudin*, tr. Richard Freeborn. London: Penguin, 1975.

Turgenev, Ivan. *Virgin Soil*. Project Gutenberg. https://www.gutenberg.org/files/2466/2466-h/2466-h.htm#link2H_4_0040.

Voska, Emanuel and Will Irwin, *Spy and Counter Spy*. New York: Doubleday, Doran, 1940.

Vowles, Judith. "Marriage à la russe," *Sexuality and the Body in Russian Culture*, ed. Jane T. Costlow, Stephanie Sandler, Judith Vowles. Stanford: Stanford University Press, 1993. 53–72.

Wells, H.G. "H.G. Wells Interviews Joseph Stalin in 1934," *Open Culture*, April 23, 2014. https://www.openculture.com/2014/04/h-g-wells-interviews-joseph-stalin-in-1934.html.

Wells, H.G. *H.G. Wells in Love, Postscript to an Experiment in Autobiography*, ed. G.P. Wells. London: faber and faber, 1984.

Wells, H.G. *Russia in the Shadows*. New York: George H. Doran, 1921.

Wilmont, Martha. *The Russian Journals of Martha and Catherine Wilmot, 1803–1808*, ed. Marchioness of Londonderry and H.M. Hyde. London: Macmillan, 1934.

Wilson, Duncan. *Leonard Woolf: A Political Biography*. London: Hogarth Press, 1978.

Wilson, Edmund. "Comrade Prince," *Encounter* 5.1 (1955): 10–20.

Wilson, Edmund. "Journey to the Soviet Union, 1935," *The Thirties, from Notebooks and Diaries of the Period*, ed. Leon Edel. New York: Farrar, Straus and Giroux, 1980.

Wilson, Edmund. *Letters on Literature and Politics 1912–1972*, ed. Elena Wilson, intro. Daniel Aaron, foreword by Leon Edel. New York: Farrar, Straus and Giroux, 1977.

Wilson, Edmund. "Meditations on Dostoevsky," *The New Republic* 56 (October 24, 1928): 274–6.

Wilson, Edmund. *Red, Black, Blond and Olive, Studies in Four Civilizations: Zuni, Haiti, Soviet Russia, Israel*. London: W.H. Allen, 1956.

Wilson, Edmund. *To the Finland Station: A Study in the Writing and Acting of History*. New Introduction. New York: Farrar Straus and Giroux, 1972.

Wilson, Edmund. *Travels in Two Democracies*. New York: Harcourt, Brace and Company, 1936.

Wilson, Edmund. *A Window on Russia*. New York: Farrar, Straus and Giroux, 1972.

Wood, James. "What Chekhov Meant by Life," *The Broken Estate, Essays on Literature and Belief*. New York: Picador, 2010.

Woolf, Leonard. *Downhill All the Way: An Autobiography of the Years 1919–1939*. London: Hogarth Press, 1967.

Woolf, Leonard. *Autobiography II: 1911–1969*. Oxford: Oxford University Press, 1980.

Woolf, Virginia. *Between the Acts*, ed. Frank Kermode. Oxford: Oxford World's Classics, 2000.

Woolf, Virginia. *Diary of Virginia Woolf*, vol. I, ed. Anne Olivier Bell. New York: Harcourt Brace Jovanovich, 1977.

Woolf, Virginia. *Diary of Virginia Woolf*, vol. II, ed. Anne Olivier Bell. New York: Harcourt Brace Jovanovich, 1978.

Woolf, Virginia. *Diary of Virginia Woolf*, vol. III, ed. Anne Olivier Bell. New York: Harcourt Brace Jovanovich, 1980.

Woolf, Virginia. *The Essays of Virginia Woolf*, vol. 3, ed. Andrew McNeillie. New York: Harcourt Brace Jovanovich, 1988.

Woolf, Virginia. *Jacob's Room*, ed. Kate Flint. Oxford: Oxford World's Classics, 2008.

Woolf, Virginia. *Letters of Virginia Woolf*, vol. 2: 1912–1922, ed. Nigel Nicolson and Joanne Trautmann. New York: Harcourt Brace Jovanovich, 1976.

Woolf, Virginia. *Night and Day*, ed. Suzanne Raitt. Oxford: Oxford World's Classics, 2009.

Woolf, Virginia. "On Rereading Meredith" (1918*), Granite and Rainbow: Essays*. London: Hogarth Press, 1958.

Woolf, Virginia. *Orlando*, ed. Rachel Bowlby. Oxford: Oxford World's Classics, 2008.

Woolf, Virginia. "The Russian View, 1918," *Essays of Virginia Woolf*, vol. 2, ed. Andrew McNeillie. New York: Harcourt Brace Jovanovich, 1988.

Woolf, Virginia with S.S. Koteliansky. *Translations from the Russian*, intro. Laura Marcus, ed. Stuart N. Clark. Southport: Virginia Woolf Society of Great Britain, 2006.

Woolf, Virginia. "Uncle Vanya," *The Complete Shorter Fiction*, 2nd ed., ed. Susan Dick. San Diego: Harcourt Brace Jovanovich, 1989.

Woolf, Virginia. "An Unwritten Novel," *The Mark on the Wall and Other Short Fiction*, ed. David Bradshaw. Oxford: Oxford World's Classics, 2008. 18–29.

Woolf, Virginia. *The Waves*, ed. David Bradshaw. Oxford: Oxford World's Classics, 2015.

Woolf, Virginia. *The Years*, ed. Hermione Lee. Oxford: Oxford World's Classics, 2009.

Yeats, W.B. "Meditations in Time of Civil War," *Selected Poems*. London: Penguin, 2000.

Youngblood, Denise J. *Soviet Cinema in the Silent Era 1918–1935*. Austin: University of Texas Press, 1991.

Zitzewitz, Josephine Von. "That's How It Was. New Theories about Anna Akhmatova and Isaiah Berlin," *Times Literary Supplement*, September 9, 2011. 14–15.

# Index

Ackerman, Robert 93, 96, 99, 228, 109 nt.2
Acmeist 215, 225 nt. 19
Akhmatova, Anna 1, 10, 54 148, 150, 207–22, 223 nt. 1, nt.3, nt. 4, nt.5 nt.7, 224 nt.8, nt. 9, nt. 11, nt. 12, 225 nt. 13, 14, 15, 16, 20, 22, 23, 226 nt. 24, 26, 227 nt.28, 30
   *Cinque* 212, 215, 222, 226 nt.24
   *The Flight of Time* 226 nt. 26
   *From Six Books* 227 nt. 27
   "Guest from the Future" 211
   "In Praise of Peace" 214
   "Instead of a Preface" 208
   *Poem without a Hero* 211, 213, 215, 216, 217
   *Poems 1909–1960* 214
   *Requiem* 208, 211, 220
   *Selected Poems* 208
   *Sweetbrier in Blossom* 215
   "The Wild Rose Comes into Bloom" 212
   *The Word that Causes Death's Defeat, Poems of Memory* 223 nt. 1
Akhmatova Museum 222
Andreeva, Maria 165 167
Archangel 71, 78, 79, 80, 82, 166
Armand, Inessa 136, 138, 139, 140, 141, 144, 161 nt. 13

Baedeker, Karl 94, 109 nt. 6
   *Russia, Handbook for Travelers* 109 nt.6
   *Russia, with Teheran, Port Arthur and Peking* 94
Bakunin, Mikhail 164 nt. 33
Balfour, Lord Arthur James 83
Ballets Russes 130, 187, 191, 192, 217
Balzac, Honoré 33
Baring, Maurice 191
Beard, Mary 98, 99, 100, 110 nt. 13, nt. 14
Bears 95, 103, 104, 105, 106, 111 nt. 21

Beasley, Rebecca 6, 45, 134 nt. 14, 201 nt.12, 23 nt. 25
Beaverbrook, Lord 72, 183 nt. 14
Becket, Samuel 111 nt.17, 126
Belinsky, Vissarion 5
Bell, Quentin 194, 203 nt. 34
Bell, Vanessa 193
Benjamin, Walter 1, 2, 9, 10, 23–44, 54, 91 nt. 10, 202 nt. 16, 207
   "Conversation on Love" 24, 42 nt. 5
   "Erotic Education" 25, 42 nt.6
   "Moscow" (essay) 23, 30, 33, 42 nt.3
   *Moscow Diary* 23, 30, 33, 42 nt. 4, 44 nt. 25, nt. 28
   "Naples" 23, 29
   "On Love and Related Matters" 25, 42 nt. 6
   "On the Present Situation of Russian Film" 30
   *One-Way Street* 23, 25, 30, 34, 35, 42 nt.7, 44 nt.27
   "Political Groupings of Russian Writers, The" 30
   "Program for a Proletarian Children's Theatre" 32, 40
   "Recent Literature in Russia" 30
   "Russian Toys" 30
   "Theses on the Philosophy of History" 91 nt. 10
   "Young Russian Writers" 30
Berberova, Nina 90 nt.4, 170, 177, 182 nt.2, nt. 5, 183 nt. 13, 229
Bergson, Henri 95, 97, 102
Berlin 13, 19 nt. 21, 22 nt. 36, 30, 31, 34, 38, 39, 41, 42 nt. 4, 73, 136, 166, 168, 171, 172, 175, 180, 192, 193, 194, 198, 203 nt. 36
Berlin, Isaiah 1, 9, 10, 54, 207–22
   "Anna Akhmatova: A Memoir" (Berlin) 225 nt.14, 225 nt. 22
   "Conversations with Akhmatova and Pasternak" 218, 225 nt.13, nt. 15, 226 nt.24

"Hedgehog and The Fox, The" 217
*Karl Marx: His Life and Environment* 217
"Madame Akhmatova," 227 nt. 28
"Meetings with Russian Writers in 1945"
    221, 224 nt.12, 225 nt.18, nt. 22
*Personal Impressions* 226 nt. 23
*Russian Thinkers* 218
*Soviet Mind, The* 225 nt. 23
Blok, Aleksandr 208, 223 nt.6
Blount, Anthony 220
Boym, Svetlana 18 nt. 14
Brecht, Bertolt 39, 153
Brodsky, Joseph 207, 223 nt.3
Buber, Martin 23, 33, 34
Buchanan, Sir George 49, 75, 76, 77
Budberg, Baron Nikolai 73, 171, 172, 181, 184 nt. 20
Budberg, Moura 2, 10, 34, 73, 78, 80, 81, 82, 83, 84, 85, 86, 87, 89, 90 n.4, 91 nt. 12, 165, 166, 167, 168, 169, 170, 174, 175, 176, 177, 178, 179, 180, 181, 182, 183 nt. 17
Bulgakov, Mikhail 86, 91 nt. 12
    *Master and Margarita, The* 86, 91 nt. 12
Burns, Mary 141, 142, 143, 144

Cambridge 93, 94, 100, 102, 108, 133 nt.4, 220
Capri 23, 25, 29, 34, 62
Cheever, John 22 nt. 42
Cheka 79, 80, 81, 83, 85, 88, 167, 171, 173
Chekhov 1, 4, 5, 6, 9, 10, 12, 16, 17 nt.8, 18 nt. 9, nt. 10, 20 nt. 27, 53, 55, 58, 120, 121, 123, 126, 127, 130, 133 nt.4, 133 nt.10, 134 nt.12, 149, 183 nt. 18, 187, 191, 212
    "A Little Game" 18 nt.11, 127
    *Cherry Orchard, The* 145, 191
    "Concerning Love," 18 nt. 12
    "Kiss, The" 4, 5, 17 nt.8, 127
    "Lady with the Little Dog" 9, 20 nt. 27, 58
    *Three Sisters, The* 121, 123 126, 133 nt.10
    *Uncle Vanya* 13, 183 nt. 18
    "Ward No. 6" 212
Chernyshevsky, Nikolay 1, 7, 20 nt. 29
    *What Is to be Done?* 1, 7, 20 nt. 29
Chicherin, Georgy V. 80, 81, 82
Churchill, Randolph 211, 212

Churchill, Winston 212
*Close Up* 193, 197
Conrad, Joseph 7, 9, 16, 19 nt. 17
    *Under Western Eyes* 6, 7, 16, 19 nt. 17
Cornford, Francis 99
Cromie, Francis 73, 80, 82, 166

Demuth, Helene 136, 143
Diaghilev, Serge 130, 185, 187, 191, 217
Diment, Galya 186, 201 nt.5, 200 nt.1, nt. 7, 202 nt. 24
Dos Passos, John 150, 153, 161 nt.4, 162 nt. 20
Dostoevsky, Fyodor 1, 2, 3, 6, 16, 17 nt.4, 19 nt. 18, 41, 44 nt. 29, 50, 53, 54, 55, 57, 62, 94, 95, 98, 101, 104, 105, 106, 112 nt. 30, 125, 149, 151, 152, 159, 163 nt. 27, 164 nt. 35, 185, 187, 188, 189, 191, 200, 201 nt. 8, 202 nt. 16, 211, 218, 219
    *Brothers Karamazov* 50, 53, 64, 106, 107, 112 nt.30, 149
    *Crime and Punishment* 13, 64, 185, 189
    *An Honest Thief and Other Stories* 188, 189, 202 nt. 17
    *Idiot, The* 3, 6, 9, 13, 18, 19 nt.18, 106, 187, 188, 189, 199, 202 nt. 16
    "Plan of the Life of a Great Sinner, The" 190
    *Possessed, The* 50, 106, 145, 152, 187, 200
    *Stavrogin's Confession* 190
    "An Unpleasant Predicament" 188
    "White Nights" 17 nt. 4, 41, 44 nt.29, 159, 164 nt.35
Dreiser, Theodore 153
Duncan, Isadore 153

Eccentrism 197
*Eighteenth Brumaire* 151
Einstein, Albert 114, 194, 195, 196
Eisenstein, Serge 210
    *Battleship Potemkin* 194
Eliot, George 99
Eliot, T. S. 16, 119
    "Reflections on Vers Libre" 16, 22 nt. 45
Engels, Fredrich 136, 141, 142, 143, 153, 154, 156
    *Condition of the Working Class in England, The* 142
Engelstein, Laura 5

Finland Station 63, 116, 135, 136, 138, 148, 156, 212, 226 nt. 24
Fokine, Michel 191, 203 nt. 28
Forster, E.M. 189
Fox, Ralph 8, 9, 19 nt. 25
   *Novel and the People, The* 8, 20 nt. 26.
   *Storming Heaven* 8, 19 nt. 25.
Freud, Sigmund 186
Fry, Roger 192, 193

Garnett, Constance 188, 191
Garnett, Edward 191
Garshin, Vladimir 210, 211
Gauss, Christian 149, 150, 152, 154, 159
Geneva 46, 67
George, Lloyd 61, 62, 64, 71, 77
Gerhardie, William 1, 6, 19 nt. 19, 113–32, 187, 207
   *Chekhov, A Critical Study* 134 nt. 13, nt. 14
   *Futility* 114, 116, 117, 118, 119, 120, 121, 122, 123, 124, 127, 129, 132, 133 nt. 5, nt. 6, nt.7, 187
   *God's Fifth Column* 130
   *Memoirs of a Polyglot* 113, 116, 118, 122, 133 nt.6
   *Of Mortal Love* 128, 129
   *Polyglots, The* 117, 121, 122, 128
   *Resurrection* 123, 134 nt. 15
   *Romanovs, The* 130, 131, 134 nt.17
Gide, André 104, 150, 169, 174
Gladkov, Fyodor 30
   *Cement* 30, 44 nt. 18, 229
Gogol, Nikolai 1, 38, 53, 125
Goncharov, Ivan 3, 17 nt.5, 107
   *Oblomov* 3, 17 nt.5, 52, 85, 107, 126, 158
Gorky, Maxim 1, 2, 10, 55, 58, 73, 75, 85, 86, 88, 90 nt. 4, 128, 165, 167, 168, 169, 171, 172, 173, 174, 175, 176, 177, 178, 180, 181, 182 nt.5, 183 nt. 17, 185, 186
   *Judge, The* 172
   *Life of Klim Samgin, The* 173
   *Life of a Useless Man* 85
Griffith, D.W. 195
   *Intolerance* 195
Gumilyov, Lev 208, 211, 213, 214, 215
Gumilyov, Nikolai 207, 220, 226 nt. 24

Halban, Aline 10, 212, 219
Hardwick, Elizabeth 2, 17 nt.2

Hardy, Henry 221, 222, 224 nt.12, 227 nt. 29, nt. 30
Harrison, Jane Ellen 1, 20 nt. 29, 93–109, 186, 187, 190
   *Alpha and Omega* 108
   *Ancient Art and Ritual* 95, 99, 100, 108, 111 nt. 16, 112 nt. 29
   *Aspects, Aorists and the Classical Tripos* 96, 97, 106, 108, 109 nt.1, 110 nt.10
   *Book of the Bear* 102, 104, 105, 111 nt.22, nt.25, 112 nt.26
   *Epilegomena to the Study of Greek Religion* 108
   "Epilogue on the War: Peace with Patriotism" 104
   *Introductory Studies in Greek Art* 110 nt.14
   *Life of the Archpriest Avvakum* 101, 102, 105, 111 nt. 19, nt. 20, 108, 186, 187
   *Prolegomena to the Study of Greek religion* 100, 108
   *Reminiscences of a Student Life* 97, 103, 108, 109 nt.3
   *Russia and the Russian Verb* 93, 95, 96, 99, 108, 109 nt. 5, 110 nt. 9, 186
   *Themis: A Study of the Social Origins of Greek Religion* 99, 100, 108
Haslewood, Jean 88
Havel, Vaclav 222, 227 nt. 32
Haxton, Gerald 45, 46, 54
Hebrew 13
*Hedda Gabler* 2, 3
Heldt, Barbara 17 Nt.6
Herzen, Alexander 217
Hicks, Captain William 74, 79, 80, 81, 87, 88, 90 nt.4, 167
Hogarth Press 22 nt. 40, 97, 102, 108, 109, 111 nt. 18, nt.19, 112 nt.28, 185, 186, 187, 190, 191, 200 nt. 1, 201, 201 nt.5, 225, 229, 234, 238, 239.
Holroyd, Michael 118, 133 nt. 6
Hubbs, Joanna 5
Hugo, Victor 213
Huysmans, Joris-Karl 119
   *À rebours* 119

Ignatieff, Michael 19 nt. 21, 20 nt. 28. 218, 223 nt.7
   *A Life of Isaiah Berlin* 19 nt. 21, 20 nt. 28, nt. 29.

Jeffreys-Jones, Rhodri 49, 67
Joyce, James 111 nt.17
   *Finnegans Wake* 111 nt. 17

Kafka, Franz 133, 226 nt. 24
Kaplan, Dora 80, 81
Kellner, Dora 29, 30, 38, 39, 40
Kelly, Gerald 55
Kerensky, Alexander 47, 48, 49, 51, 55. 56. 58. 61, 62, 63, 64, 66, 68 nt 13, 116, 175, 183 nt. 17
Kermode, Frank 126, 134 nt. 12
Keun, Odette 174, 175, 180, 182 nt.6
Keynes, Maynard 187, 191
   *Short View of Russia, A* 187, 191
Khrushchev, Nikita 214
Kiev 98, 158, 160 nt. 5
Klee, Paul 85
   "Angelus Novus" 85
Knox, Major Alfred 116, 117, 118, 119
Kotelianksy, S. S. 185, 186, 187, 190, 200, 201 nt.5, 202 nt.24
Kremlin 71, 72, 80, 81, 82, 83, 84, 86, 87, 90, 140, 147, 169, 170
Kropotkin, Prince Peter 45, 55, 56, 65
   *Ideals and Realities in Russian Literature, The* 55
Kropotkin, Princess Alexandra (Sasha) 54, 55, 56, 58, 61, 62, 64, 68 nt. 10, 75
   *How to Cook and Eat in Russian* 65, 68 nt.10
Krúpskaya, Nadézhda 135, 136, 137, 138, 139, 153, 155, 156

Lācis, Asja 2, 10, 23 ff
Lawrence, D.H. 186
le Carré, John 16, 67
Lehmann, Rosamond 113
Lenin, V. I. 1, 8, 47, 48, 49, 62, 71, 77, 80, 81, 82, 83, 88, 91 nt.8, 102, 116, 130, 135, 136, 137, 138, 139, 140, 141, 144, 145, 146, 147, 148, 149, 150, 151, 153, 154, 155, 156, 157, 159, 161 nt. 11, nt. 16, 162 nt. 21, 163 nt. 30, 164 nt. 35, 166, 167, 168, 170–1, 183 nt. 11, 186, 207, 214
   *State and Revolution* 82.
Leningrad 90 nt.4, 102, 131, 132, 144, 146, 161 nt.8, 175, 207, 208, 210, 211, 213, 215, 216, 219, 221

Lewis, Wyndham 132, 134 nt. 19
   "Letters from Petrograd" 132, 134 nt. 19
*Literary Moscow* 214
Litvinov, Maxim 72, 77, 82, 83, 89 nt.3
Lockhart, H. Bruce 1, 2, 6, 63, 71–89, 165, 166, 167, 171, 172, 173, 174, 176, 179, 180, 182 nt. 2, nt. 3, 183 nt. 14, 184 nt. 20, 207
   *British Agent* (film) 174
   *Diaries of Sir Robert Bruce Lockhart* 90 nt.5
   *Memoirs of a British Agent* 71, 72, 73, 78, 89 nt.1, 166, 174, 182 nt.2
   *Retreat from Glory* 86, 91 nt.13
   *Two Revolutions: An Eye-witness study of Russia 1917* 88, 91 nt. 15
Loti, Pierre 72

Magre, Maurice 84
   "Avilir" 84
Malaysia 72, 73, 74
Manchester 141, 142
Mandelstam, Osip 148, 150, 208, 216, 220, 223 nt.4, nt.5, nt.6, 225 nt. 20, 226 nt. 24
   "Anna Akhmatova" 225 nt. 20
Mandelstam, Nadezhda 208, 223 nt. 4, 224 nt. 7
Mansfield, Katherine 113, 114, 120, 126, 133, nt. 8, 186, 181, 191, 201 nt. 5, 133 nt. 8
   "Garden party, The" 133 nt. 9
*Manual of the Russian Language* 94
Marinetti, F.T 217
Marvell, Andrew 1, 14, 22 nt. 42
   "Definition of Love, The" 1, 14, 22 nt. 42
Marx, Karl 8, 9, 58, 136, 141, 142, 143, 144, 152, 153, 154, 155, 156, 163 nt. 3
   *The Communist Manifesto* 151, 153
   *Das Kapital* 151
   *What Is to be Done?* 138
Maugham, Somerset 1, 6, 9, 13, 16, 22 nt. 41, 45–67, 86, 207
   *Ashenden* 13, 22 nt. 41, 45, 54, 55, 56, 60, 61, 62, 64
   *Caroline* 45, 46
   *Jack Straw* 61
   "Love and Russian Literature" 55, 56
   "Mr. Harrington's Washing" 56
   *Penelope* 62
   *The Road Uphill, The* 62

*Summing Up, The* 68 nt.12
*A Writer's Notebook* 50–1, 52, 54, 61, 68 nt. 5
Mayakovsky, Vladimir 20 nt. 29, 216
McCarthy, Mary 144, 151, 157, 163 nt. 29
McDonough, Anna 6, 19 nt. 16
Meredith, George 13
Meyerhold, Vsevolod 36, 38, 41 nt.1, 151
　*Inspector General,The* 36, 38
Michelet, Jules 135, 150, 152, 153, 154, 155
Mirrlees, Hope 94, 98, 101, 102, 104, 105, 108, 109, 109 ft.1, 111 nt. 19, nt. 20, nt. 21, 112 nt. 26, nt.27, nt.31, 186, 187
　*Paris: A Poem* 108
Mirsky, D.S. 5, 20 nt. 29, 93, 97, 105, 108, 109 nt. 14, 111 nt. 19, nt. 20, nt. 21, 112 nt. 27, 148, 185, 186, 201 nt. 8
　*A History of Russian Literature* 5, 20 nt. 29, 104, 105, 186
　*Jane Harrison and Russia* 109 nt. 4
　*Modern Russian Literature* 186
Modigliani, Amedeo 220, 221, 226 nt. 26
Montage 188, 193, 194, 195, 196, 197, 204 nt. 44
Moscow 1, 8, 9, 30, 31, 32, 33, 36, 37, 39, 40, 71, 72, 73, 74, 75, 76, 77, 78, 79, 81, 83, 84, 85, 87, 88, 90 nt. 4, 97, 98, 99, 147, 161 nt.8, 165, 166, 169, 170, 171, 173, 175, 176, 178, 183 nt. 17, 187, 208, 209, 210, 211, 210, 212, 213, 217 219, 221, 222
Murray, Gilbert 97, 100, 104. 109 nt. 4
Murry, John Middleton 186, 191, 201 nt. 5

Nabokov, Vladimir 21 nt. 33, 133 nt. 4, 136, 143, 145, 159, 161 nt. 17, 160 nt. 4, 162 nt. 21, 182 nt. 1
　"Spring in Fialta" 21 nt. 33
*New Republic* 150, 153, 154, 163 nt. 32, 183 nt.16, 220, 221
Nicolson, Harold 192
Nijinsky, Vaslav 191

Odessa 71, 148, 151, 158, 159, 160 nt. 5
Orlov, Vladimir 210

Pankhurst, Emmeline 51
Parem, Olga 41
Paris 10, 55, 57–8, 64, 85, 93, 101, 103, 104, 105, 106, 108, 111 nt. 23, 120, 138, 142, 174, 180, 183 nt. 17, 186, 191, 217, 218
*Partisan Review* 150, 163 nt. 30
Pasternak, Boris 1, 10, 163 nt. 26, 201 nt. 8, 208, 210, 213, 214, 220, 223 nt. 5, 224 nt. 11, 225 nt. 17, 226 nt. 24, nt. 25
　*Doctor Zhivago* 176, 219, 224 nt.11, 225 nt. 17, 226 nt. 25
Peters, Yakov 81, 82, 83, 84, 167, 173
Petrograd 47, 48, 49, 50, 51, 55, 56, 59, 61, 62, 64, 67, 68 nt.7, 73, 75, 76, 78, 79, 81, 89, 90 nt.4, 116, 125, 135, 140, 165, 166, 168, 169, 170, 171, 209
*Poetry Day* 214
Pound, Ezra 161 nt.10
Prague 72, 86, 87, 88, 89, 91 nt.14, 173, 179
Proust 32, 33, 103, 110 nt.9, 114, 122
　*In Search of Lost time* 110 nt.9
Pudovkin, V.I. 185 192, 193, 194, 195, 196, 204 nt. 37
　*End of St. Petersburg* 194
　*Film Technique* 204 nt. 37
　*Film Technique and Film Acting* 204 nt. 37, nt. 43
　*Mother* 193, 204 nt. 42
　"On the Principle of Sound in Film" 197, 205 nt. 49
　*Pudovkin on Film Technique* 194
　"Statement on Sound" 196, 197, 204 nt. 47
　*Storm over Asia* 192, 193, 194, 198
　"Types as Opposed to Actors" 193
Punin, Nikolay 207, 211, 214, 215
Pushkin, Alexander 5, 24, 28, 29, 43 nt. 11, nt.13, 146, 151, 208
　*Onegin, Eugene* 26, 28, 29, 35, 43 nt. 11, nt. 12, nt. 14, 60, 85

Radt-Cohen, Jula 33, 39, 41
Ransome, Arthur 84
Reed, John 51
Reich, Bernhard 2, 10, 23, 28, 26, 27, 29, 31, 34, 35, 36, 38, 39, 41 nt.2
Reilly, Sidney 71, 72, 80, 81

Remizov, Aleksey 101, 105, 111
Reyfman, Irina 5
Riga 29, 30, 34, 207, 209, 210
Rolland, Romain 176
Roth, Joseph 37, 44 nt. 17
Rothenstein, John 119, 120
Rubinstein, Ida 191
Russia Abroad 104, 105
Russian 13, 53, 62, 73, 81, 93, 94, 95, 96,
    97, 98, 100, 101, 102, 103, 108,
    109 nt.1, 115
Rutten, Ellen 17 nt.1

Sachs, Hanns 193
Sackville-West, Vita 187, 192
Satie, Erik 191
Savinkov, Boris 62
Sazonoff, Sergey 76
Schlesinger, Arthur 220
Scholem, Gershom 33, 34, 40, 41
Shakespeare, William 148, 215
Shaw, G.B. 131, 150, 176
Shestov, Lev 101, 104, 105
Shostakovich, Dmitri 158
Sobol, Valeria 19 nt. 23
Solovev, Vladimir 16
    *Meaning of Love, The* 16
Sontag, Susan 32, 42 nt. 7, 44 nt. 23
Soule, George 154 155
sound 50, 99, 185, 194, 195, 196, 197, 198,
    199, 204 nt. 44, nt. 47, 205 nt. 49,
    nt. 50, 217
Sparrow Hills 86, 166
St. Basil's Cathedral 36, 37
St. Petersburg 6, 15, 43 nt. 12, 58, 90 nt.
    4, 97, 102, 115, 116, 133 nt. 4, 137,
    146, 151, 158, 159, 176, 186, 207,
    208
Stalin, Josef 35, 39, 83, 85, 128, 129, 145,
    147, 149, 150, 153, 155, 158, 169,
    175, 176, 178, 183 nt. 16, nt. 17,
    195, 176, 178, 183 nt. 16, nt.17, 195,
    208, 214, 215, 216, 217, 220, 221,
    223 nt. 5, 227 nt. 27
Stanislavsky, Konstantin 165
Steffens, Lincoln 150, 153
Stein, Gertrude 130
Stoppard, Tom 5, 18 nt.13
    *Coast of Utopia* 5, 18 nt. 3
Strachey, Lytton 185, 186, 190

Straight, Michael 220
Stravinsky, Igor 191
    *Firebird, The* 191
    *Petrushka* 191
    *Sacre du printemps, Le* 191
Stray Dog Café 207, 216
Strong, Eugénie (Sellers) 110 nt. 14
Struve, Pyotr 141, 161 nt. 15

Taunton, Matthew 5
Tchaikovsky 130, 151
    *Queen of Spades, The* 151
Thornton, Elena Mumm 144, 159
Tolstoy, Alexei 88, 17 nt. 388, 174
Tolstoy, Leo 1, 3, 5, 6, 9, 11, 16, 17 nt.7, 21
    nt. 32, 50, 98, 102, 105, 106, 123,
    127, 130, 145, 162 nt. 2, 185, 186,
    187, 188, 190, 200, 201 nt. 8, 202 nt.
    23, 211
    *Anna Karenina* 2, 7, 13, 17 nt. 3, nt.7,
    19 nt. 22, 55, 190, 211
    "Bear Prince, The" 105
    *Family Happiness* 3, 17 nt. 7
    "Kreutzer Sonata" 9, 11–12, 16, 21 nt.
    32, 28
    *Resurrection* 50
    *War and Peace* 75, 162 nt.22, 188, 190,
    202 nt.23
Tolstoy, Sofiya 12, 21 nt.33
    "Whose fault?" 12, 21 nt.33
Tomashevsky, Boris 216, 217
triangles 40, 43 nt. 12, 199, 211, 219, 224
    nt. 11
Trotsky, Leon 71, 73, 74, 77, 80, 81, 82, 84,
    116, 135, 141, 150, 151, 154, 160
    nt.1, 166, 168, 183 nt. 17
    *History of the Russian Revolution* 135,
    160 nt. 1
    *Literature and Revolution* 151
Tsvetaeva, Marina 5, 18 nt. 15, 101, 220.
Turgenev, Ivan 1, 3, 7, 10, 13, 15, 16, 18 nt.
    12, 19 nt. 20 nt. 21 nt. 24, 22 nt. 43,
    24, 25, 26, 27, 28, 29, 38, 42 nt. 9, 44
    nt. 16, 54, 55, 60, 85, 89, 91 nt.11,
    nt. 16, 99, 102, 106, 109 nt.5, 127,
    145, 161 nt. 16, 162 nt. 22, 179, 183
    nt. 18, 185, 187, 190, 200, 211, 219
    "Ásya" 25, 26, 27, 42 nt.9, 60
    "Correspondence, letter VI, A" 7, 19
    nt. 24

"Diary of a Superfluous Man" 15, 162 nt. 22
*Fathers and Sons* 55, 85, 91 nt.11
*First Love* 7, 8, 19 nt. 21, 54, 127, 162 nt.22, 219
*Month in the Country, A* 18 nt. 12, 19 nt. 21, 29
*Rudin* 7, 16, 19 nt. 20, 161 nt. 16, 179, 183 nt. 18
*Virgin Soil* 3, 89, 91 nt.16
Turner, Jean Haselwood 74, 75

Union of Soviet Writers 215, 216

Verdi, Giuseppe 145
*Otello* 145
Viardot, Pauline 10, 44 nt.16
Vienna 87, 115
Vladivostok 48, 71, 78, 117, 118, 120, 121, 126, 127, 132, 166, 223 nt.5
vodka 196
von Westphalen, Jenny 135
Voska, Emanuel 49, 50, 56, 59, 68 nt. 6, nt.11
Vowles, Judith 20 n.30
"Marriage à la russe" 20 nt. 30.

Walker, Rachel 218
Walpole, Hugh 51, 52, 75, 120
Washington 62, 63, 209, 212, 218, 219
Wellcome, Syrie 45, 46, 54
Wells, H.G. 1, 2, 6, 10, 16, 34, 73, 82, 85, 86, 90 nt.4, 126, 129, 165–82, 207
*Anatomy of Frustration, The* 181
*Apropos of Dolores* 175
*Mr. Britling Sees it Through* 82
*Croquet Player* 181
*Experiment in Autobiography* 165, 180
*H.G. Wells in Love* 169, 181, 175, 176, 182 nt. 7, nt.8
*Passionate Friends, The* 182 nt.1
*Research Magnificent, The* 182
*Russia in the Shadows* 170, 183 nt. 10, nt.11
West, Anthony 168, 177
West, Rebecca 168, 174, 175, 177, 179, 180, 181
Wharton, Edith 113, 120, 121, 126
Wilde, Oscar 119, 125, 130, 167, 168
*Importance of Being Earnest, The* 119

Wilmot, Catherine 11, 20 nt. 30.
Wilmot, Martha 11, 20–1 nt. 30
*Russian Journals* 11
Wilson, Edmund 1, 13, 135–60, 201 nt. 8, 207
*American Earthquake* 151
*American Jitters: The Year of the Slump* 149
*Axel's Castle* 135
*I Thought of Daisy* 149, 163 nt. 27
"Marxism and Literature" 150
*Red, Black, Blond and Olive* 144, 149, 156, 160 nt.5
*Thirties, The* 134 nt. 34, 144, 162 nt.19
*To the Finland Station* 135 136, 140, 141, 144, 145, 146, 147. 149, 150, 152, 154, 155, 159, 160 nt. 5, 164 nt. 35
*Travels in Two Democracies* 144, 146, 148, 155, 160 nt. 5, 161 nt.18
*Window on Russia, A* 164 nt. 35
*Wound and the Bow, The* 149
Wood, James 5, 17–18 nt.9
Woolf, Leonard 101, 105, 112 nt. 28, 185, 186, 187, 192, 193, 201 nt.4, 201nt.7, 201 nt.8, nt.9, 202 nt. 14
Woolf, Virginia 1, 13, 16, 22 nt. 37, 64, 68 nt. 9, 98, 105, 108, 112 nt. 31, 123, 185–200
"An Unwritten Novel" 188, 194, 204 nt. 39
*Between the Acts* 192, 195, 197, 203 nt. 32
"Cinema, The" 192
*Common Reader, The* 16
*Diary* 189, 194, 197, 198, 200, 201, 201 nt.6, 202 nt. 19
"Intellectual Status of Women, The" 108
*Jacob's Room* 188, 189, 192, 195, 203 nt. 31
"Modern Fiction" 123
"Mr. Bennett and Mrs. Brown" 13, 189
"Kew Gardens" 199
*Mrs. Dalloway* 189, 195, 199, 205 nt. 50
"Mark on the Wall, The" 188
*Night and Day* 188, 199, 202 nt.15
"Novels of Turgenev, The" 13, 190

*Orlando* 64, 68 nt.9, 190, 200, 205 nt.51
*Room of One's Own, A* 108, 194, 198
"Russian Point of View, The" 16, 187, 188
"Russian Sense of Comedy, The" 189
"Russian View, 1918, The" 22 nt. 40
*To the Lighthouse* 110 nt.8, 190, 192, 195, 199
*Voyage Out, The* 188, 190

*Waves, The* 189, 190, 194, 195, 197, 198, 199 202 nt.1
*Years, The* 187, 190, 202 nt. 13

Yeats, W.B. 12, 21 nt. 34
"Meditations in Time of Civil War" 21 nt.34

Zhdanov, Andrei 213, 215, 221
Zinoviev, Grigory 168
Zurich 140

www.ingramcontent.com/pod-product-compliance
Lightning Source LLC
Chambersburg PA
CBHW071823300426
44116CB00009B/1418